# Our
# Australia
# EVENTS

In memory of my parents, Marie and George,
who started me on 'Banjo' Paterson along with
*Jack and the Beanstalk*; for the grandchildren they read to,
Noah and Jack; and for their grandchildren to come.

**Publisher's Note**

This book originally appeared as part of a larger volume:
*Why We Are Australian* (2007).
It has now been divided into three volumes:
*Our Australia: CULTURE, Our Australia: PEOPLE* and
*Our Australia: EVENTS.*

The Five Mile Press Pty Ltd
1 Centre Road, Scoresby
Victoria 3179 Australia
Email: publishing@fivemile.com.au
Website: www.fivemile.com.au

Text copyright © Paul Taylor, 2007
Copy editor: Sonya Nikadie
Supervising editor: Maggie Pinkney
Designer: Michael Bannenberg
Picture editor: Janet Pheasant

Formatting this edition
SBR Productions, Olinda, Victoria 3788

Printed in China

FRONT COVER IMAGE: Bicentenary celebrations, Sydney Harbour, *Newspix*

# Our
# Australia
# EVENTS

PAUL TAYLOR

The Five Mile Press

# CONTENTS

# Preface

It's a sarcastic Chinese curse with an implied wish for calamity to be visited on you and your country – 'May you live in interesting times' – but in the Lucky Country, Australia, it just doesn't have the same sinister menace. *The Lucky Country*, the title of Donald Horne's 1960s best-seller, was meant to be derisive. Horne used the term ironically: Australia, he argued, was a country blessed but run by second rate-people.

But Australians didn't agree. We knew better. To Horne's chagrin we took the term to be a celebration of our unique selves. We recognised that we had the great fortune to live in a country that, perhaps more than any other, has a recorded history remarkably free of the levels of hatred and violence, the civil wars and the brutal conflicts – nation against nation, class against class, creed against creed, race against race – that other, less lucky countries, have endured.

And we knew, too, that this good fortune was due to the 'second-raters'; people like us, who built the nation from a struggling, starving penal colony in one of the remotest parts of the world into a stable, safe and prosperous society.

Does that mean our history is not 'interesting', our challenges and conflicts dull by comparison with other nations and the events that shaped us tame by comparison? The Australian historian Manning Clark might have thought so. He wrung his hands over the lack of 'blood on the wattle', the national upheavals and revolutions experienced again and again in Europe, Asia, Africa and the Americas.

Do we need buckets of blood to have a fascinating past?

Mark Twain didn't think so. Visiting Australia in the late 19th century the great American novelist found our history, 'does not read like history, but like the most beautiful lies; and all of a fresh new sort, no mouldy old stale ones. It is full of surprises and adventures, and incongruities, and contradictions, and incredibilities; but they are all true, they all happened.'

This volume looks at some of those beautiful lies.

Paul Taylor, *2009*

# 1

# THE FIRSTS

The almost fully intact bones of the predator *Thylacoleo carnifex* – Australia's so-called Marsupial Lion – found in a Nullarbor cave led the Museum of Western Australia to recreate it in this image.

By and large the original inhabitants of Australia were a frightful lot. And very large many of them were. Massive, vicious killers and peaceful plodders alike, some were as tall as a two-storey building, all were very ugly and too many were absolutely terrifying. Allosaurus, for instance, at five metres tall and ten metres long, was almost as huge as its relative Tyrannosaurus rex and, with its gigantic jaws that tore apart its prey, just as terrifying. More benign creatures such as Muttaburrasaurus, nine metres long; Sthenurine, the claw-footed kangaroo that weighed in at 300 kilograms; and Timimus, an ostrich-like dinosaur with the useful ability to run very swiftly, subsisted on plants.

Offshore, deep in the warm ocean waters, swam Plesiosaurs, fat-bellied and long-necked, not unlike the fabled Loch Ness monster. And high above all, the Pterosaurs, nightmarish flying reptiles with two-metre wingspans, ruled the southern skies.

Australia was still part of Gondwana, the giant continent that also included Africa, South America, India and Antarctica until, around 45 million years ago, our continent separated and began to meet the crust of south-east Asia. And from there, perhaps as long as 60,000 years ago, by boat or raft, the first people came to Australia.

With them they brought fire, and they may even have tucked into giant marsupial roasts: the three-metre-tall kangaroo; the wombat the size of a rhinoceros; and a takeaway snack on the wing, leallynasaura, not much bigger than a chicken. But with the fire and the food came a cost: the death of the super-marsupials.

In January 2007 a team of Australian scientists announced the discovery of the first complete skeleton of *Thylacoleo carnifex*, a leopard-sized marsupial lion, among more than 60 articulated skeletons of some of the largest mammals to live on this continent. Cavers had found the almost perfectly intact remains four years before, deep in three caves, in the middle of the

Nullarbor Desert. The skeletons had lain there for nearly half a million years.

Their discovery solved Australia's oldest murder mystery. Who or what killed our giant prehistoric animals? The clue can be found in the skeletons' teeth. They show that the creatures were capable of surviving in a hot, dry climate. 'There's no way you can twist the facts to say that climate change was responsible,' said paleontologist Dr Gavin Prideaux of the Western Australian Museum. The team's conclusion supports the theory that the megafauna were killed off by man.

Can the Aborigines be blamed for the extinction? Hardly. They could not have realised that the species would slowly disappear across the continent. 'Long before the rise of Babylon and Athens, the early Australians had impressive achievements,' Geoffrey Blainey says in his preface to *Triumph of the Nomads*. 'They were the only people in the world's history to sail across the seas and discover an inhabitable continent.'

Where did they come from? No one knows for sure but Blainey suggests that the first Australians came across the 'stepping stone' islands from south-east Asia and that 'the slow eastward movement of these people was one of the great events in the history of man'.

Exactly when the first man and woman set foot on Australian soil we will never know, nor will we know how long it took for them and their tribe and others like them to populate the entire country. But we have forensic evidence that from at least 30,000 BC people around Lake Mungo, in the south-east of the continent, were enjoying a diet that included crayfish and emu eggs.

They had regular trade routes, medicines and drugs; they were skilled herbalists. Aborigines enjoyed, says Geoffrey Blainey, a material life that could be compared favourably with many parts of Europe at that time and was superior to some.

Three hundred years ago when the giant marsupials had all disappeared there were probably 300,000 Australians living together in at least 500 diverse tribes. Each tribe numbered between three or four score and five or six hundred, and each had its own distinct social customs and dialect. They were intelligent and intuitive, an ancestor-worshipping society, nomads, not wandering

The rain and wind that shaped the eerie landscape at Lake Mungo, 1000 kilometres west of Sydney, has also uncovered ancient fireplaces and hearths, stone tools and remains of Tasmanian tigers, giant kangaroos and an oxen-sized animal, the zygomaturus. *Newspix*

aimlessly, but moving with a purpose and in patterns and with a communal right to hunt and gather food in a particular area. Above all they were deeply spiritual.

Central to their lives was the Dreamtime, the time in the mythological past when all things had their origins: rivers, trees, rocks, birds, mammals and man. Everything in the natural world, they believed, was symbolic of the supernatural beings, good and bad, who created it.

'Few white Australians can understand the affection felt by Aborigines for their own soil, rocks, trees, animals and sacred sites … the landscape and all living things testified to a divine presence,' Blainey wrote.

Tribal warfare was a constant but the Aborigines lived in harmony with the landscape and its flora and fauna, and had done so from time immemorial, because the land itself was their story, their Dreaming. Take it away, and you took away their past and their future: their spiritual life.

All of that, after countless thousands of years, changed irrevocably at three o'clock on the afternoon of 18 January 1788. Significantly, we know that precise time thanks to a man who was there at Botany Bay. He was not an Aborigine. He was Second Lieutenant Phillip Gidley King, a European. He froze the moment for us.

'...the boats were hoisted out and Governor Phillip and some officers belonging to the *Supply*, with Lieutenant Dawes and myself landed on the north side of the bay... where we observed a group of the natives... they called to us in a menacing tone and at the same time brandishing their spears or lances.

'...Governor Phillip then advanced towards them alone and unarmed, on which one of them advanced towards him... and seemed quite astonished at the figure we cut in being clothed... We soon after took leave of them and returned on board.'

The destruction of the Dreaming had begun.

In a photograph taken around 1860 the melancholy of the couple, artificially posed in a studio, is testimony to the alienation felt by the Aborigines in the early years of the colony.

# The first white settlers

A century and a half before the First Fleet came to anchor in Botany Bay, two young Dutchmen landed on the mainland of Western Australia. They were our first white 'settlers'. They had no say in the matter. It was settle or swing. They opted to settle and the last they saw of the civilisation they left behind was a row of corpses, hands severed, dangling on gibbets on a barren island of death.

Jan Pelgrom de Bye and Wouter Looes were put ashore, marooned, in 1629 as punishment for their part in the mutiny on the ship *Batavia*. What followed that mutiny was the most surreal and nightmarish page in Australia's history. All told, around 210 men, women and children on the *Batavia* died, mostly slaughtered, over three horrific months.

The *Batavia*, the flagship of the Dutch East India Company, set sail from Holland in October 1628. She was on her maiden voyage to her namesake city in Java in the East Indies – Jakarta, in modern day Indonesia. On board were 316 sailors, soldiers and merchants and their women and children, and in the hold, a fortune: a quarter of a million guilders in coin.

The *Batavia* was under the command of the company's senior merchant, Francisco Pelsaert, and captained by Ariaen Jacobsz, but the two were at odds from the beginning. They had sailed

Sailing into Sydney's Darling Harbour in 2000, the glorious and meticulously recreated *Batavia*. Below deck in 1628 it was a different story. Where 300 slept in cramped, claustrophobic conditions a mutiny was brewing, bloated rats and cockroaches scuttled and it was foul-going in the fairest of weather. But in the hold was the equivalent of $40 million worth of silver coin, gold and jewels. *Newspix*

together on a previous voyage to the Dutch East Indies colony and intensely disliked each other. On board, too, was a former apothecary from Haarlem, Jeronimus Cornelisz. The third most senior company man on the *Batavia*, Cornelisz was a member of a cult that conducted sexual orgies and sanctioned any crime because, its members said, man was made in God's image and therefore He must approve.

Cornelisz hatched a plot. He suggested to the captain that with help they could kill Pelsaert and any loyal soldiers, commandeer the *Batavia* and its treasure and use it as a pirate ship. The conspirators went to their bunks on the night of 3 June 1629, with weapons hidden and at the ready.

Two hours before dawn on 4 June, off the Abrolhos group of islands 80 kilometres from the west coast of Australia, *Batavia*, blown off course by storms, smashed onto coral rocks, stuck fast and began breaking up. But through the chaos Pelsaert saw an island about three leagues away, with two smaller islands, little more than outcrops of rock, beside it.

As the storm raged, 180 people were safely landed on the main island and 40 on the smallest, along with food and some few barrels of water. Some preferred to stay – carousing – on the sinking ship: 'the godless unruly troops of soldiers, as well as crew, and their women whom I [Pelsaert] could not keep in the hold on account of the liquor or wine.' On the second day they took off merchandise and some of the gold and jewels.

On the third day they set out to bring off Cornelisz and the others who were still on the *Batavia* but the seas beat them back. With a heavy heart, Pelsaert later said, he left 'with the utmost grief, my lieutenant and 70 men on the very point

of perishing on board the vessel.' Sink or swim. As conditions worsened many sank. Tragically, Cornelisz was not among them.

Exploring, the castaways found no fresh water. Pelsaert and a crew went in search of it up the coast in a skiff built from the wreck of the *Batavia*. The search was proving futile when 1000 kilometres from the wreck, he decided to make for Batavia, a further 1000 kilometres north.

Jeronimus Cornelisz meanwhile had made it to shore and taken command. Immediately he began to resurrect his fantasy. This time he planned to seize the hoped-for rescue ship. To ensure there were fewer mouths to feed and to satisfy his psychotic urges he ordered the murder of all those who were not a party to the pirate compact.

The killings began. He and other merchants, junior officers, soldiers – even cabin boys – hacked to death, drowned, bashed, beheaded or strangled men and women and children. As the murders went on, day after day, week after week, the killers became drunk with the slaughter and began hunting down their prey wearing gorgeous uniforms of red coats embroidered with gold and silver from material looted from the ship's hold.

It seemed nothing could stop the atrocities until, on one of the smaller islands, Wiebbe Hayes, a soldier sent with an unarmed scouting party of around 25, sent up a smoke signal. He had found water. A score or so men escaped at once, swimming, to the smaller island. They told Hayes their story, began making pikes, daggers and clubs from timbers and barrel hoops washed ashore, and waited for the inevitable attack.

On 27 July the first attack was beaten off. A second attack followed within a week but Hayes's men waded into the water and once again drove

Top: Encapsulated in one image: the shipwreck of the *Batavia*, stuck on the Abrolhos coral rocks, the drownings of those who failed to reach the three small islands, and the indiscriminate daily slaughter that followed.
Above: The torture of mutineers at Batavia Castle before their public execution. Seven, considered the most dangerous, had already died on the coral islands, hanged on hastily erected gibbets. Their leader, Cornelisz, defiantly roared, 'Revenge!' as he went to his death.

them back. Two weeks later, four of Hayes's soldiers died from gunshots in a third assault. Then, as the mutineers retired to re-load, a ship, the *Saadam*, with Francisco Pelsaert aboard, appeared beyond the reef. Both sides made a frantic dash to get to it first. Hayes and three others met Pelsaert as he was about to step into a skiff loaded with bread and had hardly told him the situation when two boats came alongside manned by mutineeers bristling with weapons and dressed in their lavish embroidered 'uniform'. They asked to be taken on board. Pelsaert declined and instead gave them the choice of surrendering or being blown apart. The men put down their weapons.

Seven of the most dangerous mutineers were executed then and there. They brought Jeronimus Cornelisz to a block and chopped off his right hand – the hand that had drawn up the pirate compact. Then he was dragged to a makeshift gallows. He was followed by would-be pirates, murderers, who just a few weeks before, were simply soldiers, or carpenters, merchants or cabin boys.

The rest of the mutineers – all but two – were taken to Batavia, gruesomely tortured and publicly executed. Wouter Looes, a soldier, and Jan Pelgrom de Bye, a cabin boy, who murdered another boy, were spared. When the *Saadam* sailed for Batavia they were taken to the mainland and left.

Pelsaert advised the two to behave well towards any natives they might encounter. 'If they will then take you into their villages to their chief man, have the courage to go with them willingly. Man's luck is found in strange places.' Nothing more was ever heard of Jan Pelgrom de Bye and Wouter Looes. But decades later explorers encountered blue-eyed Aborigines, and it is feasible that one of their descendants may be reading these words at this moment.

# The first blood

The hypothetical existence of Terra Australis, the Great South Land, had been mooted for more than a thousand years and had been proven, first by the Portuguese and then the Dutch, in the 16th century. And the likelihood is that in the early 15th century, even before them, the Chinese may have touched our northern coasts. The English, however, had shown little interest in the land the Dutch called New Holland, and the pirate William Dampier's distinct lack of enthusiasm, once he had set foot on it – the first Englishman known to have done so on the mainland – reinforced this.

4th January, 1688, we fell in with the land of New Holland having made our course due south. New Holland is a very large tract of land. It is not yet determined whether it is an island or a main continent; but I am certain that it joins neither to Asia, Africa nor America... The land is of a dry sandy soil, destitute of water except you make Wells... The inhabitants of this country are the miserablest people in this world... They are tall, straight-bodied and thin. They have great heads, round foreheads and great brows.

Dampier stepped ashore at a point near the present day Buccaneer Archipelago and was welcomed by Aborigines waving spears. A gun shot scattered them and then Dampier, having frightened the women and children into flight, offered the men clothing and ordered them to carry water to the boats. They declined both. His pirate ship, the *Cygnet*, was careened and its hull scraped at low tide and despite the men's fears that troglodytes walked the land – men whose heads grew under their shoulders and whose feet were so large that they served as sunshades when they lay down in the sun – the crew lived ashore for nine weeks, sleeping in huts and hunting turtles and manatees.

Dampier left the *Cygnet* at the Nicobar Islands and with seven others set off in a canoe for Sumatra. In 1691, 12 years after he had left England, he returned, accompanied by a Filipino whom Dampier told London was a member of Philippines royalty, 'Prince Job'.

He remained ashore for two years until in 1693 he sailed for the West Indies with a group of adventurers looking to recover treasure from sunken Spanish ships.

Dampier's expedition was a spectacular failure. It never reached the Caribbean, and he returned to England in February 1695. Desolate, he wrote, '[I made] very sad reflections on my former life and looked back with horror and detestation on actions which before I disliked, but now I trembled at the remembrance of.'

William Dampier is an enigma. For more than 40 years and in the course of sailing three times round the world, Dampier did the things that pirates do: looting, pillaging and murdering from South America to Sumatra. But he was much more than a pirate. William Dampier was one of the greatest explorers, a man who had seen more of the world than any man ever had – he was the first person to visit five of the seven continents – and his scientific records of those extraordinary journeys remained relevant for at least two centuries. Few have led a life more crowded with adventure.

Born in 1652, he went to sea as a boy and at 21, then in the navy and at war with the Dutch, he

Dampier began his career as a buccaneer on the Spanish Main, landed in Australia 80 years before Captain Cook, was the first person to circumnavigate the world three times, and wrote the first best-seller.

all: *A New Voyage Round the World*. The Admiralty began to show interest in the Great Southern Continent, New Holland. The diarist John Evelyn noted in August 1698: 'I dined with Mr Pepys, where was Captain Dampier, who had been a famous Buccaneer [and] printed a relation of his very strange adventures, and his observations. He was now going abroad again by the King's encouragement, who furnished a ship of 290 tons.'

Dampier intended to discover the east coast of New Holland and sailed the *Roebuck* 1450 kilometres around the western and northern coast, landing at Shark Bay and going ashore at Roebuck Bay, south of Broome. He wanted to capture an Aborigine but the situation got out of hand. He fired his gun into the air and when the Aborigines noticed that the noise had no discernible effect they charged. Dampier was forced to wound one of them – the first known bloodshed between the indigenous inhabitants and whites on the mainland of the continent.

He was tired, feeling his age, now. He fell sick but brought the rotting *Roebuck* as far as the Atlantic before it went down off Ascension Island.

Undeterred, he took ship again in 1707 with a privateer and returned with 200,000 pounds of booty and Alexander Selkirk, a man Dampier had marooned on a previous voyage and whose island exile inspired Daniel Defoe to write *Robinson Crusoe*. The old sea dog was 57 now, and his last days were spent quietly and fairly comfortably in London. His second book, *Voyage to New Holland*, was published in 1709 and again, in the course of recounting his extraordinary adventures, was disparaging about Australia.

He died in March 1715. It is not known where he is buried.

had his first taste of battle. Wounded and invalided out of the service he went home to recuperate but within a year he had worked his passage to Jamaica to manage a plantation for a neighbouring Somerset family. There he got to know the pirates and privateers who flourished in those Caribbean waters.

Dampier's written repentance of his piratical past was published in 1697 in a work that astonished

# The First Fleet

### BOUND FOR BOTANY BAY

*Farewell to olde England forever*
*Farewell to my olde pals as well*
*Farewell to the well known Old Bailey*
*Where I once used to look such a swell.*
*Chorus:*
*Singing Too-ral Li-ooral li-ad-dity*
*Singing too-ral li-ooral li-ay*
*Singing too-ral li-ooral li-ad-dity*
*And we're bound for Botany Bay*
*...Now all my young Dukies and Duchesses*
*Take a warning from what I'd to say*
*Mind all is your own that you toucheses*
*Or you'll find us in Botany Bay*
*Singing Too-ral Li-ooral li-ad-dity...*

That was the ballad they sang after the First Fleet had sailed to Botany Bay and established the colony of New South Wales. The message may have been mordant, but it was delivered with some gusto and jollity – when the colony had settled in and many of the mysteries of the unknown land were no more. But until then their exile in an upside down world frightened the convicts; the young dukies and duchesses and the old lags. 'Their constant language was an apprehension of the impracticability of returning home, the dread of the sickly passage, and the fearful prospect of a distant and barbarous country,' Marine Captain Watkin Tench wrote.

They came to this frightening new world in 11 ships. Only two of the 11, the flagship HMS *Sirius,* and HMS *Supply*, were naval warships, the rest were converted merchantmen. All were small; cockleshells by today's standards, and suffocatingly cramped. The largest transport in the fleet, the *Alexander*, was less than 35 metres long and 10 metres in beam, and the second largest, *Scarborough*, had so little headroom – four feet five inches – 134 centimetres – that lack of oxygen on the lower decks sometimes made it impossible to light a candle.

The convicts shared double bunks 90 centimetres wide, the air below deck was foul and the bilge almost beyond description, though Robert Hughes in *The Fatal Shore* has a splendid try: 'Even those whose guts have heaved at the whiff from the boat's head at sea can have little idea of the anguish of eighteenth century bilge stink: a fermenting, sloshing broth of sea water mixed with urine, puke, dung, rotting feed, dead rats and the hundred other attars of the Great Age of Sail.' Surgeon John White, on the *Alexander*, said the bilge effluents 'had by some means or other risen to so great a

height that the panels of the cabin and the buttons on the back of the officers' jackets were turned nearly black by the noxious effluvia. When the hatches were taken off the stench was so powerful that it was scarcely possible to stand over them.'

They didn't know it, but the passengers aboard the First Fleet were on a voyage that would take more than three-quarters of a year. First to Teneriffe in the Canary Islands off north-west Africa; then to Rio de Janeiro on the east coast of South America; on to Cape Town at the southern tip of Africa and from there to Botany Bay across a southern ocean where only six European vessels had gone before.

At 3 a.m. on a black mid-winter morning the signal was given: weigh anchor, and with His Majesty's frigate *Hyena* as escort the fleet sailed from Portsmouth. It was Sunday 3 May 1787. Aboard the ships were around 1500 men, women and children, of whom half – 759 – were convicts, 191 of them women, and almost all of them thieves. (Contrary to folklore few women convicts were transported for prostitution and only around 300 men were exiled for political offences.) The remainder of those on the ships, in order of rank, were civil and military officers, 245 marines, 31 of their wives and 23 of their children; and 306 ships' crew.

Most were from England but there were also 83 Irish, 33 Scots, nine Welsh and 14 North Americans and assorted Europeans, a dozen or

so black men and Jewish men and women. There were 45 children, 22 of them with their convict parents. Another eight children were born on the voyage. With them came 700 axes, 700 hatchets, 700 spades, 700 shovels, 12 ploughs, 40 wheel-barrows, six carts, 10 blacksmiths' forges, 44 tonnes of tallow, pit saws, adzes, claw hammers, bedding, chisels, fishing nets, 800 sets of bedding, 420 dozen candles. On and below deck were the commander's pet greyhounds, bulls, cows, sheep, goats, pigs, turkeys, ducks, geese and chickens and, most essential, grog. Inadvertently left behind was clothing for the women convicts, ammunition for the guns on the ship, and musket balls and paper for cartridges for the marines' firearms. Oh, and the provost-marshal.

The London *Morning Post* farewelled the fleet with the uplifting and extremely optimistic thought that those setting sail for 'the thief colony' might hold the seeds to 'a great empire, whose nobles will probably, like the nobles of Rome, boast of their blood.' The more pragmatic reason for the establishment of 'the thief colony' – New South Wales – was not to found a great new empire, but to rid England of its unwanted. America was no longer available as a dumping ground (the War of

The 11 ships of the First Fleet, left to right: *Alexander* (convict transport), *Prince of Wales* (convict transport), HMS *Sirius* (main Naval ship), *Lady Penrhyn* (convict transport), *Fishburn* (storeship), *Scarborough* (convict transport), HMS *Supply* (fleet tender), *Charlotte* (convict transport), *Golden Grove* (storeship), *Friendship* (convict transport) and *Borrowdale* (storeship).

Independence had seen to that) and Prime Minister Pitt's government wanted to relieve the pressure on its over-crowded prisons and rotting hulks. Their inhabitants, all born to be bad in the prevailing opinion, could be shipped to the other side of the world, never again to be a blot on Blighty's landscape. These first 1500 were the forerunners of more than 160,000 convicts who would be sent to Australia over the next 80 years. They were to be first in all things. And for the inhabitants of the land they were invading they were to be the first white people ever seen.

William Bradley, first lieutenant on the *Sirius*, meeting a large number of Aborigines a few days after landing, described them: 'The men we met with here were in general stout and very well-limbed. The women, excepting the very old women, were young and in general shorter than the men; very straight-limbed and well-featured, their voices a pleasing softness, they were all entirely naked, old and young.' And in that regard, Lieutenant Philip Gidley King, later to be governor of the colony, wrote, 'I think it very easy to conceive the ridiculous figure we must appear to these poor creatures, who were perfectly naked.'

The collision of two worlds was apparent to both from the very beginning.

# The first governor

The Governor of New South Wales was on the beach at Manly, trying to make an agonising run for it. He had a three-metre long spear through his body, the butt jagging in the sand.

'Get it out for God's sake!' the governor cried and young Lieutenant Waterhouse did his best, and failed, as spears rained around them.

This image of Governor Arthur Phillip is one we are not familiar with. The official depiction, the one we are accustomed to, shows him standing in the uniform of an Admiral of the Fleet, looking slightly perplexed. An almost bow-legged middle-aged man, short, with a narrow face, large nose and fleshy lips. Take away the wig and he might look like Woody Allen with a humour bypass; or the man behind the counter who tells you to keep applying the ointment.

Arthur Phillip was humourless and unprepossessing. But he was much more than that. He was human, for one, and probably kept his housekeeper, Deborah Brooks, as his mistress. Phillip, a 48-year-old man, had left his wife in England and Deborah Brooks, in the frustratingly fleeting references we have of her, was clearly an attractive woman. The two had met on an island in 1783. Sailing to the East Indies in HMS *Europe* Phillip encountered Deborah on the island of St Helena. She was stranded there with four British sailors and three other women. Edward Spain, a seaman on Phillip's ship, wrote that he 'granted leave to four women to go to sea in the ship. But don't imagine that it was out of partiality to any of them, except one, which one he had a sneaking kindness for and had he given permission to her

Arthur Phillip's precept, 'There can be no slavery in a free world,' articulated his vision for the colony and set the template for the peaceful and successful integration of the convicts.

alone the reason would have been obvious to the officers and the ship's company.'

Deborah, Spain wrote, 'had eloped from her husband... She it was that our noble commander had a partiality for... [and] had free access in and out of the great cabin.'

Spain suspected that Phillip wanted to replace him as bo'sun with Thomas Brooks, Deborah's companion, 'the fancy woman's gallant', to ingratiate himself with her, but 'The Admiral no doubt saw through the scheme,' and Brooks was not promoted. But five years later, as bo'sun, Brooks sailed on the First Fleet's flagship, *Sirius*, with Deborah and Phillip. Deborah became Governor Phillip's housekeeper in Sydney Cove and she is almost certainly the woman Bennelong fondly remembered kissing, moments before Phillip was speared.

So Arthur Phillip was certainly human. But he was also humane and resolute; a brave man for this brave new world. (Phillip suffered his spearing stoically and forbade retaliation.) He was patient; he was firm; he was far-sighted; he was intelligent; he was practical; and he was benevolent. He could be hard, too; ruthless when he felt it was necessary. Phillip treated the convicts – by the standards of the day – with justice and, often, mercy. But though he doubted 'if the fear of death ever prevented a man of no principle from committing a bad action,' he had been less than six weeks in the new land before he approved the hanging of a 17-year-old boy for stealing dried beans, salt pork and butter worth five shillings (50 cents).

And of murder and sodomy, Phillip said – though he didn't act on it – 'I would wish to confine the criminal until an opportunity offered of delivering him to the natives of New Zealand and let them eat him. The dread of this will operate much stronger than the fear of death.'

Chillingly ruthless at times, visionary, merciful, dispassionate. All these qualities Phillip would call upon in the unique challenges to come: the establishment of a penal colony for thieves on the other, virtually unknown, side of the world.

Captain Phillip's first challenge was to get his fleet

safely to the new colony. It was to be the longest voyage ever attempted on this scale, a passage across oceans unknown to Phillip and all who sailed with him. The First Fleet had been at sea for eight months and one week and had traversed over 24,000 kilometres when the *Supply* dropped anchor in Botany Bay on 18 January 1788. It had not been all plain sailing – there were two mutinies and an attempted escape along the way, but only 48 had died on the voyage: 40 convicts, five children of convicts, one marine, one marine's wife (Mary Cook, wife of the drum-major), and one marine's child.

By the time the First Fleet dropped anchor in Port Jackson, Arthur Phillip had already demonstrated that he had been an astute choice (though there is little evidence that the matter had been given much thought) for the position of the colony's commander: an autocrat – virtually a despot if he chose – of New South Wales.

But in the following four years, he showed again and again that his appointment, if fortuitous, was inspired. Everyone gave him trouble at some stage, from Lieutenant Governor Major Ross, the choleric commander of the marines and one of the most unpleasant and universally loathed individuals in the colony, down to the convicts and the Aborigines. The male convicts got among the female convicts. The Aborigines clashed with the invaders and sometimes slaughtered them. There was a partial drought. The pathetic crops failed. The sole surviving supply ship was wrecked. The colony had just three months food remaining. Then 3000 more hungry mouths arrived...

As starvation threatened he ordered that the convicts get the same rations as their captors. This infuriated the marines, the more so when he hanged some of them for stealing food. And the convicts in turn were angered by his even-handedness – bias, as they saw it – towards the Aborigines they feared and despised.

Phillip strove to comply with his orders to befriend the natives and to punish those who gave them 'unnecessary interruption'. When Aborigines killed and mutilated convicts he refused to order retaliatory attacks and flogged those who attempted to do so. (He also insisted that the convicts would not be slaves. 'There can be no slavery in a free world.') And when Phillip finally ordered a punitive raid to bring back Aboriginal heads in retaliation for the murder of his gamekeeper he was unfazed when the party returned empty-handed.

'By grit and stubborn even-handedness even in face of hopeless prisoners and near mutinous marines, Phillip pulled his wretched settlement through months of crisis,' Robert Hughes wrote in *The Fatal Shore*. Starvation presented the most frightening scenario. Phillip vowed, 'We shall not starve, though seven-eighths of the colony deserves nothing better, the present want will be done away by the first ship that arrives.'

That ship, the *Lady Juliana*, arrived on 3 June 1790. It brought more misery: 222 women convicts and some flour and the news that the *Guardian*, laden with two years' food and stores, had struck an iceberg and had been abandoned in Cape Town. It was followed by the remaining ships in the Second Fleet, spewing out their dead, dying and incapacitated.

And on and on it went: four dismal, frustrating and turbulent years in an alien, dangerous, topsy-turvy world. Yet when Phillip finally sailed for England in December 1792, a new nation had been born. Arthur Phillip's was the first distinct European footprint on the Australian landscape.

# 2

# THE DISASTERS

The televised rescue of Todd Russell and Brant Webb, trapped for 14 days in the 2006 mining disaster at Beaconsfield in northern Tasmania, thrilled a breathlessly watching nation.

Within months of the First Fleet's arrival the settlement faced a disaster. Starvation. The crops had failed and in March 1789 six marines were hanged for stealing stores. The following year an officer wrote home to say that 'In our visitings it has long been the custom to put your bread at least in your pocket; and the usual form of salutation is "Will you bring your bread and come and see me?"' The first 'conventional' disasters, however, were the shipwrecks that brought first convicts, and then free settlers, to the colonies.

Many of those shipwrecks were the result of navigation errors. But the disasters that Australia is most prone to are beyond human control. 'I love a sunburnt country,' Dorothea Mackellar wrote in 'My Country', but the Australian sun has caused untold deaths. Skin cancer from sunburn – melanoma – is a silent, cruel killer, and astonishingly, heatwaves have killed more Australians than any other natural phenomenon. Mackellar went on to list other aspects of life in Australia – droughts and flooding rains – but she could have added cyclones. In March 1899 the Bathurst Bay tropical cyclone Mahina killed more than 400 people – six times the toll of Cyclone Tracy.

The personal hardships, financial loss, and environmental damage caused by drought is incalculable. In 2006, climate experts told us that we were having the worst drought in a thousand years. Were we? Historian Geoffrey Blainey pointed out that the Federation Drought from 1894 to 1902 was far more devastating, and it was followed by the most arid years on record.

Bushfires present almost annual disasters.

And then there are the man-made disasters. In 1850 a Somerset landowner sent his brother in Victoria 24 wild rabbits and the man released them on his property to provide some sporting shooting. Within 10 years, millions of rabbits were swarming throughout the Western District, and soon right across Australia. Man-made or natural, disasters will always be with us. And we've learned to cope and live with them all.

# The 1939 bushfires

Imagine heat so intense it causes brick buildings to spontaneously combust. Imagine a towering wall of flame hundreds of kilometres wide inexorably consuming all in its way. Imagine huge trees lifting from the earth like gigantic flaming matches. Imagine a colossal flamethrower burning and roaring across the entire state of Victoria.

No matter how grotesque the images and how vivid your imagination, the holocaust that raged across Victoria on Friday 13 January 1939 – Black Friday – beggars all.

The worst bushfire in Australia's recent history, Black Friday, and the fires that preceded it, left 71 dead and many hundreds badly burnt and injured. Ash Wednesday, in February 1983, cost 76 lives in Victoria and South Australia, and Tasmania's 7 February 1967 bushfire devastated that state, killing 62 in a single day.

But Black Friday, 1939, unlike any other bushfire Australia has known, had the entire state at its mercy. Its death toll was horrendous. The heatwave that triggered the blazes claimed 438 lives. And its savagery was of biblical proportions. The ferocity of the fires horrified Australia and left a scar on the national psyche.

The nation heard how men were boiled alive, roasted in a sawdust heap, held prisoner by thorns on a blackberry bush as the fire swooped, and died from suffocation or agonising burns inside marooned cars. At Matlock, 15 died in one timber mill and another 12 in the Rubicon timber belt. Four children were burnt to death near Colac. Near Noojee an entire family perished.

The Black Friday bushfire was a monster, and the monster was everywhere. It appeared as though 'the whole state was alight', a Royal Commission judge later said.

Judge Leonard Stretton, who headed the Royal Commission, vividly described that infamous Friday the 13th. And his description tells why Black Friday is probably the worst natural disaster we have known.

Judge Stretton wrote:

Townships were obliterated in a few minutes. Mills, houses, bridges, tramways, machines were burnt to the ground: men, cattle, horses, sheep were devoured by the fires or asphyxiated by the scorching debilitated air.

Generally the numerous fires which during December, in many parts of Victoria, had been burning separately, as they do in any summer, either 'under control' as it is falsely and dangerously called, or entirely unattended, reached the climax of their intensity and joined forces in a devastating confluence of flames on Friday the 13th of January.

On that day it appeared that the whole state was alight. At midday, in many places, it was as dark as night. Men carrying hurricane lamps worked to make safe their families and belongings.

Travellers on the highways were trapped by fires or blazing fallen trees, and perished. Throughout the land there was daytime darkness... Horses were found harnessed in their stalls, dead, their limbs fantastically contorted.

Steel girders and machinery were twisted by

With Victoria engulfed in flames, a dark cloud of smoke, ashes and cinders hung over the state and even darkened the skies over New Zealand, where ashes also fell. The worst bushfire in our history, Black Friday, 1939, left 71 dead.

heat as if they had been balls of fine wire. Sleepers of heavy durable timber, set in soil, their upper surfaces flush with the ground, were burnt through... Balls of crackling fire sped at a great pace in advance of the fires, consuming with a roaring explosive noise all they touched. Houses of brick were seen and heard to leap into a roar of flames before the fires had reached them... Great pieces of burning bark were carried by the wind to set in raging flame regions not yet reached by the fires. Such was the force of the wind that in many places hundreds of trees of great size were blown clear of the earth and piled upon one another as matches strewn by a giant hand...

One day's rain could have saved the state. But when it came – on the Sunday – it was too late. Instead, much of the drought-stricken state was left blackened and smoking. Countless sheep and native animals had been devoured by the flames. Two entire townships were obliterated. Sixty-nine sawmills were burnt to the ground along with 700 homes and many businesses and farms.

The fires affected 75 per cent of the state in one way or another. They burnt 1.4 million hectares of protected and reserved forests and plantations and changed forever the lives of thousands of Victorians. The landscape, too, would never be the same. The Black Friday bushfires, the most dramatic and influential event in the environmental history of Victoria, had a huge impact on the beauty of the countryside, the regeneration of forests, soil fertility and water catchments.

Could Black Friday have been avoided?

Before white settlement, the Aborigines knew that fire is a necessary part of the environment and understood how to keep it under control. Their system of burning-off created a mosaic pattern of burnt areas which managed bushfires – accidental and man-made – and prevented any disasters. Judge Stretton found, in essence, that the Black Friday fires were lit by landowners who had little understanding of bushfires and their control. He recommended that the public be educated on the matter.

But even with the greatest of knowledge and care the combination of dry, dense forests and adverse weather – record heat of 47.7°C and a roaring 110-kilometre-per hour northerly wind – would have inevitably ignited bushfires. And the volunteer bands would have been no match for what followed.

In this hell, firefighters were powerless. The regular bushfire fighters, all men in voluntary brigades, were joined by thousands more but they could do little other than try to save lives and homes. The orthodox method of halting a bushfire is to make a firebreak clearing in the path of the advancing fire. But the intense roaring wind on Black Friday tore huge trees from the earth and carried flaming bark and trees across the firebreaks to fresh fields. The smoke was so dense that ships off the coast hove to or turned on their foghorns.

The fire spanned the South Australian border to Gippsland. In the Otway Ranges south-west of Melbourne, fire swept down almost to the sea and the resort towns of Lorne and Apollo Bay. Melbourne itself was threatened, the fires coming within 50 kilometres of the capital. In the east, at Warburton, fires menaced the township and destroyed much of the surrounding bush. In Gippsland thousands of hectares of timber went. Timber towns such as Noojee, rebuilt after being destroyed by fire in 1921, along with the picturesque old gold mining centre, Woods Point, and Matlock

were obliterated. Others such as Warrandyte, Yarra Glen, Omeo and Pomonal were badly scarred.

The fires reached into towns as far apart as Ballarat and Dromana, Mansfield and the Grampians. From end to end they burnt along the Victorian Alps. And close to Melbourne, in the Dandenongs and at Healesville, many homes were lost but the famous wildlife sanctuary was saved. Sometimes there was no warning. A Country Roads Board truck carrying 44-gallon drums of petrol was parked in the main street of Woods Point. The heat simply burst the drums and flaming petrol poured on to the street. Near Warrandyte two firefronts met and took out half the township while women and children dashed for their lives to the safety of the river.

Too often the fires caught fleeing people. The town of Narbethong was razed, and on the Acheron Way road beyond the town the fire caught a car with seven terrified passengers. They were burnt to death.

In the Matlock forest, 17 men at Fitzpatrick's timber mill – almost the entire community – perished. The owner of the mill died near his two sons. Another man climbed into an elevated water tank in a frantic attempt to escape. His remains were found in the boiled-dry tank. Others tried to insulate themselves by burrowing into a sawdust pit. Across the horrified nation prayers went up for the weather to break. And a cool change reached central Victoria in the early afternoon of Black Friday but it came with little rain.

That night there was some lessening in the intensity of the fires but morning saw them burning with renewed ferocity. Finally, late on Sunday, the wind changed and with it came blessed, drenching rain. The worst fires the nation has known were extinguished.

This scene is typical of the devastation across Victoria. At Woods Point 143 of 150 houses were in ashes. At Matlock, the remains of 15 men were found.

# HMAS *Voyager*

'The thing that unnerved me most of all was when the ship turned up on its end and started to slide under – the cries of those trapped inside... that was the most horrific experience. If you've ever seen the movie *The Cruel Sea*, men are trapped below and screams come up through the voice pipe to the bridge. The captain has to – for his own sanity – close the cover in the voice pipe to try to shut out those screams of the trapped men.'

Michael Patterson, leading seaman in the operations room on HMAS *Voyager*, 25 years on and talking to the ABC's *Four Corners*, still vividly recalled the horror of the night the *Voyager* went down, split in two by HMAS *Melbourne*, with the loss of its captain, 13 other officers and 68 seamen.

It took only minutes for the flagship of the Royal Australian Navy to slice her escort in two. But the controversy and the traumas of those few minutes remain unresolved four decades on.

'It's not something easy to describe,' Michael Patterson said. And it is impossible, he may have added, to forget. But what is most enduring about the night of 10 February 1964 is the question of who was to blame for Australia's worst peacetime military disaster.

On that February night, the aircraft carrier HMAS *Melbourne* and the destroyer HMAS *Voyager* were steaming together, 160 kilometres south of Sydney, off Jervis Bay.

*Voyager*, a Daring class destroyer of 3200 tonnes under Captain Duncan Stevens, was escorting the pride of the Australian fleet, *Melbourne*, the giant 20,000-tonne Majestic-class aircraft carrier under Captain John Robertson.

It was a moonless night, but clear, and visibility was 30 kilometres. The sun had set an hour ago, at 7.45 p.m., and the two ships, on a 'night op', were heading south, looking for a wind to allow aircraft to take off and land on the carrier.

Captain Stevens's orders were to take his ship astern of the aircraft carrier to 'Plane Guard Station', ready to come to the rescue of any aircraft that misjudged its landing on *Melbourne*'s flight deck and finished in the sea.

*Melbourne* gave the 'flying course' as 020 degrees and the speed as 22 knots. *Voyager*, about 1500 metres ahead of *Melbourne* and on her port bow, needed to allow the carrier to pass her, and then fall in astern. Usually a destroyer would do this by turning in a circle until the carrier was ahead and then fall in behind.

*Voyager* turned to starboard. Then, about 40 seconds later, Captain Robertson on duty on *Melbourne*'s bridge, saw the destroyer swing back to port. He assumed that *Voyager* was 'doing a fishtail', changing course from port to starboard, reducing speed, and waiting for the carrier to pass.

*Voyager* was more than 700 metres away when, out on the wing of the destroyer's bridge, an 18-year-old ordinary seaman, Brian Sumpter, cried out in alarm: 'Bridge!'

Brian Sumpter had been at sea only a few days and was the port lookout. What he saw worried him. *Voyager* was beginning to get uncomfortably close to *Melbourne*. On the starboard lookout was another teenager, Robin Russel, 17, who had just one hour's experience in the job.

As *Voyager* continued closing on *Melbourne*, Sumpter's call to the bridge went unanswered. Captain Stevens, for reasons never satisfactorily explained, was off the bridge, studying a chart

Captain Robertson readied *Melbourne*. 'Collision Stations!' he ordered and all watertight doors and hatchways were shut.

The biggest ship in the navy, *Melbourne* had no hope of slowing down or turning away in time to avoid the approaching catastrophe. The two officers could now only pray that *Voyager* had been ordered to alter course and swing away from their ship. The order was given – but it came too late.

It was 8.55 p.m. On *Voyager*, the officer of the watch, Lieutenant Price, presumably shouted to Captain Stevens in alarm. Stevens, it is known, got to the bridge from the chart table and ordered: 'Hard at starboard – Collision Stations!'

Twenty seconds later, at 20.56 hours, the destroyer hit *Melbourne*'s bow. Captain Stevens and those around him were killed instantly as the carrier carved through, cutting *Voyager* in half near the bridge.

The two halves of *Voyager* drifted down *Melbourne*'s sides. In the bow section were 225 of the crew of 314. When it sank, a few minutes later, it took most of the 82 men who were at the area of impact.

Not all of the dead went to the bottom, 1500 fathoms (nearly three kilometres) down. Captain Stevens's body was recovered from the sea by a helicopter from the Fleet Air Arm station near Nowra on the New South Wales coast. *Melbourne*'s boats picked up others as well as the surviving 232 officers and men from the destroyer.

No one was injured on *Melbourne* and, her decks crowded with survivors and some of the dead, she made her way back to a stunned, waiting nation, and a series of controversial post-mortems.

Just hours after the disaster the prime minister, Sir Robert Menzies, ordered a Royal Commission.

Looking like a Great White Shark, the pride of the fleet, the aircraft carrier HMAS *Melbourne*, comes home to a stunned nation and a series of controversial post-mortems. *Newspix*

under a light, which would have temporarily caused him to lose his night sight.

On the bridge of the *Melbourne*, meanwhile, the ship's navigator, Commander J.M. Kelly, had arrived to check the wind as Captain Robertson moved to the compass platform.

Commander Kelly was stunned at what he saw. 'Stop both engines – half speed astern both engines!' he shouted as almost simultaneously Captain Robertson ordered: 'Full speed astern both engines!'

It laid the blame for the collision on *Voyager*. But it was unable to account for the collision itself. 'It was not due to any fault on the part of any person on *Melbourne*. Nor is it possible to identify the individual or individuals on *Voyager* who were responsible. It is not easy to understand how the collision could have occurred if an effective lookout was being maintained on *Voyager*, and appropriate evasion had been taken as soon as any possibility of danger was observed.'

There the tragic matter might have rested. But six months later the new prime minister, Harold Holt, responding to allegations that Captain Stevens was a drunkard and that his ship handling was subject to sudden lapses, flashes of recklessness or bad temper, ordered a second inquiry that absolved Captain Robertson and his two fellow officers on *Melbourne* of all blame for the collision. The commission also absolved Captain Stevens, rejecting entirely 'any idea that the late Captain Stevens was under the influence of liquor at the time of the collision'.

The report found that he was not a drunkard, nor did he become periodically intoxicated. Of his handling of ships, the commissioners said, 'There was some evidence that from time to time the late Captain Stevens became impatient and gave officers of the watch and others a "blast". We suspect this is by no means an uncommon characteristic of some RAN officers.'

Five years after the *Voyager* disaster, HMAS *Melbourne* again ran over an escorting destroyer. The circumstances were similar, with the US vessel on a course that made collision inevitable. This time 74 American seamen died. And, once again, *Melbourne*'s captain was honourably acquitted but demoted, causing him to resign, as Captain Robertson had done before him.
*AWM NAVY15897*

# Cyclone Tracy

It was the night before Christmas, 1974, and Cyclone Tracy was coming to town. People were expecting Tracy: expecting her to pass close, but not too close for comfort. Four days before, the Bureau of Meteorology had monitored the formation of a tropical depression 700 kilometres north. When it recorded winds of 63 kilometres an hour the bureau upgraded it to a cyclone and gave it the name Tracy. Over the next few days Tracy moved closer, but it was going to pass well to the north, the bureau said, until early on Christmas Eve Tracy changed direction and headed straight for the city.

Darwin had been badly damaged by a cyclone in 1937, but few of the 43,500 residents of Darwin were there then, and cyclone warnings, for most people, were something that they had come to ignore. Cyclone Selma had been predicted to hit Darwin earlier that month but it had gone north and dissipated. 'We'd had a cyclone warning only 10 days before Tracy... and it never came. So when we started hearing about Tracy we were all a little blasé,' Dawn Lawrie told Bill Bunbury (*Cyclone Tracy, Picking Up the Pieces*). Another resident told Bunbury, 'And you started to almost think that it would never happen to Darwin even though we had cyclone warnings on the radio all the time... most of the people didn't really believe the warnings.'

By 10 that Christmas Eve they were beginning to believe. Darwin was being drenched and the wind was whipping through the city. By midnight Darwin was in the eye of a cyclone. For the next five hours Darwin was ferociously battered by a Category Five cyclone the city had treated with contempt. By seven the next morning, Boxing

The eye of the storm, photographed from space. Cyclone warnings were a fact of life in Darwin. Only hours before a ferocious cyclone mundanely named Tracy struck, people were celebrating at Christmas Eve parties. By 1 a.m. Tracy was tearing down the town. When the cyclone finally passed people emerged to see this wasteland.

Day, the people of Darwin came out from wherever they had sought shelter to find their city almost wholly destroyed.

Seventy-one people – 49 on land and 22 at sea – died. Up to 1000 were injured. More than 70 per cent of Darwin's buildings were destroyed. And Australia struggled to come to terms with the fact that one of its capital cities was no more.

Cyclone Tracy was our most compact tropical cyclone on record: from its centre it extended only 48 kilometres. But it was Darwin's ill luck to be at the centre of the storm. The wind gauge at Darwin airport recorded winds of 217 kilometres an hour before it was blown away. Unofficially the winds reached 300 kilometres an hour. Few buildings in Darwin could withstand gales of that tremendous power and intensity.

Darwin was rebuilt, of course. Today twice as many people live in the city. But newcomers or old hands, there are none who have forgotten Cyclone Tracy.

# The Granville train crash

It's 8.12 in the morning on 18 January 1977. Jack McKeown is in his newsagency shop at Granville, an outer suburb of Sydney. Outside it's raining lightly, and the 6.09 from the Blue Mountains is a couple of minutes late. Just another morning.

Jack had been an engine-driver with the railways before he retired to run the newsagency but when he glances up he sees what he's never seen in all his years: about 50 metres from a nearby rail overpass a train coming round the bend is out of control, skidding down the line at nearly 80 kilometres per hour.

Jack runs outside – stops, open-mouthed – and then dashes back in when he sees what happens next.

Jack dials. Emergency services. 'Give me the ambulance – there's been a huge train crash!'

In the next 30 seconds scores of passengers in Train No. 108 are to die instantly. Hundreds more will be trapped under 600 tonnes of steel and concrete. And at the end of that day as Australia, aghast, watches the dead and the injured taken from the wreck, the toll of this, the nation's worst train accident, will be 83 dead and 213 injured.

It was a disaster that could easily have been avoided. Train No. 108 went off the rails simply because the wide gauge track was in need of repair: poorly fastened and badly aligned.

It was a disaster of such magnitude because the train was derailed under a bridge, which then fell on it. 'If it had happened on an open line, carriages would have been damaged, and passengers shaken, but probably most people would have walked away,'

a railway expert, Dr Stewart Joy, has said. And because of the nature of the train that the regulars on the 6.09 called 'The Summit', it was a disaster that almost pre-ordained those who died in their usual seats and those who escaped.

'The Summit train was a very friendly and homely sort of atmosphere,' recalled Jeff Moran, a past president of the Blue Mountains Commuter Association.

'There was a large proportion of the train with booked seats; everyone knew pretty well everyone else's first name.'

The friendly train left Mount Victoria Station in the Blue Mountains uneventfully as usual on that day and pulled out of Parramatta Station for Sydney Central, at 8.10 a.m., three minutes behind schedule. Engine 4620 was hauling eight wooden carriages on the last leg of its 126-kilometre journey.

It was a trip most of its 469 passengers had taken hundreds of times. But within three minutes it was to be the last for many of them. Just before Granville, an outer Sydney suburb, Driver Ted Olencewicz slowed the train as it rounded a bend and he and some passengers felt three sharp jolts. To some it seemed as if the driver was putting on the brakes quite heavily. In fact the jolts were the wheels leaving the rails on the bend. The front wheel of Engine 4620 had fallen inside its rail. The other wheels followed.

The engine skidded 46 metres and slammed through all eight steel stanchions of one of two trestles supporting the upper decking of the Bolt Street overpass, and stopped, on its side, 67 metres further on.

Behind it, also derailed, were the first two carriages. Carriage 1 had struck a power pole. Shorn off at its base, the pole crashed down, ripping apart

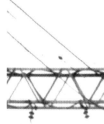

the roof, flattening the walls almost to ground level, killing eight of its 73 passengers and injuring 34. But the second carriage stayed largely on the track, virtually unscathed, and there were no fatalities among its 64 passengers. The other carriages stayed on the tracks. Much of Carriages 3 and 4 were directly under the four-lane Bolt Street bridge.

For perhaps 20 seconds there was stillness.

Then the bridge sagged and with a deafening roar collapsed on the line below: almost 600 tonnes of steel and concrete crashing down on the two carriages. In the third carriage, 44 passengers were fatally crushed. In the fourth another 31 perished. Both carriages made up the bulk of the death toll. And around half of the fatalities were men and women who had boarded at Parramatta.

At the subsequent judicial inquiry Justice James Staunton said: 'The roofs of the carriages were crushed in, the sides were burst out and the height of the carriages from floor level reduced, in some cases, to inches. The result was catastrophic.'

When Jack McKeown phoned Emergency his call was at first treated as a hoax. He had to repeat, twice, that there had been a disaster. But Emergency responded quickly and within five minutes the first of 40 ambulances arrived, fast followed by State Emergency units, police and fire engines.

They were met by a devastating scene. In a great cloud of dust still settling on the wreckage dazed passengers and people off the street stumbled among bodies and gave the injured what help they could.

The biggest peacetime rescue operation in Australia had begun, and it would go on for the

The driver of Train 108, vilified anonymously, was cleared of all blame at two hearings. The 'very unsatisfactory condition' of the line caused the crash that killed 83 and left 218 injured. *Herald and Weekly Times Photographic Collection*

next 31 hours. All the long, wet day and through the night 900 men and women worked: police rescue, ambulance, doctors and nurses, Department of Main Roads teams, electrical crews, crane operators, fettlers, the fire brigade, clergy and the Salvation Army.

Men with jackhammers worked in relays breaking up the concrete slab that had crushed the third and fourth carriages and heaving away the heavy sections of the bridge.

Each time a slab was lifted it revealed more brutally broken bodies. Not long after midnight a giant piece of reinforced concrete and the roof of one of the carriages were lifted. Inside 22 passengers were crushed in their seats.

Doctors, nurses and clergy crawled in through the wreckage, located the living by tapping and craned to hear answering cries for help. They gave morphine, amputated limbs and performed major operations. The dead they left for priests to administer the Last Rites.

Father Michael Campion was the first cleric to minister to the dead and the dying. 'It was the silence that hit me. I think I knew that everyone in the carriage was dead. It was the silence of the entombed. I remember saying, "I am a Catholic priest. Hang on, help is on the way, we will say prayers," but there was no response. Later I learned that there were at least 20 dead in the carriage.'

But there were those whose will to survive inspired rescuers: Cheryl Seymour, 17, her skull fractured and her arm broken, was trapped for four and a half hours. A corpse in front of her blocked her from sight, but rescuers could hear her: 'I'm a brave girl, aren't I? I'm not going to scream or cry like the others.' She was brave and survived.

Erica Watson, 18, a student at the Australian Academy of Ballet, made the wrong choice. As Train 108 pulled into Parramatta station she had to decide: should she stay on the slow suburban train or switch to the Blue Mountains express to the city?
She opted for the express and ran to its third carriage. Too late for a seat she looked enviously at those who had one as the train started up. Two minutes later, 'There was this terrible, wrenching, tearing, horrible sound as everything caved in on us.'

When she came to her senses she was pinned, crushed from the shoulders down. She thought of her ballet and her back. She wiggled her toes to check that her spine wasn't broken and lay there for two hours in the dark. She could feel a trapped man, trying to free himself, his hand feebly pressing her leg.

'Then I felt his hand go.'

After 10 physically and emotionally draining hours the last of the injured, Bryan Gordon, a 28-year-old man who had been trapped in Carriage 4, his thighs pinned, was carried to a waiting ambulance. There was a feeling of sad satisfaction. At last it was over. Then, two days later, they learned that he, too, had died.

By 3.20 p.m., on 19 January – 31 hours after Jack McKeown's phone call to emergency services – the last body was removed from Train No. 108.

# THE WARS

Front page of the Melbourne *Herald Sun*, 13 October 2002, tells of the killing of 202 people, among them 88 Australians.

The first of more than 100,000 Australian soldiers killed in action died on New Year's Day 1900 on the hot, dry hills beyond the Kimberley diamond mines. Four months later one of 300 Australians at a pivotal garrison between Pretoria and Mafeking wrote: 'We are in this dreadful place, and it is hard to say how long we will be kept here.' Then the Boers began shelling and shelled non-stop for 11 days. When Major-General Lord Kitchener raised the siege he was stunned to find the defenders were not only holding out but also staging night raids. 'I do hope that Great Britain will show its gratitude to those Australians for the brightest page in the history of the war,' one of his officers wrote.

The soldier's letter, the siege, the counter-attacks, the observer's praise, all were to be a constant in the next 100 years, long after Australia had forgotten its Boer War defence of the Elands River Post. The total of 251 Australian lives lost in action in South Africa over three years paled against the losses of the first day's fighting at Gallipoli. At least 2000 Australians were killed on 25 April 1915.

Australian men and women have fought countless battles over the past century. But when we saw the grin on the face of the Bali mass murderer, Amrozi, we knew that we were in a war completely new to us. A war without battlefronts, without borders and without sense. All we really knew was that the enemy – whoever they were – hated us... for being us. The Bali bombings at popular tourist meeting points at Kuta on 12 October 2002 were designed, Jemaah Islamiyah terrorists said, to ensure maximum carnage on the enemies of Islam. Eighty-eight Australians were among the 202 people from around the world who died, blown to shreds, burnt to cinders, horrifically mangled and mutilated by a bomb in a car parked outside the Sari club.

Eleven days before the third anniversary of the 2002 bombings, suicide bombers struck again in Bali. Four Australians were among the 20 dead.

And so the war goes on.

# Gallipoli

'The finest body of young men ever brought together in modern times,' John Masefield, England's Poet Laureate, wrote of the Anzacs. 'For physical beauty and ability of bearing, they surpassed any man I have ever seen.' To this unqualified adulation others completed the portrait. The Anzacs, they wrote, were recklessly courageous and resourceful; men who stuck by their mates, scorned authority and never lost their laconic, larrikin sense of humour.

That is the Anzac legend. But is it a myth?

The remarkable fact is that most of it is true and that almost a century after it was created the unique Anzac spirit is still alive and honoured.

The central storyteller of the spirit that was summed up in the acronym ANZACS – Australian and New Zealand Army Corps – was Australia's official war correspondent, Captain C.E.W. (Charles) Bean. But it was an English journalist's newspaper report, the first account Australians read of the landing at Gallipoli, that riveted the nation and overnight sowed the seeds of the Anzac legend.

Les Carlyon, in his definitive account of the Dardanelles campaign, *Gallipoli*, says Ellis Ashmead-Bartlett 'was a journalist-adventurer, the sort of man who once made Fleet Street interesting, and he knew about war. He had served in the Boer War as a Lieutenant, and reported at least seven others, several of them involving Turkey. He was the sort of man who could write "Hire of yak – £500" on an expense claim and not blush.'

Anzac Cove, soon after the landing, gives little hint of what had taken place on 25 April and what was to follow in the next nine months. On the horizon is the headland of Ari Burnu, much steeper than the flat terrain of the intended landing site, Gaba Tepe. *AWM H03500*

Reporting from the bridge of the battleship *London*, Ashmead-Bartlett, was able to take in the entire sweep of the landing on the Anzac beachhead. Then he joined the troops. Newspapers around Australia carried the sensational news on 30 April.

Its impact was immediate. Aside from the thrilling account of the battle, Ashmead-Bartlett's admiration for the Australians was astounding. It revealed to those at home, C.P. Smith of the Melbourne *Argus* wrote, 'that our men were giants, a new strange race that had no fear, and who could face almost certain death as if they sought to die. Only then did we understand what splendid fellows these were, and what a proud thing it was to be Australian.'

This is an edited account of that report:

By 1 o'clock in the morning [of April 25] the ships had reached the rendezvous, five miles from the appointed landing place, and the soldiers were roused and served with the last hot meal.

The Australians, who were about to go into action for the first time in trying circumstances, were cheerful, quiet, and confident. There was no sign of nerves nor of excitement.

As the moon waned, the boats were swung out, the Australians received their last instructions, and men who six months ago had been living peaceful civilian lives had begun to disembark on a strange and unknown shore in a strange land to attack an enemy of a different race...

The work of disembarking proceeded mechanically under a point blank fire. The moment the boats touched the beach the troops jumped ashore and doubled for cover, but the gallant boat crews had to pull in and out under the galling fire from hundreds of points.

...The Australians rose to the occasion. Not waiting for orders, or for the boats to reach the beach, they sprang into the sea, and, forming a sort of rough line, rushed at the enemy's trenches.

Their magazines were not charged, so they just went in with cold steel.

It was over in a minute. The Turks in the first trench were either bayoneted or they ran away, and their Maxim was captured.

Then the Australians found themselves facing an almost perpendicular cliff of loose sandstone, covered with thick shrubbery. Somewhere, about half-way up, the enemy had a second trench, strongly held, from which they poured a terrible fire on the troops below and the boats pulling back to the destroyers for the second landing party.

Ashmead-Bartlett's enthusiasm didn't stop at those men storming the heights.

Storming the heights: 'An almost perpendicular cliff... about half way up, the enemy had a second trench, strongly held, from which they poured a terrible fire on the troops below.' Detail from George Lambert's famous painting in the Australian War Museum. *AWM ART02873*

...I have never seen anything like these wounded Australians in war before.

Though many were shot to bits, without the hope of recovery, their cheers resounded throughout the night... They were happy because they knew that they had been used for the first time and had not been found wanting.

Bursting with pride at this first news of glorious valour, Australia, within a week, was reeling at the reality of the landing. By then, of 23,292 Anzacs who had landed on the beach, some 5000 Australians were dead or wounded. In cities and country towns, the grieving began.

There was to be another eight months of slaughter before the Anzacs left Gallipoli. And in that time the legend was nourished by the reports of bands of brave men in ferocious hand-to-hand battles, and of individual heroes like Simpson and his donkey,

and Captain Albert Jacka, VC. But the truth of the most horrific chapter of the Anzacs' Gallipoli story, the carnage — murder, it was later called — of the vital strategic point known as the Nek was never told. The senseless slaughter was the climax of Peter Weir's 1981 film *Gallipoli*. '.. so well done that for many it is the reference point on the Gallipoli campaign,' Les Carlyon wrote. 'Yet its final scenes, built around the fourth charge at the Nek, are inaccurate and unfair to the British. The film suggests the Australians at the Nek were being sacrificed to help the landing at Suvla. It also suggests that a British officer was ordering successive waves of Australians to run out and commit suicide.

'The scale of the tragedy of the Nek was mostly the work of two Australian incompetents, Hughes and Antill. Hughes was the brigade commander and he didn't command. Antill wasn't the brigade commander and he did.'

Australia's prime minister, 'Billy' Hughes, burnished the legend in this speech but ignored the culpability of the commanders at the Nek:

> The story of how the 8th Light Horse of Australia went out to die in the dark hour before the dawn, when the tides of life are at their ebb, is one by which even that of the Charge of the Light Brigade must pale its fires.
>
> There were some 500 of them, and they were to attack in three waves. They were given their orders six, eight, 10 hours before. Every man believed that he was going out to almost certain death. Yet they did not hesitate. They made their preparations. They handed to those who were to remain in the trench their poor brief messages of farewell, and waited calmly for the order.
>
> In the dark hour when night is yielding doggedly to day, these young soldiers of Australia went out to die. As the blast of the whistle sounded, the first wave leaped from the trench, but nearly all fell back dead upon their fellows who were waiting their turn in the trench. None got more than a few yards before being shot down. In the face of this awful sight the second line, undaunted, leaped out. Of these only five or six remained on their feet after they had gone 10 or 12 yards. The third wave followed in their turn and met the same fate. The wounded lay exposed to the pitiless machine-gun fire of the Turks, which poured a veritable hail of death into their poor, bleeding bodies. The colonel was killed at the head of his men 50 yards from the trench. Eighteen officers went out – two only returned. Of the men the merest handful survived.

Ever-present death. A trench at Lone Pine, its parapet lined with Australian dead. Looking up is Captain Leslie Morshead. Two decades on he was to command the 9th Division at Tobruk and Alamein. *AWM A02025*

We must look back into the grey dawn of history before we find a deed parallel with this. The Spartans of Thermopylæ have left an imperishable name, whose glory has shone through the ages with a lustre which time has not dimmed and which will burn brightly when the pyramids have crumbled to dust and the proudest monuments of kings are no more. But surely what these young Australian soldiers did that day – these men of a new nation, the last but one

in the family of the great British Empire – what these men did, too, will live for ever!

Gallipoli cost 8700 Australians lives. But the sense of the Anzacs being at one with the heroes of ancient Greece was underpinned at the conclusion of the tragedy. The evacuation of Gallipoli on 19 December was done in so masterly a fashion that it became an intrinsic part of the legend: the Trojan horse in reverse. The Turks were completely deceived by a brilliant strategy designed to convince them that the Anzacs were, as always, at their posts and firing.

There were only two minor casualties where there might have been a massacre. And the Anzacs left laconically. 'You didn't push us off, Jacko, we just left' one Australian wrote in a note left for the Turks. Strictly speaking that was incorrect. But that was the Anzac spirit.

This is an edited extract from C.E.W. Bean's hour-by-hour report of the evacuation, filed for the *Sydney Morning Herald*.

Three miles away from me, across a grey, silky sea, lies the dark shape of the land. Eight months ago, just as the first lemon-grey of dawn was breaking over that long, lizard-shaped mountain, I watched such signs as were visible of the landing of the Australian troops in Gallipoli. Now, as the night falls gradually down upon the same historic spot, I am watching for the signs of their departure.

For tonight the first and second divisions are leaving the old position of Anzac. The New Zealand and Australian division is leaving the slopes and foothills of the range. Further north, the Indian Brigade is leaving Hill 60, where for months it has overlooked Suvla flats. And further north still from across those same flats, with the chocolate hill in the middle of them, and in the distance the slopes of Kirecteh Tepe, the British are retiring from the position which the world knows as Suvla.

All the non-essential corps were sent away during the previous week. Night after night on the beach, one found trooping by along covered routes down to the piers, ambulances, hospitals, engineers, army service corps – all the men, in fact, except those actually carrying rifles.

The moon is just beginning to flood sea and

land with a light so clear that you can scarcely notice the change from twilight into night. This brightness of the moon is one of our chief anxieties, for if the enemy sees what we are doing and attacks during certain stages of the embarkation before tonight is over, then nothing can prevent one of the most sanguinary and desperate fights in history.

The movement which at this moment is going on is the one which, from the day of landing, everyone here has most dreaded. I heard it said on the day of landing, and it has been commonplace ever since, that though the experiences of landing were bad enough one thing would be worse, and that was if it ever fell to our lot to have to get off again.

The only chance is to get the troops away without the enemy, of whom there are 85,000 at Anzac and Suvla, having a suspicion of it. The enemy cannot actually see the ground round the landing point, but there is an off-shoot from the main ridge to the north, from which he could look over our inner ridge, and into Ariburnu Point and half of the North Beach. It was known as 'Sniper's Nest' because he habitually sniped from there at night with a machine-gun. From Sniper's Nest he can just see the tip of one landing site, and all boats moving to or from them.

The plan at Anzac was quite different from that employed or is ever likely to be employed elsewhere. The whole normal garrison of every section of the firing line, divided into three parties, amounting possibly to a thousand or two, would be left holding the whole five miles of the outside line, faced by 40,000 Turks. Everything depended on them keeping up the appearance of a normal night. The extremes of the line, and especially those on the far left, were as much as

three miles away, up steep, tortuous and empty gullies. Men would have to leave them at least one hour, and in some cases two hours, before they left the centre.

That last party was known as the Die Hards, they were not asked to volunteer. They were deliberately chosen, because the authorities wanted to get the men whom they themselves thought suitable. The result was quite extraordinary. Competition to stay behind in this batch was very keen, and in some units the commanding officers were flooded with complaints from men who had not been chosen, asking if there was anything against their record which had caused them to be overlooked.

... The uppermost thought in the mind of every man I have spoken to is regret at leaving the little mountain cemeteries, which every valley and hillside contains, for a week past, at any time of day, you saw small parties of men carefully lettering in the half-obliterated name of some comrade on a rough wooden cross, or carefully raking the mound, and bordering it neatly with fuse caps from fallen shells. The demand on ordnance for wood for crosses has been extraordinary. I noticed some chaplains sowing wattle and manuka on the graves. The men believe the Turks will respect these graveyards. Indeed many Australian soldiers have been writing letters to leave in their dugouts for 'Abdul', telling him what a clean fighter they think he has been, and wishing him au revoir.

# *Darwin*

The 7th December 1941, President Roosevelt said as he declared war, was a day that would live in infamy. That was the day the Japanese Imperial Navy had surprised and crippled the American Pacific Fleet at Pearl Harbor. In astonishingly rapid succession the Japanese took Hong Kong and invaded Malaya, Burma and the Philippines. On 15 February 1942, the British surrendered Singapore with its 110,000 defenders, among them 15,000 Australians.

And four days later Darwin was bombed.

Thursday 19 February 1942, is our day of infamy. And our day of shame.

The Japanese dropped two-and-a-half times as many bombs on Darwin that day as they had on Pearl Harbor on 7 December. They killed around 250 and wounded 300 to 400. The precise figure will never be known because it is unclear how many people were on merchant boats that sank.

The bombing of Darwin, the first foreign attack on our shores since white settlement, was covered up as much as possible by a government determined to prevent panic. So too was the mass desertion of hundreds of servicemen who fled south, along with about half the city's population of around 2000. Nor were we told of the looting of some who stayed behind. A decade later, on the anniversary

Japanese pilots in carrier bombers from the Imperial Japanese Navy aircraft carrier *Shokaku*. This type of aircraft bombed Pearl Harbor and, 10 weeks later, Darwin. *AWM PO2886*

of the bombing, Paul Hasluck, then Minister for the Interior and later governor-general, called 19 February 'not an anniversary of national glory but one of national shame'.

It began at 9.15 that Thursday morning. Lieutenant John Gribble of the Royal Australian Navy reserve saw a mass of aircraft that 'didn't look like ours' and at once radioed to the Naval Communications Station on HMAS *Coonawarra*. Twenty minutes later a Catholic missionary on Bathurst Island, Father John McGrath sent a message to the wireless postal station in Darwin. He'd seen 'a huge flight of planes', silver aircraft glittering in the summer sun, heading their way. What he and John Gribble had seen was an attack force of 54 land-based bombers and 188 fighters and divebombers that had taken off from four Japanese aircraft in the Timor Sea.

McGrath's message was passed on to the RAAF, but no action was taken. That failure to act on that 23-minute advance warning proved fatal for many. At 9.58 the surprise attack on Darwin began. The targets were ships, military and civil airfields and a hospital.

In the harbour below were 46 ships. Among them, just returned from reinforcing Australian forces on Timor, were the destroyers, USS *Peary* and *William B. Preston*. The *Peary*, the main target, exploding in a huge fireball, was lifted from the water when a bomb went straight down the funnel. Only 28 of the 120 men on board survived. The *Preston* escaped, guns blazing, and made it to Sydney. The passenger ship *Neptuna*, loaded with thousands of tonnes of depth charges and high explosives, was not so lucky. She went up, said a witness, 'like a volcano erupting'. The 45 aboard died instantly. Eight ships were sunk, and on the wharf 22 waterside workers having a smoko were

Smoke billows from one of the ships – sitting ducks – sunk in Darwin harbour. *AWM 128108*

hit by a 450-kilogram bomb and more than 100 buildings were destroyed in the town.

The attack lasted for 40 minutes. At 10.38 the planes turned and stunned Darwinians emerged from shelter. Eight minutes later a second wave of 54 planes rained bombs on the RAAF base, crippled Allied fighters during takeoff, and shot down others that had managed to scramble into the air.

When it came to counting the dead the Commonwealth Government announced that nine had been killed. Later this was increased to 15. The real figure, the Mayor of Darwin insisted publicly, was at least 900 people.

The attack convinced every Australian, from the prime minister and his Cabinet down, that the Japanese were set to invade. In fact Japanese military archives revealed, long after the war, that the Darwin raid was to ensure the success of their invasion of the island of Timor that night. There would be no counter-attack from Darwin on the night of 19 February.

# Papua New Guinea

'I don't know what you read in the newspapers, but this is the truth,' Padre Fred Burt began. He was talking to the Perth RSL five weeks after he had left the 2/16th Australian Infantry Force fighting in Papua. A priest and an officer of the 2/16th he had been with them in the Middle East, in Greece and in Syria before Prime Minister Curtin demanded they be recalled and sent to fight the Japanese in New Guinea.

Part of the truth about the epic battles that stemmed and then turned the tide – at Kokoda and at Milne Bay, on the beachheads of Gona and Buna and at nearby Sananda where the Japanese invasion of Papua was finally smashed – was that the fighting was conducted in jungle that Kenneth Slessor, the *Sydney Morning Herald*'s war correspondent, called 'maleficent. It is not made for man.'

'It is full of malaria, ague, dysentery, scrub typhus, obscure diseases, full of crocodiles and snakes and bloated spiders, leeches, lice, mosquitoes, fleas, all the crawling, creeping, leaping, flying, biting reptiles and insects that ever sucked human blood (and in the morning you make a habit of knocking your boots to shake the scorpion out). Its breath is poisonous. It stinks of rotten fungus and dead leaves turning softly liquid underfoot; mould and mildew put their spongy paws over everything...

'Sometimes it's so wet the wood won't burn until it's been dried by the little flame which you keep smouldering almost permanently, like prehistoric man. Sometimes it's so hot the sweat trickles like brine over your lips. Sometimes it's so cold that your bones begin to chatter. Sometimes it's so high that your ears hurt, you can't hear properly, you have to keep opening and shutting your mouth. At the end of the trail, the Japanese wait with knives and bullets. But the jungle enlists a thousand enemies before this last enemy of all. It is unending, unrelenting, unforgiving. It is maleficent. It is not made for man...'

And the truth was, too, that the men fighting in this macabre war were under the command of an insufferable American, a five-star general with carefully tilted peaked cap, endless rows of decorations, aviator sunglasses and a ludicrously unconvincing corncob pipe, his signature prop, forever jutting from his manly jaw. Long after his death General Douglas MacArthur, God's gift to cartoonists, represents the cliche caricature of American militarism.

MacArthur in fact was a walking, talking cliche: 'I am sending you in Bob, and I want you to remove all officers who won't fight... I want you to take Buna or not come back alive!' he barked, although he himself, said William Manchester in *American Caesar*, 'never saw the [Papua] battlefield... while permitting press articles from his G.H.Q. to state he was leading his troops in battle.'

Under MacArthur was General Sir Thomas Blamey, the Australian commander-in-chief, who earned the contempt of his men when, at Koitaki, he gave the veterans of Kokoda what Peter Brune called in *A Bastard of a Place*, 'the greatest dressing down of all time.'

'Blamey tells them that their country has been defeated, that he has been defeated and they have been defeated. The "stand at ease" order of a minute or two ago now becomes a contradiction in terms. There is a growing restiveness in the ranks.

Muffled insults begin to be heard from the rear...
And then the comment comes that will blow like
a whirlwind through the scattered ranks of the
entire 7th Division – the entire army in Papua.
"Remember," he says, "it's not the man with the
gun that gets shot, it's the rabbit running away.'"
This is quite simply dynamite. It is taken as a charge
of cowardice and it infuriates everyone present.'

Padre Burt was at the Koitaki parade. Here is
what he told the Perth RSL – a speech that the
*Perth Daily News* submitted to the censor for
publication and was refused.

If you can't get the truth in the newspapers
you get a sort of fear at the back of your mind
that you can't believe anything you read. War
correspondent Chester Wilmot wrote the true
story and lost his job. I hope for the sake of the
men I saw killed, and their children who are left,
that the true story of the campaign will now be
published.

We came from the Middle East and Syria to
New Guinea. From Port Moresby we went up
the Pass in a sort of lift, and jumped straight into
a different climate. We went from 45 inches of
rain a year to 165 inches. After four or five days'
camp, the brigadier told us that we were going up
the Kokoda track... that one battalion would take
Kokoda, another Buna.

We got to Owens Corner and came out onto the
track. It was a 10-day trek, up and down all the
time. The natives had no idea of going round to
take off the height. Heavy rains had fallen, and tree
roots were about six feet out of the ground. The
soldiers were carrying 60 to 100 pounds, with their
guns and packs, over the rough stony track.

We came to Myola, an open clearing where

planes were to drop stores. But there were no stores, and we had to stay there for three days, waiting. The brigadier stirred things up, and five planes came over to drop our stuff.

We got to the Gap. We were told that we could hold the Japs with a machine gun and a platoon – it would have taken a Division to hold it. Militia troops had been sent to reinforce the 39th Battalion there. They had been in the army for 12 months. They were taken to Port Moresby about two weeks after joining up, and quite a large proportion were between 18 and 19 years of age. They'd had no training. We were told that on the way up they were shown parts of a Bren gun they had never seen before. They were taught to use it along the track.

The Japs had pushed back one battalion which had done a good job, and another which never got into position when it was sent back. They were untrained, too.

When we arrived, the Japs had got five transports of troops in – fresh men from Malaya, huge fellows full of fight. Then the two battalions were left to hold it. The thing was hopeless from the start. We couldn't hold them, we hadn't the men. We were told to get out. I saw men who were supposed to be stretcher cases crawling back on their hands and knees. They had broken legs and arms, and they had to climb over rocks.

We fought for two days. Then came Euro Creek. We could see the Japs over on Alola Ridge holding 'corroborees'. Our morale was the highest, and after 24 hours' fighting our men had the game by the throat. If we'd had more men we could have pushed the Jap back as he pushed us

The boys at the Front were just that – teenagers, many of them facing and beating an army that had smashed all attempts to halt its advance. *AWM 013857*

47

back. In the middle of his corroborees he got a few grenades in his middle, and didn't like it. He came in that night, but we held him. We were told to move off at dawn. We went so quietly that six of our chaps didn't know we had gone. They woke up and saw soldiers they thought were ours. A sergeant strolled over to one and asked him for a light from his cigarette. They took a look at each other and ran.

We withdrew off the track and made a detour. There was only one battalion of about 250 men left out of the remnants of the two battalions. I saw some wonderful exploits, but it would not be fair to mention anyone in particular.

Then another battalion came up to meet us. We had been asking for them all the time, but they wouldn't send them. They said they were needed for the defence of Port Moresby. The brigadier had sent them a message: 'Send the battalion or send my successor.' Those behind could not appreciate the position.

This battalion fought at Butcher's Corner, and lost some very fine men. We tried to cut our way through the Japs, but had to make another detour. What was left of the other battalion was cut off in the bush. They wandered there for three weeks without food.

We got back to Ioribiwa Ridge, and were reinforced by a brigade and a battalion. With the remnants of the other battalion and these four battalions we still had to retire. But the Jap never came on. He just walked back. He had had enough, what with casualties we had inflicted, dysentery, disease, malaria and the difficulties of communication. We got back to Kokoda, and we were pulled out for a rest... Fellows half-dead with dysentery, who should never have been

there. Ninety per cent got malaria. They were pulled out, but as soon as their temperatures went down they were sent back into it. A lot died of wounds simply because they didn't have the resistance to fight them.

When it was over we had 120 men left, and another battalion only 80. If we'd had men to replace the sick everything would have been alright. If they had got a Division of men around the coast to Buna we could have stopped the Jap the same as he was stopped at Milne Bay, cleaned them out.

And when we got back, a general thanked us for saving Port Moresby.

Blamey got the rap, because apparently this show and the Solomons show were supposed to synchronise. There was an investigation. Blamey told the men: 'The rabbit that runs is always in more danger than the rabbit that sits.' He said he supposed we realised we had been beaten by an inferior force, that the Japs had more casualties than we had. Half a dozen of the men said then that they would like to meet some of the bowler hats, and find out the truth. It's time we had a clean-up in the army.

Under the slouch hat, the man with the archetypal Aussie face, open and pleasant, is Sergeant Tom Derrick, awarded the Victoria Cross in New Guinea on 24 November 1943. Earning a DCM at Tobruk and wounded at El Alamein, 'Diver' Derrick was one of the hardened North Africa men who fought alongside novice infantrymen – boys – in New Guinea. *AWM 016247*

# Sandakan

Private Nelson Short, 2/18th Battalion, was listening to the Japanese interpreter telling the skeletal prisoners: 'All men who can stand on their feet be prepared to march.' At the same time an Allied aircraft, 'a monstrous Catalina flying boat' flew overhead. 'You could see the airmen looking down at us. No shot was fired. I often wondered about that.'

He must often have wondered, too, why no attempt was ever made to rescue him and the thousands of other captives of the Japanese who were soon to die on that march. No one has ever been able to supply an adequate answer to that question, and the shame of the Sandakan death marches lies not wholly on the side of the Japanese.

More than 2400 men, Australians and British, were with Private Short in the camp at Sandakan, a town on the north-east coast of Borneo. He and five others came out alive. The rest died; around half of starvation, dysentery, beriberi or malaria; the rest were murdered – tortured beyond endurance, bayoneted, bashed with rifle butts or shot.

The Sandakan death marches, in 1945, the last year of World War Two, is the grimmest chapter in the story of Australian prisoners of war, a story that spans camps and forced labour sites from Poland, Germany, Yugoslavia, Russia, Italy, France, Greece, Tunisia, Egypt and the Middle East, to Thailand, Japan, Malaya, Burma, Singapore, Timor, Ambon, New Guinea, Formosa, Korea and Vietnam.

All the PoWs who came home – and of the 22,000 captured by the Japanese, one in three didn't – told the same story, in varying degrees, of deprivation, cruelty, hardship and the mateship that is an integral and distinct part of the make-up of all Diggers.

But the PoWs who survived Japanese captivity came back skeletal, hollow-eyed and subdued, telling of unrelenting horror: dark atrocities that shocked the nation. The survivors, for the most part, must have been scarred for life. And the legacy of the Japanese sadism lingers to this day. Changi, where 'Weary' Dunlop and thousands of courageous men like him were imprisoned; Sister Vivian Bullwinkle, the sole survivor of the slaughter of Australian nursing sisters on Banka Island; and the horror of the Burma railway, these and a myriad other stories from PoWs made deep and nightmarish impressions on Australians. But the Sandakan marches were, until recently, largely unknown to us. The reasons probably lie in the unspeakable horror of the story and the disgraceful failure of the Australian military command to come to the rescue of these tortured men.

When Private Short saw the Catalina flying over the Sandakan camp he and the Japanese knew that the Allies were likely to land at any moment. When the march began he had hoped that 'if they turned us to the left as we got down the bitumen road that the war was over and we were going down to the boat. But it was to the right we went, straight into the jungle.'

It was late January and the Japanese, knowing they were losing the war, were determined that their prisoners would not be liberated. They selected 470 men who they deemed fit enough to act as porters – each carrying on his back a 45-pound bag of rice – for two of their battalions being transferred to the western coast of the island. It was a forced march of around 200 kilometres and their guards were ordered to kill immediately those too weak to continue. There were to be two more such marches.

In 2006 journalist Garry Linnell, who walked in the footsteps of those men, wrote in the *Bulletin*: 'The heat smothers you. So, too, the silence. But there's a coolness running down your spine that chills the sweat and leaves the skin clammy. Something wicked passed through here a little over 60 years ago and its traces can still be felt. It fills you with disgust and loathing...

'The hills and mountains around here are formidable, even for those with modern hiking boots, adequate supplies of water and the knowledge of a warm, parasite-free bed for the night. To breathe deeply on some days, to suck in the thick combination of heat, moisture and warm earth, is to know what it is like to be buried alive.'

For the PoWs, weakened by brutality, disease and starvation – they had been rationed to 140 grams of rice and a small amount of tapioca a day – the march was impossible, an almost certain death sentence. The killings began very soon. Private Sharp, whose legs and feet were rotting, remembered: 'It was no distance before the blokes started to drop out, never to be seen again... The bloke with the machine gun coming on behind us shot them. And that happened all the way through.' Now and again they were allowed to rest, but often 20 or more couldn't get up again. They were immediately shot. Some, like Gunner Albert Cleary, escaped and were recaptured, tortured hideously and their mangled bodies thrown to the side of the jungle track. Cleary, tied to a tree and beaten viciously from morning to night, took a week to die.

Private Richard Murray, too, was bashed, but his death was quick. Murray gave his life for his mates. When the Japanese discovered that someone had pilfered a bag of rice they ordered a line-up. Everyone knew what was coming: beatings and

torture, certainly; executions probably. Richard Murray stepped from the line and told the guards that he alone had stolen the rice. He was beaten and then taken down a track and bayoneted.

Could they have been rescued?

General Blamey claimed, when questions were raised after the war, that plans were made to parachute troops into Sandakan, free the PoWs and over-run the area, but 'At the moment we wanted to act we couldn't get the necessary aircraft to take them in.' Lynette Silver, an Australian historian and the foremost expert on the Sandakan death marches, dismisses this. The failure, she says, was due to poor decision-making and a series of bungles. Blamey 'lied and blamed others,' she says.

Murray Griffin, an Australian prisoner of war, painted this harrowing depiction of an Australian 'hospital' on the Burma-Thailand railway. *AWM ART25104*

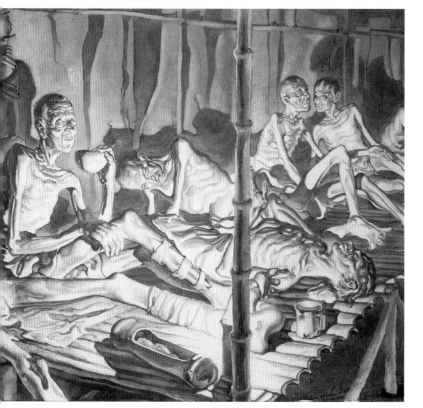

# Vietnam

On Thursday 29 April 1965 Prime Minister Robert Menzies announced to a half empty House of Representatives, and to no one's great surprise, that Australia was to commit a battalion of 800 soldiers to fight beside the Americans in Vietnam. It was the beginning of a 10-year war for Australia, the longest war in which we've been involved.

Robert Menzies represented an Australia that was passing. World War Two in Europe and the Pacific; the war in Korea, the Malaya insurgency, the Suez Canal crisis; these were things he understood. But Vietnam, as successive prime ministers were to find, was a very nasty, very different war. And the people of Australia, the young in particular, were different. Most didn't understand why we were there.

A year later the new prime minister, Harold Holt, announced that conscripts, 20-year-olds, would fight in Vietnam. Their names would be drawn from a barrel. On 5 May the first conscripts arrived in Vietnam and within three weeks, Private Errol Noak became the first to die in Vietnam.

The late 1960s were turbulent years. Fashion, music, fads and philosophies were changing throughout the West with astonishing rapidity. In America youths were demonstrating against the war with the slogan, 'Hell no, we won't go!' And in Australia the disenchantment with the war was mounting. In March 1970, Dr Jim Cairns, the charismatic ALP politician, called on workers and students to 'occupy' the streets of Melbourne. One hundred and twenty thousand people marched in Bourke Street. It took so long that it became more a sit-down than a march and the dramatic TV footage and front page photographs of Dr Cairns addressing the immense crowd was a turning point. Around the country there were other 'moratorium' marches: in Sydney 25,000; in Brisbane 8000 and Adelaide 6000 and in Perth and Hobart 3000.

The *Australian* summed it up: the march sent 'a loud message about people power and the rights of demonstration in Australia. Yesterday a nation changed for the better.'

Slowly, the Australian forces in Vietnam were reduced, but when the Whitlam government announced the withdrawal of all remaining units the troops returned home without any celebrations. There were few cheering crowds and the bitterness felt by Vietnam-returned servicemen towards those who abused and insulted them when they returned, lingers. They left behind 474 of their mates killed and 408 wounded – almost half of them conscripts.

The tipping point. Dr Jim Cairns, at the peak of his popularity, addresses 120,000 marchers calling for an end to Australia's involvement in the war in Vietnam. Media images like this proved crucial to the course of the war in Australia and the US.

# 4

# THE SPORT

One of the great sports photographs of the 20th century, John O'Gready's, *The Gladiators*, captures the moment as St George's raw-boned giant, Norm 'Sticks' Provan – perhaps the best back rower to play the game – and West's Arthur Summons, mates under the mud and different jumpers, trudge off after the 1963 Rugby League grand final.

Australians are obsessed with sport – almost all sport – to an extraordinary degree. And we succeed beyond what should be a normal country's reasonable expectations. We are a dominant nation in cricket, swimming, hockey, basketball, golf, cycling, rowing, netball, rugby league and rugby, and in most sports we make an impact that is most clearly reflected at the Olympics. On the medals tally of the last two Olympic Games, in 2004 and 2002, Australia has finished fourth behind the US, China and Russia.

But that's not good enough. We want more. We want world domination.

In a 2003 survey Australians named the death of John F. Kennedy, the landing on the moon, and winning the America's Cup as the three most memorable events of the 20th century. Twenty years after the winged keel *Australia 11* broke the New York Yacht Club's 132-year stranglehold on a sporting trophy, Australians still treasured that euphoric moment when Bob Hawke, the prime minister, summed up the jubilation: 'I tell you what, any boss who sacks anyone for not turning up today is a bum!' The America's Cup meant that much. It meant world domination.

The jubilation that seized Australia on 26 September 1983 was such it almost approached that day when, at 2.15 in the afternoon of 18 July 1876 a telegram arrived with the news that Edward Trickett was the new world champion rower. A man born and bred in New South Wales had taken on and beaten – easily, by four lengths – the great English sculler, Sadler. It was almost unbelievable. We had our first world champion.

The colony was delirious with pride and excitement. When he arrived home, 25,000 – a colossal percentage of Sydney's population – packed Circular Quay to carry Trickett off in triumph. It's safe to say that few turned up for work that day.

We've always wanted to beat the world in a way that the small boy wants to beat his big brother. In another hundred years will our America's Cup triumph be forgotten, as Edward Trickett's is today?

Certainly. By then we'll have experienced the euphoria of winning soccer's World Cup. By then we'll be going for three in a row.

# The First Test

There were 144,319,628 men, women and children in Bangladesh on 18 June 2005 and every one of them over the age of five almost died of joy. Playing in a one-day cricket match the Bangladesh XI soundly trounced the Australians on that historic day. It was – the experts were as one on this – the most unexpected and astonishing win in the long history of cricket.

Well, no. It wasn't. That distinction belongs to an Australian XI – the very first 11 players selected to play for their country. And they beat England on 15 March 1877. The joy in Bangladesh 128 years later was unconfined. But the thrill that rushed through the colonies with the news that the English had been beaten was almost palpable. Keith Dunstan, the journalist and author, has described it as cricket's Gallipoli: 38 years before the landing at Anzac Cove, the win at the Melbourne Cricket Ground welded the colonies into one nation.

England's loss, on the other hand, was a traumatic shock to the Mother Country's psyche. It badly damaged its self-image as the imperious ruler of the world, superior to all others in all ways. The very large chip which had rested on the shoulders of the young nation had been put on that of their masters. In the 310 Test matches played between the two countries since then it has remained on their shoulders.

Until 15 March 1877 it was universally acknowledged that the English could not be beaten at cricket. The game belonged to them.

Outside the fence enclosing the 'G' on New Years Day 1862, non-paying spectators lounge in the afternoon sun. Inside, the first All-England X1 lost to a Victorian XV. Played at the ground of the Melbourne Cricket Club, the game was sponsored by the caterers whose sign can be seen on the stand. Sixteen years later, on the same ground, England lost the first Test.

They invented it and they played it at a level the Australians (and the Canadians and Americans, until they came up with its cousin, baseball) simply couldn't match. The only way to give the English a run for their money was to set the odds in your favour: play twice as many men as they put on the field. And even then, even with 22 players to their 11, they'd still beat you.

The Englishmen, not surprisingly, suffered from a marked superiority complex, tinged with more than a touch of condescension. Asked what he thought of colonial cricketers, Roger Iddison, a Yorkshire all-rounder, said: 'Well, I don't think much of their play, but they're a wonderful lot of drinking men.' This characteristic was to distinguish Australian sides for the next century and more.

But pride comes before a fall and perhaps the first premonition that the English might one day come a cropper came when an all-England XI, under Mr H.H. Stephenson, started its 1861 tour of the colonies on an unheard-of note: a team of 15 New South Wales players beat the English by two wickets. Stephenson took his team to Victoria. The Melbourne Cricket Ground astonished him. England had no oval so well prepared and so suited for cricket, and the grandstand, 700 feet long, was the finest in the world. The Victorian team of 15 promptly repeated its rival colony's victory, and then New South Wales won again – this time by 13 wickets.

Stephenson came home humiliated. But despite the two embarrassing losses the tour had been a financial bonanza and it was followed by a series of tours, each showing that the gap between the two countries was closing.

On 15 March 1877 at the Melbourne Cricket Ground that had so impressed Stephenson 16 years before, it closed emphatically. For the first time the intensely competitive colonies, New South Wales and Victoria, put aside their jealousies and agreed to play a combined inter-colonial team that would be called the Australian team. In recompense for holding the game in Melbourne and not Sydney, six New South Wales players were selected, one more than Victoria. Of those selected, Frederick Spofforth, 'The Demon Bowler' refused to take his place because he would not bowl to the Victorian wicketkeeper, the brilliant J.M. Blackham, and the Victorian Frank Allen, the 'Bowler of the Century' was not inclined to play, preferring to attend the Warrnambool Fair. The wrath of the newspapers in Melbourne and Sydney was considerable.

More than 1000 spectators were there when the match began on Thursday and by the end of the day their numbers had trebled. By lunch the Australians had lost three wickets for 41 runs and the captain, Dave Gregory, had made history by being the first man run out in Test cricket. Charlie Bannerman, however, was holding things together, driving superbly while watching wickets fall. By close of play Australia was 166 for 6, and on Friday, the following day, Bannerman might have gone on to become the first man to carry his bat through a Test had he not been injured by a sharply rising ball and retired on 166, a huge total for those days. England replied with 196, leaving them 49 runs behind. Australia's second innings was a disaster: Bannerman, his hand heavily bandaged, made just four, and the top score, from Horan, was 20.

England began its second innings needing just 154. They fell 45 runs short. Kendall, who played only one more international game (he was a wonderful drinking man) took seven for 55 in 33 overs.

One hundred years later, at the Melbourne Cricket Ground, the two teams played the famous Centenary Test. And once again Australia won by 45 runs. The chip was safe.

# The Bloods

They dubbed themselves the Bloods: 22 blood brothers who privately vowed to do whatever it took to win the 2005 AFL Grand Final.

Australia knew them as the Sydney Swans, but the players reached back 72 years to when the Swans last won a Grand Final. They were known as the Bloods in those days. In 2005 it was more than an 'in-house' nickname. 'The boys will do anything for each other,' Ryan O'Keefe said after the match. 'We would spill blood for any one of us.' They spilt more than their share in the Final and came off the field carrying broken bones, fractures, lacerations. O'Keefe himself had been concussed but like Jared Crouch, who tore ligaments in his ankle during the game, was unwilling to come off. Leo Barry and Adam Schneider ran on to the MCG with fractured cheekbones. Jude Bolton had a dislocated AC joint. Darren Jolly broke his hand six weeks before the game and Craig Bolton's nose was smashed.

They were battered but they refused to bend to the West Coast Eagles, let alone the AFL supremo, Andrew Demetriou, who'd predicted, earlier in the season, that they'd lose more games than they won if they persisted with their 'unattractive' style.

Sydney finished third at the end of the home-and-away series and in the first final, against the Eagles, was beaten by four points. They had to win

With the game in the balance and seconds left – just enough time for an Eagle to mark and close enough for him to kick the winning score – the ball comes tumbling out of the blue to a waiting pack. Two million viewers leap with him as Leaping Leo Barry comes from left of screen and flings himself into a crunch of blue, yellow, red and white. It's a Grand Final mark that has not been bettered in 115 years. It's saved the Swans. It's hysteria! Tears in the west, but for the rest, exultation. After almost 150 years, Sydney has succumbed to Australia's indigenous code, the last frontier has been conquered. Like the Socceroos' triumph a month later, the fairytale ending to the Swans' 72-year premiership drought overcomes all parochialism: Rugby League fanatics, Union diehards, soccer tragics, Blues, Roos, Magpies, Tigers – no matter who you barracked for, you were barracking for Sydney in those last thrilling minutes. *Newspix*

the next two matches to stay alive. Against Geelong they were beaten, everyone but the Bloods knew, when they trailed badly in the last quarter. Then Nick Davis kicked four – the last of them a miracle snap right on the siren – and they survived, by three points. A week later they topped the glamour side, St Kilda, and the following week, against the odds, they did it again: came back from the dead to win the most heart-stopping Grand Final in decades.

You bloody beauties!

One year later the two were back again and again came up with a classic. This time it was the Eagles' turn: a one point win that extended what was now a fierce rivalry – over their past five games only 12 points had separated them.

But classic conflicts are old hat in Australian football. Two years before the most ancient sports rivalry – the Ashes Test – they were playing Australian Football in front of huge and passionately partisan crowds. Nat Gould, the American sports author and historian, was amazed at the fervour of the fans.

'It is no uncommon thing on a Saturday afternoon in Melbourne, when the famous clubs meet in a Cup Tie, to see from 25,000 to 30,000 spectators present. Considering the population [200,000] as compared with some great English cities, this, I think, is an extraordinary attendance.'

Richard Twopenny, an English visitor, too, was astonished by the size of the crowds and thrilled by the new Australian game. 'The best game of football has been found, in Melbourne,' he wrote.

'A good football match in Melbourne is one of the sights of the world. Old men and young get equally excited. The quality of the play, too, is much superior to anything the best English clubs can produce. Of course it is not easy to judge of this when the games played are different, but on such points as drop-kicking, dodging, and catching, comparison can be made with the Rugby game; and every "footballer" (the word, if not coined, has become commonly current here) knows what I mean when I say that there is much more "style" about the play of at least half a dozen clubs in Victoria, than about the "Old Etonians" or the "Blackheath", which are the two best clubs I have seen play in England.'

The Australian football code invented in 1858 and at first peculiar to Victoria had within 20 years spread to South Australia, Queensland and Tasmania, and in 1880 Victoria played against New South Wales. Victoria won with ease and *Punch* magazine perceptively said the code would never be popular in Sydney as long as it continued to be called Victorian Rules Football.

'Victorian Rules... had they dubbed the game Scandinavian Rules, well and good, but VICTORIAN – perish the thought! The sooner the game is altered to Australian Rules of Football the better!'

# The Ashes Third Test, 2005

From the day it began at Lords on 21 July when England sent out the first of a never-ending series of shock waves – dismissing Australia for just 190 – the 2005 Ashes series of five Tests was a gripping, gladiatorial contest. In the following 54 days until the damp squib anticlimax of the last hours, when bad light and a South African batsman with rainbow hair and a death or glory bat brutally wrenched the Ashes from Australia's grasp, the entire cricket world – around a billion and a half people – was in thrall to its ebb and flow.

It was, all but the churlish agreed, the most thrilling series played in 128 years of Test cricket. Five matches that came down, in the end, to two runs. Two runs from 1543. It was a series that rested on events that took on great significance: the weather that saved Australia in the Third Test; umpiring that seemed to go marginally against Australia; 100 no-balls from Australia and 18 dropped catches – one of them, Warne's, that would surely have meant the Ashes were safe; captain Ricky Ponting allowing his players to come off because of bad light in the Fifth,

*'...the extended opera – hymns and arias, solos and chorus, tumbling upon each other for passage after passage, day after day – did cricket the world of good. Sport as a whole came up beaming to take a bow. Undoubtedly players and followers of other games, professional or amateur on vast packed arenas or village 'recs' were forced to look at themselves and take serious note. Challenge, defiance and character, entertainment, enjoyment – and valour. The honouring of the foe has been the template these last few weeks; the nobility of both sets of cricketers has been heart-warming, edifying and salutary.'*
*– Frank Keating in the* Spectator

and Ponting losing the last three toss of the coins.

But of all the factors in and out of the players' control, Australia's demise can be traced back to Ponting's decision to bowl first in the Second Test at Edgbaston. Almost certainly it cost Australia the match. Ponting's bizarre decision dismayed all Australia (in hindsight) and gave England a tremendous boost: the arrogant, all-conquering Aussies, it was clear, were loath to face their fast bowlers until the pitch played slower. Had Australia won – and it was just three runs and a wrong, final, umpiring decision short of a win – the side would have gone on to the Third Test two up, and England's spirit would have been broken.

Australia's batting – tailenders excepted; they fought like cornered cats – was appalling. Incredibly, it took six innings before an Australian batted for longer than 154 balls. Until Ponting's match-saving and magnificent 156 off 275 balls in the second innings of the Third Test – the first century in the series from an Australian – he had averaged 23. Hayden's average was 22, Katich's 26 and Martyn's 27. The greatest striker of the ball that Richie Benaud has ever seen, Adam Gilchrist, a man with a Test average of more than 50, had a dismal time batting and his keeping was worse.

Lee had a fine series in many respects, his last

ditch batting stand helped save and almost win the Edgbaston Test, and he was there at the end for the heart-stopping draw at Old Trafford. Yet he ultimately failed as a bowler: each of his 20 wickets over the 10 innings came at an average cost of 40 runs. Of the other bowlers, only Shane Warne could point to a magnificent series. Three wickets were lost to no-balls. McGrath, who bowled one of them, unbelievably, had to withdraw from the Second Test after injuring himself horsing about in the hours before the match. Gillespie took just three wickets at an average cost of 97 and Kasprowicz was almost as inept.

But there were other fatal flaws. Australia's fielding, for decades the best in the world, was abysmal. England's import, Pietersen, who single-handedly snatched the Ashes from Australia on the final day, was dropped three times early in his innings. It was Australia's worst performance in a Test series in almost two decades.

Yet Australia cheered its team as never before. And England was in ecstasy. The matches were played with a chivalry and bravery on both sides that had long been lamented as lost. It was too much for many men to bear. In England they took refuge behind couches, unable to cope with the tension of watching the telecast. In Australia men and women switched off the television and went to their beds in despair, lay awake in the dark wondering, got up and switched the television back on, punched the air with surprised glee, were plunged back into despondency, went back to bed, lay awake wondering, got up...

The twists and turns of the Tests were endless and all five would make thrillers to warm the heart of

One of the most astonishing of all Test match moments: congratulations from the English after Lee and McGrath held them at bay.

Hitchcock, but the Second, Third, and Fourth, in particular, were heart-stoppers, and can be ranked among the half dozen most exciting Tests ever played. Richie Benaud, in his preface to *Test Cricket Lists*, wrote: 'Until that magnificent summer [2005] I had three views about outstanding matches: that the greatest series in which I took part was the Tied Test series of 1960–61, from the purely selfish personal point of view the best match was Old Trafford 1961 and the finest series, 1981, when Ian Botham at Headingly began his season of mayhem against Australia.

'All that changed with Edgbaston, Old Trafford and then Trent Bridge in 2005, plus Kevin Pietersen's century at the Oval, and the twists and turns and extraordinary excitement of the final four matches made it a series never to be forgotten.'

And of one of those Tests Steve Waugh wrote: 'Rarely have consecutive Tests qualified as memorable matches, but the Edgbaston epic was paralleled by a masterpiece at Old Trafford.'

The Old Trafford ground at Manchester has hosted Tests since 1884. It was here that Victor Trumper scored the first-ever century on the opening morning of a Test match and helped Australia win the 1902 Test by three runs. It was here that Jim Laker destroyed Australia, in 1956, on an old-fashioned 'sticky wicket' with match figures of 19 for 90. And it was here that Ian Botham's crash-bang 118 in a sixth-wicket stand of 149 with Chris Tavare clinched the 1981 Ashes for England.

Now, for the Third Test of the 2005 series, Old Trafford was about to see a game to match any staged at Lancashire cricket's venerable home.

Ponting lost the toss on day one and England batted. At the end the innings, as it had in the Second Test, England had piled on more than 400

runs, the first time since 1986–87 that Australia had conceded more than 400 runs in successive first innings.

It could have been far less. England's captain Michael Vaughan was dropped on 41 off McGrath. Four runs later he was bowled off a no-ball by McGrath. He was dropped again and he should have been run out. And he went on to make 141.

This was new territory for Australia. The side was being out-batted, out-bowled – the old reliable Jason Gillespie went for more than 100 runs before claiming a wicket – out-fielded and out-eyeballed. The Englishmen were acting like Australians, strutting, laughing, looking hungry and with a spring in their step. The Australians, coming off the Second Test defeat, looked shell-shocked. Their heads hung low. Ricky Ponting, under withering fire back home for his Second Test decision to put the Englishmen first, seemed to be incapable of lifting his side. He made seven when it was Australia's turn to bat, and like all the recognised Australian batsmen, was bewildered by the devastating reverse-swing of Simon Jones, who took 6–44. Only Shane Warne, agonisingly close to his maiden Test century, with 90, could hold his head high. He came to the crease with Australia foundering at 5–129, avoided the follow-on with Jason Gillespie and put on 86 runs with the fast bowler before he went, another Jones victim. The dour Gillespie, having a nightmare time bowling, was doing heroically at the crease, blocking, blocking and blocking until he allowed himself to open his shoulders and smash a slashing six over square leg. McGrath was not out, one, and Australia had stumbled over the psychological 300 run mark.

Still, England was 142 ahead when the openers

Strauss and Trescothick came out and once again saw off the Australian attack. Strauss made a century and Michael Vaughan the skipper was happy to declare the innings close with England leading by 422.

In 69 Tests at Old Trafford only one team, England, in 2004, had successfully chased more than 200 runs to win on the last day, and Australia had to make twice that amount and more or bat out the last day to survive.

Making the runs was out of the question. Australia flirted with the idea and came nail-bitingly close. It was a new Australia, led by a new skipper. For more than seven hours, Ricky Ponting crafted a masterpiece, 156 chanceless runs in 411 minutes. But when he gloved a catch off Harmison all thoughts of reaching and passing the massive total were forgotten. His was the ninth wicket to fall and there was only Lee, who had already shown at Edgbaston that he had the skill and the grit to bat out an innings, and McGrath, the batting bunny, the world's finest number 11, by his own admission.

Four overs, 24 balls, remained.

'The crowd at Old Trafford,' wrote the *Herald Sun*'s London correspondent Bruce Wilson, 'was like a living, separate entity, a vast, noisy, passionate being.' (There were 20,000 in the ground and another 25,000 locked out of the ground). 'The din as Steve Harmison bowled the last over may have been heard in Leeds. It was not the crowd that failed to take that wicket, but England.'

Here's how the final over went.

**1st ball**. Australia's 12th man, Stuart McGill, rushes out to McGrath and tells him to bat out of his crease to Harmison. The ball goes harmlessly past, down the leg side.

**2nd ball**. McGrath plays and misses, and wicketkeeper Geraint Jones, who has had a disastrous time behind the stumps, once again blunders. With McGrath out of his wicket he throws the ball back to Harmison.

**3rd ball**. McGrath bunts the ball to mid-wicket and scampers through for a single. To the immense relief of Australia, this brings Lee to face the last three balls.

**4th ball**. A fullish delivery down the leg side. Lee watches it go.

**5th ball**. Once again, Lee doesn't have to play a shot.

**6th ball**. Harmison, predictably, tries a yorker but the ball arrives on Lee's bat as a full toss. He clips it to the boundary. The two Australians embrace and England's despair throws a shroud of misery over Old Trafford.

The match is drawn and the Ashes series levelled. Two more Tests to go.

## THE SERIES RESULTS

*1st Test, Lord's*
*Australia won by 239 runs*

*2nd Test, Edgbaston*
*England won by two runs*

*3rd Test, Old Trafford*
*Match drawn*

*4th Test, Trent Bridge*
*England won by three wickets*

*5th Test, The Oval*
*Match drawn – England wins the Ashes 2-1*

# Cathy Freeman

Cathy Freeman's sister Anne-Marie was born with cerebral palsy. She died of an asthma attack in 1990, three days after Freeman won her first gold medal at the Auckland Commonwealth Games. At her funeral Cathy vowed that every race she ran from that day on would be for Anne-Marie. Anne-Marie first inspired her when Cathy, as a young girl, took up running. Lying in bed, not wanting to train, Freeman's mother Cecilia shamed her: 'You've got two good arms and two good legs, now get out there and use them!'

Now, 10 years after Anne-Marie's death, Cathy Freeman took her block. She seemed to start slowly – or was she coasting? – running without a hint of the strain that must have been in her head. She was running for herself and for Anne-Marie, for her mother Cecilia and all her people, and for Australia.

She seemed to have been running for an eternity without us really knowing where she was placed in the field. Around the last bend and now we all knew. She was going to win this, win this 400 metre race, win this going away!

It was over in 49.11 seconds. Cathy Freeman had become the 100th Australian to win gold and the only Olympian to light the torch and win gold at the same Olympics.

She let her legs go after she had crossed the line, slowed to a stroll, and taken the congratulations of her rivals. She slumped to the ground, sat for a while and soaked in the roar. Someone gave her two flags, the Australian flag and the Aboriginal flag and she took them entwined, and skipped down the track. The glorious grin was back now, bigger and more joyful than ever.

# Socceroos

For 31 years they've been losers. Now, after going down 1–0 in the first leg of the 2006 World Cup qualifier the Socceroos are staring at another four years in the wilderness. They come to face the Uruguayans – there's bad blood between them – again. Eighty thousand are at Sydney's Telstra Stadium for the decider. At home another two million watch the match: for many it's the first they've seen in its entirety. Marco Bresciano scores in the 35th minute and the two teams are level. The second half see-saws into extra time. Another 30 agonising minutes and the referee signals: penalty shoot-out. Australia groans. Our goalie – the Socceroos are now 'ours' – makes two superb saves. John Aloisi steps up, converts and starts running as if he's in a huge hurry to get to Germany and the World Cup. His team mates are running. In living rooms around the nation we're pumping the air. We're going to the Cup – and we're all in a hurry!

*Photograph courtesy Newspix*

# 5

# THE CRIME

A rare mugshot of Abe Saffron, the 'Mr Sin' at the centre of Sydney corruption. Many believe he was behind the 1979 ghost train fire in Sydney's Luna Park. Six children and the father of one of them died in the flames. *Newspix*

There's no escaping it. Crime is at Australia's core. Pickpockets, highwaymen, bushrangers and forgers, more than 150,000 transported felons literally laid the foundations for the new colony. What's more, for the last 130 years, Ned Kelly, a man who murdered two policemen and planned to kill many more in a train derailment, has remained, unchallenged, our most admired and heroic figure.

There's not another country in the world that can claim that, or would want to. Yet, in a bizarre paradox, it's something that most of us are proud of. Because when the chips are down we know that this nation, a country that criminals helped build, became within a few decades one of the most law-abiding societies the world has known.

It still is. We return library books on time. We are not by nature riotous, racist or rabid. Not disputatious, violent, vengeful or bloodthirsty. We're easy-going, we're affable, we're she'll-be-sweet-mate law-abiders.

But then there are those others whose instinct is not to return the library books. The convict 'bolters' of the colony's first half century, and the more romantic home-grown bushrangers were in truth the villainous antecedents of the mid-20th century underworld characters whose activities centred on illegal gambling, grog and prostitution – segments of life that hardly affected the average Australian.

In 1983 the *Age* tapes, covertly recorded telephone conversations, rolled over a colossal rock and scores of slimy creatures scuttled for cover: magistrates, judges, politicians, police, businessmen, bureaucrats, racing 'identities'; all part of a murky world called organised crime. Then came the white shoe brigade, paper shufflers who made billions, but were just another bunch of crooks.

Two decades on and Melbourne's gangland war opened our eyes afresh. This was not about illegal bets, or sly grog, or shady ladies under street lamps. This was a war for control of the multi-billion dollar drugs trade. In that war, almost all of us are destined to be involved. And millions of us will be the losers.

# The Melbourne gang wars

It's given to few of us to open our morning newspaper and read that we're about to be murdered. Over breakfast in his East Doncaster home in February 2005, Dominic 'Mick' Gatto read the front page story. It conjectured: MICK GATTO NEXT? The headline may have caused the charismatic and generally well-liked big man to gulp a little more cappuccino than he intended. But the story itself would not be news to him and the chances are that he paused only briefly before taking another bite from his brioche.

For 10 years, almost to the day, from the time his friend Alphonse 'Al' Gangitano shot dead a standover man in St Kilda on 7 February 1995, to the morning of 6 February 2005, when another close friend was gunned down, Mick Gatto had become accustomed to seeing his circle diminish – almost daily it seemed – in a ferocious power struggle. In those 10 years as many as 33 died in the gangland war for control of Melbourne's billion dollar amphetamines industry. It was a war between the 'Carlton Crew', backed by the Mafia and centred around the Lygon Street cafés and coffee shops of Melbourne's 'Little Italy,' and a brash but vicious gang of young up-and-comers who believed they better understood the ever-expanding drug world and its oceans of money there for the taking. It was crime's venerable Establishment up against the vulgar trash from the western suburbs. It was a fight to the death and, on a body count, the Westies were winning the fight.

Melbourne has underworld wars like other cities have cultural festivals. They are part of the calendar and go back to and beyond the 1920s and the brutal Fitzroy vendetta that culminated in the mutually fatal ventilation of Squizzy Taylor and Snowy Cutmore, killed in a blaze of gunfire in Snowy's Carlton terrace house.

From the late 1950s (on the waterfront) and for the next 30 years there was the Painters and Dockers Union's internecine war. That struggle for power claimed at least 40 lives. At Melbourne's Queen Victoria market, the biggest growers market in the world, decades of killings followed the 1962 death of Domenica Italiano, the head of the Honoured Society in Victoria, the Mafia controllers of the market's many rackets. On 16 January 1964, Vincenzo Muratore, Italiano's financial advisor, was shot dead as he left his Hampton home at about 2.30 a.m. Thirty years later and 150 metres away, at 1.30 in the morning outside *his* Hampton home, his son Alfonse Muratore, went in almost exactly the same way.

Domenico Italiano, Il Papa, had his elaborate funeral service – more like that of a head of state – in December 1962 at the church of choice for gangster send-offs with style, St Mary's Star of the Sea, West Melbourne. And it was here, 36 years on, that Alphonse 'Al' Gangitano, was also buried with great pomp – as he would have expected.

Gangitano was the epitome of the Carlton Crew's fondness for aping the Goodfellas of Hollywood movies. He postured in Italian suits, slicked back his hair and wore dark glasses. He saw himself as a young Andy Garcia, handsome, suave, and charismatic:

The Melbourne *Herald Sun*'s front page report on what proved to be the last killing in the gangland war that claimed as many as 33 lives.

Gangland victim: MARK

# GANGLANI EXECUTION

## Underworld accus shot dead at hom

Holly Lloyd-McDonald, Mark Buttler and Geoff Wilkinson

GANGLAND figure Mario Condello was shot dead at his luxury Brighton home last night.

The body of Mr Condello, 53, a senior member of the so-called Carlton Crew and a key figure in Melbourne's underworld war, was found dead in his garage by his wife shortly before 10pm.

His killing ended a 20-month pause in the bloody gangland war that has claimed 28 lives.

A police source said his wife and one of his children found his body.

His daughter ran screaming towards the police line and had to be held back by ambulance officers. She then fell into her mother's arms as they both sobbed.

Mick Gatto, last year acquitted of the murder of gangland hitman Andrew "Benji" Veniamin, and three of the Carlton Crew arrived 10

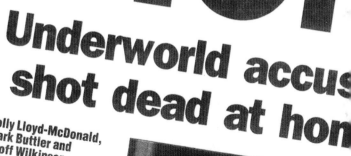

**Crime scene:** distraught family members com each other last night. Picture: REBECCA MICHAE

last night Mr Gatto said: "Leave me out of it."

He and Mr Condello had been seen earlier last night at The Society restaurant in Bourke St.

Mr Condello was known as a smooth talker who roamed high-roller rooms of Crown casino, even securing prized status as a "premium club" me...

police Chief Commiss ner, Christine Nixon.

Underneath Mr Conde lo's polished exterior wa a man who sometime used violence and intimi dation to get his way.

The Purana taskforce which was formed to stem the ganglan bloodshed

Murder plotter Mario Condello leaves a court b...

Crew arrived 10

the Black Prince of Lygon Street. But when he opened the security door of his home, late one night on 16 January 1998, the prince was wearing his pyjama top and blue underpants: clothes he wouldn't have been seen dead in, had he a say in it.

At the door was Graham 'The Munster' Kinniburgh, a long-time friend and an Elder Statesman among Melbourne's criminal fraternity. Despite the respect he commanded, The Munster later told the Coroner, Al told him to clear off for half an hour. He was expecting another, unnamed, visitor.

Kinniburgh dutifully drove to a convenience store for cigarettes, where, as he anticipated, he was recorded on a video camera. While he was away, he claimed, Gangitano's killer arrived. Through the mesh of his security door Gangitano would have seen the man – or men – his sometime partner in crime, Jason Moran and, possibly, Jason's half-brother, Mark. That morning Jason and Al had appeared in court over a brutal bashing in a city bar. For no apparent reason – other than to demonstrate what they could do if they didn't get protection money – the pair laid into the patrons with billiard cues and an iron bar, sending 10 to hospital, one of them a woman.

Twelve hours after the chums left court Al opened the door and shortly after, when words led to a fearful falling out, he was running for his life. He made it to the laundry before someone, Jason, or Mark, shot him three times: in the back, head and nose.

For a week or so Melbourne's underworld was awash with sentimentality. Mark 'Chopper' Read

Top: Jason Moran peers over a coffin top and, left, big Mick Gatto whispers a confidence. *Newspix*

nostalgically recalled how, 'We started off as friends; I was the first person to give him a sawn-off shotgun... he was about 16 and... I could see the delight on his face, he'd never had one before.'

Mick Gatto inserted his standard death notice – one of 208 in the *Herald Sun* – underpinned by what discerning readers cherished as his familiar theme line: 'Sorry to see you go this way.' Mick had been inserting death notices in the classifieds since 1982, when Brian Kane – Jason Moran's uncle – went down in a hail of bullets at the Quarry Hotel in East Brunswick.

Jason Moran had a notoriously quick temper. In the following year it went on show again, this time sparked by another middle-ranking criminal wannabe, an amphetamines manufacturer, Carl Williams. Williams dropped out of school at the age of 16 to try his hand at drug dealing and over the next decade, was so successful that he had a price on his head of $150,000.

On 13 October 1999 the Moran brothers met Williams in a park to discuss money they said he owed them. Jason got straight to business. He pulled a .22 Derringer and while Mark urged, 'Shoot him in the head!' Jason shot Williams in the stomach. Jason wanted Williams to live so that he could pay his six figure debt.

It was a mistake, the beginning of an obsessive vendetta by Williams that would wipe out the Moran crime family and lead to the incidental death of as many as 10 men. The killings started on 15 June 2000 when Williams blasted Mark Moran with a shotgun as he stepped from his car outside his house. (Mark's father had been similarly ambushed 18 years before.)

Top: Lewis Moran, one of the last to be murdered, and (right) Alphonse Gangitano, the first to go. *Newspix*

Next on the list was Jason. Williams had planned to kill him at the gravesite of Mark, and, for added piquancy, on the anniversary of Mark's murder. Two contract killers assigned to the job arrived to find Jason had left his card on the grave and gone. With Williams, they concocted a new plan and waited for the following Saturday. That morning, 21 June 2003, while Jason and his bodyguard, Pasquale Barbaro and six children sat in a van watching a football clinic for kids, one of them, a man known as The Runner, rushed to the car and killed the two. Moran was carrying a handgun, but The Runner got in first with a shotgun and a handgun, the same weapons Carl Williams used to kill Mark Moran.

Six months later, on 13 December 2003 The Munster was gunned down in the driveway of his upper-class Kew home. Kinniburgh, a close friend of the Morans, knew he was a target. 'My card's been marked,' he'd say.

Lewis Moran, too, knew he was living on borrowed time but, shattered by the death of his sons and his close mate The Munster, he didn't seem to care. On 31 March 2004 the patriarch of the notorious family was caught and killed by two masked men who walked into his favourite Brunswick bar as he downed a VB. 'I think we're off!' Moran said by way of farewell to his drinking mate as he saw the masked men and made a half-hearted run for it. His mate was shot and severely wounded. Lewis fell dead by the pool table.

Lewis Moran was gunned down the day after Andrew 'Benji' Veniamin, surrounded by the usual Central Casting thugs, had been laid to rest. Benji had died on the floor of La Porcella, a Carlton restaurant frequented by Mick Gatto. He had been dispatched with two bullets to the head, put there by Gatto. It was self-defence, the big man said, and the jury agreed. In a dark back passage of La

Porcella, Veniamin, a vicious punk, pulled a gun on him, the former heavyweight boxer said. In the struggle it went off.

Mick Gatto, many thought, would be next to fall in the grim line that now numbered in the dozens. But the next – and last to go – was the Carlton Crew kingpin, Mario Condello. Shot repeatedly in his garage on 6 February, 2006, Condello had put out a $150,000 contract on Carl Williams.

Police and most of Melbourne had no doubt that Williams and an associate were behind the killings but there was no real proof. Then, in March 2007, came news of a stunning betrayal. The gangland killers who had carried out Williams's orders finally turned on him – rolled over – in return for reduced sentences. Two of the killers, The Runner, and The Driver, told how Williams and 'Fat Tony' Mokbel had paid around $150,000 for rivals to be murdered.

Faced with the certainty that their testimony would guarantee that he would be sentenced to life imprisonment, never to be released, Williams decided to try the same plea bargaining ploy. He admitted to the murders of Jason and Lewis Moran. 'Fat Tony' Mokbel, too, was charged with Lewis Moran's murder. He had jumped bail on a cocaine charge and was living the high life in Greece until he was caught in June 2007.

Before Williams agreed to the plea bargain deal, however, he stipulated that police get a message to Mick Gatto. He wanted Gatto to know that no matter what, he wished him no harm. Hearing that, Big Mick may have sprinkled another grain of salt on his osso buco.

Carl Williams and the coffin of his hitman Benji Veniamin. Williams arranged the murder of Jason Moran in front of his children. The Morans had hired two men to kill Williams at the christening of his daughter. *The Age*

# Sydney, the crime capital

'Organised crime consists of the criminal milieu, the men in the black hats plus its support system in the white hats: politicians, accountants, journalists, lawyers, bureaucrats, police and judges,' Evan Whitton wrote in *Can of Worms*.

Organised crime is nowhere better organised than in Australia's crime capital, Sydney – the most corrupt town in the western world,' says Whitton, 'except of course for Newark, New Jersey, and Brisbane, Queensland.'

And no one better exemplifies the corruption of Sydney's 'white hats' than Abe Saffron, the man the tabloids called Mr Sin. Saffron died in 2006 aged 86. For most of his life he had been making his fortune supplying illegal services, alcohol, drugs, gambling and prostitution. He'd been closely linked – together with the crooked police Deputy Commissioner, Bill Allen – to US mafia figures and to murder. Yet in all that time he was only twice convicted of a crime, once, in 1938, when he was still a teenager working as a runner for illegal bookmakers, and again, 50 years later, when he went to jail for two-and-a-half years for tax fraud.

Wendy Bacon, writing in the *Bulletin*, after Saffron's death, said, 'He paid millions in bribes to NSW police and politicians... To protect himself from challenges, he hired people who handed out threats, beatings, "dobbed in" people to the police and, if necessary, murdered.'

A noted crime investigative journalist, Wendy Bacon was a university student editor when she became embroiled in the fight to stop the high-rise development of beautiful Victoria Street, Potts Point, a block from Saffron's Kings Cross trip clubs.

'Hundreds of tenants were issued with eviction notices. Suddenly the thugs who controlled Saffron's Kings Cross clubs were patrolling the street... A resident activist, Arthur King, was violently kidnapped... When he returned he was too frightened to tell us what happened. Only some years later did he report that he had been dragged into the boot of a car that was later parked outside Saffron's Venus Room club.'

Two years later, Juanita Nielsen, the wealthy editor of the local newspaper campaigning against the development, got a phone call and visited Saffron's Carousel Club. On Friday 4 July 1975 she was seen leaving the club but never seen again. Three men were charged with conspiring to abduct her and two served jail terms, but the coroner found: 'There is evidence to show that the police inquiries were ignited by an atmosphere of corruption, real or imagined.'

The Juanita Nielsen case, marked by callous and cynical disdain, shocked Sydney. Ten years later the dark side of the city was once again shockingly revealed. Once again the victim was a young, attractive woman, campaigning against corruption through the media, but where Juanita Nielsen was said to be the heiress to the Mark Foy wealth, Sally-Anne Huckstepp was a heroin addict and prostitute. Huckstepp, like Juanita Nielsen, got a phone call that caused her to hurry to a meeting, telling her flatmate she'd be back shortly. Next morning her body was found floating in a pond in Centennial Park.

Roger Rogerson (far right) looks on as a detective, one of 18 policemen staked out in Dangar Place, Chippendale, examines the corpse of heroin dealer and armed robber, Warren Lanfranchi. *Newspix*

In 1996 the notorious Neddy Smith, now serving a life sentence for a road rage killing, was charged with Sally-Ann Huckstepp's murder. He had been secretly recorded confessing to a cellmate that he had strangled her, 'the most satisfying thing I ever did in my life', and then standing on her back to keep her head submerged. Smith was acquitted in 1999, claiming he knew he was being taped and he wanted the publicity for a book he was writing, *Neddy: the Life and Crimes of Arthur Stanley Smith.*

Sally-Anne Huckstepp was seen frequently on TV current affairs programs before she was murdered. Her lover, a heroin dealer, Warren Lanfranchi, had been shot dead by Detective-Sergeant Roger Rogerson. Huckstepp – and, after her murder, Neddie Smith, an informant for Rogerson – alleged that Rogerson had murdered Lanfranchi as retribution for robbing another heroin dealer.

Now in his mid-60s, Roger Caleb Rogerson is Australia's most infamous ex-policeman. A good cop/bad cop, the winner of a policeman of the year award – 'a polished performer, an extremely enthusiastic worker, an outstanding detective' – Rogerson shot, or was present, when a number of criminals were gunned down by police. Warren Lanfranchi was a violent criminal, a gunman wanted for armed robberies and for trying to shoot a traffic policeman. But his killing left unanswered questions.

Rogerson claimed that he was attempting to arrest Lanfranchi on suspicion of five bank robberies when he took 18 policemen with him to a meeting in Dangar Place, Chippendale. Neddy Smith in his book claimed that Lanfranchi had asked him to negotiate a bribe with Rogerson, up to $50,000, to avoid arrest over the heroin theft. And Sally-Anne Huckstepp said that she had ironed 'a warm shirt' for Lanfranchi and saw him off, unarmed and carrying $10,000. He had expected to meet Rogerson alone in Dangar Place.

Instead, 18 policemen had staked out the vicinity when Rogerson and three others went into the lane on Saturday afternoon, 27 July 1981. Lanfranchi drew a gun and aimed it at Rogerson, they said, who drew his gun and fired two shots in close succession. Two girls who heard the shots differed. They estimated the shots were 10 or 11 seconds apart.

Police told the inquest that Lanfranchi had a handgun but they denied he was carrying $10,000. The inquest found that Rogerson had been trying to arrest Lanfranchi but refused to find he acted in self-defence or in the execution of his duty. No action was brought against Rogerson and he was commended for bravery.

Three years later, on 6 June 1984, Michael Drury, an undercover policeman, was standing close to his daughter when he was shot twice through his kitchen window. Drury was badly wounded and, believing he was dying, made a 'dying deposition' in which he claimed Rogerson had tried to bribe him in a heroin trafficking case.

The mounting suspicions over Roger Rogerson came to a head when he was filmed waiting to take secret money from bank accounts: he had $110,000 in bank accounts under false names. 'In my day, the New South Wales police force was the best police force money could buy,' he once said. He was charged, spent nine months in jail, appealed and lost and spent a further three years in jail.

Roger Rogerson carrying a pump action shotgun and (far right) actor Richard Roxburgh who played Rogerson – and looked uncannily like him – in the chilling ABC series *Blue Murder. Newspix*

# The Thorne kidnap

'I have told the boy that I was to take him to school. He sed why, where is the lady. I sed she is sick and cannot come today. Then the boy got into the car and I drove him around for a while and over the Harbour Bridge. I went to a public phone box near The Spit Bridge and I rang the Thornes. I talked to Mrs Thorne and to a man who sed he was the boy's father. I have asked for 25 thousand pounds from the boy's mother and father. I told them that if I don't get the money I feed him to the sharks and I have told them I ring later. I took the boy home in the car to Clontarf and I put the car in my garage. I told the boy to get out of the car to come and see another boy. When he got out of the car I have put a scarf over his mouth, and put him in the boot of the car and slammed the boot. I went in my house and the furniture removalist came, a few minutes later. When it was nearly dark, I went to the car and found the boy was dead. That night I tied the boy up with string and put him in my rug. I put the boy in the boot of the Ford car again, and then I threw his case and cap near Bantry Bay, and put the boy on a vacant lotment near the house I went to see with a real estate agent, to buy sometime before.'– *S.L. Bradley*

The boy was eight-year-old Graeme Thorne. S.L. Bradley was Stephen Bradley, his murderer. And the Thorne Kidnap, as it is always referred to, was a freeze-frame moment for Australia.

Child-killers are all too frequent in our society. And every child murder comes with a shudder of horror and outrage. But the murder of Graeme Thorne shocked the nation because Australia understood it to be a bitter precedent: an awful sign of what was to come – the kind of criminal society that we knew only from Hollywood movies.

Kidnapping was unknown in Australia when Steven Bradley lured the Bondi schoolboy into his car and killed him. His confession – which he later denied – tells the story from a sanitised but fairly accurate viewpoint. He had demanded the then huge ransom of £25,000 after reading that the boy's parents had won £100,000 in the tenth Opera House lottery. The lottery, established to build the proposed Sydney Opera House, was big news in 1960 and the prize was enough for a man to live comfortably for two lifetimes.

Where Bradley's version of the kidnapping differs from the truth is in the manner of the boy's death. Bradley hadn't 'found' Graeme Thorne's dead body in the boot of his car. Graeme Thorne hadn't died of asphyxiation: two policemen, breathing air from the boot for seven hours proved that. And he hadn't died after accidentally striking his head on the rim of the spare tyre, as the defence was to claim. Graeme Thorne's body was found on 16 August, 75 days after he was taken, on a vacant block of land at Seaforth. He was wearing his Scots College blazer. Around his neck was a knotted silk scarf. The body was wrapped in a car rug. The boy's skull had been fractured by 'a good force' and he may also have been strangled. His hands and feet were tied. It was chilling, brutal, murder.

The police investigation into the Thorne kidnapping is a classic of forensic investigation. Bradley was convicted and sentenced to life imprisonment and died of a heart attack eight years later. No one lamented him. But with Graeme Thorne, part of our innocence died.

# The Bogle-Chandler mystery

The January morning was already steaming up when the two boys came across the body in the bush. The dead man, blue in the face, blood trickling from the nose, lay on his stomach on a bank of the Lane Cove River in suburban Sydney. Rigor mortis had set in. Arms spread-eagled, legs extended and shoes mud-caked, the corpse was half naked, clad only in shirt, tie, socks and shoes. Neatly folded trousers covered the legs and under them was a grimy piece of carpet, about one by one-and-a-half metres, over the naked loins. The man's jacket – fresh semen traces on it – covered his back. The sleeves followed the spread of the arms. It seemed clear this wasn't a suicide, or death by natural causes.

It was around 7.45 a.m., on New Years Day, 1963.

About three hours later, when police arrived, they found the dead man's wallet and identified him as a Dr Gilbert Bogle of Turramurra. They had presumed, in all likelihood, that the body was that of some old dero. But a dead doctor found in this bizarre pose – well, that was something different. Then, a shout from a motorcycle policeman around 15 metres away, closer to the river.

'Hey! Sarge! There's another one down here!'

Margaret Chandler, her body still warm, was lying on her back, a leg protruding from three sheets of a flattened-out beer carton put together to cover her nakedness. She too was nude from the waist down and a man's underpants were between her ankles. Her dress was rolled up to her waist and her strapless bra was pulled down to expose her

In a not entirely accurate simulation, Dr Gilbert Bogle's body is shown as it was found: trousers and jacket laid over back and legs. *Newspix*

breasts. She had crawled or stumbled around – or been dragged by someone. Her white panties and brown shoes and Dr Bogle's belt were down by the dry river bed.

Bogle and Chandler, the police quickly discovered, were married – to others.

The coroner, on this public holiday, couldn't be found and the bodies baked in the sun until the middle of the afternoon when the sickening sight and stench of the vomit and diarrhoea that surrounded them was almost overpowering. The corpses were refrigerated overnight and the autopsy performed the next day – too late to trace possible poisons.

The Bogle–Chandler mystery, four decades on, still baffles, still intrigues. But in 1963 the shock of the discovery of the bodies and the mystery of their deaths reverberated around the nation. Here was a Rhodes Scholar, a brilliant scientist at a famous research laboratory, a married man with four children. Here was this estimable and remarkable man, found dead with his trousers off and a reputation already in tatters.

And Margaret Chandler. She was the mother of two little kiddies – and she had been a nurse! – also half naked, and found with a man's underpants between her ankles. Worse, it transpired, her husband, also a CSIRO man, didn't give a hoot that his wife was having an affair with Dr Bogle – in fact he encouraged it! And he too was having a bit on the side.

On the surface Geoffrey Chandler, 32, and his wife Margaret, 29, seemed to be a happily married couple with had two small children and common interests in dachshund dogs and veteran cars. He was a scientific photographer at the CSIRO.

Dr Gilbert Bogle, 39, a colleague of Chandler's, was also a seemingly happily married father of four,

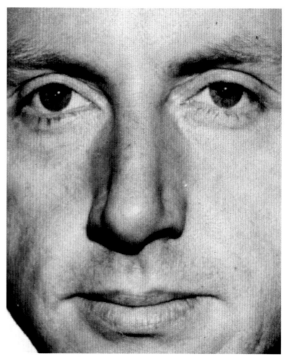

'Gib' Bogle a practiced seducer of colleagues' wives and (right) Margaret Chandler. 'It's always gratifying to have one's choice in one's wife borne out by another man's attention to her,' her husband wrote. *Newspix*

whose wife Vivien was the daughter of an Anglican bishop. At the CSIRO he was working – blazing a dazzling trail – on solid state physics, specialising in masers, the precursors of lasers. His work was not classified top secret but its ramifications for military use were extremely significant.

'Gib' and Margaret met at a CSIRO Christmas barbecue and there was instant rapport. 'They struck a spark, one off the other,' Geoffrey Chandler later wrote in his book, *So You Think I Did It?* (Chandler was the prime suspect in the minds of most of the police and many members of the public.) 'In a way I was flattered. At least two women had told me that Gib was a fascinating man and it is always gratifying to have one's choice in one's wife borne out by another man's attentions to her.'

Chandler didn't know Bogle well, but he knew

that Bogle made a practice of seducing the wives of friends and colleagues. Bogle, he later learned from one of Gib's former conquests, was a man who was apparently not particularly ardent, but who liked to 'renew himself' with other women.

Geoffrey Chandler, too, liked to renew himself. He was a member of the Sydney 'Push', a loose tribe of intellectuals who saw themselves an anti-Establishment. 'Casual love-making was part of the Push life,' he wrote. 'There were always a number of good-looking young girls around.'

At the time they met, 'Gib' Bogle was having an on-and-off affair with a woman, Margaret Fowler. Geoffrey Chandler was 'constantly seeing' an attractive member of the Push, Pam Logan. And Margaret Chandler had come out of an affair with an unmarried man who told police that Geoffrey Chandler had suggested that he visit Margaret when he was not at home.

Driving home from the barbecue Geoffrey Chandler could see his wife was excited. Margaret wondered what he would be like as a lover. Geoffrey told her, 'If you want to have Gib as a lover, if it would make you happy, you do it.'

On New Year's Eve, after the Chandlers had left their children with Margaret's parents at Granville, the three met again at the Chatswood home of Ken and Ruth Nash on Sydney's North Shore. Ken Nash, a dapper man, was Chandler's superior in the photographic branch at the CSIRO. The Chandlers, it transpired, had been invited at late notice – and only at the prompting of Gib Bogle, the star guest among the 22 who came– suitably dressed – to the party. Only Geoffrey Chandler declined to come in the stipulated jacket and tie for men.

Inside the '30s suburban home Geoffrey Chandler looked around and didn't much like what he saw:

about 20 people talking quietly and not doing a lot of drinking. 'Pretentious and effete,' he described it in 2006. He slipped out around 11 p.m. and went to a Push party in Balmain, where he met Pam Logan. They went to her bedsitter in Darlington for about half an hour before Geoffrey returned to the Nash's party at between 2 a.m. and 3 a.m.

No one seemed to have missed him and as supper was served Margaret told him cheerfully that Gib was going to drive her home. The three of them sat 'in what I think Ken Nash called his den... it was at this time I should have said to Margaret, "Come on, we're going home." But I didn't. So it was really I who forced the issue.'

Chandler asked Bogle if he still wanted to drive Margaret home. Bogle, he said, looked at him intently for a moment and then said 'Right.' It was taken for granted that Chandler would go to Granville to pick up the children, leaving the Chatswood home empty.

Chandler mooched out of the house, not bothering to say goodbye to anyone, sat outside for a while smoking – waiting to see if Margaret might change her mind – and had a last cigarette in his car before starting the engine and driving his silver vintage Vauxhall to Pam Logan's.

He woke her up and she went with him to pick up the boys. The distinctive car was seen on the Parramatta Road between 4.45 and 5 a.m. by two witnesses, one of whom recognised Chandler and said to his wife that the woman in the car wasn't Margaret Chandler. At Granville, while Pam waited at a discreet distance from the house, Chandler picked up his children and they all returned to the Logan flat at Darlington. It was 6.30 a.m. There Chandler stayed until 10 a.m., when he returned to his Croydon home, tumbled into the empty double bed and slept.

Lovers, Pam Logan and (opposite page) Geoffrey Chandler were seen in his car around the time Bogle and Margaret Chandler were dying from what the baffled coroner could only conclude was 'acute circulatory failure'. *Newspix*

Fifteen minutes after Geoffrey Chandler had driven off, disconsolate, Gib Bogle said goodnight to Ruth Nash and in his Ford Prefect beeped farewell to the remaining partygoers. Margaret Chandler waited a few minutes, got into Bogle's car and they drove off. They were seen driving into Lane Cove River Park, five kilometres from the Nash's, around 4.30 before Bogle turned on to a narrow dirt track, on the eastern bank of the Lane Cove River, a well-known Lover's Lane.

Bill Jenkings, the veteran *Mirror* crime reporter, thought he knew how Margaret Chandler and Gib Bogle died. It was not murder, he said. In *As Crime Goes By: The Life and Times of 'Bondi' Bill Jenkings*, he wrote: 'I have no doubt it was a stupid practical

joke that badly misfired. This I base on my own investigations and the many frank discussions with that shrewdest of detectives, Jack Bateman... I believe that one of the guests at the party slipped [dog worming] tablets into cups of coffee Dr Bogle and Mrs Chandler drank just before they left the party.' (Mrs Chandler had bought worming tablets for her dachshund dogs the day before her death. She had asked the vet if they could be harmful to humans and had been told they could, in sufficient dosages.)

In September 2006, the ABC screened a documentary by filmmaker Peter Butt. He proposed that the couple had been asphyxiated: that the Lane Cove River was so polluted with waste from leaking sewage and nearby factories that the couple had quickly succumbed when a deadly cloud of hydrogen sulphide gas – better known as rotten egg gas – had bubbled up from the waters and gathered in the shallow hollow where the couple lay.

Kevin Perkins, then a young reporter for the *Daily Telegraph,* told the *Australian* the documentary 'didn't ring true. They didn't mention the fact that both Chandler and Bogle had been violently ill or the fact that one of the bodies had clearly been dragged away from the other. At that time, the local kids used to swim and fish in the river all the time, so I'm not sure it was as polluted as the film-maker would have us believe.'

In 1976 on the 13th anniversary of the death of Gilbert Bogle and Margaret Chandler, Ken Nash, the New Year's Eve party host, wedged a .22 calibre semi-automatic rifle between his legs, stooped his head over the barrel and squeezed the trigger.

Nash was said to be obsessed by the Bogle–Chandler case.

The rest of us are still intrigued.

# Alan Bond: the corporate criminal

*'He was our national hero, an entrepreneur who strutted the world stage, who mesmerised all with that Grand Canyon smile... medical experts were called to testify that Bond was a brain-dead ignoramus who could not take the stand... A couple of days before he was released after less than four years in jail for fraud involving $1.2 billion, a Northern Territory man was sentenced to one year's jail for stealing $23 worth of cordial and biscuits. Had the same formula been applied to Bond, he would have been in jail for 50 million years.'*

– *Sydney Morning Herald*, 7 October 2000

You'd have to have a heart of stone not to laugh. There on the front pages and leading the nightly television news was Alan Bond, leaving after another tough day in court. Bewildered, eyes fighting back the anguish, he was pitiful. And limping. Limping like a weather-beaten old pirate making his way uphill to the George and Dragon after too many years of yo-ho-ho-ing and too much plunder.

Alan Bond's legal team, surrounding him with matching worried mien, insisted that his limp was the result of severe depression. But other, unkind souls, said Bondy's gait would have improved markedly if he'd taken the trouble to empty his shoe of the large pebble it surely held.

Cynics have always been cruel to Alan Bond. 'Some people think they can say what they like about me...Well, it hurts, I can tell you. It hurts,' he complained. 'I'd just ask people: "Isn't it about time they gave Alan Bond a fair go?"'

Bond, who has fathomless chutzpah, went on Andrew Denton's Enough Rope to talk about the cynics and his colourful career. Denton, the finest and funniest interviewer Australian television has known, began: 'Whenever I mention to people, "I'm interviewing Alan Bond," they say, "Oh, has he got his memory back?" Because they remember you from those court cases in 1994 where you were apparently very, very sick. How sick were you?'

These days Alan Bond seems to have regained his memory, is reputed to be worth $60 million despite the hundreds of millions he owes, and lives in a penthouse in London with his second wife, Diana Bliss.

Alan Bond was the most egregious of the corporate cowboys – 'Last Resort' Laurie Connell, Robert Holmes à Court, Christopher Skase, George Herscu, Abe Goldberg, Larry Adler and the like – dodgy high-fliers on the Australian financial landscape over the last quarter of a century. Most of them were patently unpalatable. But for a time, Alan Bond was the Australian Idol.

The man who financed our successful America's Cup Challenge, Bondy seemed to have no limit to his imagination or his purse. (The reality was, of course, that winning the unwinnable America's Cup gave Bond the credentials he needed to borrow huge amounts from the Western Australian state government and the banks, whose generosity to men like Bond – $28 billion, all of it lost – was boundless.)

At the height of his entrepreneurial career his public company Bond Group and his private company Dallhold owned major breweries in Australia and North America, the Nine television network, West Australian newspapers, property

The high life for Alan Bond. The hero of the America's Cup triumph, he's seen here in his Swan Airship, enjoying a convivial can of his own Swan Lager. Bond loved the limelight. *Newspix*

developments, mining operations, the discount chain Norman Ross and the department store chain Waltons, Thorn EMI film studios, New York's swish St Moritz hotel, and most of an English village.

The newspaper image on the previous page sums it up: Bond, photographed from outside his Swan Airship is seen in the capacious cabin grinning through the window, a sumptuous meal on the table before him, while behind him brewery execs, beer cans in hand like Bond, beam with the wonder of it all.

Bondy was garrulous and gregarious, unlike his fellow Western Australian entrepreneur Robert Holmes à Court, a man who, Les Carlyon wrote, 'spoke the way pharmacists used to dispense arsenic: carefully, slowly, every syllable weighed. He seldom said what he meant or finished a sentence.'

Bondy, for his part, loved the limelight. He was photographed with prime ministers and the Pope, and he was President of the Richmond Football Club: proof positive that Bondy was a dinki-di Aussie who just happened to be a billionaire.

But that was before the Bond Corporation's $8.23 billion crash. 'Tiny' Rowland, a tough and shrewd English businessman – whose conglomerate, Lonrho, faced a takeover by Bond– precipitated the fall. The Bond Corporation and Bond himself were then at the height of their fame. Bond had just – supposedly – paid $53 million for a not particularly good Van Gogh, and he seemed set to assume the throne of the emperor of international commerce.

Tiny Rowland said the emperor had no clothes. Or if he had, they were threadbare.

People began looking closely at the emperor, and shortly after Tiny Rowland's view was confirmed. Bond Corporation went into receivership. Alan Bond was declared bankrupt, paying his personal creditors $3.25 million to settle debts of more than half a billion.

In 1992 he was jailed for 30 months for dishonesty, released after a retrial but then jailed for three years over some creative accounting involving another very costly work of art. He was jailed for a further four years in 1997 for deception to the tune of $1.2 billion. It was at this trial that he claimed to be suffering from amnesia caused by depression and brain damage. On appeal by the Crown the sentence was increased to seven years, but the High Court overturned that sentence on a technicality and Bond was released on parole.

In 2003 in Perth Bondy was back in the spotlight, part of the 20th anniversary celebrations of the America's Cup win.

Paul Barry, who so incensed Bond that, on camera, he tore up Barry's media pass, wrote that, 'For 20 years Alan Bond plundered his public companies... at the end of it he left a black hole of around five billion Australian dollars which was losses borne by shareholders, creditors, bankers and the rest... He then managed to hang on to a private fortune of something like $100 million... what he did in the 1980s and the 1990s was a disgrace to this country and he brought us into disrepute around the world... he made a fool of the legal system and he made a fool of all of us too.'

That's why most people don't think it's about time to give Alan Bond a fair go.

# 6

# THE UPHEAVALS

On 5 March 1804, Major George Johnston and 56 soldiers caught up with the Irish convicts who had broken out at Castle Hill. What did the rebels want, Johnston demanded. The contemporary illustration shows their leader Cunningham's reply – 'Death or liberty!' – and Johnston's response: 'I'll liberate you, you scoundrel!' as he clapped a pistol to Cunningham's head and ordered his troops to fire. Within minutes a dozen Irishmen lay dead and the troops moved in with fixed bayonets. Cunningham was summarily hanged on a staircase and two days later eight others swung.

Castle Hill, and Eureka Stockade half a century later, remain the only battles fought on Australian soil.

In September 1993 the commentator Peter Ryan dealt a devastating blow to the reputation of the revered historian Manning Clark. Writing in Quadrant Ryan regretted that he had, as head of Melbourne University Press, published Clark's famous six-volume A History of Australia – 'a vast cauldron of very thin verbal soup... a construct spun from fairy-floss, and much of that false.' Ryan wrote: 'If our history were really as black as Clark so wickedly paints it, children would just have to face it. But in fact, by the standards of comparison which the real world allows, the Australian experience of life has been unrivalled in its spaciousness and freedom.'

Australia's historians circled the wagons. One said Ryan had gone mad. Another that he was a coward. A third that he was a cannibal. But some, like Don Watson, who wrote Paul Keating's famous Redfern Address, admitted that Manning Clark's version of our history was marred by 'errors or absence of fact', and Geoffrey Bolton conceded 'there may be cause to remove [Clark's] icon to a lower shelf'.

What became known as the History Wars exploded with renewed fury in 2002 when Keith Windschuttle showed that in Tasmania the recorded number of Aborigines who died violently between 1803 and 1834 – the height of the clashes between Aborigines and settlers – was 120. (The death toll for the colonists over the same three decades was 187.) And, he found, the Black Line campaign of 1829–1830 – said by some to be an early example of 'ethnic cleansing' – cost a total of three Aboriginal lives. Only one trooper was killed by Aborigines in the history of Tasmania, Windschuttle said, belying the claims of the historian Henry Reynolds that an Aboriginal guerilla war waged against the whites was 'the biggest internal threat Australia has ever had'.

Fact or fiction? Historian, politician and, later, governor-general of Australia, Paul Hasluck wrote in 1942: 'There have been two colossal fictions in popular accounts of the treatment of natives in Australia. One suggests that settlers habitually went about shooting down blacks: the other, framed as a counterblast, is that every settler treated natives with constant kindness. There is no evidence to support either statement in Western Australia.'

Whatever the truth of the History Wars, rooted as they are in the question of the treatment of Aborigines, the truth about Australian history as a whole is that since Captain Cook landed at Botany Bay in 1770 we have known far less tumult and trauma than any large-scale nation. North and South America, Europe and Russia, Asia, India and Pakistan, Africa and the Middle East have all been wracked by centuries of almost unremitting wars: civil, religious, ethnic and tribal; by uprisings and rebellions; by regicides; by the cyclical rise and fall and rise of despots and dictators; by constitutional crises, coups d'état and civil disobedience.

Australians, with one tragic exception, have known very little of that. Our history since Cook has been remarkably free from the class warfare and religious conflict – the 'blood on the wattle' – that Manning Clark seemed almost to yearn for. Ethnic clashes, too, have been rare. The ferocious riots at the Lambing Flat goldfields in 1861 saw hundreds of Europeans attack Chinese miners and kill at least two. Police, in turn, shot dead one of the European rioters. But Lambing Flat is remembered – just – because it is a terrible exception. Racial tensions, present throughout our history, seldom erupt.

Blood on the wattle – other than that of the convicts, flogged relentlessly for the most trifling offences in the first 50 years of the colony – came in the 1804 convict uprising at Castle Hill, one of only two armed rebellions in our history. The other, at Ballarat's Eureka Stockade 50 years later, cost the lives of 24 goldfields miners, four soldiers and a trooper, killed in a protest against remote and overbearing government.

Anti-government industrial turmoil has seen brutality and violence, but seldom deaths. In 1890 shearers on Jondaryan Station in Queensland's Darling Downs won the right to allow only union shearers in the shed. This emboldened the union to ask others to refuse to handle wool shorn by non-union labour. That winter the Maritime Strike of seamen and wharf laborers was joined by the shearers and by miners from Newcastle and Broken Hill. In Sydney an armed escort accompanying volunteers carting wool towards Circular Quay was met by a rowdy crowd of 3000. A police officer read the Riot Act and mounted troopers went in. The Maritime Strike failed, but out of the defeat of the unionists the Australian Labor Party was born.

Only two fatalities can be directly attributed to industrial strikes. More than 600 Melbourne policemen mutinied over pay and pensions in 1923 and criminals and hooligans took to the streets. One man was kicked to death, 237 were taken to hospital and 85 looters arrested before order was restored by volunteers, mainly returned soldiers, wielding pick handles. Six years later, in 1929, police threatened by a mob of 300 strikers in the Hunter Valley shot dead a miner. His was the only violent fatality of union action in the Depression.

Though it took four years of misery and grinding poverty, Australia emerged from the Depression relatively unscathed. It was, certainly, among the most traumatic periods in our history, but in 2006 David Potts' *The Myth of the Great Depression*, overturned many conceptions of the period. Potts claimed that historians had presented a distorted picture of starvation and despair when, in fact, the shared Australian instinct of 'fair go' helped battlers cope. There was little real starvation, he says. In fact, because people drank less alcohol and ate more vegetables the nation's health actually improved.

The upheavals that followed the Depression and World War Two were mainly social changes, for

*The Eureka Stockade.*
A photographic print hand-colored by Beryl Ireland and based on a cyclorama of the battle exhibited in 1891, gives some idea of the hand-to-hand fighting that left 24 diggers, four soldiers and a trooper mortally wounded or dead.

good and bad, that we live with today. In the fifties, Bill Haley and the Comets, a visiting band playing the new and curiously named 'rock and roll' music came to Australia. Overnight, one Haley song, 'Rock Around the Clock', changed the lives of every teenager in the land. In the sixties came the astonishing sexual revolution. In the seventies, feminism and no-fault divorce laws. In the eighties, conspicuous consumption and Bob Hawke's economic reforms. In the nineties the IT tsunami.

Which left just one stratum of our society virtually untouched by the recent decades of upheaval: the Aborigines. Almost from the moment that Captain Cook hoisted a boat to go ashore and was met by two men brandishing spears, 'resolved to defend their coast to the uttermost, though they were but two and we were forty', the Aborigines have inevitably been overwhelmed.

The new millennium brings fresh hope. Supported by such Aboriginal leaders as Noel Pearson it offers an end to the welfare and legal systems which treat Aborigines as victims, and the beginning of a new vision of economic advancement and property rights. But is it too late?

Gary Johns, a former federal Labor minister, and president of the Bennelong Society, warned in an article in the *Australian* in March 2006 that, 'Within a generation the Aboriginal lands will begin to empty. The camps at the fringe of regional centres in Northern Australia will begin to swell. The young will leave their homelands to find a job, women will leave to find protection from violence, elders will leave to find medical attention, children will leave to attend school. Many will leave to find there is nothing much for them. What then, policy makers? How will you manage out-migration?

'Slowly the penny drops, the land rights revolution has failed... As effective as guns, germs and steel, the very forces meant to save them – abundance – are wiping out the last of the Aborigines in remote Australia. Abundance has caused death by kidney and heart disease, through car accidents, through the rape and murder of women and children.

'... Reality has a way of intervening in boasts and gestures. Reconciliation walks over Sydney Harbour Bridge did not help Aborigines. Aborigines from remote areas need to walk over their own bridges. They need to follow in the path of thousands of their fellows, to walk the bridge of knowledge... Knowing what produces abundance, knowing how to reproduce it, knowing how to cope with it...'

That walk has now begun. It may lead to the biggest and most welcome upheaval of all.

# Immigration

Nino Culotta, the hero of *They're a Weird Mob*, has just arrived in Sydney and is phoning for a job as a builder's laborer:

'Joe Kennedy here. Who's that?'

'This is Mr Culotta.'

'Who?'

'Culotta.'

'You ringin' about that job?'

'Yes, please.'

'New Australian are yer?'

'I am Italian, Mr Joe.'

'Don' make no difference to me, mate. Long as yer can do the job.'

'I have not the experience, sir. But I am big and strong.'

'Yer'll wanter be, mate. Ut's hard yacker. Diggin' foundations. Where yer livin'?'

'I am at the Mayfair Hotel, Kings Bloody Cross.'

'Gawd yer wanna get outa there, mate. Yer'll go broke stayin' there. 'Ow long yer been there?'

'I only arrived from Italy today.'

'Only ter-day? Don't waste any time, do yer? 'Ow y'orf fer togs?'

'I do not understand.'

'Workin' togs, clothes.'

'Oh, I am clothed. Yes, thank you.'

'Okay. I'll give you a go. If yer no good yer don' get paid. Fair enough?'

'Do I understand I have the job?'

'I'll give yer a start, mate. Be 'ere about seven in the mornin'.'

Written in 1957, *They're a Weird Mob* was the most sensational Australian publishing success since *The Sentimental Bloke*. Like C.J. Dennis's *Bloke*, John O'Grady used his hero, Nino Culotta, the novel's supposed author, to hold the mirror up to the urban working class Australians. Tabloid newspaper serialisations alone were devoured daily by hundreds of thousands, and the book was reprinted 13 times in its second year of publication. Readers found Nino and the weird mob he encountered – Australians - irresistibly hilarious.

Fifty years on John O'Grady's humour may seem on the lite side, and unlike *The Sentimental Bloke*, O'Grady's best seller will never be recognised as a classic. But it was a first. The precursor of Australian books and films to come (in many ways it mirrored *Crocodile Dundee*'s adventures in New York), the shock-of-recognition humorous novel instilled a pride among Australians for being the way we were – little knowing that we would never be quite that way again.

O'Grady's dialogue between Nino and Joe accurately presents the attitudes of the times. On the whole 'Old Australians' had an offhand, take 'em or leave 'em attitude to 'New Australians.' If there was some antipathy there was little animosity. Migrants were seen as odd: they reeked of garlic, it was agreed; they did curious things – collecting and cooking clusters of mussels from pier pilings, for instance, unlike Aussies who hopped into half a cray and minimum chips on Friday nights. Still, you could get through to the newcomers if you articulated …v-e-r-y s-l-o-w-l-y and v-e-r-y loudly… though for some reason they didn't feel the need to answer in the same way. They'd get used to us, was the attitude and they did. What few dinki-di Aussies realised was that in the process the newcomers were transforming the nation's somewhat plain Anglo Celtic face.

Tom ROBERTS
born Great Britain 1856, arrived in Australia 1869, died 1931
*Coming South* 1886
oil on canvas
63.5 x 52.2 cm
National Gallery of Victoria, Melbourne
Gift of Colonel Aubrey H. L. Gibson in memory of John and Anne Gibson,
settlers (1887), 1967

The post war arrivals were the last mass wave of immigrants to change Australia and its inhabitants. The first came courtesy of the British government - 160,000 convicts and their keepers transported from England over a period of 80 years. Almost entirely English and Irish and only 15 per cent of them women, they dislocated the original inhabitants, the Aborigines, in almost every sense of the word. From the 1830s a new immigration era of free settlers began, giving birth to South Australia and Western Australia, rejuvenating Sydney and slowly turning Melbourne from a village to a small town.

In 1854 the Gold Rush brought a sudden and dramatic wave of immigrants. Within six years almost half the population of Australia was in Victoria and Melbourne was its biggest city. The gold rushes in Victoria, New South Wales and Queensland brought men from around the world: among the 13 men on trial for their lives after the battle at Eureka Stockade were an African American from New York, a Jamaican, a Swede, a Dane, a Dutchman an Italian, Irish, English and Australians. The rushes also attracted Chinese. Mostly law- abiding, hardworking gold fossickers, they kept to themselves, built their joss house temples, fan tan parlors, opium dens and laundries on the goldfields and sent home the money they made. Twenty thousand Chinese came to Victoria in the 1850s and another 12,000 landed in Sydney when new gold fields were discovered in south-western New South Wales. European miners' resentment of the Chinese, who seemed to be able to find gold when they could not, flared in the murderous Lambing Flat riots of 1861. The Palmer River gold rush in Queensland in 1877 brought another 20,000 and eventually the colonies passed laws to keep them out. The White Australia policy, with bi-partisan political support, was officially put in place in 1901, the first year of Federation. It was to stay in place for another 73 years.

# Conscription

The great and bitter battles of World War One had an uneasy echo halfway round the world. Australia, the land that had never known civil war, faced a crisis that threatened to swirl over into sectarian violence. It was brought on by Britain's call for more Australian men – 16,500 a month for 12 months, to take up arms – and the determination of the Australian Prime Minister, William Morris Hughes, to meet that quota.

The way to meet Britain's request for another 200,000, he said, was to call on 'the shirkers' to enlist, but also to let the people vote on whether conscripted troops should be sent overseas.

The issue of conscription brought class divisions and hatreds to a dangerous level, set Protestants against Catholics, caused many loyal Australians to be denounced as traitors, and consigned the Labor Party to years in opposition. In this dangerous vortex were two men. Both were Celts and both were brilliant speakers, but in almost every other way, physically and philosophically, they were diametrically different. Daniel Mannix, the Catholic Archbishop of Melbourne, was Irish, handsome and charismatic. Tall, with a rare elegance and charm, he was a persuasive speaker whose sharp wit was delivered in a warm brogue. Prime Minister 'Billy' Hughes was Welsh; wily, ruthless, fiery-tempered – as prime minister he tore into a mob throwing eggs at him and emerged with bloodied knuckles – and God's gift to cartoonists.

'It may be doubted whether he loved any man,' wrote Manning Clark. 'Endowed by nature with a short, almost dwarfish frame, and made deaf by his harsh experiences ... he brought to politics the cunning and determination of a man who had graduated in a hard school of survivors.'

Around these two, though Mannix only twice spoke out against conscription in 1916, the debate centred. Mannix's enemies were many and vehement. The Anglican synod in Melbourne declared the war was a religious war. Irish Catholics, traditionally treated as an underclass by the Anglo-Scottish Establishment, were seen as potentially disloyal; and when Mannix denounced the European conflict as 'just a trade war' he was called a traitor. The *Argus* called him 'belligerent and provocative,' and Billy Hughes branded the man of God 'a liar and a criminal'.

Hughes, for his part, had enemies within. He led a Labor party pledged to oppose conscription for overseas service. The trade unions were implacably against it, and though Hughes fought tooth and nail and even ordered soldiers to break up anti-conscription meetings the electors narrowly voted against it in October 1916 and he found himself punished, losing a vote of no confidence in the party room. 'We feel no sympathy for Mr Hughes. His tactics have been brutal and his abusive language unparliamentary to say the least of it,' the party's journal *Labor Call*, railed. 'What does he think of the parasites, vipers, disloyalists, anti-Britishers and pro-Germans in our midst? There are only 723,142 of them. With all his vitriolic verbosity he has condemned all anti-conscriptionists as these. But he lacks statesmanship and diplomacy. He is a pettifogger, inflated with gas. He is like a soap bubble; he comes puffed up and then disappears in vapour, Billy the Mighty Atom. The Australian Napoleon has met his Waterloo. Blithering Billy is blown out.'

Blithering Billy walked out on the party he had

Conscription propaganda, on both sides, made strong and emotional appeals to women, and mothers in particular. Some women sent white feathers – a symbol of cowardice – to men who refused to join up.
*AWM ARTV05167, AWM RC00337, AWM ARTV05469*

done so much to build, taking four ministers and 26 rank and filers with him and leaving it in ruins. All were expelled from the party. Hughes, with the Liberals, formed a new coalition party.

Hughes's defection devastated Labor and his new National Party swept to power in May 1917.

He announced that there was to be a second conscription referendum.

This time Archbishop Mannix was more to the fore. Hughes saw to that. Much of what Mannix said about the war and conscription was what most of the Labor Party was saying, but it coincided with the republican uprising in Ireland and Hughes used the uneasy feelings it sparked in some to exploit sectarian antipathies. This time the country was even more bitterly divided. On the one side was Hughes, the impassioned champion of the Empire and Australia. On the other was Mannix, the dry observer who argued that Australia had sent enough men to the Front. 'Conscriptionists will not be satisfied until Australia is denuded of her manhood,' he said. 'Australia, they think, has not done her part... We are told over and over again that we are not doing our share but I say that we have done more than our share compared to other parts of the Empire.

'... I have made it perfectly clear that England and the Allies were quite justified in coming to the rescue of Belgium and other small nations. Of that I am absolutely convinced, and I wish I could be equally certain that there were not ulterior motives of which no man could approve... while there was every justification for England's coming into the war to protect Belgium and France, and to protect herself, there was – and is – no justification for that country to go into the war or to remain at war for the purposes of securing the economic domination of the world.'

The Prime Minister urged Australians to stiffen their sinews and summon up the blood. 'Duty and national honour alike beckon us on,' Hughes said. 'What Australian will consent to partial withdrawal from this life and death struggle? Who among us will support a base abandonment of our fellow citizens who are fighting for us to the death with deathless heroism? Tens of thousands of our kinsmen in Britain have died that we might live free and unmolested.

'...Australians! This is no time for party strife. The nation is in peril, and it calls for her citizens to defend her. Our duty is clear. Let us rise like men, gird up our loins and do that which honour, duty and self-interest alike dictate.'

On 20 December 1917, a little over a million voters who agreed to gird the loins were outvoted by a margin of 165,000: men and women who disagreed that honour, duty and self-interest dictated that unwilling men be sent to the Front.

Mannix once dubbed Hughes 'the little Czar,' and after his defection he was despised by the Labor Party. But the troops loved him and dubbed him 'the little Digger', hoisting him on their shoulders and cheering him whenever he appeared among them, as he often did. At war's end he pugnaciously strode the stage at the Versailles peace conference, demanding reparation and resisting the attempt to allow New Guinea, a former German colony, freedom of migration (opening the door to the Japanese). 'The soldiers died for the freedom of Australia,' he said. 'Australia is safe.' The Little Digger was hailed as a national hero.

By the end of the war Mannix too was triumphant, revered by the Catholics and Irish. He had opposed the Dublin insurrection of 1916 and condemned Irish nationalist violence, but in

Prime Minister Hughes, 'the Little Digger', enjoyed immense popularity among Australian troops overseas. Back home the country was bitterly divided.

1919 – following the death of a hunger-striker, the archbishop led an Irish republican funeral cortége through the streets of London. In 1920 he was photographed at the St Patrick's Day parade with 14 Australian Diggers who had won the Victoria Cross. Most of them were non-Catholics, but seated beside him was John Wren, the wealthy entrepreneur and Labor Party fixer whose shady beginnings seemed not to concern Mannix. (Later they both played major roles in Frank Hardy's *Power Without Glory*.) Wren, infatuated with Mannix, had paid the 'expenses' of the VC winners. He put them on white horses (one had never ridden before) as a guard of honour to the archbishop, who solemnly raised his biretta to 10,000 marchers.

The archbishop, like Hughes, had those who loathed him. The Establishment ostracised him and would not invite him to official functions. In 1919

he was stopped from landing in Ireland to visit his ailing 89-year-old mother. The British, fearful that he could ignite more unrest in Ireland, took him in a Royal Navy destroyer, from Cork harbour to England, where once again he clashed with his old adversary. Prime Minister Hughes was suspected of making moves to prevent him from returning to Australia unless he swore an oath of loyalty, but Mannix brushed aside the possibility: 'Mr Hughes is no more my ecclesiastical superior than the Shah of Persia'.

Hughes fell from power in 1923 and when Labor won government six years later the Little Digger was consigned to the political wilderness. He waited in vain for reconciliation with the party that he had torn apart. A quarter of a century on, like Billy Hughes, Daniel Mannix was to play a part in another, even more disastrous split; one that was to keep the Labor Party out of office for 23 years.

# The Split

It was, wrote the eminent British novelist Rebecca West, 'a political battle of a fury not previously known in the country, [Australia] nor ever known in most others.'

But it was much more than that. It was a spy story, a Cold War confrontation played out in front of press cameras that sent the dramatic images around the world. A story with a cast of characters that included a prime minister who couldn't believe his good luck; his bitter rival, brilliant but increasingly unstable; an urbane counter-espionage agent; the man he manipulated – a drunken Russian KGB officer who feared he was about to be eliminated; the Russian's attractive wife, also a spy; and, later, an archbishop in the shadows who had once before played a major role in a time of tumult.

It was a story that might have been written by John Le Carré, but the end of the spy story began another much more catastrophic sequel. It pitted old political friends against each other, it divided families, sometimes forever, and it consigned Australia's oldest and proudest political party to 17 years in Opposition.

The Petrov Affair and The Split that followed were momentous. Together they re-shaped Australia's political landscape and their legacy, more than half a century on, persists.

Vladimir Petrov and his wife Evdokia came to Australia in 1951, ostensibly as ordinary members of the Soviet Embassy. In reality they had been sent by Lavrenti Beria, the degenerate and dreaded head of Soviet security, the KGB. The Petrovs were, in fact, high-ranking KGB agents: he was a colonel and his wife a captain in the KGB.

But in March 1953, Joseph Stalin died. Beria was arrested by Nikita Khrushchev and his frightened colleagues, who decided to liquidate him before he liquidated them. In Canberra Vladimir Petrov's colleagues accused him of being a Beria supporter. Petrov feared he would be recalled to Russia and, like his master, given a bullet in the back of the head.

Petrov had a friend in Australia, a handsome and sophisticated Polish emigré, Dr Michael Bialoguski. Together they visited the prostitutes of Kings Cross and had whisky-fuelled and maudlin conversations, increasingly steered by Bialoguski to the subject of defection. Bialoguski, like Petrov, led a double life. He was a part-time spy with ASIO, the Australian Security Intelligence Organisation.

In early 1954 Petrov made up his mind. He would defect on the day his KGB successor arrived. He covertly met an ASIO agent who offered him £5000 to do so. He didn't tell his wife.

On 13 April, on the eve of Parliament rising for the election campaign, Prime Minister Robert Menzies announced that a Soviet spy in the Canberra embassy had defected. It was the height of the Cold War and the Russians responded by claiming that their embassy official had not defected but had been kidnapped.

Evdokia Petrov had no way of knowing what the truth was. But in mid-April, two burly Russian 'couriers' came to Australia to take her back to Moscow. To the delight of reporters staked out at the Canberra embassy the party left for the airport at high speed. Shrouded in the back of a huge black Cadillac and flanked by the couriers, Zharkov and Karpinski – in name and in their appearance, characters from Central Casting – the car arrived

Terrified Mrs Petrov, hand to her heart, is hustled to the Moscow-bound plane by the Russian 'couriers'. Moments later burly Federal police dragged the pair away from her and disarmed them. *Newspix*

at Sydney's Mascot airport just as the plane was preparing to leave. Waiting for them was an angry crowd, many of them Soviet refugees. The two dragged Mrs Petrov to the gangway of the plane, and pushed her up it as the crowd swarmed around them.

The plane was due to touch down for refuelling in Darwin at 5.15 the next morning. Mrs Petrov, pale and exhausted, was clearly terrified of going back to Moscow. Equally, as she later revealed, she was afraid that her family would be killed if she defected. Seated next to the Russian Ambassador and in front of Karpinski and Zharkov, she burst into tears and asked if she could smoke a cigarette. She was told she couldn't, but she lit up in any case.

The stewardess, Joyce Bull, accompanied her when she asked to go to the lavatory. Joyce Bull asked her if she was in danger, and did she wish to defect? Mrs Petrov told her the couriers were armed and indicated that if her husband had indeed defected voluntarily she too wanted safety in Australia. Joyce Bull told the captain who radioed the news to Darwin. At Darwin, police were waiting.

The drama that followed was encapsulated by one of the iconic Australian press photographs of the '50s: it showed the swarthy Karpinski squirming to break free from a headlock applied by a towering Northern Territory policeman, a gun in his holster. The Russians, too, were armed. Karpinski had a .32 Walther automatic on his hip and Zharkov had another in his shoulder holster.

Australia thrilled. It was the height of the Cold War and the sight of a tough, lanky Aussie bearing down hard on a communist thug – who might as well have been wearing a black hat – confirmed the superiority and virtue of the West in its struggle against the USSR. But the extraordinary drama and the graphic front-page images were not, as many

still believe, the final nails in Labor's electoral coffin.

'Despite the mythology of the Labor party, there is no evidence that the Petrov defections determined the result,' Robert Manne wrote in the *Age* when Mrs Petrov died in July 2002, 11 years after her husband. 'According to the Gallup Poll support for the [Liberal/Country Party] Coalition was slightly higher before the defection than it was on election day.

'Robbed of his long-anticipated victory, Dr Evatt [leader of the Labor Party] – one of the most brilliant but unstable politicians in Australian history – almost altogether lost his mind. Conspiracy theories overtook him.'

The Petrov Affair, Dr Evatt came to be convinced, was a gigantic plot hatched by Prime Minister Menzies, Colonel Spry, the head of ASIO, and the Catholic anti-communist activists led by a lawyer, B.A. Santamaria.

Bob Santamaria was a protégé of Dr Daniel Mannix, the charismatic Catholic archbishop whose opposition to Conscription four decades before had led to the Labor Prime Minister Billy Hughes walking out on his party, taking colleagues with him and causing a disastrous Labor split. Now, a far more damaging and tumultuous division in the party was about to unfold.

Herbert Vere 'Doc' Evatt, the man at the centre of the calamity that kept the Australian Labor Party out of power for the next 17 years, was a respected statesman, brilliant scholar, renowned lawyer and fatally impetuous politician. Above all, he was an enigma.

Dr John Burton, private secretary to Dr Evatt, and later head of the External Affairs Department, said 'Doc' Evatt, his boss, 'was the most charming person and he was a delight to be with on

occasions. Yet he was about the rudest person you could come across. All of these qualities in extremes, and there would be a quick switch: one never knew what to expect.

'Hence there was tremendous tension, tremendous nervous tension right throughout his department – and I suspect throughout Parliament House, because his colleagues were experiencing the same nervous tension. One would meet someone and say, "Well, I wonder what the mood is today?"

'This duality, these extremes and the quick switch from one to another, is to my mind the secret to understanding his whole personality, and indeed his whole political career... in later days this duality in character became accentuated. It was almost a split personality...'

The Petrov defections led the unpredictable Dr Evatt to embark on a mounting series of astonishing blunders. At the subsequent royal commission into the defections he appeared for two members of his staff, named in documents Petrov gave to ASIO as having delivered information to the Russians. During the commission his behavior became increasingly strange; it led to deep unease, and, eventually his leave to appear was withdrawn.

On 5 October 1954, he issued an astonishing denunciation of his party's Victorian State Executive. Most of the State Executive were Catholics and anti-communist. Catholics, overwhelmingly, were Labor voters and anti-communist. Soon after, he extended the attack to include Santamaria (a man Evatt had covertly approached offering a pact) and Dr Mannix. They were, he claimed, a right-wing clerical fascist group that had infiltrated the ALP.

The erratic behaviour of Dr Evatt during the Petrov Affair disastrously tipped over when he attacked the party's anti-communist Victorian State Executive, a move that led to the Split.

It was true that Santamaria, though not a member of the ALP, headed an activist Movement aimed at fighting the communists' influence in unions (at one stage after the war they controlled 25 per cent of Australia's unions) and influencing Labor policy. But in attacking the Movement and the party's Industrial Groupers – Labor politicians also fighting communists in the unions – Evatt was alienating a huge section of ALP supporters.

Then Evatt read to Parliament a letter from Molotov, the Soviet Foreign Minister. He had written to Molotov, Evatt told Parliament, asking him if the Russians were spying in Australia. Molotov had assured him they weren't, he announced triumphantly. Amid the uproar, appalled anti-communists in his Opposition ranks hung their heads. Menzies and the Coalition laughed with delight. A week later Menzies announced another election, a double dissolution, that he won in a landslide.

Within the ALP Left and Right were now at war. Good friends feuded. Families fell out. The first battle ended with a purge of the Industrial Groupers and of politicians considered to be sympathetic to the Movement. These expelled Labor men then formed the ALP (Anti-Communist) which became the Democratic Labor Party and which, through its balance of power in Senate seats and allocation of preferences, was able to influence Coalition policies and keep the ALP out of power for the next two decades.

# The Dismissal

Late in November 1975, Gough Whitlam asked the Men and Women of Australia to vote for him in the coming 13 December election and urged them to recall November 11. 'Remembrance Day 1975. Remember that day. Mr Fraser's day of shame.' And then he went on to further qualify it: 'a day that will live in infamy.'

Whitlam adapted the phrase from the famous opening to President Franklin D. Roosevelt's address to his nation: 'Yesterday, December 7, 1941 – a date which will live in infamy – the United States of America was suddenly and deliberately attacked by naval and air forces of the Empire of Japan'.

The parallels were there. A few days earlier, on 11 November, Gough Whitlam had been sunk by an attack he had never expected: his dismissal as Prime Minister of Australia by the man he thought was 'on side,' the man he appointed governor-general, Sir John Kerr.

'The dismissal of Whitlam, to shrewd observers,' Professor Geoffrey Blainey wrote in 2005, 'seemed to be one of the most momentous and far-reaching events in Australian history – an event like the start of World War 1 in 1914 or the acute Depression of the 1930s. Now, 30 years later, while the dismissal appears less momentous, it still stands as a major and nation-shaking event.'

This nation-shaking event, our greatest Constitutional crisis, was brought about by the egos of three very different men.

Urbane and autocratic, eloquent and witty, with a droll habit of addressing his colleagues as 'comrade',

Like a monarch in the tumbrel on his way to the guillotine, Gough Whitlam's dignified demeanor gives little hint of the rage inside as he hears the governor-general's secretary read the proclamation of the dissolution of parliament.

Prime Minister Gough Whitlam, 59, was adored by millions. They saw him as The Messiah who after 23 years had led them from the Opposition wilderness. His charisma was indisputable. But not even his ecstatic idolators would deny that Gough, as they called him, was a man of prodigious vanity.

Malcolm Fraser, 45, his political opponent, was stiff and aloof, utterly ruthless and with a boundless command of indignation. His face had all the emotion of the Easter Island monoliths it resembled. A Western District grazier, he showed no discernible charm or wit, but like Whitlam had an ego to match his towering height. Both men displayed the imperious confidence that comes with a wealthy family and a good school.

The man in between, Sir John Kerr, the silver-maned son of a boilermaker from working-class Balmain, had made his mark as a flamboyant lawyer. He had joined the ALP as a young man and was a unions legal advisor before being elevated to Chief Justice of New South Wales. Although he was said to be a 'pre-war socialist' he enjoyed the good life, respected the Monarchy and relished the pomp and perks of his high office.

Kerr's upbringing was very different, but like Whitlam and Fraser, his vanity was considerable. When the Prime Minster injured it, using him as little more than a rubber stamp and taking the governor-general's consent for granted, he signed his political death warrant.

On the day Kerr issued the warrant, 11 November 1975, Australia was going through the most volatile and turbulent period in our modern political history.

Less than three years before, in December 1972, Gough Whitlam's Labor Party had been swept into office on a tsunami of excitement. Whitlam, virtually single-handedly had done it, and even many Liberal voters agreed that, as his campaign slogan had it, 'It's Time'. In an astonishing first few weeks in government Whitlam, once again virtually single-handedly, initiated radical reforms. Aborigines, foreign affairs, the arts, the environment, social welfare – the changes were so rapid, so dramatic and so wide-ranging that most Australians felt a surge of patriotic pride that was fresh and new. Many felt their country was undergoing a Renaissance that reinvigorated a nation that for too long had been moribund, drifting under the torpor of lacklustre Liberal administrations. By the end of the following year Whitlam could point with pride to 250 bills running to 2200 pages – three times as many pages as the Liberals in their last year in power. It was an exhilarating roller-coaster ride.

But there were those who wanted to get off the roller-coaster, slow it down or preferably stop it. The Coalition of the Liberal and National parties, which controlled the Senate had blocked 20 per cent of these 250 bills – some of them election promises – and had tried to provoke a new election by blocking the government's supply bills. Without supply the government had no money to run the country.

Whitlam called the Coalition's bluff and agreed to the double dissolution elections – both Houses of Parliament were dissolved and a new election was called for May 1974. Labor was returned to government, although with a smaller majority. 'We were not defeated. We just didn't win enough seats to form a government,' said the Opposition Leader Billy Snedden, providing the nation with a welcome belly laugh and a laugh line that lives on to this day. But the truth was, the election was one of the closest in our history. It took ten days for the results to become clear and when they did Labor and the Coalition each had secured 29 Senate seats. Two conservative Independents won the remaining Senate seats and when the Snedden laughter subsided the threat to block supply was still on the Coalition's agenda. 'From May 1974,' Whitlam's speechwriter Graham Freudenberg, wrote, 'the Labor Government was under siege. At no time thereafter could it plan confidently on more than six months of existence at a time. It lived in the expectation that each November and each May it would face another fight for Supply in the Senate.'

And now the Coalition had a new leader, the ambitious and aggressive Malcolm Fraser. If the government's actions were sufficiently 'extraordinary and reprehensible', and unless the Prime Minister called a double dissolution before June 1976, Malcolm Fraser promised that the Coalition, with its narrow majority in the Senate, would once again block supply. The opportunity came soon enough in a rolling series of 'Affairs.'

Gough Whitlam, a visionary, was never noted for his interest in economics. Others in the Cabinet were no better: his soon to be sacked Treasurer, Frank Crean, likened the Cabinet's budget discussions to a debate in a lunatic asylum. Paul Keating, a minister in the last weeks of the government, said the Cabinet meetings 'were mayhem... much of it entirely undisciplined'. And the feeling that, economically, things were spinning out of control was exacerbated by the man who replaced Crean as Treasurer, the Deputy Prime Minister Jim Cairns. Loved by some, loathed by others – there was no half way – Jim Cairns, though he coyly denied it, was clearly smitten by Juni Morosi his sultry principal private secretary, the first woman to hold such a position to a senior federal minister. Inevitably the romance became known as The Juni Morosi Affair. Cairns was also making a series of grossly incompetent and bizarre errors involving memory loss, his son (and staffer) Phillip's business dealings – involving overseas Arab loans – and a signed authorisation giving a Melbourne businessman a 2.5 per cent 'brokerage fee' for loans he might raise for the Commonwealth of Australia. Cairns's blunders and his barely concealed love life eventually forced Whitlam to sack him for misleading Parliament. A few days later Caucus removed him as Deputy Leader and installed dull but dependable Frank Crean.

Bill Hayden replaced Cairns as Treasurer and began to rein in Labor's economic excesses. By now, however, more than a million people were living below the poverty line. Petrol prices were leaping, unemployment had trebled since 1972 to a quarter of a million, inflation, at 16.9 per cent, had quadrupled, and interest rates soared to 11.5 per cent. Budget expenditure was set to increase by 42 per cent, double the figure for 1973–74, which was itself the largest increase in two decades. In nine months since the 1974 election Whitlam's approval rating had plummeted from 57 per cent to 35 per cent and, worse, his disapproval rate doubled to more than 50 per cent. It was not the time for another double dissolution.

But that was what the Coalition was determined to have. All he needed, Fraser had said, was an 'extraordinary and reprehensible circumstance'.

The Juni Morosi Affair, the Loans Affair, and its bizarre offshoot, the Khemlani Affair, gave him plenty of circumstances.

Rex Connor initiated the Loans Affair – an audacious attempt to raise a colossal $US4 billion, the: biggest foreign loan ever authorised by the federal government and an amount that exceeded the combined foreign debt of all Australian governments. Connor was determined to 'buy back the farm', to give Australians ownership of its booming gas, oil and minerals industries. It would be a 'temporary loan' – a 20-year temporary loan.

In December 1974, while Sir John Kerr and his wife were at the ballet, a hasty night meeting of the executive council – Whitlam, Murphy, Cairns and Connor – authorised the raising of the $US4 billion. Foolishly, the governor-general agreed to sign the minutes of the meeting, at which he was not present and to which he had not been invited. Whitlam had used Kerr as a rubber stamp. Kerr resented this but kept his peace, and by staying silent reinforced Whitlam's confidence that he had the governor-general's support.

The public knew nothing of the proposed loan. Few Cabinet ministers knew. 'By even thinking of raising money to govern without the Senate's approval of supply,' Clive James wrote, 'Whitlam was preparing to govern without a parliament – the very thing the governor-general's powers are designed to stop.

'While proposing to govern without a parliament, Whitlam was already governing without a cabinet. Scarcely anyone knew about the Loans scheme being cooked up, its secrecy a tacit avowal of its fundamental unreality.' By the following month the authority to raise the loan was withdrawn. By February it was back on the agenda as a $US2 billion loan. By May, Whitlam believed the attempts to raise foreign loans had once again been abandoned. Too late, however, to prevent the unravelling of the Loans Affair.

In May 1975, helped by drip feeds from an alarmed Treasury, the media was beginning to publish details of a covert and extremely unorthodox attempt by the Government to raise 'petrodollars' from Middle East oil sheikhs. The broker, Tirath Khemlani, a fly-by-night Pakistan commodity dealer living in London, was named in Parliament. Khemlani was later jailed in the US, for trying to pass stolen travellers cheques.

But on 2 September, Whitlam told Parliament that the Minerals and Energy Minister Rex Connor had assured him that there had been no further negotiations with Khemlani after May 20 – a claim Connor repeated on 9 October, the day after the Melbourne *Herald* carried fresh and dramatic news of what was now called the Khemlani Affair. The paper claimed that Connor wanted to raise up to $US8 billion in two parts at 8.22 per cent interest over two years. The terms of the loan meant that Australia would have to pay back $US39 billion – around $US250 billion in today's terms.

Nicknamed 'the Strangler,' Connor was a taciturn politician feared on both sides of the House. He denied the report and said he would sue the *Herald*.

A *Herald* reporter, Peter Game, who had chased Khemlani around the world, met him again in Melbourne. Khemlani brought with him telexes that contradicted Connor's claims. They showed that Connor had continued to ask Khemlani to negotiate loans after Whitlam had assured Parliament that Connor had told him he had stopped. Just five days after the *Herald* broke the news Connor was sacked for causing Whitlam to mislead Parliament. He was replaced by the young up-and-comer, Paul Keating.

The next day Malcolm Fraser announced that, because of the extraordinary and reprehensible circumstance he would defer finance for the government. 'The Opposition now has no choice,' he said in his sanctimonious monotone. 'The Labor

Government 1972–75 has been the most incompetent and disastrous government in the history of Australia.' His party would block the budget in the Senate until Whitlam called an election.

Whitlam responded predictably in his own, booming, even more distinctive tones; his government had survived the same tactic in 1974. 'We will not yield to blackmail. We will not be panicked.' It was coming down to a battle of egos, a question of which man would break first.

For three weeks the constitutional crisis heightened as the parties confronted each other in Parliament and around the country. Whitlam was confident that the Senate was on the point of passing the supply bills, that the Liberals would lose their nerve. If Whitlam was wrong Government money for payment to public servants and government contractors would run out by 30 November. The crisis could then end in one of only two ways. He would buckle and call an election or the governor-general would sack him. Whitlam, however, was confident that he wouldn't be sacked.

Two men begged to differ. Bill Hayden, the new treasurer, met Sir John to brief him on alternative financial arrangements. Hayden was disturbed to find that the governor-general was more interested in discussing Whitlam's fighting abilities. 'How do you think you'd go if there was an election?' he asked Hayden. Hayden told him, 'We'd be done like a dinner,' but Kerr thought that Whitlam was a fighter, and could come back. Hayden, alarmed, left Yarralumla and ordered his driver to take him not to the airport, but direct to Whitlam's office. A former policeman, his 'copper's instinct' told him that Kerr was going to sack Whitlam. He found

The son of a boilermaker and a Labor Party man, Sir John Kerr liked the pomp, and took seriously the power, that came with his office. *AWM 136161*

Whitlam entirely at ease. 'He was standing against the wall even larger than life. He was fiddling his spectacles around in his hand. He said to me, "No comrade, he wouldn't have the guts for that."'

As a young lawyer, Bob Ellicott QC, a junior minister in the Opposition, once had an office on the same floor of the same chambers as Whitlam's and Kerr's, and the three knew each other well. Ellicott had risen to become Commonwealth solicitor-general, and, as it transpired, knew Kerr better than Whitlam. Ellicott believed that Kerr might use the reserve power that the Queen's representative in Australia had to act on his own behalf. In a media release Ellicott warned that, 'The Prime Minister is treating the Governor-General as a mere automaton with no public will of his own, sitting at Yarralumla waiting to do his bidding. Nothing could be further from the truth...

'The Governor-General has at least two clear constitutional prerogatives he can exercise: the right to dismiss his ministers and appoint others and the right to refuse a dissolution of the parliament or of either house.'

Whitlam said that Kerr phoned him to say, 'This Ellicott thing, it's all bullshit isn't it?' and Whitlam asked his attorney-general and solicitor-general to prepare a 6000-word opinion confirming that blunt assessment. He was confident that Kerr was 'on-side.' When colleagues asked him about the governor-general's position, Whitlam would reassure them: 'Kerr will do the right thing comrade. I'm as confident of this as I am about anything in my career.'

Kerr meanwhile privately consulted Sir Garfield Barwick, the chief justice of the High Court, who concurred with Ellicott. The governor-general had the power to sack Whitlam and instruct the incoming prime minister to promptly call a new federal election.

The debate over the legality and ethics of blocking supply to force an election was not new. In Opposition Whitlam and Lionel Murphy, later to join the High Court bench, had affirmed the legality of such tactics and had tried them no fewer than 170 times while out of office. The Liberals, when in office, strongly disagreed on the question of their legality and fair play. Now the two parties were performing backflips on the question. Now it was the Liberals threatening to block supply and Labor taking the high ground.

Less than four weeks later, at 12. 40 p.m., on 11 November 1975, Whitlam went to Government House to formally request that Kerr approve a half-Senate election. He had rejected Malcolm Fraser's compromise of an election for both houses in May 1976 and instead pinned his hopes on an immediate half-Senate election that he hoped would give him power in the upper house.

In the governor-general's Yarralumla study, as he reached into his inside pocket to pass over the formal

Burly Rex Connor towers over Al Grassby. Ministers in the Whitlam Cabinet, the two could hardly be less alike. But both damaged Whitlam's legacy. Connor's stubborn deceit finally led to the Dismissal. Grassby's deception was much more insidious.

The Minister for Immigration, popular with the media for his extrovert ways, Grassby was dogged throughout his public life by rumours of criminal links. When Griffith anti-drugs campaigner Donald Mackay disappeared Grassby, it was alleged, secretly mounted a campaign to implicate Mackay's wife Barbara, his son and his solicitor in his murder. He was charged with criminal defamation but was eventually acquitted on a technicality.

After Grassby's death in 2005 the Melbourne *Herald-Sun* reported: 'The detective who arrested controversial federal MP Al Grassby 18 years ago claims the National Crime Authority bowed to political pressure not to fully investigate his mafia links. Retired NCA senior investigator Bruce Provost said he had no doubt the Whitlam Labor government minister was paid to commit crimes and do favours for the Calabrian mafia.

'Speaking publicly for the first time about the NCA's inquiry, Mr Provost said Mr Grassby was firmly in the mafia's pocket. He said there was more than enough intelligence on Mr Grassby to warrant a full investigation, but he was held back by the NCA.'

In an editorial the *Herald-Sun* said: 'Mr Grassby died last month aged 79 and has since been eulogised as a flamboyant idealist and a father of multiculturalism. But if claims of his underworld dealings are true — and today they come from senior figures on both sides of the law — such tribute is a travesty.'

In 2007, against bitter opposition led by Donald Mackay's family, the ACT's chief minister, John Stanhope, authorised the erection of a $72,000 life-size statue of Grassby.

advice, Whitlam found that Kerr, instead, was passing him a letter. It outlined his reasons for refusing the half-Senate election and notified Whitlam that he was dismissing him and his government.

Kerr had been suspicious of Whitlam and possibly planning this moment ever since Whitlam had made a flippant remark less than three weeks before. At Government House he had said to Kerr that it might be 'a question of whether I get to the Queen first for your recall, or you get in first with my dismissal'. Laughter all around – but Kerr was not amused. 'Quite devastated,' he said later. Now, metaphorically, the governor-general had beaten the prime minister to the phone.

'He had his warning,' Kerr said later. 'The ball was in his court.' Kerr said that in the fraction of time between his telling Whitlam of his intention to dismiss him and his passing over of the letter Whitlam had one lifeline, to 'negotiate to go to the people as Prime Minister... had he done so I would have agreed.'

'Things then happened as I had foreseen,' Kerr said in his autobiography, *Matters of Judgement*. 'Mr Whitlam jumped up, looked urgently around the room, looked at the telephones and said sharply, "I must get in touch with the Palace at once."' It was too late for that, Kerr told him. 'He said, "Why?" and I told him, "Because you are no longer Prime Minister. These documents tell you so and why."'

Whitlam heard Kerr say, 'We shall all have to live with this.' The former prime minister had the presence of mind to reply, 'You certainly will,' and the good grace to shake hands with Kerr as the governor-general wished him farewell and good luck in the coming election. It was their last conversation. At 1.30 p.m., Malcolm Fraser, waiting in another room, was sworn in as a caretaker prime minister on condition that he immediately call an election.

Whitlam, meanwhile, went back to the Lodge and sat down to a late lunch, a steak. Why he chose to have a substantial lunch without notifying any of his Cabinet is perplexing. Whitlam finally summoned a small circle of colleagues, the deputy prime minister, the leader of the House, the attorney-general, the head of the prime minister's department and his scriptwriter and told them the news. 'We all sat there like stunned mullets', said Fred Daly, the leader of the House of Representatives. None thought to notify Labor's leader in the Senate, Ken Wriedt, that he was now the Opposition leader in the upper house, and not two hours after Whitlam had left Parliament to get the governor-general's rubber stamp on a half-Senate election Labor Senators, ignorant of the fact that they were out of government, passed the Budget, imagining that Fraser had finally caved in.

At 3 o'clock Whitlam returned to Parliament and on his way met young Paul Keating, three weeks a minister. 'You're sacked!' he said as he brushed on by, leaving a bewildered Keating plaintively calling after him, 'What for?' In Parliament Whitlam moved a motion that the House express no confidence in the caretaker prime minister and it was approved. The Speaker was instructed to see the governor-general and ask him to commission Mr Whitlam again but was told Sir John Kerr was unavailable until 4.45.

At that time, Whitlam, his eyes glowing with self-righteous indignation and staring fiercely into the middle distance, was standing on the steps of Parliament House behind the governor-general's secretary, David Smith. There was the hint of a grim smile on his lips as Smith read the proclamation dissolving Parliament. Smith concluded, 'God save the Queen,' and Whitlam stepped to the microphone: 'Ladies and gentlemen, well may we say "God save the Queen," because nothing will save the Governor-General. The proclamation you have just heard read by the Governor-General's official secretary was countersigned "Malcolm Fraser," who will undoubtedly go down in history as Kerr's cur.'

As the crowd roared and cheered, he ended with this rousing command: 'Maintain your rage and enthusiasm throughout the campaign for the election now to be held and until polling day.'

Around Australia the news stunned everyone. There was agitation for a national strike – Bob Hawke, the unions' leader, defused it. In the pubs of Balmain and Carlton, hotheads leapt on bars and called for the barricades to go up. There were no takers, though there were demonstrations around the country; Fraser was egg-bombed; and real mail bombs were posted eight days later, one of them injuring two staffers of the Queensland premier. But though the country was fiercely divided and the respect for the position of the governor-general almost irrevocably damaged, the army was not called out. Gough Whitlam had too much respect for the Constitution, and the country went peacefully enough to the polls.

On 13 December 1975, the Coalition won the election in a landslide. In 1977 Labor's vote plummeted even further and Whitlam retired, a Labor martyr. Sir John Kerr died a lonely and tragic man. Fraser governed until 1984 when, beaten by Labor's new Messiah, Bob Hawke, he made a tearful apology to the Liberal Party.

Thirty years on Whitlam is still revered and – astonishingly – reconciled with his tormentor, Fraser, who by now had turned his energies to ceaseless attacks on... the Liberal Party.

# *Azaria Chamberlain*

We all knew – well, most of us knew – that she was guilty; Lindy Chamberlain, the mother of the missing nine-week old baby girl, Azaria. Lindy had said her baby was carried off by a dingo at their tourist camp site at Ayers Rock. We all knew – well most of us knew – that wasn't the case and that Lindy Chamberlain had killed Azaria with the help of her husband Michael.

Australia was riveted by the case, and the world watched it with some bemusement. What intrigued Australians was the demeanour of Azaria's parents. But what fascinated all, those who followed every minute detail of the story in Australia and those around the world whose curiosity was aroused, were the circumstances and the setting. A dingo, you say? And at Ayers Rock?

Had the Chamberlains been holidaying anywhere else in the Australian Outback the case, though sensational – 'A dingo has taken my baby!' – would not have gripped the nation. The dramatic backdrop of 'the Rock', however, turned the story into a drama watched globally.

Lindy Chamberlain and her husband Michael, undeniably, were a curious couple. On the night of the disappearance of Azaria and in the days after, their reactions to the gruesome fate of their baby seemed bizarre. When almost all the camp site near Ayers Rock went into the night searching for Azaria Lindy and Michael stayed at the site: incomprehensible behaviour to those whose

Young and attractive, the Chamberlains held Australia in thrall as millions wondered: how could they murder their baby? The truth was, they didn't.

maternal and paternal instinct would be to run into the darkness screaming the name of their child in the forlorn hope of hearing a pitiful answering cry. A few days later Michael, a photography enthusiast, rang the Melbourne *Sun News-Pictorial* and asked if the newspaper would like to publish his shots of Ayers Rock. And on leaving the place where a dingo had trotted off into the darkness carrying their little girl in its jaws they stopped to buy souvenir coffee mugs bearing images of the Rock.

In Alice Springs court Lindy continued to confound. She seemed unmoved as the prosecution introduced a parade of forensic experts who testified that it was likely that the baby's throat had been cut, probably with scissors, and that a spray of foetal blood had been found in the couple's Holden Torana.

Damning, expert, evidence. But most damning was the circumstantial 'evidence:' the detached demeanour of Lindy, as we all called her. A Seventh Day Adventist, she looked anything but. She pouted, she seemed sulky, almost sultry. She appeared at court each day wearing fresh outfits that might have been chosen for their effect on the camera crews who jostled outside the courthouse. (Some journalists at the trial admitted to being affected. One had a mild crush on her.)

Lindy Chamberlain just didn't look or act the way we expected of a grieving mother on trial for the murder of her daughter. But there were those who staunchly believed in her innocence. 'Bastards!' reporter Malcolm Brown yelled – not showing the demeanour or acting in the way we expect of journalists – when the jury brought in its verdict of guilty.

And then in January 1986 police investigating the death of a British tourist near the Rock found the little matinee jacket that Lindy had claimed Azaria was wearing when she disappeared. The jacket had tooth marks. Doubts about Lindy Chaberlain's guilt began to gather.

Sixteen months later a Royal Commission began looking afresh at the evidence that had sent Lindy Chamberlain to jail for life. This time forensic experts called by Lindy's barrister told the commission that what had been alleged to be a bloody adult handprint on the baby's jumpsuit had in fact been nothing more than red sand; that the blood in the car was sound deadener and sealant, standard in Holden cars.

In 1988 Lindy Chamberlain successfully appealed against her conviction. The Northern Territory Government paid her $1.3 million in compensation and we all agreed – well, most of us, anyway – that we had always known her to be innocent. It always had been a disgraceful miscarriage of justice.

In the following decade, when John Bryson wrote *Evil Angels*, his forensic dissection of the case and its forensic experts (and Meryl Streep starred in the film version) the fault, we all agreed, lay with 'experts' and with the rednecks of the Northern Territory who refused to believe that a dingo would carry off a baby, and certainly not at the sacred heart of the nation, the icon, Uluru, as we were now all happy to call it.

# Author's Acknowledgments

I am indebted to David Horgan of The Five Mile Press, who suggested I write *Why We Are Australian*; to Maggie Pinkney who oversaw its challenging production; to Janet Pheasant, for her tireless work in obtaining the many images in this book; to Michael Bannenberg for his excellent design; to Susan Gorgioski for her invaluable assistance; and to my wife Suzie Howie whose patience was tested but triumphed. I also owe a debt to the works of such historians, authorities and journalists as Patsy Adam-Smith, Robyn Annear, Geoffrey Blainey, Michael Cannon, Les Carlyon, Don Chapman, Manning Clark, Peter Coleman, Frank Clune, Mike Dash, Keith Dunstan, Geoffrey Dutton, Tim Flannery, Harry Gordon, Richard Haese, Geoff Hocking, Robert Hughes, Clive James, A.K. Macdougall, Andrew Mercado, Diana and Michael Preston, Ian Jones, Cyril Pearl, Andrew Rule, Bernard Smith and Terry Smith, Bill Scott, Gerald Stone, John Silvester, Bill Wannan, Don Watson, Charles White and Evan Whitton.

# Pictorial Acknowledgments

The author and Publishers thank the following organisations for permission to publish the images in this book:

Australian War Memorial, Canberra, pages 28-9, 36-7, 38-9, 40-41, 43, 44, 46-7, 48-9, 50-51, 93, 104-5

Fairfax Photos, pages 72-3

Getty Images, pages 21, 61, 64-5

Herald and Weekly Times Photographic Collection, page 33

National Gallery of Victoria, Melbourne, pages 90-1

National Library of Australia, Canberra, pages 19, 87, 95, 109

Newspix, pages 8, 10-11, 27, 57, 66, 67, 70, 71, 75, 77, 79, 80, 81, 82, 83, 84-6, 97

John O'Gready, page 53

State Library of Victoria, Melbourne, pages 9, 89

University of New South Wales, Sydney, page 30

Western Australian Museum, Perth, page 7

# Our
# Australia
# PEOPLE

In memory of my parents, Marie and George,
who started me on 'Banjo' Paterson along with
*Jack and the Beanstalk*; for the grandchildren they read to,
Noah and Jack; and for their grandchildren to come.

**Publisher's Note**

This book originally appeared as part of a larger volume:
*Why We Are Australian* (2007).
It has now been divided into three volumes:
*Our Australia: CULTURE, Our Australia: PEOPLE* and
*Our Australia: EVENTS.*

The Five Mile Press Pty Ltd
1 Centre Road, Scoresby
Victoria 3179 Australia
Email: publishing@fivemile.com.au
Website: www.fivemile.com.au

Text copyright © Paul Taylor, 2007
Copy editor: Sonya Nikadie
Supervising editor: Maggie Pinkney
Designer: Michael Bannenberg
Picture editor: Janet Pheasant

Formatting this edition
SBR Productions, Olinda, Victoria 3788

Printed in China

FRONT COVER IMAGES: (left to right): Ned Kelly, *Victoria Police Museum*; Cathy Freeman, *Getty Images*; Don Bradman, *National Library of Australia*

# Our Australia

# PEOPLE

PAUL TAYLOR

The Five Mile Press

# Contents

# Preface

On 4 January 1688 when William Dampier stepped ashore on the far north-west coast of the continent his fellow pirates feared that they would encounter troglodytes – men whose heads grew under their shoulders and whose feet were so large that they served as shades when they lay down in the sun. Well, every nationality has its distinct characteristics.

In the case of Australia, three centuries on, it's generally accepted that we are an easy-going lot, good at sport and, er… that's about it.

The truth is, we're better than that, and much more complicated, much more incongruous. Incongruity may be our distinguishing feature.

What other country holds a murderer's memory sacred? Hanged and then decapitated, his remains buried in an anonymous prison lime pit, Ned Kelly, in the minds of many, is among our half dozen most admired Australians. The memory of Howard Florey, on the other hand, a man who saved millions, honoured on his death with a Memorial Service in Westminster Abbey, is almost entirely gone.

What other country can boast of a leader – its first – speared, and who took the wound, one he thought fatal, and used it to build bridges with his attackers? What other country could honour one of its most popular artists on a postage stamp but send him – Albert Namatjira – to prison for sharing a bottle with a mate?

Is there anywhere else with a prime minister who could have the nation roaring with delight as he appeared on television in a jingoistic jacket and proclaimed: 'I'll tell you what, any boss who sacks anyone for not turning up today is a bum!'?

That prime minister seldom said no to a drink. The Father of the Year, he was a notorious womaniser. He could get weepy. He could turn nasty. But Australians, most of them, loved Bob Hawke. He had something of the 'ratbag' about him. And many of our greats share this same quality. Germaine Greer can be infuriatingly perverse. But the Mistress of Surprise remains, for many, a heroine. Percy Grainger, perhaps our finest pianist and composer, seemed to make being a ratbag his life's work.

We admire those who buck authority: bushrangers, like Cash, Brady, Kelly and Ben Hall, we generally hold in high regard. We love sport, it's true, but – until very recently – we never really knew much about Don Bradman, the idol above all our sporting idols. He was the most popular sportsman we have had – except among some who played alongside him.

But if we knew little about 'the Don', we knew much less about the man who was, internationally, the best known, most respected and, yes, best loved of all Australians: Steve Irwin. Don Bradman was revered in cricket-playing nations. But Irwin, a man we knew very little and cared less about, was universally loved.

He was, we came to see, the quintessential Australian the world wanted.

Paul Taylor, *2009*

# 1

# THE ABORIGINES

'From what I have seen of the Natives of New Holland they may appear to some to be the most wretched people upon the earth; but in reality they are far more happier than we Europeans; being wholly unacquainted not only with the superfluous but the necessary Conveniences so much sought after in Europe, they are happy in not knowing the use of them. They live in a Tranquility which is not disturbed by the Inequality of Condition; the Earth and Sea of their own accord furnishes them with all things necessary for life.'
— Captain James Cook, 1770

Thousands of years ago a man waded ashore to the continent we call Australia. He and his tribe were the ancestors of millions of us Australians. Millions of us? 'Let me state one undeniable fact,' the Chief Justice of New South Wales the Honourable J.J. Spigelman said on 27 October, 2005. 'Many, probably millions of Australians, have an Aboriginal ancestor.' Many family trees, he said, had points at which the origins of particular forebears were left blank. 'These are all telltale signs of Aboriginal origin...This should be recognised as an important bond.'

At the time of the First Fleet there were, it's estimated, somewhere around 300,000 Aborigines living in Australia. Each community – perhaps 500 of them – had survived in their ways for a seeming eternity. But when the whites came their ancient and unchanging way of life was doomed. Today the confrontation and conflict of two centuries has gone, to be replaced by battles for land rights, some kind of 'treaty', and agitation for an Apology from the Federal Government on behalf of white Australians.

Should there be a treaty or an Apology?

Historian John Hirst rejects calls for a treaty, saying it is driven by ideological fantasy. Aboriginal intellectual Noel Pearson, too, argues for an end to the welfare and legal systems which treat Aborigines as victims, and for the beginning of a new vision of economic advancement and property rights.

'Neither of the political parties has made the changes in thinking that are necessary for Aboriginal people to turn around our social disaster. To simplify the policy contrast: the Australian Labor Party will be strong and correct in their policies in favour of the rights of Aboriginal people – particularly land rights and native title – and they will be weak and wrong in relation to the breakdown of responsibility in Aboriginal society occasioned by passive welfare dependency, substance abuse and our resulting criminal justice predicaments.

'The Coalition will better understand the problems of responsibility but will be antipathetic and wrong in relation to the rights of Aboriginal people.'

# Bennelong

They were chatting around a beach barbie at Manly. One an extrovert, the other reserved, the way friends often are.

A bystander wrote later about the extrovert's 'pleasure to see his old acquaintance, and inquiring by name for every person whom he could recollect at Sydney; and among others of a French cook, one of the governor's servants, whom he had made the constant butt of his ridicule, by mimicking his voice, gait and other peculiarities, all of which he again went through with his wonted exactness and drollery.

'He also asked particularly for a lady from whom he had once ventured to snatch a kiss; and on being told that she was well, by way of proving that token was fresh in his remembrance, he kissed Lieutenant Waterhouse and laughed aloud.'

After this alpha male horsing-about and mockery of the French cook, the blokey atmosphere turned nasty. It can happen at the best of barbies.

'Matters had proceeded in this friendly train for more than half an hour,' wrote the observer, 'when a native with a spear in his hand came forward, and stopped at the distance of between 20 and 30 yards from the place where the governor [Phillip], Mr Collins, Lieutenant Waterhouse and a seaman stood.

'His Excellency held out his hand and called to him, advancing towards him at the same time, Mr Collins following close behind... The nearer the governor approached, the greater became the terror and agitation of the Indian. To remove his fear, Governor Phillip threw down his dirk which he wore at his side. The other, alarmed at the rattle of the dirk, and probably misconstruing the action, instantly fixed his lance in his throwing-stick.

The spearing of Governor Phillip. Although seriously wounded, he forbade reprisals. Only 'the most absolute necessity would ever compel him to fire upon them', an officer on his ship wrote.

'To retreat His Excellency now thought would be more dangerous than to advance. He therefore cried out to the man, weree, weeree (bad; you are doing wrong) displaying at the same time every token of amity and confidence. The words had, however, hardly gone forth when the Indian, stepping back with one foot, aimed his lance with such force and dexterity, striking the governor's right shoulder just above the collarbone, the point glancing downward and out at his back, having made a wound many inches long. The man was observed to keep his eye steadily fixed on the lance until it struck its object, when he directly dashed into the woods and was seen no more.

'Instant confusion on both sides took place.'

Henry Waterhouse, who accompanied Phillip, wrote, 'I immediately concluded the governor was killed... and turned around to run for the beach as I perceived Captain Collins running that way and calling to the boat's crew to bring the muskets up.

'The governor also attempted to run holding the spear with both hands to keep it off the ground, but owing to the length the end took the ground and stopped him short (I suppose it could not have been less than 12 feet long).' Phillip begged

Waterhouse to pull out the spear and as Waterhouse broke it off, a spear grazed his hand. 'The governor attempted to pull a pistol from his pocket, but I told him the spears were flying so thick that if he stopped he certainly would be speared again... With the help of a seaman I lifted the governor into the boat, as he was very faint... We pulled the boat to Sydney Cove with all our might. The governor bore it with the greatest patience... made his will and settled his affairs not expecting to live...'

Fortunately for the colony and its inhabitants, black and white, Phillip survived.

From the beginning relations between the white man and the Aborigines have been marked by misunderstanding, violence and confusion. Governor Phillip had been chatting to Bennelong, a member of the Eora tribe, when he was wounded. Six months before he had ordered Bennelong captured along with another Aborigine, Colbee. Phillip wanted to put an end to 'petty warfare and endless uncertainty', to learn the Aborigines' attitude to the invasion of their land, and to assure them that they had nothing to fear.

Colbee's life is largely unrecorded but thanks to Watkin Tench, the bystander at the wounding of the governor, we know a considerable amount about Bennelong. Tench, an equable marine officer, kept a record of his time in the infant colony and published it as *A Narrative of the Expedition to Botany Bay*. It is a journal marked by its humanity and understanding – though Tench confessed that understanding was not always easy, and often impossible:

'During the intervals of our duty, our greatest source of entertainment now lay in cultivating the acquaintance of our new friends, the natives. Ever liberal of communication, no difficulty, but no understanding of each other subsisted between us. Inexplicable contradictions arose to bewilder our researches, which no ingenuity could unravel, and no credulity reconcile.'

No Aborigine was more contradictory than Bennelong. A tall, handsome man in his mid-20s, intelligent and quick-witted and with a love of laughter, he readily picked up enough English to make himself understood 'and willingly communicated information; sang and danced and capered; told us all the customs of his country'.

He was a great fighter and, by his account, a great lover who shared a wife, Barangaroo, with Colbee.

Portrait of Bennelong.

*Page 299 Vol. 1.*

*Portrait of Bennelong, a native of New Holland, who after experiencing for two years the Luxuries of England, returned to his own Country and resumed all his savage Habits.*

At first Bennelong revelled in the company of the newcomers, but when the colony's food supply was dangerously low and Phillip ordered rationing Bennelong's mood changed. 'Hunger made him furious and then put him in what might be called a decline, and in this melancholy state he made his escape.'

Four months later Bennelong and Phillip came face to face when the governor's party encountered him and around 200 Aborigines broiling meat from a dead whale on fires along Manly beach. The spearing of Phillip united the two – Bennelong called often to ask about Phillip's health – and sparked an unusual friendship. He called the white man 'beanga' or father and Phillip treated him almost as a son, ordering a brick house be built for him at what is now Australia's best-known stretch of land, the site of the Sydney Opera House, Bennelong Point.

Before sailing to establish a settlement in New South Wales, Phillip had been ordered, 'to endeavour by every means to open an intercourse with the natives, and to conciliate their affections, enjoining all our subjects to live in amity and kindness with them', and Phillip, a conscientious and kindly man, did his best to obey orders.

As a result Bennelong was introduced to rum and wine, put in the confines of European clothing and sat down at the table to eat in the European manner. In 1792, Bennelong with another from his tribe, a 12-year-old boy, Yemmerrawanne, voluntarily took ship to England with the ailing Arthur Phillip. He met King George III and was much feted as an example of the Noble Savage. Inevitably his novelty faded. Yemmerrawanne had died of pneumonia and in 1795, with the settlement's new governor, John Hunter, Bennelong returned to Sydney Cove. 'Homesickness had much broken his spirit,' Hunter recorded.

Now he was a man torn between cultures. On 29 August 1796 Bennelong wrote to a friend he had made in England, Lord Sydney's steward: 'I am very well. I hope you are very well. I live at the governor's. I have every day dinner there. I have not my wife; another black man took her away. We have had murry [great] doings; he speared me in the back, but I better now; his name is now Caruey. All my friends alive and well. Not me go to England no more. I am at home now...'

But of course, he wasn't 'at home'. He was a man without a true home, a stranger to his tribe who dressed and often acted like a white man but who was largely shunned by the settlers. Introduced to alcohol, Bennelong had taken to it with alacrity. 'He would drink the strongest liquor, not simply without reluctance, but with eager marks of enjoyment.' And he relished a fight. Inevitably the two led to him being badly wounded in tribal skirmishes before, on 3 January 1813, Bennelong, a tragic symbol, was killed fighting at Kissing Point.

# *The Black Line*

'The liberal imagination, appalled at European violence on the frontier, tends to cast the Aborigines as victims merely and not fine practitioners of violence themselves,' historian John Hirst says in *How Sorry Can We Be?* In fact, Hirst says, unlike the European societies with their professional armed services, all Aboriginal adult males were warriors. As a result violence was more central to Aboriginal society and warfare was endemic.

T.G.H. Strehlow grew up with the Aranda tribe and spoke their language as his mother tongue. Strehlow understood the religious and linguistic significances embodied in the land and made his life work the monumental recording and translation of the Aranda songs, *Songs of Central Australia*. His understanding of the indigenous culture of the Aranda was unparalleled. Strehlow wrote that the 'unbridled expression of blood lust' in the tribe's warrior songs 'was relished by old and young' and he presented this example, told by one Aranda warrior who took part in the massacre of a rival tribe:

'Spears and boomerangs flew with deadly aim. Within a matter of minutes Ltjabakuk and his men were lying lifeless in their blood at the brush shelters. Then the warriors turned their murderous attention to the women and older children, and

A pictograph, made around 1828, of Governor Davey's view of race relations: blacks and white could live together in peace. But the murder of one by the other would be dealt with by hanging.

John GLOVER
born England 1767, arrived Australia 1831, died 1849
*The River Nile, Van Diemen's Land, from Mr Glover's farm* 1837
oil on canvas
76.4 x 114.6 cm
National Gallery of Victoria, Melbourne
Felton Bequest, 1956

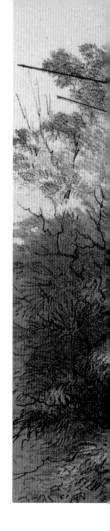

either speared or clubbed them to death. Finally...
they broke the limbs of the infants, leaving them to
die "natural" deaths.'

The Aborigines were formidable fighting men and
in Van Diemen's Land an undeclared war had been
sporadically fought almost from the first landing
in1804. By the time Governor Arthur arrived, in
1824, retaliatory raids by Aborigines, spearing the
sheep and shepherds, butchering settlers and burning
their huts, had the colony in an uproar.

Governor Arthur, who laid the blame for the
violence on the whites, and in particular the
convicts, urged that '... much ought to be endured
in return before the blacks are treated as an open
and accredited enemy by the government', a
sentiment shared by his predecessors, Collins,
Davey and Sorrel. All issued proclamations
against provoking or persecuting the Aborigines
and pointing out that they enjoyed the same full
protection of English law as the settlers.

This kind of thinking did not accord with that
of Andrew Bent, an ex-convict himself, a strident
opponent of Governor Arthur, and the publisher of
the *Hobart Town Colonial Advocate*.

On 1 May 1828 the *Colonial Advocate* carried this
call for drastic remedies:

Unless the blacks are exterminated or removed,
it is plainly proved, by fatal and sanguinary
experience, that all hope of their ceasing in their
aggressions is the height of absurdity. All the
conciliations – all the mercy – all the kindnesses
– all the entreaties and endeavours that have
been bestowed to render these unhappy tribes
sensible of the benefits of civilisation, have been
thrown away, and the only return they have
made is to murder and plunder, and express their
determination to exterminate every white man
that comes in their way.

It is no vain and idle theory which dictates
the removal of the blacks. It is a step which is,
in every sense of the word, practicable. Fit out
your parties of volunteers from the Prisoners'
Barracks – place tickets of leave, emancipations,
and free pardons as the rewards, and soon would
the blacks be hunted down and taken, without
bloodshed – lodged in safe custody, and removed
to King's or some other of the Islands in the
Straits. Then some hope might be entertained of
civilising them...

We predict, that unless the blacks are removed
by the Government, the time is not far distant,
when the whole of the Settlers, with one accord,
will set about the dreadful work of Aboriginal
extermination. Since our last, the following
attacks have been made by these worthless
creatures:-

Mr Gilles's hut attacked; the inmates saving
their lives by flight.

A servant of Mr Cotterel's killed at his hut.

A man on horseback attacked near the Lagoon
of Islands; escaped with great difficulty.

...Mr Kearney's stock-keepers attacked within
a hundred yards of his dwelling, after having just
before kindly entertained two Natives there. It
was with the greatest difficulties that he escaped
to the hut, where he and his companion were
kept prisoners the whole of that night and the
following day, the blacks guarding the door. At
length, their patience exhausted, they fired at
one of the savages, and wounded him about the
posteriors, severely. The rest then collected and
retired, carrying off their wounded companion.

Having attacked another stock-hut, among the

*Attack of the Store Dray*, 1865, by S.T.Gill

Western Mountains, and failed to kill any of the men, they proceeded to spear and drive away the cattle, 30 of which are missing, and two have died from spear wounds!

One of Mr Mackersey's men wounded to death! and the hut robbed of every movable.

Another man dangerously speared, near Mr Presnel's new house, at Sorrell Springs.

Mr Eddington's stock-hut, at Quamby's Bluff, set on fire!

A man of Mr Robertson's speared, and is missing!

Another man, in the same neighbourhood, dangerously speared in five places!

Such, then, is the dreadful catalogue of crimes committed by the Natives, within one little month, which have come before the Public, and it is very probable, that there are many more instances...

They are too ignorant – too truly barbarous to understand any thing but force; and, although we cannot but admit, that a greater protection is afforded by the present Proclamation, still it is not efficient. The Natives are never, in our opinion, to be quieted, otherwise than by one of two methods, viz. their extermination or their removal...'

Governor Arthur chose the latter course. In 1830 he brought every white on the island into a concerted effort to drive the Aboriginal tribes from the settled areas, where they had become such a menace, to the Tasman Peninsula, where they could be contained. More than 2200 men – the Black Line – converged on the Peninsula. It took them seven weeks and they caught just two Aborigines, a man and a small boy.

# Myall Creek

One June day in 1838, about 40 Aborigines camped near a hut on the Myall Creek station, looked up to see 12 stockmen galloping towards them. All but one of the riders were convicts.

From the very first days of settlement the convicts hated the Aborigines. They saw that where convicts were flogged or hanged for stealing food, Aborigines who did the same got off scot-free. When convicts escaped they were often killed by Aborigines or caught by them and returned to be punished. Later, Aboriginal black-trackers led troopers and police to convicts and criminals in hiding. And later still, 'Native Police' captured and brought in law-breakers. For their part, the Aborigines despised and – with good reason – feared the convicts.

Fifty years after they first clashed the mutual hatred was high when the 12 stockmen galloped up to the Myall Creek hut.

Edward Smith Hall, the crusading editor of the *Sydney Monitor*, picks up the story:

> All the Blacks, it appears, were residing at the hut of Kilmaister, in peace and confidence as usual, when a party of men, mounted, and armed with swords and pistols, galloped up to the place. From the manner of the party, the Blacks, who are by no means so deficient in intellect as they are represented in books, perceived the danger, and ran for safety into the hut. They were taken out, and tied one by one to a long rope, used to catch cattle by the horns.
>
> Perceiving their fate, they began to weep and moan. The women, though tied, contrived to carry their infants in a net slung from their shoulders. Being all secured, men and boys, women, girls, and sucklings, one of the horsemen led the way, with the end of the rope attached to himself or horse. The other 10 horsemen divided into two parties of five each, five placing themselves on one side of the rope, one behind the other, and five on the other side.
>
> The funeral procession then commenced its march, amid the tears and lamentations of the victims. It must have been a heart-rending sight to see the aged Black, named 'Daddy', led to the slaughter, a man of giant-like stature, and probably brave as he was magnificent in his form; the tears rolling down his aged cheeks at the sight of his wife, children and relatives. The children perhaps scarcely knew their sufferings until the sharp steel had passed through their bodies, and put a speedy end to their troubles.
>
> Arrived at the place chosen for the catastrophe, the slaughter began. All, however, we can glean from the evidence is that two shots were fired. The sword it should seem did the rest without noise, except the cries of the victims. Decapitation appears to have been considered the readiest way of despatching them, from the great number of skulls afterwards found.
>
> After the slaughter, a fire composed of dead trunks of trees, and many yards in extent, was kindled, and the headless bodies and skulls were placed on the pile. But the party did not stay to see the bodies completely consumed. Perhaps they got alarmed, or were compelled to return home in a given time. It would however have been prudent for one or two of the party to remain at the fire another day. In the course of 24 hours every skull and every bone, even the little bones of sucking children might, by

diligent searching among the ashes, have been found and consumed, and then what yesterday formed eight-and-twenty living human beings, would have been a mere heap of ashes.

No Aboriginal massacre is so well documented – and none had such a profound effect – as the 1838 Myall Creek slaughter at Henry Dangar's sheep station near Inverell in northern New South Wales. The 12 stockmen had claimed to be acting in retaliation for the theft of cattle. At the trial that followed the discovery of the remains of the Aboriginal victims the stockmen's defence was paid for by an association of landowners and stockmen. The jury deliberated for just 20 minutes and came back with the verdict: not guilty.

Smith Hall was outraged:

'... The verdict of acquittal was *highly popular!* It was with exertion that the chief justice could prevent the audience *from cheering* – such was their delight! The aristocracy of the colony, for once, joined heart and hand with the prison population, in expressions of joy at the acquittal of these men.

We tremble to remain in a country where such feelings and principles prevail.'

Before the men could be released, however, the attorney-general ordered that seven of the men be charged with the murder of one of the children. This time the seven were found guilty and, on 5 December 1838, hanged. Their public execution was a turning point. It was the first real test of the justice of English law when it was applied to Aborigines. After Myall Creek, Aborigines knew that the law would punish those who murdered them.

Contemporary illustration of the murderous stockmen who descended on about 40 Aborigines, rounded them up, and massacred them at Myall Creek. Seven of the 12 killers were later executed.

# Nicky Winmar

It's 1993. St Kilda's Nicky Winmar, a brilliant, take-no-prisoners forward, was playing a blinder against Collingwood. Neil Elvis 'Nicky' Winmar was a renowned hard man and a spectacular match winner. And he was black. At the most notorious home ground in the nation, Victoria Park, rabid Magpie fans were screaming racist insults. Winmar responded by lifting his jumper and pointing to his skin. The gesture contained equal measures of dignity and contempt, but above all it was a symbol of the pride of a man in the colour of his skin. Overnight the striking image was recognised around the nation as a statement that Aborigines would no longer accept racism.

It was a turning point. After Nicky Winmar, racist louts watching Australian Football were mute, and when Essendon's idol, Michael Long, complained about an on-field incident the AFL brought in a code to stop racism among players and spectators.

Michael Long went further – a lot further. Retired in 2001, he walked into history. On 20 November 2004 Long went to the funeral of an Aborigine. He came home bitter and depressed by the needless deaths among his people. He felt he had to do something. The next day he set out to walk from his Melbourne home to Canberra. He wanted to talk to the prime minister.

Michael Long began his walk alone. By the time he reached Canberra and walked into the prime minister's office he had been joined by thousands who went part of the way with him, and some who were beside him for almost all the 650 kilometres. Around Australia, in their hearts, millions more walked with Michael Long and the Aboriginal race.

The first Aborigine to play 200 VFL/AFL games, Nicky Winmar was also one of the most dazzlingly talented men ever to play Australian Football. But he will be forever and best remembered for this moment. *Newspix*

# Eddie Mabo

Eddie Koiki Mabo, a Torres Strait Islander, grew up believing that he owned his family land on Murray Island. It was not a lot of land, not much more than a few garden plots on the small island, but it was Mabo land, and it had been Mabo land for generations.

So when Eddie was having lunch one day with a young academic, and he brought up his ownership of the land he was shocked – 'as if I had punched him in the face' Henry Reynolds said – when the young historian told him that he didn't own the land: it was Crown land.

'No way! It's not theirs, it's ours!' Eddie said.

That was in 1974. Eddie was 38, working at James Cook University in Townsville, married to Bonita Neehow and bringing up 10 children. He had tried a number of jobs: on pearling boats, on the railways, but when he began work as a gardener at the university he discovered the rewards of learning. He'd sit in on lectures, spend hours in the library, and immerse himself in books about his Melanesian heritage.

His love of learning interested Henry Reynolds and seven years later Reynolds was there to encourage him when Eddie Mabo spoke at a Land Rights Conference at the university. A lawyer who heard him suggested that Eddie should mount a test case to claim land rights through the courts.

'It was a 10-year battle and it was a remarkable saga, really,' Reynolds said. 'After listening to the argument and investigating it, Justice Moynihan came to the conclusion that Koiki Mabo was not the son of Benny Mabo and declared that he had no right to inherit Mabo land.'

Mabo and his legal team. *Newspix*

Eddie appealed to the High Court. Six of seven judges decided in his favour.

The landmark case altered the foundation of land law. It gave legal recognition to the fact that indigenous land ownership existed before European settlement and was not, in some cases, extinguished by the Crown. The court's decision meant large tracts of Australia would be 'native title', property that could be held only by indigenous people.

Prime Minister Paul Keating hailed the judgement and said it overturned *terra nullius* – Latin for land belonging to no one: 'the bizarre conceit that this continent had no owners prior to the settlement of Europeans'.

British claims to the possession of Australia were said by contemporary Australian historians to be based on that 'bizarre' *terra nullius* doctrine of 18th-century British rulers and explorers.

But terra nullius was not an 18th-century doctrine. It was a 20th-century term. In *The Invention of Terra Nullius,* a Tasmanian historian, Dr Michael Connors, called into question the use of the Latin term, pointing out that it had no place in common law or in the thinking of the 18th century. The High Court had wrongly relied on terra nullius, when Australia's settlement was actually based on the annexation of territory, followed by settlement.

One of the judges who made the decision, Sir William Deane, later to be governor-general of Australia, argued against the doctrine of *terra nullius* while praising the work of Australian historians who had shown the nation, he said, that it had inherited 'a legacy of unutterable shame'.

Foremost among those historians was Henry Reynolds, the James Cook University professor who had encouraged Eddie Mabo and who promulgated the existence of the *terra nullius* doctrine. In retrospect, Reynolds admitted in March 2006 'It might have been a good idea if we had said when we mentioned *terra nullius:* "Say, by the way, they didn't use this term at the time."'

In any case, he argued, 'The one utterly unquestionable fact about Australian history is that when the British arrived in 1788 they didn't recognise the Aborigines owned any land.'

Eddie Mabo died in January 1992, five months before the historic High Court decision. But his name will never die. And Paul Keating was surely right when he said: 'Mabo is an historic decision – we can make it a historic *turning point*, the basis of a new relationship between indigenous and non-Aboriginal Australians.'

The crucial page from the High Court's Mabo judgement recognising the original occupants' right to possession of their traditional lands.

122

Declare –

(1) that the land in the Murray Islands is not Crown land within the meaning of that term in s.5 of the *Land Act* 1962-1988 (Q.);

(2) that the Meriam people are entitled as against the whole world to possession, occupation, use and enjoyment of the island of Mer except for that parcel of land leased to the Trustees of the Australian Board of Missions and those parcels of land (if any) which have been validly appropriated for use for administrative purposes the use of which is inconsistent with the continued enjoyment of the rights and privileges of Meriam people under native title;

(3) that the title of the Meriam people is subject to the power of the Parliament of Queensland and the power of the Governor in Council of Queensland to extinguish that title by valid exercise of their respective powers, provided any exercise of those powers is not inconsistent with the laws of the Commonwealth.

This page and the preceding 121 pages comprise my reasons for judgment in *Mabo & Ors v. State of Queensland*.

# 2

# THE LARGER THAN LIFE

'Weary' Dunlop's statue, one of many commemorations of those who served, at Melbourne's Shrine of Remembrance.

Some are born great, some achieve greatness and some have greatness thrust upon them. Charles Kingsford Smith would seem to fit the first mould. 'Smithy' was destined for big things from the moment he made news as a nine-year-old, saved from drowning at Bondi. Charismatic, a daredevil, he thirsted for fame, got it, and paid the price.

Melba, Bradman and Florey achieved greatness, working hard for many years before winning international recognition. Like Kingsford Smith, they were larger-than-life figures who went beyond mere fame to greatness.

And then there are those who have greatness thrust upon them.

*'We know all about you and your [wireless] set. You will be executed, but first you will talk.'*

'Weary' Dunlop's arms encircling the trunk of a tree were manacled at the wrists. Facing him was his Japanese interrogator and behind him, soldiers with fixed bayonets. He was not going to talk, he resolved, and in the few moments he expected to live the past rushed up. He recalled *'... a time at school when for an escapade I anticipated expulsion and disgrace'.* Now, facing an excruciating death, he reflected wryly that the schooldays threat of disgrace seemed far worse than the bayoneting he was about to get. Weary shook off those memories and told his interrogator what he thought of him. He talked so defiantly, so proudly, that the man, admiring the prisoner's courage, relented and ordered him tortured instead.

Sir Edward 'Weary' Dunlop saved the lives of hundreds of his fellow Australian PoWs at Changi, Singapore. He was knighted for his services to medicine and given many awards, yet larger-than-life Sir Edward Dunlop's achievements remain largely ignored in the roll-call of Australian heroes. In books dedicated to famous Australians his name is often missing from the index. 'Weary' Dunlop didn't yearn for greatness. But he couldn't help being larger than life.

# Ned Kelly

**W**as Ned Kelly, the most legendary figure in Australian folklore, nothing more than a murderous thief? It's a view that some have held for more than 125 years.

'We are aware that the opinion will seem strange to many who still hold the belief that under other circumstances Ned Kelly would have been a hero,' said *Melbourne Punch* on 1 July 1880.

'Under no circumstances could the wretched nature have been altered. He murdered with the ferocity of a wild beast, when there was no chance of retaliation. He swaggered with the bravado of a bully before powerless men when he himself was armed to the teeth, but he displayed no bravery. He was at heart a thorough coward, whose hand shook so when he was menaced with real danger that he was unable to take aim at one of his pursuers.

'And Ned, the leader, the man who would never be taken alive – is captured, roaring with physical pain like a wounded bull, and the hero straightaway commences with lying statements to pose a brave fellow, when every act of his lawless career, from the brutal end of Kennedy to his attempt to leave his comrades in the lurch, shows unmistakable signs of his being a white-livered cur, even if a bloody poltroon... a wretch without one redeeming point... Edward Kelly, Murderer, Traitor, Hypocrite, Liar and Coward.'

Is this so? The truth is that every sentence in *Punch*'s tirade is wrong, and, for the most part, grossly wrong.

Could he have been a hero under other circumstances? In an interview with the London *Observer*, Peter Carey, author of the 2000 Booker Prize-winning novel, *True History of the Kelly Gang*, quoted Dame Mabel Brookes, who said: 'If a cog had slipped in time, the Kelly boys would have been on Gallipoli, one probably a VC winner.' That one, most likely, would have been Ned.

Did he murder 'with the ferocity of a wild beast, when there was no chance of retaliation'?

Kelly killed two policemen, Lonigan and Kennedy, who were out to kill him. Joe Byrne, probably, killed Scanlon, the third in the party. Disguised as prospectors, Kennedy, Scanlon and Lonigan had gone hunting for Ned and Dan Kelly in the Wombat Ranges. They went with body bags and their intention was to bring back the Kellys in those bags – 'those men came into the bush with the intention of scattering pieces of me and my brother all over the bush,' Kelly said in his 'Jerilderie Letter'. The Kellys, Hart and Byrne could have shot all three in cold blood. Instead they emerged from cover and called on the policemen to 'Bail up!' The Stringybark shoot-out began and the three policemen all died in an exchange of shots.

The rest of *Punch*'s claim – that Ned was a bullying coward – has no basis in fact. At times he was bombastic and given to bluster, but he was not a bully. And he was certainly not a coward. ('His hand shook so when he was menaced with real danger that he was unable to take aim at one of his pursuers,' because in the opening exchange of the pitched gun battle at Glenrowan, when Kelly had put a bullet through the wrist of Superintendent Hare, he received in turn, a hail of about 60 bullets. One shattered his left elbow and another smashed through the sole of his right foot. He was captured,

'I always said this bloody armour would bring us to grief,' Joe Byrne told Ned Kelly before being fatally shot in the groin. Ned posed for this photograph, taken for his family, the day before his execution. *Victoria Police Museum*

still firing, riddled with 28 bullet wounds and close to death. 'He could not raise his arm properly,' said one who returned fire with Kelly. 'He seemed to be crippled.')

Badly wounded, Ned could have ridden away from the Glenrowan siege, leaving his brother Dan, Joe and Steve. Instead he limped to where his mare was tethered, struggled onto her and rode to waiting sympathisers, turning them away from the battle. And far from 'his attempt to leave his comrades in the lurch', he came back to them at dawn. 'Come out, come out boys, and we'll beat the beggars,' he rallied them as he beat his revolver butt against his iron breastplate.

Cowardly? When two troopers came within 10 yards and fired both barrels of their shotguns, 'Ned only laughed,' one said. 'Fire away you buggers, you cannot hurt me!' But of course they could. Shotgun blasts to his unprotected knees cut him down. He sagged and as they rushed him, collapsed to the ground, revolver still in hand.

'As game as Ned Kelly,' is an Australian expression that he earned at Glenrowan and that has survived since 1880, when he stood up to a sanctimonious judge in court and then went to the gallows with dignity.

Peter Carey sums up the case for Ned Kelly.

'It is easy to look at this boy as a product of his class and circumstances, one more example of what happens when you imagine you can change your penal colony into a decent nation.

'Yet the story of Ned Kelly, and the reason Australians still respond to him so passionately, is that he was not brutalised or diminished by his circumstances. Rather, he elevated himself, and inspired a particular people with his courage, wit and decency.'

# Melba

For seven decades after her death in 1931 the good sisters of St Vincent's Hospital in Sydney guarded Dame Nellie Melba's secret. Finally, at the beginning of the new century it emerged: the great soprano had died when a facelift went wrong.

She was almost 70.

Of all the stories that revolve around Melba, of her ego, scandalous love life, legendary jealousy, temper, sweet voice and foul tongue, this surely is the most revealing – and the most typical.

Melba was a woman 70 years ahead of her time. The revelation that she had undergone vanity surgery at such a venerable age was almost predictable when her character and her career are examined. Because Melba fitted the persona of a modern Material Girl – Madonna, more than Danni Minogue comes to mind – and those scores of wannabe pop stars enslaved by Botox and breast implants.

The 20th century's first great diva – at her peak she earned more for a single performance ($250,000 in today's terms) than any other performing artist. She was also first in so many areas other than opera. Decades before the phrase product spin-off was dreamed up, Melba was turning her name into a brand (celebrated in the classic peach and ice cream dessert created for her by the great French chef, Escoffier; in a toast; and in wafers. There was even a Melba doll.

Above all, Nellie Melba, born Helen Porter Mitchell in Richmond, Melbourne, on 19 May 1861, was the first internationally famous Australian. Nellie Melba was a one-off: first among the prima donnas, the original pop diva, the Prima Madonna.

Top: Melba in maturity, still the Diva and at the pinnacle of her success.
Above: The young Nellie. *Newspix*

Left: Rupert Bunny's portrait, *Madame Melba*, shows the Diva, imperious and magnificent, beginning her artistic partnership with tenor Enrico Caruso

Rupert Bunny
Australia 1864–1947, lived in Europe 1884–1933
*Madame Melba* (c.1902)
oil on canvas
245.5 x 153.0 cm
National Gallery of Victoria, Melbourne
Purchased through The Art Foundation of Victoria with the assistance of
Henry Krongold CBE and Dinah Krongold, Founder Benefactors, 1980.

# Charles Kingsford Smith

Kingsford Smith, a master pilot, never lost the daredevil spirit that pushed him to set aviation records but ultimately led to his death. Below: The three-engine *Southern Cross*, the first aircraft to fly the Pacific, took off from San Francisco and touched down in Brisbane, where she can still be seen at Brisbane airport.

**W**as it the Tall Poppy Syndrome: the compulsion to reduce lofty achievers to your own lowly level? Or was it hubris, the fatal flaw of arrogance and self-confidence that leads to retribution and destruction?

Either way, Sir Charles Kingsford Smith – 'Smithy' – suffered because of it. His fall was worthy of a Greek tragedy: a national idol, brought low by bad luck and bureaucrats, gossip and innuendo, and the imperative to seek redemption in one last great adventure, flies into the night, never to be seen again.

Kingsford Smith, Don Bradman and Phar Lap were and remain giants on the Australian landscape. Their careers coincided closely. Smithy and Bradman even looked alike. Both were short: at 173 centimetres, Bradman, the Little Don, was actually six centimetres taller than Kingsford Smith. Both had calculating blue eyes balanced by wide grins. Both were driven to push themselves to the utmost: to break all records. But there the resemblance ends. Where Bradman, a non-smoking teetotaller, might be found relaxing at the piano, Smithy

would be in the bar demonstrating how to down a schooner standing on your head. A drinking man, a womaniser with a reckless and at times irresponsible streak completely foreign to Bradman, Smithy lived hard and fast.

Small though he may have been, Kingsford Smith was tough, with powerful shoulders and

hands and an indomitable spirit. In 1928, a year after Lindbergh crossed the Atlantic in 33 hours, Kingsford Smith, Charles Ulm, a navigator and a wireless operator, crossed the Pacific in the *Southern Cross* in 83 flying hours. For ambition, audacity and extraordinary physical challenge, the flight dwarfed Lindbergh's. The *Southern Cross* was met by the governor-general and 300,000 deliriously happy Sydneysiders. Overnight 'Smithy' became a national idol above all others. (Bradman and Phar Lap were beginning their careers that year: Bradman in first-class cricket, Phar Lap as a two-year-old.)

By 1930 all three were at the peak of their powers. That year Kingsford Smith broke the England to Australia solo record, Bradman was astounding the cricket world with a string of centuries including a Test innings of 334 and Phar Lap had 21 starts for 19 wins including the Melbourne Cup.

Adored by the entire country. Smithy was recognised internationally as the world's greatest aviator. But in Australia he was not universally applauded. Over him hung a cloud of rumour and gossip. He was sent white feathers in the post and he was hissed in the streets by some.

Smithy, many believed, was the cause of the death of two men – one of them a man who was once his mate.

Charles Kingsford Smith first made news in 1906, when, aged nine, he was swept out to sea and rescued by lifesavers using the new line and reel at Bondi beach. He was next in the news at Buckingham Palace 11 years later, where he hobbled on crutches to be given the Military Cross by King George V. After joining the army and going to Gallipoli, Kingsford Smith had transferred to the Royal Flying Corps and distinguished himself as a pilot in France. Badly wounded in the foot he made it back to the squadron through sheer grit.

Smithy went to the US, stunt flying for silent movies in Hollywood and making news again in a flight in Death Valley. He came home with a dream of flying the Pacific and linked up with another young pilot who shared the dream: Keith Anderson. The pair set out to get sponsorship for the venture and, as a way to win attention, invited three paying passengers to accompany them on a flight across the continent from Carnarvon to Sydney.

The first commercial passenger flight in Australia made headlines and attracted the attention of another young Gallipoli veteran, Charles Ulm. Ulm joined the partnership and Anderson found himself on the outer as Kingsford Smith and Ulm made a record-breaking flight around Australia. The three went to the US on the promise of financial backing from the New South Wales premier, Jack Lang, but when the state governor sacked Lang and the new premier refused to honour the commitment Anderson returned to Australia. Smithy and Ulm stayed in the US, and eventually found a backer. The flight from Oakland, California, to Brisbane, Australia, is one of the great epics of aviation.

Smithy and Ulm now began a series of record-breaking flights that won world attention and thrilled the nation. But in April 1929, heading for England on another attempt to set a record, they got lost and had to put down on a mudflat in the Northern Territory. Bogged and unable to take off, they'd also lost radio contact. Keith Anderson, with Bobby Hitchcock, hastily and ill-prepared, took to the skies to find his old mate. His plane, *Kookaburra*, went down in the Tanami Desert. Anderson and Hitchcock died of thirst.

Smithy and Ulm were found after 12 days but by now there were allegations that their disappearance was a publicity stunt and that Anderson and Hitchcock, his mechanic, had died for nothing. There was malicious gossip; the government ordered an inquiry that cleared Smith and Ulm, but now the idol's pedestal had become rocky.

Smithy never recovered the adulation that had once been his in his home country. Internationally he was feted but at home, despite his continuing success at setting long-distance flight records, his business ventures failed. The Depression had set in.

He and Ulm started a passenger airline company, Australian National Airways. The pride of the fleet, *Southern Cross*, crashed somewhere in the Snowy Mountains. The company folded.

Then Ulm disappeared on a flight over the Pacific.

The pressure kept mounting. In 1934 Smithy bought himself a plane in an attempt to win an England to Australia Air Race and get back on his feet. He wanted to call it *Anzac*, but many found this an affront to the memory of those who had fallen where Smithy himself had fought. Once again the government stepped in and made him change the name. He re-named the plane *Lady Southern Cross* but pulled out of the race when authorities ruled he had exceeded the fuel capacity. More bad press followed. Now he was criticised for failing to compete and cowardly letters questioned his courage.

At 38 Charles Kingsford Smith was feeling the strain.

In a last ditch attempt to win back the press, Smithy and Tommy Pethybridge followed the route taken by the Air Race he had been forced to abandon and were on track to break the record when his luck ran out.

On 8 November 1935 an Australian pilot, Jimmy Melville, saw flames from the twin exhausts of *Lady Southern Cross* 320 kilometres south of Rangoon. That was the last sighting. Smithy almost certainly died in the way he had feared from childhood: in the black waters of the Andaman Sea.

Charles Ulm (left) taught himself to fly. Both he and 'Smithy' were charmers, but neither man was ever able to shrug off the whispered accusations that they had faked their desert disappearance, causing the deaths of two mates who set out to find them. Ironically, in separate flights, Ulm and Kingsford Smith disappeared flying over the sea.

# Don Bradman

At any time of the day or night, it's been said, someone, somewhere, is talking about Don Bradman.

Sir Donald Bradman in 20 years as a Test batsman made 6996 runs including 29 centuries at an average of 99.94. He made a century on average every third time he went to the crease. He is without question Australia's greatest sportsman and one of a handful of sporting figures unchallenged as supreme in their field.

He was idolised by Australians from the moment he made his astonishing innings of 334 – the first 300 coming in a day – at Leeds. Bradman came at just the right moment in our history. When the Little Master went in to bat the Depression, the lingering sectarian aftermath of the bitter Conscription fight, and the terrible legacy of the lost and maimed from the Great War were forgotten. Bradman unified the nation as no one ever has.

Yet he had and has his enemies and detractors – some of them team-mates, like Jack Fingleton and 'Tiger' Bill O'Reilly – and others like Ian Chappell who makes no secret of his feelings towards 'the Don'.

Fingleton, the Australian opener, once said that you didn't bat with Don Bradman, you ran for him.

Cricket writer David Frith claims that the enmity between the two arose from Fingleton's claim that in a game played at the WACA in the run-up to the Bodyline series

Bradman had approached him in mid-wicket and asked him to face the fast bowling of 'Gubby' Allen. Bradman had said: 'I think they're going to have a pop at me.'

This clearly implied that Bradman was a coward. Bradman never publicly responded but he was, rightly, enraged. In a letter to his closest friend, the journalist Rohan Rivett, he said, 'Well I would prefer not to even recognise Fingleton. He has spent virtually a lifetime of using me as a meal ticket for his own monetary reward [Fingleton by then was a journalist] and falsely attacking me by attributing to me attitudes which I did not possess... I prefer to ignore him. He is not worth recognising.'

The Bradman/Fingleton animosity could also be traced back to one of cricket's most notorious moments: the visit of England's tour manager to the Australian locker room at the height of Bodyline. Australia's captain Bill Woodfull told the England manager, 'Plum' Warner: 'There are two teams out there but only one of them is playing cricket.' The press printed the story and although neither was in the room at the time Bradman and Fingleton both blamed each other for the leak.

There was mutual dislike, too, later in his life between Bradman, on cricket's Board of Control, and Ian Chappell, who was campaigning for better pay for top-level cricketers. Chappell and his team-mates were paid a derisory fee to play for

PLAYER'S CIGARETTES

Bradman the idol, on a cigarette card aimed at children. Right: The Don takes the field. The smile on his face almost always stayed as he went on to punish bowlers.

their country and Bradman – who in his time had bucked the board to increase his own earnings – opposed giving them more.

Chappell is the grandson of Victor Richardson. Fourteen years older than Bradman, Richardson's career overlapped Bradman's and there were tensions over the captaincies of Australia and South Australia when Bradman moved to Richardson's home town, Adelaide.

'...The ambitious Master Bradman climbed right over the heads of his contemporaries, some of whom felt that priority entitled them to the plums of captaincy,' said Arthur Mailey, the great slow bowler, who, like his team-mates Fingleton and O'Reilly, became a journalist on his retirement.

Four decades on the bitterness lingered. Ian Chappell, 'a rebel in his youth, was a superb leader of men in his prime and a deep thinker and writer on the game with the mellowing of middle age,' Cricket historian Chris Harte said. 'His family's feud with Bradman has lasted to this day with the clash of iron wills and personalities [helping] cause the eruptions of later years.'

It was also a clash of personality. Chappell was a swashbuckler whose temperament was the antithesis of the older man's. Bradman told his friend Rivett that he would not attend an award presentation for Chappell. 'On principle I refused to attend – my mute protest at his approach to life.'

Bradman's private, introvert nature was a source of his unpopularity with other cricketers. He wasn't 'one of the boys'. He didn't drink with the team or opponents after the game. He was more likely to be found in his room writing, or listening to classical music. And at the crease he was cruel. 'Poetry and murder lived in him together,' an English journalist wrote. 'He would slice the bowling to ribbons, then dance without pity on the corpse.'

Arthur Mailey wrote this on the weekend when Bradman made his final bow, at the Melbourne Cricket Ground in December 1948:

Don Bradman will be remembered as one of the most remarkable sportsmen who ever graced the sporting stage of any country.

Bradman, playing in his testimonial in Melbourne this weekend, is an enigma, a paradox; an idol of millions of people, yet, with a few, the most unpopular cricketer I have ever met.

People close to Bradman either like or dislike him; there is no half-way. To those who dislike him there is no compromise.

... Bradman is a law within himself. This has been proved over and over again, and it is his amazing success as a cricketer, plus his perfect timing and tremendous respect and faith in his own judgement, that have demanded attention where others have been ignored – in some cases ridiculed.

... Bradman was brought up the hard way, the lonely way. That's why he practised as a boy hitting a ball against a brick wall, and when he felt the cold draught of antagonism within the ranks he kept his counsel, remained unperturbed, and knew his greatest weapon was centuries and more centuries.

# Howard Florey

Florey shunned publicity on the discovery of penicillin. He knew it would create a huge public demand, and there simply wasn't any to be given. It would be immoral, he thought, to raise false hopes.

In the year 2000, 35 prominent Australians nominated their Australians of the Century. Among the 80 names they came up with were a bushranger, a batsman, four Aborigines, an archbishop, sportsmen and women, politicians aplenty, a press baron, a soprano and a scientist.

The scientist topped the poll: Howard Florey.

'Sorry,' millions of Australians – and billions around the world – would say. 'Howard who?'

Howard Florey developed a drug that saved the lives of 50 million people. A drug we all are likely to have use of when we are ill. A drug that revolutionised medicine, allowing once deadly infections – pneumonia, diphtheria, syphilis, meningitis and more – to be cured. The drug that is the wonder antibiotic, penicillin.

The Nobel medicine laureate, Lord (Edgar) Adrian, told mourners at Howard Florey's memorial service in Westminster Abbey that Lord Howard Florey was to be honoured alongside Pasteur, the father of vaccine therapy; Jenner, who developed the smallpox vaccination; and Lister, the pioneer of antiseptic surgery. All four men made discoveries that have saved untold millions of lives.

Howard Florey was a great man but he has never been given the honour he deserves in Australia or internationally. Florey's face was on Australia's $50 note for a time, until it was removed in 1996. Part of the reason for Florey's relative obscurity lies in the fact that he was a modest man who insisted on sharing the credit for his work, but mostly it was a cynical decision to claim the honour for a Scot. In the midst of World War Two, Britain, anxious to wring propaganda out of the miracle cure, seized on this to claim that the discovery was Sir Alexander Fleming's. The 1945 Nobel Prize for Physiology and Medicine which was to be awarded for the introduction of the drug was very nearly given to Alexander Fleming alone, so great was the public perception that he, and only he, was responsible for it. (In the end the Nobel Prize was shared equally between Florey, his partner Chain and Fleming.)

Howard Florey had a right to be infuriated by the purloining of his landmark discovery, but he simply said, 'I'd like to emphasise first of all we didn't work with Sir Alexander Fleming; I hardly knew him. Fleming's work was done 10 years before the work in Oxford, but we just happened to work on the substance that he'd discovered.'

He was that kind of a man. Blunt, sometimes brutally plain speaking, not easy to get on with, but driven by a passion for science, and uncaring about his vanity or his material needs, he might have made himself enormously wealthy had he patented his discovery.

He was born into a wealthy family in Adelaide in 1898 but in 1918, in his second year of medical studies at Adelaide University, the business went bust and his father died of a heart attack. The loss of family financial support didn't deter Florey who, in 1922, left Adelaide to take up a Rhodes Scholarship at Oxford. He was 23, a tall, blunt and prickly man with what a colleague called 'a great fire burning within him'. At the same time Alexander Fleming, small, neat and dapper with a mild Scottish accent, was working on antibacterial substances in the laboratories of St Mary's Hospital in London. The two were destined to share the 1945 Nobel Prize yet they never worked together

and were never friends. Fleming was to accidentally discover penicillin, and Florey to develop it.

Fleming's discovery was pure fluke. On holiday, he left a petri dish with a culture of bacteria uncovered on his desk. In the cold weather the bacteria grew and when it turned warm the mould flourished. By another stroke of luck Fleming put his petri dish on top of a pile of others in a tray of disinfectant, ready to be cleaned. At the top of the pile, by a matter of mere centimetres, the mould escaped being washed away to oblivion by soapsuds.

Two weeks later Fleming returned to find the mould was about the size of a 20-cent coin, and around it, the bacteria had died. He was only mildly intrigued. A colleague came in, saw it in a bucket, and said, 'That's interesting.' Fleming was interested enough to inject it into a healthy rabbit and found it didn't hurt the rabbit. But he didn't say that it cured diseases in the living system. He didn't go further than the rabbit. He wrote a paper of 15 lines and left it at that. 'The trouble of making it seemed not worthwhile,' he said two decades later when he was getting his Nobel Prize.

Florey, on the other hand, liked going to considerable trouble. A man who relished experiments and challenges, he had the gift of attracting brilliant and dedicated people around him, not least Ernst Chain, a highly excitable but brilliant biochemist.

The discovery of penicillin is marked by an extraordinary sequence of chance. Lennard Bickel, a biographer of Florey's, told how 'Chain was reading Fleming's old paper of 15 lines when he had a sudden memory of a woman, one of the ladies who worked at the Dunn School, walking along a corridor with a dish in her hand on which a mould was growing. And he went to see this lady, and he

said to her, "This mould that I saw you with." She said, "Yes." He said, "What is it?" She told him it was *Penicillium natartum*, this species of mould, and he said, "That is the very mould that Fleming found in 1928." She said, "Yes, he cultured it and he gave us a piece of it, and we've kept it alive ever since."'

Florey and Chain decided to investigate Fleming's mould.

They had few funds and had to grow the mould in bedpans. To extract the penicillin they built a Heath Robinson contraption constructed from such things as a bathtub, a letter box, an aquarium pump and milk bottles. On Saturday 25 May 1940 they performed one of the most important medical experiments in history. Florey's team took eight mice and infected them with a fatal dose of streptococcal bacteria. Four of the mice were treated with penicillin, while four were used as controls. By the next day, the treated mice had recovered and the untreated mice were dead.

Chain danced with delight. Florey was as laconic as usual. But when he telephoned a colleague, Dr Margaret Jennings, a short time later, he couldn't conceal his excitement.

Norman Heatley, a key member of the team, recalled, 'It had taken some weeks to prepare enough penicillin for the mouse experiments, but Florey knew that a man is 3000 times the size of a mouse, and that if tests were ever to be carried out in man, an enormous increase in production would be needed. The first difficulty was to obtain enough containers to grow the fungus in. All kinds of lab glass were pressed into service, as well as domestic things like biscuit tins, trays and enamelled

Louis Kahan
*Lord Florey*
Pen and ink on paper
National Portrait Gallery, Canberra

bedpans. The bedpans were particularly good but alas, there were only 16 of them.'

Then a firm in the Midlands produced made-to-measure ceramic culture pots and soon there was enough for a human trial. A young doctor, Charles Fletcher, was to give the first injection of penicillin.

'There was a policeman who'd been in what was called the Septic Ward, a terrible sort of ward which we don't have now, with people with abscesses and boils all over them,' Fletcher said. 'And this policeman was particularly bad; he'd had a sore on his mouth about a month previously, the infection had spread over his scalp, he had abscesses there, it had spread to both his eyes, one of which had had to be removed. He had abscesses which had been opened on his arm, he had abscesses in his lung. He was well on his way towards death from this terrible infection. And we'd nothing to lose, and everything to gain. So we thought we'd have a try.

'The shortage of penicillin was such that after the first day, I collected all his urine (his urine had been saved) and I took it in a bottle over to the Dunn Laboratory where Florey was working, so that the penicillin could be extracted from the urine. 'On the third day he was having the same penicillin as he had on the first day, and on the fourth day he really was dramatically improved. And he was sitting up in bed and his temperature had come down.'

Tragically, the story doesn't end happily. Florey contained his excitement because he knew that the supplies of penicillin were running out. If the penicillin ran out before the man was completely cured he would die. The supplies ran out.

Howard Florey's penicillin factory at Oxford couldn't hope to produce the necessary quantities of penicillin needed to meet the now urgent demands of Britain, a country at war. Florey went to America with the help of the Rockefeller Foundation, and tried to get American firms interested. A friend of Florey's suggested Florey visit an obscure little laboratory in Peoria, Illinois, where chemists experimenting with growing the penicillin mould on corn steep liquor discovered that the mould increased its yield tenfold.

In December 1941, America joined the war and the United States Government saw the need for mass production of penicillin as of national importance. Only the race to develop the atom bomb was more important. Funds were found. Peoria was doing its bit but not nearly enough to meet military demand. Around the world US servicemen and women collected handfuls of samples of soil, which were flown to Peoria for analysis of the moulds they contained. Local townspeople were asked to bring in every bit of mould they could find. Mouldy Mary, the tea lady in the Peoria laboratory, was so called because of her enthusiasm for collecting bits and pieces from rubbish bins: old socks, soggy newspapers, rotting food. One day she brought in a decaying piece of rockmelon. The mould on it produced the best penicillin of all: 3000 times more than Fleming's original mould. Soon US factories were making billions of units a month and penicillin, saving thousands of lives and getting ill soldiers back into battle, was to play an effective role in winning World War Two.

Florey's first wife, Mary, died in 1966. They had two children. The following year he married his special assistant for more than 30 years. He was happy, but eight months later, in February 1968, Howard Florey died of a heart attack.

# 3

# THE MONSTERS

For a time Frederick Deeming, the Melbourne serial killer, ranked with his contemporary Jack the Ripper as the most wicked man in the English-speaking world. Deeming cut the throat of his wife, strangled his eldest daughter and slashed the throats of his other three children, cut the throat of his second 'wife', and was set to make it three in a row but for an astute bit of detective work by a Melbourne newspaper reporter. His next intended victim was stopped by police as she got off the train in Melbourne to meet the man she thought was Mr Right.

So you think we live in a society stamped by savagery? Think again. Think of the world of John Giles Price... if you are able.

'John Giles Price has remained one of the durable ogres of the Australian imagination for more than a century now,' Robert Hughes said in his account of the convict settlement of Australia, *The Fatal Shore*. Not so. The name John Giles Price means nothing to most Australians. It may once have been invoked to frighten naughty children, but it will never again cause a shudder to run down a child's spine. Just as well. Of all the monsters we have known John Giles Price is surely supreme: the overlord of the macabre psychopaths who ruled our penal settlements until the mid-19th century.

For six years of unremitting and almost unbelievable cruelty Price strutted the blood-soaked earth of Norfolk Island until, finally, he met his own brutal end. Price's private nightmare – it must surely have been – came true when he was buried beneath a mass of bodies, convicts tearing at each other to get at him. His murder in 1857 coincided with a reformist push for the abolition of Transportation and the arrival in Australia of thousands of free men; free-spirited, free-thinking gold miners. The tyrannical floggings, hangings and torture subsided as if by common consent. Henceforth our history of horrors would include depraved serial killers like those at Truro, Snowtown and the gruesome torture fields at Belanglo State Forest. But the sadists of the penal settlements, men like Price, Captain Logan (whose killing is still celebrated in song), the grotesque Morisset and his bloodthirsty underling Foster Fyans, are long forgotten.

For the children of the 20th century, after the end of the Victorian era, there were new ogres. The hairy dark bogeymen – The Big Bad Banksia Men – the villains of May Gibbs's masterpiece *The Complete Adventures of Snugglepot and Cuddlepie* frightened generations of New South Wales schoolchildren. And, for other states, tromp, tromp, tromping through the trees, came the Hobyahs, to cut up and carry away the little old lady and the little old man. In time their names, too, faded. Today the nightmares are made in Hollywood.

# John Giles Price

J ohn Giles Price, commandant of Norfolk Island, was the very model of countless monsters of fiction and film who followed him: the galley slave driver; the Boss man of the Deep South chain gangs; the heartless warder in a hundred movies and more. And, as Commandant Frere, he himself was thinly disguised in Marcus Clarke's *For the Term of His Natural Life.*

'Over six feet in height, he had a round bullet head,' a convict, Henry Beresford Grant, later wrote. '... a light complexion and hair, the last almost sandy and slightly inclined to curl, a rather large but well-shaped mouth, a thick bull neck, square massive shoulders, no waist but ribbed down to the hips like an Atlas, legs strong and slightly bowed, his whole frame as indicative of immense strength as his face was of ferocity.'

When Price arrived on Norfolk Island in 1846 he mustered the 500 prisoners. Garrett was among them and his description of that defining moment shows us the man in all his naked fear and hatred of humanity:

'The yell of defiance from 500 throats rather startled him. He turned tail. It may have been either fear or anger. He stepped back a couple of paces, looked round at his attendants and up at the soldiers in the gallery and nodded. The soldiers brought their rifles to the ready and the snick of the locks was audible. Every man around him drew his cutlass and pistol and things began to look ugly.

'Let me describe him as he then stood. He was dressed something after the style of a flash gentleman. On his round bullet head a small straw hat was jauntily stuck, the broad blue ribbon of

'I am come here to rule,' Price, the psychopathic commander of Norfolk Island penal colony barked, 'and by God I'll do so and tame or kill you... I know you mean, cowardly dogs, and I'll make you worry and eat each other.' *Tasmanian Museum and Art Gallery Collection*
Right: Rob Blackburn's evocative photograph shows the main gate of Norfolk Island prison as it is today.

which reached down between his shoulders, a glass stuck in one eye, a black silk kerchief tied sailor fashion, round his bullneck, no vest but a bobtail or oxonian coat, or something like a cross between this and a stable-man's jacket seemed to be bursting over his shoulders. A pair of rather tight pants completed his costume, except for a leather belt, six inches broad, buckled round the loins. In the belt two pepperbox revolvers were conspicuously stuck.

'The yells subsided and, assured by the presence of the soldiers and the guard, he struck an attitude by placing his arms akimbo, and again spoke.

'You know me, don't you? I am come here to rule, and by God I'll do so and tame or kill you. I know you mean cowardly dogs, and I'll make you worry and eat each other.' What else he would have said was lost in another burst of yells...

Price quickly instituted an efficient system of floggings for the least offence.

'Under John flogging became an art. Men were trained to it as to a trade. Sheets of bark were stretched on the triangles and the novices made to practise on them. It became a task, too, as rigidly enforced as the task of field labour, and woe to the flogger whose victim's back did not show the desired amount of mutilation. He was sure of the same number of lashes as the other had received, laid on, too, by the severest of floggers.

'... Men's backs, ragged and bruised from the lash, were baked in the sun like crackling pork. They swarmed with flies and maggots, with not a drop of water to moisten them. They used to make poultices of lemon and lime pulp, and where these could not be got they poured their urine on to each other. Each was like a naked fire to their backs. Men ill with dysentery, their trousers wet with discharge and smothered with flies and maggots, and weak from disease, starvation and punishment, staggered to and from labour, until, no longer able to do so, they lay down and died, or committed suicide. The stench of their festering backs in those packed dormitories and their groans were horribly offensive to smell and pitiable to hear.'

In 1849 the former chaplain on the island, whom Price had lobbied to be relieved, wrote a blood-curdling account of life under the commandant. The Reverend Thomas Rogers, Chaplain of Norfolk Island during Major Childs's time and part of John Price's rule, was the man on whom Marcus Clarke based his character, Reverend North in *For the Term of His Natural Life*. Rogers, who died aged 99 in Melbourne in 1901, wrote a damning indictment of Price. In his book *Correspondence*, published in 1849, he talked of 'the ground on which the men stood at the triangles... saturated with human gore, as if a bucket of blood had been spilled on it covering a space three feet in diameter and running out in various directions in little streams of two or three feet long. I have seen this.'

And: 'A man named Dytton was chained down to the floor of the hospital and gagged for getting up

The faces of 'old lags' – transported convicts – are a brutal indictment of the system. Yet most of the 161,700 taken to Australia over 80 years became free men and women whose descendants look back on them with pride.

to the window in the hospital cell for air. He had been ill at the hospital for six or seven weeks, has never been well since a beating he received whilst in the chain gang.

'He had abused a constable for removing pegs on which hung his clothes and rations, so was gagged, taken to the New Gaol, chained down and dreadfully beaten by several constables. He lay in a puddle of blood. Next day a constable came in and jumped on his chest.'

In 1853, after more than six years of unrelenting cruelty, Price left Norfolk Island and returned to Tasmania to retirement on a farm. But the following year he was invited to be inspector-general of penal establishments in Victoria, and he was pleased to have the whip hand once again.

He should have stayed on the farm. On 26 March 1857, he was at the quarry at Williamstown where convicts from the five prison hulks were moored nearby.

The hulks – where 15 years later Ned Kelly was lto spend a year – were, Robert Hughes says in *The Fatal Shore*, 'a new byword for ferocity. The worst of Norfolk Island had come to the mainland: the tube gagging and spread-eagling, the bludgeon handle jammed in the mouth in tobacco searches, the rotten victuals, the loading with irons, the beatings, ringbolts and buckets of sea water. Before long, a warship had to take up station next to the hulks, its guns double-shotted so that if the prisoners motioned and the guards had to flee, it could sink the hulk and send its ironed men to the bottom.'

The working parties in the quarry must have been relieved to be given work out in the open, away from the misery of the rotting pensioned-off war ships, a feeling that would have vanished once the word spread that John Price was coming.

Price strode into their midst with his usual arrogance and, when a convict named Dan Kelly asked him if his recent three-day solitary sentence would affect his imminent ticket-of-leave to freedom, Price told Kelly the sentence certainly would postpone his day of freedom.

It was too much for Kelly. 'You bloody tyrant, your race will soon be run!' he shouted. And he was right. As convicts milled about him, and one threw a clod of earth, Price did run. He was almost through them when he stumbled and they got to him. He lingered, unconscious, and died a day later.

John Giles Price was, Robert Hughes said, 'one of the durable ogres of the Antipodean imagination for more than a century'.

# *Caroline Grills*

Tiny – 122 cm short – butterball round and sweet, Caroline Grills was kindness itself, forever visiting folk, bringing them lollies and cakes made with her own plump little hands. She wouldn't hurt a fly: in her prison cell humming hymns, she would shoo them out the bars rather than swat them with the handkerchiefs she embroidered to pass the time. She was doing time – life – for attempting to murder a relative, one of a number of relatives and friends she poisoned.

Caroline Grills was 57 when, in 1947, she killed her stepmother with the deadly metallic toxin named thallium. Months later she killed a family friend. And, later that year, her husband's brother-in-law. Twelve months later it was her sister-in-law's turn. And two years after that, in 1951, she set about thallium poisoning – simultaneously – three other relatives.

What began as envy had become a very bad habit. There was no inkling of that, however, when, in 1907, Caroline Mickleson, 17, wed Richard William Grills and began a long and happy marriage that lasted 53 years. They had four sons and Caroline was Grannie to numerous grandchildren. Her father died 20 years later and left his new wife, Caroline's stepmother, Christina, the family home in the desirable Sydney suburb of Gladesville. Caroline was living in a less than desirable inner-city house in Goulburn Street, an area infested at the time with very large rats. Mrs Christina Louisa Adelaide Mickleson was living in luxury while Mrs Caroline Grills was living with giant rats. The rats or Mrs Mickleson: one of them had to go.

The local council endorsed the rat poison Thrall-rat as the most effective way to rid houses of rodents and Mr Grills laid it around their house. It killed big rats very quickly. Watching it work set Mrs Grills's mind in motion. Her father's will had ceded the big, comfortable family house to his widow... for as long as she lived. Then it would pass to her, his daughter, Caroline.

One afternoon in 1947 Caroline popped over to Gladesville to visit her stepmother. Over a chinwag Caroline quietly slipped a deadly dose of Thrall-rat into Mrs Mickleson's tea and the old lady went into convulsions. There was no autopsy. A few days later Mrs Mickleson's remains were cremated and Mrs Grills moved into the Gladesville house.

No more rats now. But there was another house. It belonged to a friend of her husband. Mrs Angelina Thomas was 84 and had known Richard Grills since he had lived with her as a child, at Leura in the Blue Mountains. She was very fond of Richard, considered him her foster son and had written him into her will, as she often reminded

Richard and Caroline. They would inherit the house when she eventually passed on. On 17 January 1948, after afternoon tea with Caroline, Mrs Thomas fell ill and died.

Now Caroline Grills had two very nice houses. But the thrill of killing had taken over and almost immediately she selected a fresh target. This time the luckless victim was a man, her husband's brother-in-law, John Lundberg. Once again doctors failed to order an autopsy and he was cremated. A year later Caroline Grills's sister-in-law, Mary-Anne Mickleson, died after a long illness. She too lost her hair and her sight, and she too had been given tender loving care by Aunt Carrie.

Then her attention turned to her surviving sister-in-law, Mrs Eveline Lundberg, the widow of John Lundberg. Once again the deadly symptoms manifested themselves: hair loss, blurred vision, agonising cramps, depression. Once again doctors were at a loss. And once again Aunt Carrie was a frequent visitor. But this time Caroline Grills was thwarted. Eveline Lundberg's daughter Christine Downey and her husband John lived across the road from her at their Redfern home in inner-Sydney, and they decided that the bedridden and almost completely blind Eveline had to be admitted to hospital. There, she began to rapidly recover.

The Downeys knew doting and dependable old Aunt Carrie as a distant relative and close friend. Each week they played bridge with her and Eveline Lundberg at their home. Aunt Carrie could always be relied upon to put on the kettle for another round of tea and she always turned up with the cakes and tempting little sweets.

With Eveline beyond reach under the watchful eye of the hospital staff, Caroline Grills took out her frustration on the Downeys. The weekly card games continued but suddenly the Downeys, Christine and John, were having problems with agonising cramps in their arms and legs. They suffered nausea, their hair was falling out, and their vision was failing. Aunt Carrie was feeding them just enough thallium to make their life a misery, but not enough to kill them.

The Downeys might have been headed for an extremely slow and painful death but for Mrs Yvonne Gladys Fletcher, who was arrested for the murder of her two husbands. Police had exhumed the husbands' bodies and found thallium in both and in August 1952 Yvonne Fletcher was sentenced to life imprisonment. Christina and John Downey read the reports of the case with morbid fascination. They learned that Desmond Butler and Bertram Fletcher had both died from the same symptoms that afflicted them and Christina's mother Eveline. The Downeys put two and two together.

The police laid a trap for Aunt Carrie, the jovial old rat. They told the Downeys to carry on as usual when Aunt Carrie called, but to avoid eating or drinking, without rousing her suspicion, and to keep samples of the food and tea she prepared. In April, Mrs Eveline Downey, blind but now out of hospital, was sitting on the verandah when Aunt Carrie came out of the kitchen with a nice cup of tea for her. John Downey saw her sprinkle something into the cup and give it a good stir. His wife diverted Aunt Carrie's attention long enough for him to switch the cups and the trap was sprung.

Caroline Grills was sentenced to life imprisonment in Long Bay jail – Aunt Thally, they called her there – and died of peritonitis on 6 October 1960, an hour after she was taken to hospital.

Her victims had lingered much longer.

# *The Beaumont children's killer*

Only a child killer could boast of killing children.

In October 2006 the ABC screened a dark documentary, *The Fishermen: A Journey Into the Mind of a Killer*, in which Gordon Davie, a retired senior detective, talked with the most evil man he had ever met, James Ryan O'Neill, jailed for life for the murder of a nine-year-old Tasmanian boy. O'Neill was on his way to collect his wife and newborn son from hospital when he abducted the boy. O'Neill admitted murdering another Tasmanian boy three months later but Davie believes he may have killed another five children around Australia, making him our worst serial child-killer.

O'Neill, Davie says, lived in a number of places where children disappeared suddenly and were never found. Among those missing were Adelaide's three Beaumont children. Nine years after the children's disappearance O'Neill was named as a suspect after his arrest in Tasmania, but told the police he had never been to South Australia. 'But he had,' Davie said. 'He went there frequently, especially between 1965 and 1967 when he drove from Melbourne to Coober Pedy – via Adelaide.' Davie believes the Beaumont children may have been thrown down a mineshaft at Coober Pedy. 'I've heard from several sources that he had boasted he was responsible for the deaths of the Beaumont children.'

In 1984, almost 20 years after the children's disappearance, Bevan Spencer von Einem, 37,

a tall blonde accountant, was sentenced to life imprisonment for the abduction, rape and murder of a 15-year-old boy, Richard Kelvin. Richard was kept alive and drugged for several weeks. Like four other young Adelaide boys whose bodies were found over three years, he had been grotesquely mutilated before and after being murdered. At von Einem's committal proceedings a witness for the prosecution, an accomplice, said he believed von Einem had killed 10 young people, including the Beaumonts. Von Einem had told him, he said, that he had picked up the three children and performed 'brilliant surgery' on them, before dumping their bodies at Moana or Myponga, south of Adelaide.

Did von Einem kill the Beaumonts? Was their killer the urbane Scotch College-educated, James Ryan O'Neill?

What isn't in dispute is that both child killers were men of limitless evil, but it's unlikely now that we will ever know who abducted and, presumably, murdered the children. Four decades after Jane, nine, Arnna, seven and four-year-old Grant Beaumont vanished from Adelaide's Glenelg beach on Australia Day, 1966, their fate is as much a mystery as ever.

On that hot and steamy morning they hopped on a bus for the beach. The Beaumonts lived at suburban Somerton, not far from Glenelg beach, and Jane had promised her mum they'd be back for lunch. Jane was jokingly known within her family circle as 'the little mother', and Nancy Beaumont felt sure her daughter would keep her word. Until the next morning, when Australia woke up to the sickening news that three small children had disappeared from a suburban beach crowded with

Perhaps the most disturbing image in this book, the three innocents: Arnna, seven, Grant, four, and Jane, nine. *Newspix*

holidaymakers, no one had ever considered it risky to send three kids on a bus to the beach without giving it a second thought.

They were last seen with a tall, gaunt-faced young man, a blonde or light brown-haired man in navy blue bathers. (Both von Einem, a blonde, and O'Neill, a handsome, brown-haired man, are tall, and both, in 1966, were young: von Einem was 21, O'Neill just 19.) A number of people said they saw the children with the young man in the navy-blue bathers. One woman said he was dressing the children. This puzzled her, because they seemed old enough to dress themselves. Another said the children were laughing and holding his hand as they walked away from the beach towards their home at around mid-afternoon.

The mystery of the Beaumont children sparked a chain of cruel hoaxes. A clairvoyant, Gerard Croiset, wrote a letter from Holland to the Adelaide *News* claiming he had visions of where the children's bodies could be buried. He had helped solve an axe murder case in Holland, advising police that they would find the axe in a canal, as they did. The Beaumont children were not kidnapped and murdered, he announced. They had suffocated in the collapse of a sandhill. Search parties dug where he said they could be found. Then he came to Australia, this time with a fresh vision: the children had been killed and buried beneath a recently concreted warehouse near the children's school. That 'vision', too, only raised, then dashed, the desperate hopes of Jim and Nancy Beaumont.

In 1968, two letters, one purporting to have been written by Jane to her parents, and the other from the children's alleged 'Guardian' were sent from Dandenong, an outer Melbourne suburb. The Beaumonts travelled to Melbourne to meet the 'Guardian'. The letters were written by a vicious hoaxer.

The agony of Nancy and Jim Beaumont continued over the following decade as cranks, frauds and armchair detectives took it in turns to leave clues to or 'solve' the case. But they never stopped hoping. Nancy once told the Adelaide *News* that her husband wanted to live somewhere else, away from the associations Somerton and Glenelg beach held. She wouldn't go.

'I can't in case the kiddies come home,' she said. 'You see I'm waiting for them to come back here. I never know. Perhaps someone could drop them at the front gate. Wouldn't it be dreadful if I wasn't here.'

Nancy and Jim Beaumont did move, in the end. But of course it never did end for them.

# The Port Arthur massacre

The world's worst spree killer stood in court smirking as he listened to the reading of the 72 charges. At the 50th count, the murder of a mother and her two children, he broke into giggles. 'Then you knew he was mad, bad – and evil as well,' wrote journalist John Hamilton.

But was he mad? And how is it possible, no matter how wicked and how insane, to kill so many men, women and children and never – not then and not now – show the slightest remorse?

The news of the massacre at Port Arthur stunned Australia as no other mass slaughter. On a bright Sunday in sleepy Tassie, one man had shot dead 35 people and wounded and injured another 28. This just didn't happen in our country. Later we'd learn of the monster of the Belanglo State Forest and the sickening killings at Snowtown. And later still we would recoil aghast at the bombings in Bali. But Port Arthur, 1996, represented a moment where, we all knew, part of our innocence was lost. After it, nothing could quite shock us so.

The man who robbed us of that innocence was 27, a loner, tall and insipid with long blonde hair and so pale that he was almost an albino. Supreme Court Justice William Cox said Bryant was a pathetic social misfit. The village idiot who happened to be a millionaire. His motives for the mass murders are still debatable, although it is clear that he wanted to take revenge on the world in general and those he thought had spurned him and crossed his father Maurice, in particular. Bryant's father, his only close friend, had – apparently –

killed himself three years before. The coroner ruled it was suicide. But days before Maurice Bryant's death, in August 1993, Martin Bryant had told Marian Larner, a woman he had known from childhood, 'Dad's missing. He's at the bottom of the dam.' Maurice Bryant's body was found a few days later, face down at the bottom of a dam, Martin's diver's weight-belt tied around his neck.

Martin Bryant had lived in a Victorian mansion near Hobart with its owner, an eccentric toothless old lady, Helen Harvey, who had died in a car crash the year before. Bryant was seriously injured in the crash but there remains some suspicion about his part in that, too. Helen Harvey had left Bryant the house and her share of the George Adams Tattersall's estate worth around $1 million.

Martin Bryant woke to the sound of his alarm clock at 6 a.m., on Sunday 28 April 1996, and prepared for the day ahead. At 9.47 he set the house alarm, left the house with its room full of television sets, its library of bestiality pornography and its collection of 200 teddy bears, got in his yellow Volvo with its surfboard strapped to the roof and drove down the Tasman Peninsula.

The Volvo stopped at the Seascape guesthouse not far from Port Arthur. Inside were the owners. For many years Maurice Bryant had tried to get the owners, David and Sally Martin, to sell him a small piece of land but they had declined. He shot the 72-year-old man and then his 68-year-old wife, smashed her head with a blunt object and mutilated him with the hunting knife.

He drove to Roger and Marian Larner's neighbouring farm and parked inside the gate. Roger Larner walked out to meet him. Larner was wary. Bryant had been harassing Marian Larner for the last three years, ever since she had told the police of his conversation with her about his dad at the bottom of the dam. She had taken out an intervention order. Bryant asked where Marian was and Roger Larner lied and told him she was out. They talked for about 10 minutes and then Bryant said: 'Gotta go. I'll come back later.'

Port Arthur is one minute away in a car. About 20 minutes later the Larners heard gunshots.

In August 2000 Mark 'Chopper' Read was released from Hobart's Risdon jail. He had met Martin Bryant inside. 'I couldn't help myself,' Read told the media. 'I said: "Why did you do it?" And his exact words were, "I don't know. One minute I'm eating my trevally and peas and the next the room is full of dead people."'

Martin Bryant is said to have the intellectual ability of an 11-year-old and the emotional development of a two-year-old. But he is cunning. He knew what he was doing that Sunday afternoon. He had come to kill. In the boot of Bryant's Volvo was a blue sports bag holding an arsenal he kept hidden inside the piano of his house: an AR-15 semi-automatic rifle, an SLR military style semi-automatic rifle, a semi-automatic shotgun, ammunition, two sets of handcuffs, a hunting knife, rope and jerry-cans of petrol.

At Port Arthur he parked and got out.

Port Arthur, in 1996, was one of Australia's premier tourist destinations. Set in an area of stunning natural beauty, it presented a sanitised, but still eerie glimpse into its past: the most feared and loathed penal colony in Van Diemen's Land. Port Arthur, established in 1830 to replace Macquarie Harbour, the brutal and barbaric penal colony, is 150 kilometres from Hobart.

Outside the Broad Arrow Café paramedics treat the wounded. Inside 20 people – men, women and children – lie dead. *Newspix*

One hundred-and-sixty-six years after its foundation the penal settlement that had been the cause of untold misery and suffering was a museum: a tourist magnet displaying the ruins of a Gothic church, the penitentiary, the watchtower, the model hospital, and the Broad Arrow Cafe. Bryant sat there, on the cafe's verandah, and ordered sandwiches and fruit juice and proceeded to have his lunch. There were around 500 people at Port Arthur that Sunday; most had finished lunch and there were 60 or so finishing up at the Broad Arrow. It was 1.30.

Martin Bryant had a conversation with a woman, finished sipping his drink and unzipped the sports bag. He took out the AR-15 and began firing. The first to die were two Malaysian tourists. In the first 15 seconds another 10 died. In the next 75 seconds as he moved through the cafe he killed eight more.

In that minute-and-a-half men and women lived and died performing extraordinary acts of selflessness and bravery. Some tried to disarm the wild-eyed man with the shoulder length blonde hair, spraying the cafe with bullets. Tony Kistan pushed his wife out the cafe door, but rather than follow her, he went back and tried to grapple with the madman. He was shot dead along with his friend, Andrew Mills.

Carolyn Loughton threw her 15-year-old daughter Sarah to the floor and shielded her with her own body. Bryant killed the daughter and wounded the mother.

A retired Melbourne property developer, Robert Elliott, lunged towards Bryant and was shot in the head. He survived. Bryant turned his semi-automatic on the table where Kevin Sharp, down in Tassie from Kilmore with a golfing party, was sitting with his wife Marlene and a friend. Kevin pushed them under the table and was shot dead. Leslie Lever died the same way. Adelaide nurse Jennifer Moors bundled two elderly ladies out of sight and hid with them, soothing them as Bryant shot three people before their eyes and walked on.

Some tried to escape through a back exit but couldn't force a faulty lock and nine died, trapped. Brave Brigid Cook, the cafe's catering supervisor, did get out. She fled from the back door of the kitchen and ran into the car park screaming for people to take cover. At the same time Bryant emerged from the cafe and began firing. Brigid ran across his line of sight but he ignored her as he shot and killed another four. Then he came back for her. He shot her in the right leg but left her alive.

He got into his Volvo and drove along Jetty Road. Nanette Mikac and her daughters, Madeline, two, and Alannah, six, ran towards the car, thinking the driver could take them to safety. When she saw the gun Nanette dropped to her knees and pleaded: 'Please don't hurt my babies.' He shot her and he shot Madeline. Then he stalked Alannah, who had tried to hide behind a large gum tree, and shot her.

He shot four in a BMW, dragged the bodies out and drove the BMW back towards the Seascape guest house.

Sydney lawyer Glenn Pears made the supreme sacrifice. When Bryant stopped at a general store on the way Pears offered himself as a hostage if Bryant spared his friend, Zoe Hall. Bryant agreed, forced Pears into the car boot, and shot and killed Hall. Then he drove back to Seascape where he shot and wounded four people in passing cars.

At Seascape, after an all-night siege and 19 hours after the killings began, he set the building alight. In the inferno his ammunition stockpile exploded with a roar and Brant ran out, fired a shot and ran back into the blaze. Minutes later, at 8 a.m., he meekly

surrendered, lying naked in the foetal position, smouldering skin, burnt in the fire, peeling from his back and buttocks. Inside the blazing guesthouse he left the bodies of Pears, handcuffed to the stairs, and the proprietors, the Martins.

In 2006 Jim Morrison, a former policeman who led the tactical planning at the guesthouse, told the *Sunday Herald Sun* that Bryant had planned to kill many more at Port Arthur. 'He put a lot of planning into what he wanted to carry out and unfortunately it led to the death of 35 people. But he failed in his original mission.' He said Bryant had planned to join and kill 150 others on the

Port Arthur ferry to the Isle of the Dead, the burial ground for the prison's convicts. But he was turned away from the ferry because he had illegally parked his Volvo nearby. Instead, Bryant went to the Broad Arrow cafe. Jim Morrison believes Bryant was bad, but not mad.

Martin Bryant is in Hobart's Risdon jail hospital and will remain there for the remainder of his life. He is certainly unbalanced and, it's said, becoming more and more withdrawn. But for all that, he still has shown no remorse, the small sign of being human.

The smoking ruins of the Seascape guest house, the stage for Bryant's last cowardly killings. He set fire to the building, then ran out to end the siege, lying curled in the foetal position. *Newspix*

# Ivan Milat

In custody, Ivan Milat stares out at us as if defying us to understand how any man could sink to such evil. *Newspix*

The most frightening thing about Ivan Milat is that he's in but his accomplice is out. Ivan Milat, the Belanglo Monster, has been in jail since 1996 and will never be released. But his accomplice – and it seems he had an accomplice in at least some of the murders he committed – is still at large.

The high-profile Sydney lawyer John Marsden, sacked by Milat during his trial, believed Milat's accomplice was a woman. The assistant police commissioner in charge of the investigation said a second person could have been involved, particularly in the last murders. The Crown prosecutor said the Crown was not able to prove that he acted with one or more accomplices, but the trial judge said: 'In my view, it is inevitable that the person [Milat] was not alone in that criminal enterprise.'

In that case at least one more Belanglo Monster is among us: a second man or woman – or more – who took part in the indescribable horror of the murders of seven backpackers in the Belanglo State Forest.

Strictly speaking, of course, the horror can be described in all its gruesome detail. A cursory narration of the killings alone is revolting. And the cruelty – some of the victims were paralysed while they were slowly tortured – and the savagery of, finally, their no doubt longed-for death, is unbearable for most of us even to contemplate. Yet thousands of Australians paid to see *Wolf Creek*, a film with ugly parallels to the killings. Some enjoyed it. (Sydney's *Sun Herald* crime reporter Frank Walker, who covered the case, was not among them. 'I walked out... It sickens me to see these terrible murders played out as sadistic entertainment on the big screen.')

Sexual serial killings were not new to us in the late decades of the last century when the Belanglo Monster was at large. In 1977, with an accomplice, Christopher Worrell, a 23-year-old rapist, killed seven young women outside Truro, north-east of Adelaide. Two years later the city was rocked again by the mutilation and murder of five young men by a 'Family' of paedophiles. Ten years on, in the Mosman area of Sydney, 'the Granny Killer', John Wayne Glover, a 58-year-old father of two girls, brutally murdered six elderly women. In seven weeks in 1993 at Frankston, near Melbourne, a maniac stabbed and killed three women. And the 1999 images of barrels holding the decomposing remains of eight bodies at Snowtown north of Adelaide – victims of a gang of serial killers – will forever repulse. But the mid-'90s backpacker murders in the beautiful and serene Southern Highlands of New South Wales sent a shudder through us unlike any other.

All seven were adventurous, joyful young people in love with life and the promise it held. The peculiar and unforgivable evil of Ivan Milat is, you suspect, that he relished robbing them of that promise.

# 4

# THE LAST WORDS

Ned Kelly, in the dock, 6 November 1880. Asked if he had anything to say before sentence was passed Kelly said, 'It is not that I fear death; I fear it as little as to drink a cup of tea…' It was the beginning of the most famous exchange in Australian legal history. *Australasian Sketcher*

On 29 October 1880 the jury in the trial of Ned Kelly, charged with the murder of Constable Lonigan, reached its verdict. Justice Redmond Barry, who had conducted what lawyers today concede was a deeply flawed trial, asked Kelly if he had anything to say.

Kelly responded: 'Well, it is rather too late for me to speak now, I thought of speaking this morning and all day, but there was little use, and there is little use blaming any one now. Nobody knew about my case except myself, and I wish I had insisted on being allowed to examine the witnesses myself. If I had examined them, I am confident I would have thrown a different light on the case.'

The two had already had exchanges, with Kelly drawing Barry into a debate that had the judge blustering and on the back foot. Finally, however, Barry seemed to have the last word. 'There is unfortunately a class which disregards the evil consequences of crime,' he told Kelly, and went on to list some 'samples of felons' and their 'ignominious deaths'.

The men in this chapter were felons but it's safe to say that none of them would have agreed that their ends were ignominious. Their last words, in most cases – Breaker Morant's for example – were brave; in others defiant; and, in the case of Ben Hall, poignant. Ned Kelly's last words to Sir Redmond Barry at his trial, and finally at the scaffold, were, typically, a blend of all three. The felons are remembered still for their last words. No one remembers what Sir Redmond told Ned Kelly in his last public utterance.

'I have now to pronounce your sentence. You will be taken from here to the place from whence you came, and thence on a day appointed by the Executive Council to a place of execution, and there you will hanged by the neck until you be dead. May the Lord have mercy on your soul.'

Kelly, calmly, replied: 'I will go a little further than that, and say I will see you there, where I go.'

Ned Kelly was hanged in Melbourne on 11 November. Redmond Barry died 12 days later.

# Alexander Pearce

The little blue-eyed Irishman Alexander Pearce was playing a deadly game. A kind of Musical Meals, where, one by one, whenever the music stopped, a man would be killed. And eaten.

Now there was just him and Greenhill. And one of them had to face the music...

Alexander Pearce, 26, had faced death before and survived. He had been sentenced to hang for stealing six pairs of shoes, but instead was transported to Van Diemen's Land where, in 1822, he and seven others escaped the horrific penal settlement at Macquarie Harbour and set out through the bush for Hobart Town. For a week it poured with rain, a heavy, drenching rain, and then it turned to gales and sleet. They could not build a fire and by the ninth day they had eaten their rations. They went another two days before one voiced what they had probably all been thinking: 'I'm so weak I could eat a piece of a man.'

'The next morning there were four of us for a feast,' Pearce said. 'Bob Greenhill was the first who introduced it and he said he had seen the like done before, and that it ate much like pork. Mathers spoke out and said it would be murder; and perhaps then we could not eat it. "I'll warrant you," said Greenhill, "I'll eat the first bit; but you must all lend a hand, so that we'll all be equal in the crime."

'We consulted who should fall and Greenhill said, "Dalton, he volunteered to be a flogger, we will kill him."

'We made a bit of a breakwind with boughs and about three in the morning Dalton was asleep. Then Greenhill struck him on the head with an axe and he never spoke again. Greenhill called Travers and he cut Dalton's throat to bleed him. Then we dragged

Soon after these post-mortem pencil sketches, the head of 'Cannibal' Pearce was cut from the corpse and turned up, decades later, among 1000 skulls in the collection of of an American phrenologist. It is now in the Museum of the University of Pennsylvania.

him away a bit and cut him up.'

That set the pattern and one after another the convicts were murdered – poleaxed mostly, when their guard was down. Finally only Greenhill and Pearce remained.

One to go. They walked apart. When one stopped the other stopped. Greenhill never let go of the axe. Neither man slept. Finally, near dawn one morning Greenhill fell asleep at last. Pearce stealthily slid alongside, slipped the axe from his hand and dispatched him.

On 11 January 1823, the 48th Regiment of troopers surrounded a camp after a tip-off and found Pearce with two outlaws, Davis and Cheetham, both

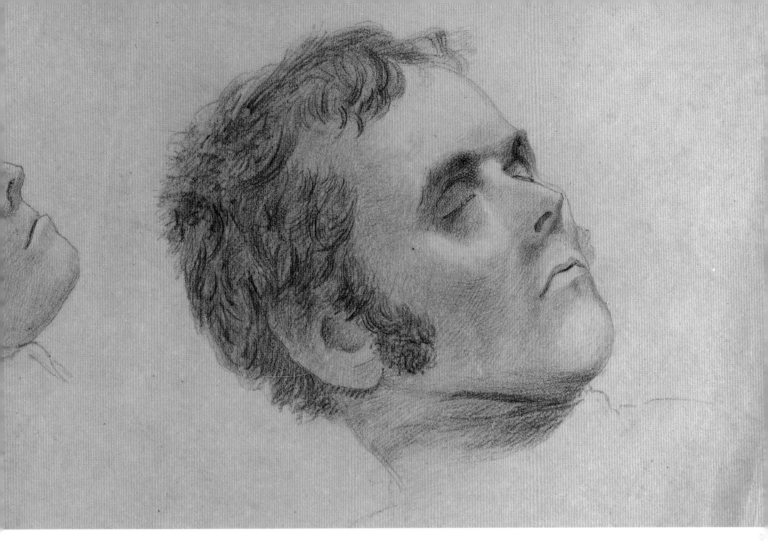

of whom a few weeks later dangled from the Hobart Town gallows. Pearce, the great survivor, didn't join them. He was not tried for bushranging but instead was returned to Macquarie Harbour, where the prisoners lauded him as a hero. More so when Pearce told what had happened.

It was, as it were, a deliciously macabre story but the authorities wouldn't wear it. Pearce was concocting this tale of culinary adventures simply to protect the missing convicts, they said: they were undoubtedly still in hiding but would inevitably be flushed out and suitably punished or simply perish miserably in the bush. In the meantime Pearce was flogged and put in solitary confinement, but now all he had to do was to keep his head down and stay out of trouble while he served the remainder of his seven-year sentence.

He escaped from Macquarie Harbour once more. This time he had only one companion, Thomas Cox, a young Shropshire lad who hero-worshipped 'Cannibal Pearce'. Five days later a schooner cruising down Macquarie Harbour saw a figure on the shore waving to alert them, and rowing ashore they were met by Alexander Pearce. Cox had drowned he said, trying to swim a river. He wanted to surrender. But then he was searched. In one pocket they found human flesh.

On the way to the gallows a guard asked Pearce what drove him to eat another. Pearce replied: 'No man can tell what he will do when driven by hunger.'

But then he said, 'Man's flesh is delicious, far better than fish or pork.'

# Ben Hall

Ben Hall, the most likeable and romantic of all the bushrangers, was riding to Cubbin Bin on Sandy Creek, in the Lachlan district of western New South Wales. His heart was high. He was coming home after being acquitted of being an accessory in a minor hold-up by Frank Gardiner, a charge of which he was almost certainly innocent.

But he had spent a month in detention and now, a free man, he could scarcely wait to be with his wife and baby. He found his home, a rough slab hut, with an earthen floor on a selection of 16,000 acres. But it was burned to the ground and his herd – 600 head of cattle – scattered.

Ben's wife Bridget, too, was gone. She had run off with an ex-policeman, taking their young son Harry with her.

Even the most good-natured man is apt to snap when his wife runs off and his home is burned to the ground. Ben Hall bought a gun and swore vengeance. First he joined Gardiner's gang, then he stole the horse of the man who had charged him: the English baronet in charge of the police at Forbes, the arrogant Sir Frederick Pottinger. Hall believed it was he who had ordered his house burned.

In June 1862, at Mandagery Creek, Ben Hall, Frank Gardiner, Johnny Gilbert and five others pulled red scarves over their noses and rode out from their cover at Eugowra Rocks. Guns in hand they bailed up teamsters driving two bullock wagons loaded with stores for the goldfields and made them turn their wagons to block the road.

Right on time came the Ford & Company mail coach.

John Feagan was driving the four-in-hand coach. Beside him was the guard, Police Sergeant James Condell. Inside the coach were three armed troopers and £14,000 in gold and bank notes on its way from Forbes to Sydney. Feagan acted quickly, braking and trying to wheel his horses when he saw the road block, and then eight men firing in a volley.

Horses reared, Feagan jumped to the ground but Condell, wounded, dropped his rifle and fell as the horses broke free from the overturned coach. Some of Gardiner's men kept the troopers covered while the others lashed the bullion to the coach horses. Then the gang rode off to the safety of their hideout high in the Whoego Mountain. There, while Sir Frederick Pottinger, pursuing a hunch, led his men 450 kilometres south to Hay, they divided the shares.

But then things began to go awry. When one of the gang, Dan Charters, took it into his head to visit his property and came across a party of police he panicked. He wrenched his horse around and rode furiously for the safety of Whoego, the police in pursuit. With them was Billy Dargin, a renowned native tracker and, working on the run, he took them to the summit not long after the gang had fled, leaving behind some of the gold bullion. The gang now went their separate ways. Gardiner and his mistress Kate Brown headed for Queensland. Gilbert took sail

to New Zealand until things quietened down. Ben Hall buried his gold in a place that is still to be discovered and went back to his homestead.

Charters, however, was captured and soon was talking, giving Sir Frederick the names of all but one of the Eugowra gold-robbers. To Pottinger's rage he refused to give up Ben Hall. Nevertheless, Pottinger rode out to arrest Hall, ordered his troopers to once again put the Sandy Creek homestead to the torch and took Hall to Orange where, once again, he was freed for lack of evidence. The charge against another gang member, O'Meally, like Hall's, was dropped for lack of evidence, and two others, Fordyce and Bow, were sentenced to life imprisonment. Henry Manns was hanged.

Hall ranged the Lachlan with Johnny Gilbert and Johnny O'Meally. In three years they raided 21 towns and homesteads – once, at Canowindra, they had occupied the town for three days – bailed up 10 mail coaches, and, when they shot dead two policemen, were outlawed. Now, with a price of a thousand pounds on their heads, they were liable to be shot on sight.

Hall made plans to leave the country. He visited his wife and got her promise that his

Celebrated in folk songs and remembered as the gentleman bushranger, Ben Hall was back in the news in 2007 when relatives called for a fresh inquest into his death, saying that as the Felon Apprehension Act had not yet come into force when Hall was killed, he had been illegally 'assassinated'.

son Harry would get his property and any money he could send from overseas. He never got there. 'Coobong' Mick Connolly, who promised Ben he would see his wishes carried out, is thought to have led the police to him.

On 6 May 1865, Billy Dargin was at the head of a party of six police surrounding Hall's camp. While he slept Dargin slid on his belly through the grass towards him. Then a horse snorted and Hall jumped to his feet. Dargin shot him in the chest.

Hall staggered, clutched the wound, saw Dargin whom he had known all his life, and gasped, 'So it's you, Billy – at last! Shoot me dead, Billy! Don't let the traps take me alive.'

Billy Dargin obliged. The police, out from cover now, joined in, firing volley after volley into Hall's body, 'pierced with bullets and slugs from his feet to the crown of his head'.

Ben Hall died with his boots on and £74 in his pockets. He was 27. With him he carried three revolvers, a gold watch, three gold watch chains and a gold locket holding a miniature portrait of his sister Polly. He was buried the next day.

'Shoot me dead, Billy!'

# Ned Kelly

'It is not that I fear death; I fear it as little as to drink a cup of tea,' Ned Kelly had told Sir Redmond Barry in his famous pre-sentence debate with the man about to condemn him. But when the time came, like all sane men, he showed some emotion. One witness thought he saw a slight shudder as Ned stopped under the rope. But just before he took that final step, he spoke. Journalists at the hanging – Alfred Deakin of the *Age* was among them – differed in their account of what he said. The *Herald* heard him mutter: 'Such is life', something the *Beechworth Advertiser* had quoted him as saying when he learned the hour of his death. The *Argus* reporter believed he said, 'Ah well, I suppose it had to come to this.' And the *Telegraph* had him starting the same sentence but trailing off: 'Ah well, I suppose...'

Of the three, history has preferred Ned's last words to be the first, philosophical comment, 'Such is life.' Commonsense says the *Argus* and the *Telegraph* were probably closer to the truth.

The *Australasian Sketcher* depiction of the execution shows Ned, his arms strapped behind his back and the execution hood ready to be pulled over his face, confronting the hangman, Elijah Upjohn.

It was over very quickly. Ned moved his head to the side to allow Upjohn to adjust the noose, looked up at the skylight as Upjohn dropped the cap, and the hangman sprang back and pulled the lever. The trapdoor slammed open and Ned Kelly dropped. He died instantly.

The last moments of Ned Kelly, accurate in almost every detail, although the artist, Carrington, was not at the hanging. *Australasian Sketcher*

# Harry 'The Breaker' Morant

Just before dawn on 25 February 1902, Harry 'The Breaker' Morant refused the blindfold. He looked down the 18 gun barrels levelled at him by a detachment of Cameron Highlanders and barked: 'Shoot straight you bastards! Don't make a mess of it!'

Morant and his fellow-Australian, P.J. Handcock, faced the firing squad after being found guilty of murder. But was it murder, or were they following orders?

'Breaker' Morant and Handcock had come to South Africa, along with 16,000 other Australians, to fight two Dutch South African republics: the Transvaal and the Orange Free State, the Boers. Morant and Handock joined the Bushveldt Carbineers, an irregular unit fighting a brutal guerrilla war in which both sides committed atrocities. The Boers sometimes wore British khaki uniforms to deceive, had no respect for the white flag of surrender, and dynamited trains. General Kitchener responded in kind, issuing orders to the British – verbal orders – to 'take no prisoners'.

The Carbineers had shot seven prisoners before Morant arrived and when Captain Percy Hunt, his best mate and superior officer, reprimanded him for bringing in prisoners Morant took no notice. Then Hunt led an unsuccessful attack on a farmhouse and was wounded and left behind during the action. The next day they found his naked body battered and mutilated. Morant set out for revenge. His patrol captured a Boer who was using Hunt's trousers as a pillow and Morant ordered him shot.

Morant and three other officers had apparently decided they would follow orders: they would shoot all Boer prisoners. When they shot a Dutch padré who saw the bodies of eight executed Boers – Morant said he believed him to be a spy – Kitchener had the Bushveldt Carbineers officers arrested. 'He had always been the underdog,' A.B. 'Banjo' Paterson wrote in the *Bulletin*, 'and now he was up in the stirrups it went to his head like wine.'

'The Breaker' was a noted horseman, something of a dare-devil, and like Paterson – 'the Banjo' – wrote bush ballads for the *Bulletin*. Paterson's assessment of incidents half a world away may have been a little subjective. Morant himself wanted people to know his side of the story that he had been acting under the Army's direction. '...see the *Bulletin* people in Sydney town and tell 'em all the facts,' he wrote to a friend. The court martial, meantime, heard all the facts and sentenced Morant and Handcock to death. A third officer, Witton, got life imprisonment and was freed within three years.

Was the sentence just? Geoffrey Robertson, Australia's noted barrister and human rights advocate, gave Nick Bleszynski, author of *Shoot Straight You Bastards,* this legal opinion: 'Morant's trial was a particularly pernicious example of using legal proceedings against lower ranks as a means of covering up the guilt of senior officers and of Kitchener himself, who gave or approved their unlawful "shoot to kill" order. Morant may have been all too happy to obey it, of course, in which case he deserved some punishment. But it was wrong to use him as a scapegoat for an unlawful policy. I regard the convictions of Morant and Handcock as unsafe.'

Edward Woodward as Breaker Morant in Bruce Beresford's successful 1980 film. Morant is portrayed as a victim of Kitchener's wish to conciliate the Boers with the lives of Morant and two others.

Bruce Beresford's 1979 film, *Breaker Morant*, starring Edward Woodward as Morant, Bryan Brown as Handcock and Jack Thompson as counsel for the defence, took the same view.

The *Bulletin* was cynical: 'He died game. That is the most charitable epitaph which a truthful acquaintance can put over the tomb of "The Breaker" – assuming that his acts were, as alleged, the result of cruelty, and not the result of "orders" which he had no alternative but to obey. It may be said of him as of many another of his kind: There was nothing in his life that so befitted him

Fred Lowry (right) whose last words gave the *Bulletin* its epitaph for Breaker Morant (left): 'He died game'.

as his way of going out of it; and that in his case, as in the case of so many others, that graceful exit will atone in many minds for sorry stumblings whilst playing his little part on the world's stage.

'...he kept to the very last his utter incapacity to appreciate the fact that he had done wrong. Picturing himself as a patriotic Robin Hood, as an empire-builder sacrificed for his zeal, "The Breaker" wrote in jail these verses...'

# Fred Lowry

On New Year's Day 1863, after a bungled hold-up when he shot and wounded a man, Fred Lowry was arrested and imprisoned at Bathurst jail. Six weeks later, while the exercise yard sentry dozed, a low whistle alerted Lowry to a crowbar that was sailing over the wall. With a knot of prisoners to cover him, lanky, gawky Fred dug a hole in the wall

big enough for him and seven others to wriggle through. On 13 July, with Larry Cummins and Jack Foley, he rode up to the Mudgee Mail coach as it groaned up the Big Hill in the Blue Mountains.

'Bail up!'

Quaking within was Henry Kater, an accountant at the Mudgee branch of the Australian Joint Stock Bank, carrying a bag bulging with bank notes worth £5,700 ($11,400) The proceeds from the Mudgee Mail hold-up could have allowed Fred and his men to retire but the reward posted for him – £500 – was enough for an informer to turn him in. On Saturday 29 August the police got a tip-off that Lowry and Larry Cummins were at Fardy's Limerick Races pub at Cooks Vale Creek, 20 kilometres from Goulburn. Lowry and Cummins were snoring peaceably in the room opening onto the front verandah when, at daybreak, Senior Sergeant Stephenson banged on their door: 'Police! Come out and surrender!'

In reply a bullet smashed through the door and seconds later Lowry came out, a revolver in each hand, bellowing, 'I'm Lowry! Come on, I'll fight you fair!' His first shot hit Stephenson's revolver, the second whistled through his tunic. Stephenson, simultaneously, got off two shots. The second hit Lowry in the throat.

Fred Lowry took 24 hours to die. His last words, a request to the priest attending him, went almost immediately into the language.

'Tell 'em I died game.'

# 5

# THE INDIVIDUALISTS

Arthur Orton was no fool. Near illiterate, coarse and uncouth, he was also intelligent and quick. His outrageous confidence trick, passing himself off as a lost, slim English aristocrat, was based on his ability to start a conversation and then get the other person talking. He retained what he was told and repeated it to the next person, in turn gathering more information.

He was a grossly unattractive man. She was the head of one of England's most illustrious families, the ninth richest in the land. The two had never met. Yet when Arthur Orton the oafish butcher from Back o' Burke arrived in Paris in 1867 to meet the immensely wealthy dowager widow of the Baronet Sir Roger Tichborne, she 'recognised' him as her long lost son Roger and settled an annual allowance on him of £1000.

One thousand pounds a year was then a tidy sum. Labourers in Britain at the time got around £30 a year. But it was just a fraction of the wealth that came with the family's hereditary title. And Arthur Orton wanted to get his hands on that hereditary title.

The legal battle he instigated became one of the most controversial and comical in British legal history. It had half the population of the British Isles and Australia – 'the lower class' – fervently convinced that this fat uncouth man was indeed the man he claimed to be, the aristocratic Roger Tichborne. And it had the other half outraged at the idea that a member of the aristocracy could so much as conceive of being a butcher in Wagga Wagga, Australia. All that was debatable. The real question was not whether Arthur Orton was Roger Tichborne, nor how he managed to convince even one solitary soul that he was, but how on earth he convinced himself that he could get away with it.

Arthur Orton is one in a long line of Australians whose belief in themselves is so iron-clad that the world marvels. Germaine Greer is extremely intelligent, but not a genius. She succeeds because she is sure that she is an intellectual giant and that we all wait on her words. Shane Warne, perhaps the greatest bowler of all time, succeeded because of his certainty that he could dismiss any batsman, swing a Test any time... and no perhaps. Annette Kellerman was totally unfettered by timidity and for that reason derided the Hollywood biopic based on her life. Our next individualist? Could she be a kid in khaki, seemingly without fear, charismatic, and full of boundless belief: a little girl called... Bindi?

# Annette Kellerman

Annette Kellerman was the most famous Australian of her day. Apart from being our first movie star and a swimmer who could beat the best women – and some of the best men – in the world, she was a pioneer of the women's movement, perhaps 70 years ahead of her time. Above all she was a propagandist for the joys of life: 'If only you could know what it is to walk and work and play and feel every inch of you rejoicing in glorious buoyant life.' A vegetarian, her attitudes to health and beauty anticipated today's attitudes and she was a forthright advocate for the cause of women left at home with children.

Along the way she invented the classic black one-piece swimsuit and was pronounced The World's Perfect Woman.

Annette Kellerman was born in Marrickville, Sydney, in 1886. Crippled by poliomyelitis as a child, she was encouraged to take up swimming to strengthen her legs. She swam, as the cliche has it, like a fish: by the time she was 16, she was swimming among them twice daily at the Melbourne Aquarium and getting paid the considerable sum of £5 a week to do so.

Annette's father took her to London. They were going to make their fortune. She was a flop. No one showed the least interest in a girl from the Antipodes who could swim. Then, as a publicity stunt, she swam 27 kilometres up the Thames River and the press and promoters from all over Europe scrambled. The Prince of Wales, a man famously fascinated by the female form, asked her to give an exhibition of her swimming at the London Bath Club. Kellerman agreed – provided she could wear the one-piece costume she had designed and made.

She was still a teenager, vibrant, fresh and attractive, and the swimsuit – she stitched black stockings into a boy's costume – revealed her slim, athletic body. The middle class was scandalised but the future king, whose mistresses included Lily Langtry and almost all the great courtesans of France, was delighted. Annette's fame was assured, and women's swimwear, which until then had consisted of smocks and stockings designed to obscure the female form, were about to change forever.

She did a brief season at the London Hippodrome – by now she had a vaudeville act that consisted of aquatic feats and was later to encompass acrobatics, wire walking, singing and ballet dancing before mirrors – and later that year went to America.

She was a sensation. For a huge fee, $1250 a week, the 20-year-old 'Australian Mermaid' swam in a glass tank at the White City fairgrounds in Chicago, then Boston and New York. A year later she won priceless press coverage when she was arrested on Boston beach – where else? – for wearing a brief one-piece swimsuit. She won the landmark case and changed the design of women's swimsuits irrevocably.

In 1912, inevitably, Annette Kellerman went to Hollywood.

She starred in several films. In one, she had to dive 28 metres from a cliff top into the sea, a world record for a woman. In *Daughter of the Gods*, the first film with a $1 million budget, she had to dive 19 metres into a pool filled with crocodiles. When

Kellerman as Anita, fully clothed, in a scene from *Daughter of the Gods*. In other scenes she wore much less. 'Anita, after wandering round like the sewing machine that doesn't have a stitch on, is captured and taken to the Sultan's harem,' one reviewer jovially noted.

a Harvard professor, after a much-publicised search, announced that Annette's measurements made her 'the perfect woman' she became one of the world's best-known performers, in such demand from rival studios and theatrical promoters that she could afford to turn down a five-picture deal with 20th Century Fox.

Three decades later she was the subject of a – very loosely based – Hollywood bio-pic, *The Million Dollar Mermaid*, with Esther Williams. Although a consultant on the movie, she didn't care for it, calling it 'namby pamby'.

She gave lecture tours on health and beauty and wrote books on the subject before she returned to Australia in 1970 to live on the Gold Coast where, on 6 November 1975, just as the women of the world were catching up with her, Annette Kellerman died.

Annette Kellerman on the French Riviera in the one-piece swimsuit she introduced to the world.

# Hugh D. McIntosh

'Huge Deal' McIntosh had gone to a lot of trouble and not a little expense to build the world's biggest outdoor stadium. He built it to stage the world heavyweight title fight. There were 20,000 people seated in it this steamy Boxing Day morning and there were thousands more outside begging to get in and now, with just minutes to go, one of the fighters, the formidable Jack Johnson, was trying to squeeze another £500 from him.

Johnson had sent the message out to 'Huge Deal': he wouldn't leave his dressing room until he got more money.

McIntosh was a small man. But he was every bit as tough as Johnson. And with him he had his Persuader. He burst into Johnson's dressing room, aimed the revolver and bellowed: 'Get into the ring you black bastard or you'll be carried in on a stretcher!'

It wasn't the first time McIntosh had pulled a gun on Johnson. Soon after they met, Johnson, not liking the fact that the promoter was friendly with Tommy Burns, the man he was to fight, warned 'Huge Deal': 'If any dirty sucker double-crosses me I'll knock him cold.' McIntosh replied by pulling his revolver and telling Johnson, 'If you ever lift your hand to me I'll blow your black head off your body. They'll identify you by your clothes.'

Hugh D. McIntosh was tough, but he got things done. He was a millionaire by the time he was 25 and by the time he was 45 he was possibly the richest man in Australia. By the time he was 55 he was bankrupt. He made several near stabs at regaining his fortune but he died broke in London aged 65. Friends passed the hat for his funeral expenses.

The first, perhaps the most audacious, and unquestionably the most interesting of Australia's international entrepreneurs, 'Huge Deal' McIntosh didn't die wondering. He started as a pie boy, went on to mix with Winston Churchill, Nellie Melba, William Rockefeller and H.G. Wells, bedded a long line of beautiful women and died a virtual pauper.

But along the way he had lived a life that was outrageously glamorous, a fantasy made real and composed of endless affairs with beautiful women; a fleet of Pierce-Arrow limousines and the world's fastest cars; a stately home in England and a Sydney dream mansion; newspapers; a chain of theatres and the friendship of the rich and famous. McIntosh, said journalist John Hetherington, was 'a blend of charlatan, genius, dreamer and bandit, an unrepentant buccaneer'.

Hugh Donald McIntosh was born in Sydney's tough inner suburban Surry Hills, on 10 September 1876, the son of a private in the 42nd Highlanders, the Black Watch. His father went to India soon after the Mutiny of 1857 and, invalided from the army, came to Sydney 10 years later. He died when his son was four and the boy's mother, Margaret, brought him up to study and respect the lives of the great men so that he could emulate their methods.

Young Hugh did so and throughout his life he sought and gained the friendship and confidence of scores of famous men and women.

He caused Winston Churchill to wince when they shook hands. He took Charlie Chaplin to church. He told H.G. Wells he'd read none of his books. He danced the foxtrot with Anna Pavlova, who couldn't dance the foxtrot. He manipulated Australian politicians from Billy Hughes to Jack Lang. He was on first name terms with Rockefeller, Melba, Kreisler, Valentino, Ziegfeld and the great boxers, cyclists and cricketers of his day – and he tried to seduce his wife-to-be with a ring from Tutankamen's tomb. The giants of politics, literature, finance, the arts and sport knew Huge Deal McIntosh and many admired him.

His own road to success began when he was seven, he used to say. 'One day when my mother was baking scones I asked her casually if I might go to Adelaide with a man I knew. Not taking me seriously she said, "Yes, go wherever you like." I went. Strange as it may seem, it is the truth that I walked out of the house, told my friend that I had my mother's permission and landed in Adelaide a few days later.'

McIntosh's 'friend', he said, was a 'travelling jeweller' and he was his apprentice. More likely the man was a tinker, a near gypsy, but they parted soon after and the boy found himself picking ore from quartz at Broken Hill.

He earned 30 shillings ($3) a week and regularly sent some of it home to his mother. He hated the work and left after a year. At 12 he was back in Sydney, hanging around Larry Foley's gymnasium in George Street, the site of today's Strand.

For a time he worked in a doctor's surgery before once again roaming, picking up jobs as a farm labourer, an engine driver, tar boy in a shearing shed, baker's boy, stagehand, chorus boy and finally, pie salesman. He was so successful at this quintessential Australian business endeavour that he soon had a chain of pie sellers working for him at sports grounds, beaches, racecourses, and the open air boxing rings that were plentiful around the suburbs.

He married Marion Backhouse, a pretty teacher of painting, when they were both 21, and remained married to and fond of her despite years of serial infidelity until his death, 44 years later.

Hugh D. McIntosh won his nickname, Huge Deal McIntosh, in 1908 when the artist Lionel Lindsay, like his more famous brother, Norman, a close friend of McIntosh, heard, 'On a tram one day two roughs... discussing the coming [Burns–Johnson] fight and I heard one apparently mystified moron say, "Ai, Bill, oo is this Huge D. McIntosh?"'

In between the time of his marriage and the Burns–Johnson fight McIntosh had become an entrepreneur in a number of catering, sporting and theatrical ventures, most of them successful. At 36 he paid £100,000 for Rickards' Tivoli Theatre circuit in Sydney, Adelaide and Melbourne, a

company that brought to Australia such stars as W.C. Fields, then a silent comedian and the world's greatest juggler; the Cockney comic singer Marie Lloyd; and the escapologist Harry Houdini.

The Tivoli circuit gave him money and a plentiful supply of chorus girls and leading ladies, but it was the world heavyweight championship fight at Rushcutters Bay on Boxing Day 1909 that was to catapult Hugh D. McIntosh into international fame and a considerable fortune.

The Burns–Johnson fight grossed almost twice the previous world record gate: £13,200, which McIntosh had established at the same stadium a few months before. But those gate takings were just the beginning. McIntosh was decades ahead in his marketing techniques, and his understanding of what only recently has come to be called 'add ons'.

He hired a cinematographer who delivered a film of the bout. It cost McIntosh £1500 to produce and only three days later he had it screening around the country. He netted £2000 from training exhibitions before the fight, sold 10,000 postcards and souvenir programs, and, after the bout, netted more from boxing exhibitions by both men on the Tivoli theatre circuit.

He took the film of the fight to London. The *Sporting Life* reported, 'The increase in his treasury is rolling at the rate of £1000 a week... £50,000

should be added to the bank account. Think of it, ye opponents of boxing – £77,000 profit from one world's championship contest!'

He seemed unstoppable, an awesome, dynamic man who had a genius for making millions. Here are two descriptions of McIntosh, written around 1913 by journalists on both sides of the Atlantic. Don't bother to try to Spot the Difference. In essence each paints a remarkably similar, almost fawning, portrait of a determined, deceptive Australian whom people were prone to underestimate.

'In appearance he is the personification of the hustler,' *Punch*, the London magazine said. 'Thick-set and muscular, a little below medium size, with the broad shoulders, broad back and the set figure of the physically strong man, he has the face of a fighter – strong-jawed with a mouth like a steel trap. Black, close-cropped hair, black eyebrows, a close-clipped black moustache, a tanned face and piercing black eyes complete the make-up of a man who positively bristles with energy and nervous force. There is no doubt about the man. He is not arrayed in sheep's clothing.

'Part of his strength lies in the fact that those with whom he deals invariably underrate him. He is too bluff, too openly and frankly compelling; but those who underrate him inevitably wake up afterwards to the unpleasant consciousness that he has gone straight on over them, and that they have been badly beaten.'

So what went wrong?

Two decades later, Sydney *Truth*, encapsulating the rise and fall of McIntosh said, 'What days they were! There was money to burn – and Hugh Donald McIntosh, who is now to face the Bankruptcy Court, burnt it.

'Champagne suppers, elegant affairs of oysters, lobsters, grilled chicken and the rest were turned on to celebrate anything and everything. Glittering girls, laughter, and maybe a headache or two afterwards.

'Oh, yes, Hughie, he was a great host! They were all tossed into the pot and Hugh D. McIntosh made merry as zealously as he made money... from pieman, promoter of pugs and presenter of pretty girls he became a politician, the Honourable Hugh Donald McIntosh, MLC... He saw fresh fields to conquer, and blossomed out as a newspaper magnate, proprietor of the Sydney *Sunday Times*...

'He hied him to England and the life of majesty in the late Earl Kitchener's elaborate home down in Kent. However such places need money to keep up. The *Times* was going broke, the Tivoli had long before been leased to other hands, the bottom had fallen out of the boxing business, and there was little else left.'

That, basically, was what went wrong. It had been a roller coaster ride but now, in 1932, it was over.

McIntosh sued *Truth* for libel. The jury deliberated for three days and found in his favour. They awarded him one farthing's damages – a quarter of a penny. And he was ordered to pay *Truth*'s costs, £700. He was finished, but still he wouldn't lie down. The journalist John Hetherington met him in London in 1935.

'I called to see him at the Royal Automobile Club. He was a shortish, burly man, with a bullet head growing bald in front, powerful shoulders, swinging gait and combative jaw. His brown suit was shabby. He was an undischarged bankrupt: his estate had been compulsorily sequestered some three years earlier, and his liabilities were only a fraction below £300,000. If this load of debt weighed on his mind, I was never aware of the fact. He was 58, yet he pulsed with all the adventurous ambition of youth, forever looking not backward, at his recently shattered past, but forward to a shining future.

'He remained aggressive, unpredictable, and irrepressible. He was bidden one day to lunch with a London actress whom he had had a tempestuous love affair with some years earlier. Her summons had directed him to meet her reigning lover in Piccadilly Circus and await her arrival. The two men were chatting on the pavement when they were hailed by a third man – the very man who had supplanted McIntosh in the actress's capricious favour, only to be supplanted himself, in his turn, by McIntosh's companion. McIntosh surveyed the others quizzically.

'"You know," he said, "all we need is one more and we'll have a quorum."'

# Percy Grainger

**M**rs Rose Grainger, the widow of the distinguished architect and the mother of the world renowned pianist, stepped out of the window of the Manhattan artists' management agency 18 storeys up. She had been ill for years but the letter she left behind to her son Percy – one of thousands she wrote to him and he to her – showed that the reason she had taken her life lay in the dark rumours that had begun to circulate: that mother and son were lovers.

My dear son,
...You must tell the truth, that in spite of everything I said – I have never for one moment loved you wrongly – or you me – not for one moment or thought of doing so. The whole thing has driven me insane and I have accused myself of something I have never thought of. You and I have never loved one another anything but purely and right. No one will believe me – but it is the real truth as you know.

Every day gets worse. I am an idiot and no one seems to realise it. I am so sorry – I have loved you and so many others so dearly.

*Your poor insane mother*

You have tried so hard to be all that is noble – but your mad side has ruined us dear. God knows the truth – man will not believe the truth I am writing.

Percy Grainger and his mother Rose had an intense relationship. They wrote each other thousands of letters but this last letter to him shows that the speculation that had grown about their relationship had unbalanced her. Rose Grainger was wrong when she said Percy had a mad side: he was eccentric by any standards, certainly, and this and the stories spread by Rose's death may be why, more than 80 years on, the memory of Australia's most eminent composer and one of our greatest pianists is not more honoured.

Everything about Percy Grainger was, most right thinking folk agreed, distinctly odd. He was short, only 160 cm. But to add to that there was his vivid orange hair. Percy wore it brushed high so

The many faces of Percy Grainger.

that from tip to toe he measured around 180 cm. His bizarre clothes and his decidedly different slew on things can be seen in the Percy Grainger Museum at Melbourne University. Percy himself designed it, paid for it and even had a hand in its construction. There are extraordinary clothes he designed for himself, his mother's clothes, pubic hair and thousands of letters, books, tapes, recordings and sheet music. There are pianos, an early Edison phonograph and his unique free-form music machines, devices made from found objects like brown paper rolls, valves, pulleys, oscillators.

Percy's wish for his skeleton to be exhibited in the Grainger Museum was not granted but there are other skeletons from a closet he kept closed until after his death: his large collection of whips. Narrow, bamboo-handled whips with a variety of lashes in different sizes and weights according to which part of the body Percy wanted to whip or be whipped are on display alongside a brown paper envelope on which Percy had scrawled: 'Not to be opened until 10 years after my death' and in which he described his love of the whip.

Percy's obsession probably began while he was just 13, around 1895, when his mother's health began collapsing with the onset of syphilis. She had contracted the disease from her husband John, a brilliant Adelaide architect who designed many fine public buildings around Australia. John and Rose Grainger came to Melbourne for him to supervise the building of Princes Bridge, which he designed, and George Percy Grainger was born, at the couple's upper-class seaside home in Brighton in 1882.

The marriage was unhappy, and by the time Percy was five or six Rose's syphilis had emerged. When her husband came home amorously inclined Rose would take to him with a whip and this may be the root of Percy's fascination with 'flagellantism'.

The couple separated in 1890. John Grainger became an alcoholic, supported for many years, like his wife and half a dozen others, by Percy. By the time he was 10 his mother had launched Percy as a child prodigy, taking him to London and then to Frankfurt, where she supported them both by giving English lessons. There she began suffering the manifestations of syphilis. Its shadow, and her fear of poverty, preoccupied her but her emotional health was linked to the relationship she had with her son. In turn, he was bound to her. The need to support his parents and others kept Percy on the concert hall circuit when he should have been free to compose.

Rose's death was softened when he met Ella Ström. They married before 22,000 at the Hollywood Bowl in 1928. In his last year, 1961, Percy wrote to her, 'My own heart's dearest Ella... I consider it a miracle of good luck that we met and wedded. I am so endlessly thankful to my darling wife.'

Percy Grainger's amazing Technicolor terry-towelling outfit at the Grainger Museum in Melbourne, and (right) modelled by its designer. Percy travelled with 30 kilos of music sheets, but took only two shirts for a three-month tour: 'I don't even have to iron the shirts – they don't show from the stage, you know'.

# Germaine Greer

On 23 April 2000, Germaine Greer was overdue at a dinner party. Worried guests went to her Essex farmhouse and found her lying on the floor, bound and distressed. A 19-year-old girl was clinging to her legs and repeatedly crying, 'Mummy! Mummy!'

The teenager, who had been obsessed with Germaine – her first name is usually enough, there is only one Germaine – had broken in, tied her and gone on a rampage, ripping the telephone from the wall and smashing anything within reach with a poker. It was a terrifying ordeal. Yet Germaine held a doorstep media conference in which she said, 'I am not angry, I am not upset, I am not hurt. I am fine. I haven't lost my sense of humour. I am not the victim here. Ever since I published *The Female Eunuch* there's been an off-chance that some nutter is going to pick me off, judging by the hostility in the letters.'

Germaine didn't say, but she surely realised, that the teenage girl clinging to her and shouting, 'Mummy! Mummy!' was a reflection of herself. All her life Germaine has been obsessed with her mother Peggy, and the love she feels both her parents denied her. And for most of her life, it seems, Germaine has been on the rampage, shrilly demanding we pay attention, give her that love.

Millions did give her that attention, and many still give her their love. For them, Germaine Greer is a role model, a woman who changed their lives. Some divide their lives into two sections: BG, Before Germaine, and AG, After Germaine. She has been named one of the 100 most influential people of the 20th century. And though she has made an art form of outrage, performed the most

bewildering 180 degree philosophical turns, and enraged men and women internationally, Germaine Greer has earned this respect. A unique and dynamic woman, 180 cm tall while still a teenager, attractive and vivacious, indomitable, she is certainly larger than life. Christine Wallace, her unauthorised biographer, a woman Germaine called a dung-beetle, wrote: 'This is the key to why she has been an inspiration to so many other women. She has never surrendered her sovereignty. Germaine Greer never was tamed.'

All her life Germaine Greer has been a wild one. Now, as she faces her oncoming 70s, though their impact is markedly lower and they no longer come as a surprise, the shockwaves still regularly reverberate. So many of her pronouncements seem calculated to offend and uttered with a headline in mind.

'It is true that men use the threat of physical force, usually histrionically, to silence nagging wives: but it is almost always a sham. It is actually a game of nerves, and can be turned aside fairly easily,' she wrote to the rage of millions married to brutal bullies. Most women were fascinated by violence; 'they act as spectators at fights, and dig the scenes of violence in pubs and dance-halls. Much goading of men is actually the female need for the thrill of violence.'

On the other hand, women could be serene instruments against violence. In 2002, she called on the women of Australia to wear veils in silent protest against war in Iraq. 'Imagine if Australia became a sea of black veils... it would be a protest that would be undeniable. When I was a young hippy I thought marching naked would be a strong protest but I don't think it would be as effective now. But if every woman were veiled, it would be very disturbing, at least to the clothing industry.'

The views of *The Female Eunuch*'s author on Middle Eastern black veils, however, paled in comparison to her stance on the region's practice of female castration – clitoridectomy. She likened it to the Western world's cosmetic surgery. Unreconstructed feminists and male chauvinist pigs alike were appalled.

In 2003, aged 64, she agreed with Andrew Denton on *Enough Rope* that she was attracted to boys – and their 'semen that runs like tap water'. Germaine turned to the audience and said, 'That's not such a bad idea, is it, girls?' She got faint laughter in return. Germaine was plugging *The Beautiful Boy*, a coffee-table book, with 200 photographs, drooled the *Guardian*, of 'succulent teenage male beauty'. The *Guardian* then went on to have it both ways, saying that Greer had reinvented herself as 'a middle-aged pederast'.

'If there's a taboo left, she'll break it,' Miranda Devine wrote in the *Daily Telegraph*. 'And since one of the few remaining taboos in Western liberal democracies is pedophilia, that's the arena she's most recently entered.'

In *Whitefella Jump Up: the Shortest Way to Nationhood*, she argued that we should become a republic, the Aboriginal Republic of Australia.

'I live in an Aboriginal country,' she told Jana Wendt. (In fact, of course, she lives in Essex, England.) 'I was born in an Aboriginal country, I'm third generation born in an Aboriginal country. If I was saying that about France, it would be understood that I was French. If I say it about Australia, could it be understood that I'm Aboriginal?'

So, Jana asked, 'You're suggesting that we reinvent ourselves as a nation of 20 million people, for the sake of 400,000 Aboriginal inhabitants?'

'No, no, I didn't say that we'd do it for them. In fact,

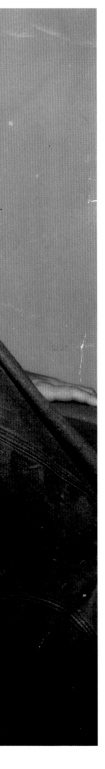

they may be extremely disobliged by the whole idea.'

'So we're doing it for us?'

'Ourselves, we're the people who need to do it.'

In 2005, by now to the surprise of only Greer True Believers, Germaine agreed to be one of eight contestants in the British reality show, *Celebrity Big Brother*. The Mistress of Surprise had previously said that the show was 'as civilised as looking through the keyhole in your teenager's bedroom door'. To absolutely no one's surprise, after five days inside the *Big Brother* house, she walked out. It was a grubby, dirty environment, she said, the show's producers were bullies, and – the horror, the horror! – some of her fellow housemates were publicity seekers.

And there was the humiliation of her fellow contestants. 'What I wouldn't do is be drawn into complicity with the degradation and humiliation of others who I consider, rightly or wrongly, to be weaker than myself.' She was then drawn out on some of her female *Big Brother* housemates.

'Brigitte... Damn right I don't like her or her habit of grabbing her store-bought breasts, banging them together like cymbals and shouting "Hot diggity!" at the top of her lungs, by way of signifying that she is having a good time. At no time did Brigitte ever display the least respect for me, not as a woman, an older woman or even a human being.

'The guys were different. Kenzie had been afraid that he would be the odd one out in the house because he was only 19; with his sweetness, simplicity, mental suppleness and capacity for fun, he'd never be the odd one out anywhere. The difficulty with Kenzie was to get enough of him. Unlike Lisa and Brigitte he seldom took centre stage. When he did, unlike them he had something to say.'

Women can make Germaine Greer, the female

misogynist, as she has been dubbed, very angry. In the '90s she railed against Suzanne Moore, a feminist journalist: 'So much lipstick must rot the brain... hair birds-nested all over the place, f----me shoes and three fat layers of cleavage.'

The Genius of the U-Turn, Germaine, who once preached eroticism and set about her numerous seductions with predatory fervour, was now, in her 50s, espousing celibacy and steaming with fury because a younger woman was wearing shoes that invited copulation. The woman who sang the song of sexual liberation – who told of her experiences with lesbian sex, abortion, rape and pornography; the woman who posed nude for the underground magazines *Oz* and *Suck*, who described the joy of being a rock super groupie and who warned against 'the bourgeois perversion of motherhood' – confounded her remaining disciples by announcing, in 1999 in *The Whole Woman*, that 'we were sold the lie of the sexual revolution'.

Germaine Greer has mellowed.

Reviewing *The Whole Woman*, Midge Dector wrote, 'It is as if the author is at long last desperate to feel some genuine love and respect for women. This eagerness, to be sure, can be signalled in strange ways. She will not, for instance, bring herself to oppose female genital mutilation, since in her view (insofar as one can actually make sense of her view) female circumcision and other like horrors are something frequently practised and always approved by women themselves.

'Nor can she bring herself to endorse freedom of abortion, on the grounds that abortions, too, turn out to be means for men to cause suffering to women. But being no great admirer of children, as well as a rather pious leftist, she cannot at the same time endorse the pro-life position. So, in a tone suggesting she has found a wholly satisfying new position, she declares her commitment to... "women's choice".'

Andrew Denton asked her in 2004, 'Germaine what wisdom do you think you've gained from life?'

She told him: 'I think one thing I did learn is that... happiness is a positive achievement, that it won't be given to you, it can't be granted you by anybody else. You have to actually work at being a happy person. And that was hard for me to learn because I was a sort of haunted, doomed hippie youth and to just decide that all my grandstanding and self-dramatisation that you do when you're young was a waste of energy, and that to be depressed is completely pointless.

'Because I am subject to depressions and I have my own way of dealing with them – I fast and stay out of bed, really, until I feel as though I'm in control again, but it's a risky procedure. Not everybody can do that. But it seems to me that happiness is actually a kind of self-discipline and it's just more useful to be... to work at being... not contented, because your discontent is what drives you, but... Well, principally, I think happiness comes from being unselfconscious – just forgetting about yourself. It's the most important thing you can do. You just become a pair of eyes. And if you're really looking, then there's endless astonishment and delight to be had.

'This is the most wonderful, wonderful world. I love it. And I think it's so funny that I should decide that I really, really love it when I'm getting to the point where I'm probably going to have to leave it, you know? I've probably got my terminal disease already... and I've just figured out how to live on this planet!'

As Steve Irwin might have said: Crikey!

# Shane Warne

'**I** looked up and saw this chubby cheeky bloke with blond spiked hair,' Terry Jenner, the Australian Test spin bowler of the 1970s, wrote in his book, *TJ Over the Top*. "What do you want me to do?" he asked.

'"Just bowl me a leg break."

'Without any real warm-up he bowled this leg break which curved half a metre and spun just as far! It was seemingly effortless, yet a magnificent delivery.

'"&%#@ me," I said to myself. "What have we got here?"'

What we have here – it goes without saying – is Shane Warne, one of *Wisden*'s five cricketers of the 20th century, perhaps the greatest bowler cricket has known and certainly the supreme spin bowler. The man who has taken more Test wickets and turned the course of more Test matches than any other. The man who has made more headlines than Bradman, Lillee and the entire current Australian XI and the 12th man put together. Too many headlines, alas, along the lines of the *London Daily Mirror*'s: 'Shame Warne. Married cricket legend harasses a mum for sex with obscene phone calls.'

From 20 metres Shane Warne can hit a 50 cent piece at 100 kilometres an hour but off the pitch he can't seem to stay on the straight and narrow. One of the boys, he seems recklessly determined not to grow up. It is an attitude that has cost him dearly.

'At the end of the day, it's cost me probably... a chance to captain Australia,' he told Jana Wendt in the *Bulletin*. '...my marriage is breaking down, we're getting a divorce. It's cost me all that and it's cost me a sponsorship. It's cost me lots of stuff. But

Mark Knight's spin on Warnie. In the way of the great cartoonists, Knight's line triggers immediate laughter.

I don't sit here and think every day about "why did I do this?" I don't think like that... It's done and the more you harp on it, the more you whinge about it... the more it stiffs with your head, the more it plays on your mind and the more it affects your general life, everyday life... It affects absolutely everything... What can I do about it? Sit here and cry and whinge?'

The tragedy is, Shane Warne brings so much happiness to so many Australian men. (Women rarely admit to liking Warney.) On the field he is sublime, the magician who rediscovered the black art of leg spin bowling, thought, until he came along, to have gone the way of the dodo. Watching Warne bowl is bliss. Simplicity itself. He grips the ball, turns, takes a few steps and rips it

down, fizzing, curving, jumping or shooting low, staying straight or breaking almost at right angles: with Warne you never know. And, time and again, his baffling ball – take your pick from the zooter, the flipper, the drifter, the topspinner, the wrong 'un – takes wickets at the psychological moment: unexpected, just when the game seems to be getting away from Australia, or so anticipated that you would put money on it.

And best of all, he saves his best for the big stage.

Warne's most famous ball, the Ball of the Century, the Wonder Ball, That Ball, as it has become variously known, typically came at the perfect psychological moment: the very first ball he bowled in a Test against England. Paul Barry in *Spun Out. The Shane Warne Story*, describes it:

'The bare facts of it are that at 3.06 p.m., on 4 June 1993, a leg break from Warne landed outside [Mike] Gatting's leg stump at Old Trafford and spun 60 centimetres or roughly two feet to the left, clipping the top of the stumps and removing the bail. But that doesn't begin to describe how amazing it was. I remember thinking it was impossible for the ball to have spun past Gatting's bat and hit the wicket. And that's clearly what Gatting thought too. Looking back at the tapes, what immediately strikes you is how quickly the ball comes through and how slowly the batsman departs.'

Gatting departed slowly because he was completely discombobulated. England's stout skipper stayed in his crease, looking at the umpire, for a good 10 seconds. He simply couldn't believe that the ball had got past him and hit his wicket. Some commentators felt the same way: 'How anyone can spin a ball the width of Gatting boggles the mind,' English sports writer Martin Johnston observed. Graham Gooch, an English captain of the same era, pointed out, 'If it had been a cheese roll it would never have got past him.' That was much later or course. For a long time the Ball from Hell was no laughing matter to the English. In effect, they lost their Ashes bid in those few astonishing seconds.

He was 23, an overweight boy from Black Rock, when he bowled Gatting and after it his life could never be the same. 'That ball sort of changed my whole life,' he told Jana Wendt. 'Suddenly people wanted to know who I hung out with, where I hung out... what I was actually doing... I'm not trying to say, "Oh, poor Shane-o" but it was bloody difficult getting followed around all the time... leave your hotel room and there'd be four photographers following you and jumping in a car and you'd go down the pub or you'd do whatever and they'd be waiting out the front. That was hard.'

The index to Paul Barry's book tells the sorry story: AIS Cricket Academy, departure from; unwillingness to train; Australian Test team, sacking from; betting scandal; drug scandal; gambling, betting on cricket; Indian Central Bureau of Investigation; rock star treatment; schoolboy's photo incident; sex scandals; sledging; smoking; suspension; women; world Anti-Doping Agency. None of it amounts to much, and most of it borders on farce. Still, with a little commonsense and a lot of character, Shane Warne could have been, like Keith Miller, a rebel revered as a brilliant cricketer and a fine man.

The joke goes that a poll of 600 women was asked if they'd sleep with Shane Warne. Seventy-two per cent of respondents said: Never again!

If only Shane had said the same.

# 6

# THE DEATHS

Phar Lap, idol of the nation, and his strapper, Tommy Woodcock. The horse Tommy called 'Bobby' died in his strapper's arms. *Newspix*

'Nielsen told me to keep Phar Lap on the move until he returned with assistance. On no account must I allow him to stop, but when Phar Lap had swollen to half his size again and was groaning in pain, I took him to the barn.

'He whinnied. He groaned. Dementedly, I rushed about to make him more comfortable. Coming toward me he nosed affectionately under my arm. Then something inside him burst, he drenched me in blood and fell dead at my feet.'

Tommy Woodcock's account of the last moments of Phar Lap – the horse Woodcock affectionately called Bobby – remains, seven decades on, deeply moving. Imagine, then, the feeling when Australia heard the news. Far away, in California, Phar Lap, who only two weeks before had set the racing world ablaze, was dead.

The great horse's death left a nation sharing the stunned disbelief that is seen only once or twice in a lifetime. And for Australians the sudden death of a sporting idol adds immensely to the shock. Like Phar Lap, the jockey Tommy Corrigan was adored because in the Depression of the 1890s he kicked home hundreds of winners. Corrigan fell in the Grand National at Caulfield and Australia saw one of its biggest ever funeral processions. The boxer Les Darcy had two funeral processions in 1917, one in San Francisco where fans paid homage, and a second, where most of Sydney asked his forgiveness: Darcy had gone from being a sporting idol to vilification as a coward who had ducked war service. In death he was a hero once more. And the 1863 state funeral of Burke and Wills, said to have been the biggest event in Australia's history to that time, drew 100,000 of Melbourne's population of 120,000 to view their remains lying in state.

But no Australian's death and funeral, surely, compares with Steve Irwin's. The world reeled when news broke that the crocodile man had been killed by a stingray. His televised memorial service had Australia choking back tears: like those for Les Darcy, they were tears tinged with guilt.

# Pozières

Imagine shaking the hand, one by one, of 23,000 young Australian men.

Imagine being trapped in a place where it rained continuously for seven weeks.

Imagine that rain as a bombardment of artillery shells – at its height, raining down on you at the rate of 20 shells a minute.

Now imagine every one of those young Australian men, the men you had shaken hands with, blown apart – again and again – bayoneted, bludgeoned, shot, drowned or suffocated in a sea of mud and blood. For that is what happened to those 23,000 in those 42 days in 1916 at Pozières, a small French village in the Somme Valley where Australians fought 19 ferocious battles and withstood one of the heaviest artillery barrages of World War One. Day after day, shells exploded on and around the Australians; at its height, they rained down at the rate of 20 a minute.

And all for this patch of land little more than a kilometre in size. Just a patch of land, but it was the crucial point on the entire Somme front. And it was more densely sown with Australian blood than any place on Earth, said the Australian war historian C.E.W. Bean.

The Somme will forever be remembered as a gigantic slaughterhouse, the folly of Field Marshal Lord Haig. The commander of the British forces in France, General Haig was determined to break the German Western Front. On the first day of his Big Push, 1 July 1916, 60,000 British troops fell. A fortnight later, and five days after their arrival

Frank Hurley's eerie image of Diggers crossing duckboards in the surreal landscape of the Somme. *AWM E01220*

in France, the Australians were about to have a taste of the same. In just a few hours on 19 July at Fromelles, in what Haig's headquarters called 'some important raids' – in fact a fiasco, an inept, pathetically planned feint that failed to deceive the Germans – 5100 Diggers were killed and wounded. That was a casualty rate equivalent to Australia's entire losses in the Boer, Korean and Vietnam conflicts. And there was much worse to come.

Four days later, the Australians went in to capture Pozières. Pozières, standing on a low but commanding plateau, was pivotal to the entire offensive on the Western Front. The Germans were determined to hold it and the British had tried and failed to take it. The Australian 4th Division was sent in.

'With a rush every man went forward. Bullets hissed past us as we followed,' a French liaison officer with the Australians recorded. '... the waves in front were merged in smoke... I just caught glimpses of ghost-like faces as a group of Germans surged through us shouting "Kamerad!"... We struggled on through a line of blown-up barbed wire... The noise was deafening.

'Every machine gun was spouting tongues of flame... Our reserves were coming up from behind all the time, appearing in stumbling groups. Men and prisoners now filled the trench... We were deeper into the village than we had first thought.'

The Australians took Pozières in just six hours. The Germans had to have it back.

'Then the storm burst,' historian Bill Gammage wrote. 'A furious bombardment fell upon the captured positions, pounding the earth and tearing the fragile air with noise. For seven weeks the merciless shells rained almost continuously, the men powerless beneath them. They dug trenches; the guns obliterated them. They crouched in holes; the guns found them out and blew them to oblivion or buried them, and dug them out and buried them again.'

AIF Sergeant Archie Barwick told how 'Men were driven stark staring mad' by the incessant shelling. Some shot themselves, others deserted. '...more than one of them rushed out of the trench towards the Germans. Any amount of them could be seen crying and sobbing like children, their nerves completely gone.'

As well as the shelling there was the horror of seemingly endless and ferocious hand-to-hand fighting. A Digger wrote to his brother: 'God we have been playing tig with death for seven days and nights... I have seen the most gruesome sights it has been my cruel lot to witness.'

It was truly a living hell, as Sergeant E.J. Rule wrote. The survivors of Pozières, he said, 'looked like they had been in Hell. Almost without exception each man looked drawn and haggard and so dazed that they seemed to be walking in a dream.'

The English poet John Masefield saw it differently. 'I've passed the last two days on the Australians' amazing battlefield at Pozières, and that is a place almost like Troy to me, with a kind of daze of beauty about it; for it was the crown of all the Somme battle; and it has a unity that none of the other bloody ghastly blasting and death come near to having.

'It is a small plateau, 500 yards square, and in its important part 200 years square, and 10,000 men were killed on that plateau and buried and unburied and buried and unburied, till no bit of dust is without a bit of man upon it.'

A Digger put it less poetically. Pozières, he said, a place where more than one in every two Australians was killed, wounded or captured, was 'so terrible... that a raving lunatic could not imagine the horror'.

# Ronald Ryan

Ronald Ryan's life and death were 'a tragedy in miniature' says Julian Burnside, the lawyer noted for his fight on behalf of asylum seekers. 'But he achieved a far greater good than he had ever intended or dreamed of.'

Whatever Ronald Ryan dreamed he surely never imagined this:

'He died silently,' wrote Patrick Tennison, one of 14 journalists who saw Ryan hang on 3 February 1967.

'His face was white but impassive. His thin lips together but not clenched. His face was strangely like a small child who had composed himself into calm bravery just before the doctor gives a needle. Only once did this change. The hangman readying the knot jolted his head with the rope. Ryan turned his head slightly towards him. That was all. The hangman stepped back, the body fell from view. The rope dragged taut and swayed just slightly. The voice of the priest was heard reading his prayers.'

Ronald Ryan, the last man to be hanged in Australia, broke out of Melbourne's old, grey and grim Pentridge jail, six days before Christmas, 1965. With him was Peter Walker. Both were tough, cunning, career criminals.

Their escape might have been scripted for a Hollywood B movie. On Sunday 19 December, the day of the warders' Christmas lunch, using knotted bedspreads and a makeshift hook, Ryan and Walker scaled two walls inside the jail and ran along the catwalk of the second wall to Tower One. There, the warder, distracted by other prisoners near the exit

Ronald Ryan, flanked by detectives, knows he faces the gallows. He was right to be worried. The Victorian premier, Bolte, was determined that he would hang. The death sentence polarised the community. *Newspix*

gate, suddenly found Ryan behind him, and an M1 carbine rifle, taken from a rack, at his ear.

The pair forced him to open the gates and with a human shield – a Salvation Army brigadier– they were out in the street. Now all they had to do was take the Salvo and his car and disappear up Sydney Road, one of the main roads out of Melbourne. But the Salvo was stubborn. He refused to hand over the car keys and, as the prisons sirens wailed, Ryan bashed him to the ground with the butt of his rifle and held up a car at gunpoint.

One courageous warder, George Hodson, followed the men out and, an iron bar in his hand, caught up with Walker. Ten witnesses – though their accounts differed markedly – said they saw Ryan get out of the car, point his rifle at Hodson and fire.

There was the sound of a shot and Hodson fell dead across the tram tracks of busy Sydney Road. The escapers sped off to their hideout, a flat near St Kilda, where Christine Aitken, the ex-girlfriend of a Pentridge inmate, lived.

Four days later the pair held up a bank. They ordered the manager and the staff into the vault and Ryan warned them that the rifle he was holding was the rifle that 'killed a man the other day'. They got away with £4000.

On Christmas Eve, cashed up and confident, the fugitives were partying at Christine Aitken's when she came home with her boyfriend, Arthur Henderson, a tow truck driver. Walker went with him to get more beer. Walker came back to the party but Henderson didn't. He didn't know who Walker was, but he'd said to him, conversationally, 'That's Ronald Ryan in there, isn't it?' He was found dead next morning, shot in the back of the head on the floor of a beachside toilet.

The fugitives drove to Sydney and holed up in a flat near Coogee Beach. Walker, bored, phoned an old girlfriend for a date. She phoned the police, who set up a 'blind date' for Ryan – supposedly a nurse at Concord Repatriation Hospital. Armed police in various guises surrounded the hospital and, after a violent struggle, caught and subdued Ryan and Walker when they arrived.

Walker got 12 years on two charges of manslaughter. He had claimed that his gun had gone off accidentally when he had fought with Henderson. Ryan was found guilty of murder by a jury that probably believed that the death sentence would be commuted, just as every death sentence had been since 1951.

It was not.

The case polarised the community. An anti-hanging committee, led by Barry Jones, lawyers, churchmen, the media, all pleaded for Ryan's life

The body of warder George Hodson lies in Sydney Road. Ryan and Peter Walker made their escape in a hijacked car. Five days later Walker (below) killed in cold blood. He escaped the noose. *Newspix*

to be spared. Ryan had denied shooting the rifle – the bullet that killed Hodson went through his body and was never found – and many argued that Hodson had been accidentally shot by a fellow warder firing his M1 from the watchtower. But the premier, the shrewd and brutally blunt Henry Bolte, was unwavering. He wanted Ryan to hang.

At the very end, when the last hope of a reprieve had gone, Ryan admitted to the killing. Ian Grindley OBE, the governor of Pentridge, had played an important part in Ryan's life. They had met when Ryan was a prisoner in Bendigo jail and Grindley had encouraged Ryan to study to pass his Intermediate (year ten) exam and his Leaving Certificate (year 11). He was studying for his Matriculation – the university entrance qualification – when he was released and went back to crime.

Grindley wrote later that he had said to Ryan, 'You know full well that you shot him,' and that

Ryan had 'looked at me squarely in the face and said: "Yes, that's true. I did shoot him. But I didn't mean to kill him... only stop him."'

'Ryan died this morning, hanged by the neck until he was dead, at a time when his fellow Catholics were celebrating candle-mass,' journalist Ron Saw wrote. 'They hanged him quickly, expertly, terribly. They did the job in exactly 25 seconds.' Four minutes later Ryan's heart stopped beating.

'With that last heartbeat, capital punishment ended in Australia,' Julian Burnside said. 'It was abolished progressively in each of the states over the next 17 years, but no one was executed during that time.

'Ryan's conviction, we now know, was right; his death was wrong. But the controversy sparked by his sentence and execution brought an end to capital punishment in Australia.'

# Michael Hutchence

The naked dead man kneeling on the floor and facing the door inside suite 524 of the Ritz-Carlton seemed to have had it all: talent, charisma, good looks, the adulation of millions and even more millions in money. But he didn't have Fifi Trixibelle, Peaches Honeyblossom and Pixie. And that, and the cocktail of substances he had taken, the Sydney coroner found, was why Michael Hutchence ended his own life.

The biggest rock star Australia has produced hanged himself on 22 November 1997. He was 37. Eighteen years before, Michael Hutchence and INXS had released their self-titled debut album and went on to record five Australian hit albums in the next six years. In 1987 they broke through on the world market with 'Kick'. The album sold nine million copies, was the catalyst for four hit singles and won a Grammy nomination. Hutchence and INXS were suddenly huge: 75,000 fans were screaming when a helicopter took INXS to Wembley Stadium and they were all screaming for Michael.

That same year, 1991, he ended his affair with Kylie Minogue, the kid from *Neighbours* he had allegedly sexually transformed. He began a relationship with the supermodel Helena Christensen. For four years she seemed to act as a calming influence on Michael's tempestuous temperament, a personality disorder that led him to increasingly frequent and violent clashes with paparazzi. In September 1995 one of them snapped him leaving a hotel after spending the night with Paula Yates, the wife of Bob Geldof. Hutchence assaulted the photographer and was fined $6000, and GQ summed up the feelings of Hutchence's worldwide fans, putting Christensen on its cover and asking: Would you trade her in for Paula Yates?

But trade her in Michael did. Paula filed for divorce and Bob began a bitter battle to have custody of his three daughters, the sadly named Fifi Trixibelle, Peaches Honeyblossom and Pixie. On 22 July 1996 Yates had a fourth baby, fathered by Hutchence, and labouring under the name Heavenly Hiraani Tigerlily. Two months later, while the couple was in Sydney, London police raided their home and found opium in a Smarties packet. Little Fifi, claimed the *Mirror,* also found erotic photographs of the pair. No charges were laid, and Hutchence told friends that the tip-off and the raid had been a set-up. Whatever the truth, the scandal helped Geldof win a temporary residence order for his three girls.

In November 1997 Hutchence flew to Sydney to join INXS for the band's 20th anniversary tour. The band badly needed a hit. Their last album had been a failure and Hutchence himself had to suffer the ignominy of being labelled a 'has been' – the worst insult in pop music – by Noel Gallagher of the up-and-coming Oasis. In an attempt to add injury to insult Gallagher's equally obnoxious brother Liam challenged Michael to a fight after he presented Oasis with a televised award.

His career on the downslide, his domestic life in turmoil, Michael checked into his suite at the Ritz-Carlton, Double Bay. He had dinner with his father and drank in his suite with an ex-girlfriend and her partner until around 5 a.m. During the night he phoned his manager in New York, saying, 'Marth, Michael here. I've f___ing had enough.'

And he twice phoned Bob Geldof. A couple in the adjoining room heard Hutchence scream, 'She's not your wife anymore!'

The next morning he phoned an ex-girlfriend, sounding drunk the first time, she said, and distressed and crying during the second call, at 9.45. She hurried to the hotel and when she was unable to get through to him left a note under his door. At around noon a maid came to clean suite 524 and found him.

Immediately tabloids around the world speculated that Michael Hutchence had died from an act of auto-eroticism that went too far: asphyxiated searching for a sexual thrill. The coroner would have none of it. Hutchence was depressed, the coroner found, and in his blood were traces of alcohol, cocaine, an anti-depressant drug and other prescription drugs. 'I am satisfied that the deceased intended to and did take his own life.'

The funeral was a celebrity circus. It was followed by a squabble over his ashes and a long drawn out and very bitter public feud between Paula Yates and Hutchence's family. In June 1998 Yates was admitted to hospital after being found on the floor with a belt around her neck and, in September 2000, she died of an accidental heroin overdose. Tigerlily found her body. The following day Bob Geldof was given custody of the orphaned Tigerlily.

Sex, drugs and rock and roll – and Fifi Trixibelle, Peaches Honeyblossoom and Pixie – the ingredients for Michael Hutchence's fatal cocktail. *Newspix*

# Kerry Packer

Kerry Packer came back from the dead and told his son that he had been to the other side and it was a void – or words to that effect. That was in October 1990. With the vexed question of life after death answered to his satisfaction, the big feller got on with business. In the next 15 years before he died – again – Packer's fortune grew by at least $6 billion, a million dollars and more a day.

Packer's death attracted saturation media coverage – more than any Australian man or woman in memory. It dwarfed the coverage for Australia's longest serving prime minister, Sir Robert Menzies; the drowning death of Harold Holt; or, even, the death of Bradman the demi-god. Packer's state funeral, a 75-minute service in the Sydney Opera House broadcast live to the nation by the Nine Network, attracted, if not the great and the good, a peerless parade of the rich and the powerful. In order of importance they included five Australian cricket captains, two prime ministers, three Hollywood stars, five state premiers and assorted billionaires.

Kerry Francis Bullmore Packer's was a riches to loads-more-riches story. Like his only son James he inherited a family empire that has dominated the Sydney media scene for a century.

His father Sir Frank Packer died in 1974, anointing Kerry as his successor. Sir Frank had always intended that his eldest son Clyde would take over. Clyde was the clever one. But Clyde fell out with Sir Frank in 1972 and that left Kerry, the man Sir Frank called Boofhead.

No one ever called Kerry Packer Boofhead from the day his father died.

The businesses he inherited were worth around $50 million. Within two years he had bought out his brother's share of the business for $2 million, and today PBL is worth almost $12 billion.

The Packer private fortune is estimated at around $6 billion. As well as his magazine empire, his Nine Network of television stations and his casinos, Kerry Packer was one of Australia's biggest landowners, with 200,000 cattle grazing on millions of hectares. He had interests in real estate, chemical plants and heavy manufacturing. His gambling was almost beyond belief. He could lose $20 million and take it in his stride but his consuming interest was in winning. And most of the time Kerry Packer won.

Packer was born into a life of wealth, power and privilege, on 17 December 1937. His early years were marked by diversity and misery. The little boy was packed off to boarding school, just a few hundred metres from his parents' home in Bellevue Hill. Between the ages of five and nine he saw his mother only a handful of times and his father not at all.

When Japanese submarines attacked in Sydney Harbour he was sent to his aunt's in Bowral where he fell seriously ill with polio. He spent six months in an iron lung in hospital and two years recuperating in Canberra with a nurse.

He was the class dullard, his father called him Boofhead, and his academic record was abysmal. He took six years to pass four academic years of high school and he failed to get his Leaving Certificate, the basic academic qualification at that time.

What no one knew, or bothered to discover, was that Boofhead was dyslexic. He saw letters back to front or jumbled.

David Rowe's brilliant caricature of Kerry Packer, published the day after Packer's death, rewards close study. Almost every line gives a clue to the tycoon's crowded life of immense wealth and power.

He went straight into the family business. Sir Frank never bothered to ask him if he had other ambitions, and he went to work in the bowels of the Consolidated Press building, cleaning presses, stacking rolls of paper. Is it any wonder that Kerry Packer grew up with a bleak view of the world that never left him? 'I don't make friends easily,' he told Michael Parkinson, 'I've had my share of being attacked... when I meet people I don't expect them to like me.'

In fact Kerry Packer won the affection of many people, some of them unlikely admirers. Bob Hawke was hated by Frank Packer but counted Kerry as a friend. John Howard gave him the rare honour of a state funeral and praised his passionate commitment to the interests of Australia (though cynical souls might read this as Packer's passionate commitment to Australian cricket). His employees remembered him as a bullying boss with a temper, but he inspired loyalty and he was capable of extraordinary acts of generosity, most of them in secret. 'He was a very generous philanthropic person,' Mr Howard said, 'and I know for a fact that many of his kindest and most generous and charitable deeds went unreported, which is precisely how he wished it to be.'

On Monday 26 December 2005, he died. In October 1990 he had suffered a cardiac arhythmia while playing polo. For seven or eight minutes his heart had stopped beating but by a one in a thousand chance an intensive care ambulance was passing by. He was resuscitated.

But on 26 December 2005 there was no miraculous rescue. He would have refused it. He was tired of living in poor health. He had seen the insides of too many hospitals. 'It was a lonely, difficult period,' Packer said. At 18 he was in hospital for a long stay, recovering from a car accident in which three men died. The car that hit his was on the wrong side of the road. He had his first suspected heart attack in 1983 – his father and his brother had heart problems – and three years later he had a diseased gall bladder and cancerous kidney removed. In 1988 and again in 1999 he had more heart surgery, and two years later had a kidney transplant donated by a close mate, his helicopter pilot.

Days after his 68th birthday, dispirited and knowing his end was near, he nevertheless delivered, with typical boldness, the biggest deal in Australian sporting history – a $780 million bid for the AFL television rights for his Channel Nine network. Three days later he told his doctors he had had enough, no more hospital: 'This is my time.'

Packer personally signed off on the deal on the Friday, the last working day before Christmas to ensure as much disadvantage as possible to the bids of his rival consortium, the networks Seven and Ten. The consortium had first and last option to respond within 14 days – effectively giving it seven working days to weigh the options. In fact the consortium topped Packer's bid, but he'd have been pleased that he had cost them dearly to do so. Packer's last business deal blended those pursuits that perhaps most interested him: gambling, sport and commerce. 'There's a little bit of the whore in all of us,' he told the Australian Cricket Board when bidding for broadcast rights. 'Gentlemen, name your price.'

In cricket he was a revolutionary. His day-night games introduced matches beamed live – and in full – to television audiences around the nation. His World Series Cricket, an audacious and ultimately successful attempt to shake the game's establishment to its foundations, gave players huge

*Kerry Packer's gambling inspired outrageous stories and rumours – most of them true.*

*Bruce McHugh, the former Sydney bookmaker who used to 'accommodate' Packer, told the* Age, *'There were two Kerry Packers – the one before he sold Channel Nine (for $1 billion to Alan Bond) and the one after.'*

*Until the sale of Nine, he said, Packer would consider the loss of 'a few hundred thousand' a bad day, a big loss. After the sale it was different. Packer's first bet with McHugh was $40,000 to $20,000, but in their final days of McHugh laying the odds to Packer, the big man might have had $2.5 million to $1 million. Or $5 million to $500,000. Then it would get to $9 million to $3 million. Or $11 million to $4 million.'*

*In four days of punting at Sydney's autumn carnival in 1987 he laid out almost $60 million in bets, most of it with McHugh. Packer was losing, down to about $27 million, when he persuaded McHugh to accept three more bets, each to win $10 million. All thee horses won.*

*'At the end of the day I owed him $300,000 or $400,000. He won that time,' McHugh said. The following day the bookmaker told the Australian Jockey Club that he was surrendering his licence.*

*At the casino Packer's betting was even more awesome. He went to Las Vegas three or four times a year to play blackjack or baccarat. In one three-day stay at the Bellagio he lost $27 million and at the MGM Grand he won $25 million. 'I take risks which are for my recreation,' he once said. 'I don't take risks with the company.'*

salary increases and, for the very best, an afterlife as highly paid commentators wearing oversized hats. Drop-in pitches, white balls, helmets, coloured uniforms – hard to imagine, but it's true, the hard men of the '80s West Indies team made their one-day debut in lipstick pink – they all came into cricket as a result of Packer's intervention. And with television replays, animated graphics, stump-cam, Hawkeye and the slowest of slo-mo he changed the way we watched sport. 'I believe people are interested in the expression on a man's face when a ball is whizzing past his head,' he said.

Packer was brutal in his business dealings. Nearly two metres tall and about 130 kilograms, he was a daunting figure bullying the boardroom or mauling politicians at a televised Senate hearing. 'You have a damned hide for bringing this up under privilege,' he told a chastened MP attempting to question him about allegations that had been shown to be false. But his devil-take-the-hindmost attitude at parliamentary inquisitions, on the racetracks or in casinos was not reflected in his business dealings. His biographer Paul Barry said Packer 'was a very cautious businessman and I think he was really always out to prove to his father that he could succeed. His father spent a lot of time telling other people that Kerry was an idiot, and made no secret of the fact that he would have preferred to have Rupert Murdoch as his son.'

As to that, Rupert Murdoch gave him this accolade: 'He was both a lifelong friend and a tough competitor. He was the most successful businessman of our generation.'

That is how Frank Packer and Kerry Packer would have liked him to be remembered.

# Steve Irwin and Peter Brock

Steve Irwin died on Monday 4 September 2006.

On that day we discovered that a man we barely knew, someone many of us 'didn't get' or disliked, was the best-known and best-loved Australian who has ever lived.

Crikey!

Steve Irwin was one of two Australian heroes who died suddenly and violently in the span of five days in September 2006. Irwin, the man who became an authentic Australian hero posthumously, the man who had seemed to be master of the animal kingdom, went first. He was killed almost instantly when a stingray stabbed its barb into his heart. Five days later, on Friday, Peter Brock, the peerless motor racing driver, lost his life when his Daytona sports coupe skidded into a tree.

The ironic tragedies, at opposite ends of the continent – Irwin off the Great Barrier Reef, and Brock near Perth – sent Australia into shock. Peter Brock's career was unparalleled in Australia and his genius at the wheel was such that he had never had a serious accident. His death at the wheel was shocking because it was unexpected. He was 61 and long retired from top-level racing. For two weeks the press carried scores of stories about Peter Perfect. He was given a state funeral. And at Sandown Park raceway 10,000 fans in a sea of Holden red cheered as Brock's sons drove a

lap of honour. But it ended there. The mourning and the media focus were confined to Australia.

Steve Irwin's death rocked the world. In America it led the NBC national news. A White House spokesperson said, 'The president and Mrs Bush are saddened by the news of his passing and their prayers are with his wife and two young children.' The *New York Times* gave over its editorial to him. US talk show host Jay Leno said 'I think for many Americans he's become the face of Australia and he was a great ambassador. He represented all that was good about the country.' CNN's Larry King showed drawings by his children. 'I love you,' wrote his six-year-old and Chance King, seven, had drawn a crocodile with the message: 'We will miss you.'

In the UK, David Bellamy, the television eco-personality with whom Irwin was often compared – harshly by some Australians – said, 'The world has lost one of the great natural historians and I am very, very sad about it.'

In France, Germany, Spain, Italy, Canada, New Zealand, Brazil, Mexico, South Africa, Egypt, Iraq, Tokyo, Hong Kong, Singapore – in almost every one of the 160 countries where Irwin's shows were broadcast in 24 languages to a worldwide audience that topped half a billion – Steve Irwin's death was front-page news.

Australia woke up, the day after Irwin's death, to discover that he was one of the most talented television performers this country has produced. It was just that we really didn't see that talent. Around the world he was celebrated for his television shows. Here he was mostly seen on talk

'My daddy was my hero...' Bindi Irwin delivers her remarkable eulogy to 'the best daddy in the whole world'. *Newspix*

shows, playing, we thought, wrongly as it turned out, a caricature character, a comical Aussie anachronism, a boy/man (Irwin was 44) horsing about in King Gee khaki shorts six sizes too small and talking in a vernacular that had disappeared along with the ice-chest, the corset and the Sunday roast.

The world saw him differently. 'My whole reason to be on this planet is to educate people about wildlife,' Irwin told an American reporter. 'I will die doing that. I have a gift.' And the world, energised and inspired by this eternally buoyant and disarmingly innocent man, agreed.

What was Irwin's appeal? Discovery cable TV's vice president said, 'He redefined the way natural history is presented on television in a way that was much more immersive, much more engaging and inspiring,' and, as for his 'cliche' Australianness: 'Americans really identified with the spirit he had as an Australian, a kind of "roll up your sleeves and just get in there and do it"'.

The day after Steve Irwin's death we rolled up our sleeves and did our best to catch up with the world. Prominent Australians scrambled to eulogise. Germaine Greer, predictably, refused to join the chorus. Irwin was a 21st-century version of a circus lion tamer, she wrote in the *Guardian*, in a piece headed: THE ANIMAL WORLD GETS ITS REVENGE.

She was dubbed a snake in the grass by editorial writers who were quick to point out that she herself had appeared on the ultimate populist television program, *Celebrity Big Brother. TIME Australia* hit back on behalf of most Australians: 'Greer made her point with a sustained, supercilious sneer that gracelessly combined

*S*eventeen days after his death, the prime minister, the leader of the Opposition, famous movie stars, and sports idols joined 5000 who had queued for the memorial to Steve Irwin at his Australia Zoo. Millions of Australians watched the service from 9 a.m. – most watched replays throughout the day – and almost all of us, like the 300 million viewers watching internationally, brushed away tears.

Brave Bindi Irwin, eight and pint sized, left her mother Terri and her two-year-old brother Bob, the image of his Dad, to read a tribute she had written. In a clear, unwavering voice, and tracing the words with her finger, she said it for the world:

'My daddy was my hero, he was always there for me when I needed him. He listened to me and taught me so many things, but most of all he was fun. I know that Daddy had an important job. He was working to change the world so everyone would love wildlife like he did.

'He built a hospital to help animals and he bought lots of land to give animals a safe place to live.

'He took me and my brother and my mum with him all the time. We filmed together, caught crocodiles together and loved being in the bush together.

'I don't want Daddy's passion to ever end.

'I want to help endangered wildlife like he did.

'I have the best Daddy in the whole world and I will miss him every day.

'When I see a crocodile I will always think of him and I know that Daddy made this zoo so everyone could come and learn to love all the animals.

'Daddy made this place his whole life and now it's our turn to help Daddy.'

ignorance with exhibitionist pseudo-erudition...

'I can find no record of what Greer has done to preserve habitat, but Irwin bought many thousands of acres of wilderness in Australia and the US, in Fiji and Vanuatu. He made a lot of money from his business and used millions of dollars to purchase land and keep it wild...

'Of course, for the Greers of this world Irwin's real sin was his lack of sophistication, his puppy-like boisterousness, his artlessness, his showmanship. Good lord, the man was little better than a common entertainer. People with joyless lives circumscribed by cynicism could never comprehend his mad enthusiasm, and needed to mock it to justify its absence in themselves.'

Unanimously, those who knew Irwin well, or met him only briefly, agreed that in private he was exactly the same person as the one the world saw on screen. 'The queer thing about Irwin, legions would offer through the week, was that the man on camera was identical to the private character,' Jonathan Green wrote in the *Age*: 'Irwin was, gulp, sincere. He had no difficulty staying in character primarily because there didn't seem to be one.

'Crikey. How did this happen?'

Prime Minister Howard offered Irwin's family a state funeral. Family and friends declined and instead, buried him in private – the site remains secret – then sat around a campfire swapping memories of him.

Peter Brock was born in Victoria, but spent most of his 61 years in macho heaven. Nine-times Bathurst winner, King of the Mountain,

king of the road, a woman magnet, married to a former Miss Australia, Brock lived, foot to the floor, in the fast lane. Then, overnight, he spun 180 degrees. For a time he gave up drinking and chain smoking, became a vegetarian and turned to alternative therapies and new-age spirituality. He went perilously close to going broke with an 'energy polariser' device – not much more than a couple of batteries – that sparked a rift with Holden. In 2004 he left his de facto wife of 28 years for her closest friend.

He seemed to have finally settled down to celebrity appearances as a rally driver and community service through the Peter Brock Foundation, established to encourage communities to mutually support each other. Throughout, 'Peter Perfect' remained idolised.

White-haired and a grandfather – of just two months – Peter Brock got behind the wheel of a car for the last time on Friday 7 September 2006. He had flown in from the UK, where he had competed in a rally, and was co-driving in the Targa West, a three-day sealed roads rally east of Perth. This was his third Targa, an event he enjoyed. But Brock admitted just before starting the race that he had not yet 'come to grips with' his car, a silver grey $100,000-plus Daytona Coupe, a limited production car virtually hand built. He told Perth morning radio the Daytona was 'sliding around everywhere, and I thought, "No, this is not going to go fast." ...So for this weekend – first time we've done it – we've actually got a pretty staid tyre-wheel suspension combination.'

But staid wasn't Peter Brock's style. Mike Hone, an old friend but an inexperienced navigator who had raced with Brock only twice before, suggested that on a course that neither had ever driven: 'We'll just take it easy through the [first] stage...Just get warmed up and see how we go after that.' Brock's response was to clock the second fastest time in the field of 79, averaging just over 120 kmh.

He was in the second stage of the Targa when at 11.50 a.m., on a tightening downhill left-hand bend on O'Brien Road, near Gidgegannup, the car 'just started to slide,' Hone said. 'Pete tried to correct it but we just slid off the side of the road and basically collected the biggest gum-tree there. We knew what was happening, we could see it coming.'

Hone held his mate's hand, but he believed Peter Brock died almost instantly.

CHASING CANCER THE GENETIC KEY TO FINDING A CURE

The **Bulletin**

Newsweek WITH

SEPTEMBER 19, 2006
$5.95 INC GST
NZ $6.50 INC GST

PRINT POST APPROVED PP25500300555

SPECIAL TRIBUTE ISSUE

PETER BROCK 1945-2006

FAREWELL THE KING

INSIDE THE FAST LIFE OF OUR GREATEST RACING

# 7

# THE SPEECHES

Ben Chifley, with the first Holden, icons both. Admired by all – his political opponent, Robert Menzies held him in respect and affection – the post-war battles with both striking miners and banks took its toll. The best-loved of all Australian Prime Ministers 'Chif' left his party with its inspirational 'light on the hill' aspiration.

By nature Australians are not loquacious. We are suspicious of those who 'rabbit on'. Governor Phillip, a shrewd, practical man, made the first speech recorded on Australian soil on the morning of 7 February 1788. There was not a hint of bulldust in it. He warned the convicts that 'attempts to get into the women's tents of a night' would be fatal. He couldn't have put it fairer than that.

Few Australian speeches survive the test of time. Paul Keating's Redfern Address is celebrated, but is unlikely to be as quoted in 50 years time, as is the speech given by a man he dismissed as 'a plodder': Ben Chifley.

In 1949 Chifley told the Labor faithful: 'We have a great objective – the light on the hill – which we aim to reach by working for the betterment of mankind not only here but anywhere we may give a helping hand. If it were not for that, the Labor movement would not be worth fighting for.'

Ben Chifley's 'Light on the hill' speech has endured and will continue to inspire, but perhaps the most important series of speeches made by any Australian was given by an Aborigine, the Cape York leader, Noel Pearson. In the last decade of the 20th century, and for more than seven years – against a background of intense struggle over Aboriginal policy – Pearson argued that indigenous rights must be balanced by responsibilities, and that passive welfare corrupts and ultimately destroys societies.

In June 2007, after the release of a report that revealed rampant child sexual abuse in indigenous communities in the Northern Territory, Prime Minister John Howard declared a 'national emergency' and took control of remote and indigenous communities, banning alcohol and pornography and sending in police and military to rebuild desperate and degenerating communities.

Howard's sweeping reforms 'could not have been contemplated in anyone's wildest imaginings, 10 years ago, five years ago or perhaps even just last year,' Dennis Shanahan wrote in the Australian, but bi-partisan support was immediate and unqualified.

Noel Pearson's almost lone plea for his people to be given the chance to shape their destiny had been finally and dramatically vindicated.

# Lalor

On 29 November 1854 an angry 'monster meeting' of 10,000 at Bakery Hill on Ballarat's goldfields decided that the miners would no longer show their licences on demand. The next day troopers provoked a fracas with a general licence hunt and violence and shooting broke out. Agitated diggers gathered again at Bakery Hill. An Irishman, Peter Lalor, who had spoken publicly for the first time at the monster meeting, seized the day. Pistol in hand, he jumped on to a tree stump. Above him the diggers' deep blue Southern Cross flag fluttered in a sultry breeze.

'I looked around me: I saw brave and honest men, who had come thousands of miles to labour for independence,' Lalor later wrote. '...I called for volunteers to come forward and enrol themselves in companies. Hundreds responded... I then called to the volunteers to kneel down.' With heads uncovered and hands raised they joined Lalor as he recited the diggers' oath:

'We swear by the Southern Cross to stand truly by each other and defend our rights and our liberties.' Then they began building a crude stockade for the inevitable battle.

Three days later, just before dawn on 3 December, about 200 infantry, cavalrymen and 100 mounted Troopers attacked. The battle of Eureka Stockade was over in less than 20 minutes. It cost the lives of 24 diggers, three soldiers and a trooper. Seventeen soldiers and 20 diggers – among them Peter Lalor, who lost his arm – were wounded. A landmark in the birth of democracy in Australia, the battle 'may be called the finest thing in Australian history,' wrote Mark Twain, somewhat overstating things.

'We swear by the Southern Cross to stand truly by each other and defend our rights and our liberties.' *Ballarat Fine Art Gallery*

December 1st 1854

Swearing allegiance to the "Southern Cross"

# Blamey

Candour was Thomas Blamey's speciality. He liked to speak his mind. Accepting the surrender of the commander of the Japanese 2nd Army, he told him: 'I do not recognise you as an honourable foe, but you will be treated with severe but due courtesy in all matters. I recall the treacherous attack upon our ally, China, in 1938. I recall the treacherous attack made upon the British Empire and the United States of America in December 1941, at a time when your authorities were making the pretence of negotiating peace. I recall the atrocities inflicted upon the persons of our nationals as prisoners of war and internees, designed to reduce them by punishment and starvation to slavery.'

'In the light of these evils, I will enforce most rigorously all orders issued to you, so let there be no delay or hesitation in their fulfilment at your peril.'

He was equally blunt with his fellow Australians, saying in an April 1945 nationwide broadcast: 'In no other country have the achievements of a very successful army been so belittled as in Australia'.

But the truth was no one had belittled Australian troops in a more brutal, stinging and grossly unfair fashion – implying they were cowards – than the commander of the Australian Military Forces: Blamey. What he said, in just 19 words, ensured that, in some quarters at least, his name would be forever reviled.

Blamey's aide-de-camp, Norman Carlyon, in his biography *I Remember Blamey*, gives this sanitised account of a despicable attack.

'I well remember one example of Blamey's close attention to the performance of his fighting men. It concerned the 21st Brigade, after a setback in their thrust forward from Ioribai Ridge.

'This brigade, which had a fine record in the Middle East, was fighting its first jungle action. When its flanks were infiltrated by the enemy, the brigade made a limited retirement. This was a successful operation in which very few casualties were suffered. However, this check displeased Blamey. He ordered the entire brigade be paraded at Koitaki so that he could address them... he was in a most aggressive mood. He was soon addressing them in harsh words.

'He told the men that they had been defeated, that he had been defeated, and Australia had been defeated. He said this was simply not good enough... he concluded with a remark which I think was particularly ill-chosen and unfair. Some others who heard it have claimed that it was not offensive.

' "Remember," he said, "it is not the man with the gun that gets shot; it's the rabbit that is running away." '

The ABC investigative journalist Chris Masters, in a 1998 *Four Corners* program, had this to say about the speech:

'By now, fresh Australian troops were in pursuit of the Japanese. In more desperate fighting, they were chased back to the north coast... On November 2 Kokoda was retaken. A week later an unchecked Blamey called to parade at a place called Koitaki, the men who had saved Australia and unequivocally condemned them.'

Bob Thompson, Sergeant 2/14th AIF, recalled the speech: 'And we went to this parade where Blamey came down to speak to us, and he gave a great dissertation to our troops about... it's the rabbit that runs that gets shot, and he all the time was virtually

saying that cowards can't live.'

John Burns, Corporal 2/27th AIF, said: 'It stirred them up like I've never seen troops stirred up before and, personally, I reckon Blamey was lucky to get out of it alive that night.'

Harry Katekar, Captain 2/27th AIF, said: 'It was a shameful, call it cowardly, attack on men that had given their all.'

Chris Masters concluded the program: 'Kenneth Slessor [a war correspondent] wrote a poem about Blamey saying the men had given him everything, except respect... On the Owen Stanleys they were fighting for neither career nor promotion... On the Owen Stanleys they overcame the lot – inexperience, the jungle, the enemy and weakness in some of their own leaders. They fought without the world watching... with less of the pointless bravery of the old ANZACS... but with all their forebears' tenacity and some mature good sense. Without exception, they call themselves ordinary Australians.'

General Blamey was Australia's only Field Marshal, but his address to the 21st Brigade ensured his memory would be forever sullied. *AWM 090106*

# *Evatt*

It was, said Graham Freudenberg, speechwriter to three Labor prime ministers, the most disastrous speech in the history of the Federal Parliament.

Writing in *A Figure of Speech,* of the turbulent 1950s ('It beats me,' he said, 'why the retrospective image of Australia in the 1950s is of a boring and uneventful place') Freudenberg sets the scene for the 19 October 1955 speech of Dr Herbert Vere Evatt, Leader of the Opposition.

'It was the year of the Great Labor Split,' Freudenberg writes. 'Following the ALP Federal Conference in Hobart in March, the reconstituted Victorian Executive expelled 18 members of the Victorian Parliament and six members of the House of Representatives who formed the Anti-Communist Labor Party, later the DLP. At state elections on 28 May the Cain Labor Government of Victoria was defeated and Henry Bolte became premier. In September the Petrov Royal Commission presented its final report and on 19 October Doc Evatt made the most disastrous speech in the history of the House of Representatives, revealing, to Labor disbelief and Liberal delight, that he had written to Molotov, the Soviet foreign minister, to ascertain the truth of the defecting spy Petrov's evidence about Soviet espionage in Australia. Menzies called an election for 10 December, 18 months ahead of time and the sixth anniversary of his victory over the Chifley Government.'

'What is the upshot of this Petrov affair?' Doctor Evatt asked Parliament. 'Two foreigners, the Petrovs, and one foreign-born Australian

'Mr Molotov,' Dr Evatt announced in parliament, '…informed me that the documents given to the Australian authorities by Petrov can only be… falsifications.'

spy, Bialoguski, have made a lot of money. The forum in which they appeared cost the taxpayers £140,000, plus unlimited security service expenses. The nation has suffered heavy loss in trade, and the breaking of diplomatic relations with a great power. There has been the attempted smearing of many innocent Australians, and grave inroads have been made into Australian freedoms by attacks on political non-conformity.

'Determined to ascertain the truth of these grave matters, I took two steps, as follows: first of all, I communicated with His Excellency the Foreign Minister of the Soviet Union. I pointed out that most of the Russian language documents in the Petrov case were said to be communications from the MVD, Moscow, to Petrov, MVD resident in Australia. I pointed out that the Soviet government or its officers were undoubtedly in a position to reveal the truth as to the genuineness of the Petrov document.

'I duly received a reply, sent on behalf of the Minister of Foreign Affairs of the Union of Soviet Socialist Republics, Mr Molotov.

[Honourable members interjecting.]

'Honourable members can laugh and clown but they've got to face up to some facts tonight. They will not put me off by their organised opposition. They have to listen to this because this is the truth of the affair. The letter to which I have referred informed me that the documents given to the Australian authorities by Petrov can only be, as it had been made clear, at that time and as it was confirmed later, falsifications fabricated on the instructions of persons interested in the deterioration of the Soviet–Australian relations and in discrediting their political opponents.

'I attach grave importance to this letter which shows clearly that the Soviet government denies the authenticity of the Petrov documents. It seems to me that in these circumstances the matter cannot be left where it is, and that, if possible, some form of international commission should be established by agreement with the Union of Soviet Socialist Republics to settle the dispute once and for all. The Soviet Union was not represented at the hearing. It will be in a position to prove clearly, definitely and unequivocally that the letters were fabricated.'
– Abridged

# Blainey

Professor Geoffrey Blainey's John Latham Memorial Lecture in 1993 posed the question of the treatment of Aborigines. Was it an ineradicable stain on Australian history? There are many answers, he concluded, each of them a part answer. The Lecture passed without attracting controversy or great attention, but, three years later, when John Howard used an evocative and powerful phrase from it – 'the black armband view of history' – Professor Blainey found himself, once more, at the centre of fierce debate. Here are some of the points he made in that Lecture:

'To some extent my generation was reared on the 'three cheers' view of history. This patriotic view of our past had a long run. It saw Australian history as largely a success. While the convict era was a source of shame or unease, nearly everything that came after was believed to be pretty good. Now the very opposite is widely preached... a rival view, which I call the 'black armband' view of history. In recent years it has assailed the generally optimistic view of Australian history... [and which]... might well represent the swing of the pendulum from a position that had been too favourable, too self-congratulatory, to an opposite extreme that is even more unreal and decidedly jaundiced.

'... Many Australians see the treatment of Aborigines, since 1788, as the blot on Australian history. Fifty years ago, fewer than 50,000 Australians probably saw this as the blot. Now maybe several million are convinced that it is the main blot and maybe half of the population, or even more, would see it as highly regrettable. Irrespective of whether deep shame or wide regret is the more appropriate response, this question will be here to vex or torment the nation for a long time to come.

'My own view on this question is much influenced by my own particular interpretation of Australian history. My starting point you might disagree with, but I have held it for some twenty years, have often reconsidered it, and will hold on to it until contrary evidence arrives.

'The meeting of the incoming British with the Aborigines, at a thousand different parts of Australia spread over more than a century, was possibly a unique confrontation in recorded history. No doubt a version of the episode happened somewhere else, hundreds of years earlier, on a smaller scale. But there is probably no other historical parallel of a confrontation so strange, so puzzling to both sides, and embracing such a huge area of the world's surface. If we accept this fact we begin to understand the magnitude of the problem that appeared in 1788, puzzled Governor Arthur Phillip, a man of goodwill, and is still with us. It will probably remain with us for the foreseeable future, defying the variety of quick-fix formulas that sometimes attract the federal government, tempt the High Court, and tantalise thoughtful Aboriginal leaders.

'In 1788, the world was becoming one world. Europe's sailing ships had entered nearly every navigable sea and strait on the globe, and the ships' crew were alert for anything that was tradable, and so they were sure to return to any place of promise. In 1788, the industrial

'How conceivably could a treaty have been signed – given the differences in language and understanding?'

revolution was also beginning. Here landed representatives of the nation which had just developed the steam engine, the most powerful machine the world had ever known, and also the semi-mechanised cotton mill. On the other hand Australia represented the way of life that almost certainly prevailed over the whole habitable globe some 10,000 years earlier. The Aborigines had no domesticated plants and animals and therefore a very different attitude to the land – this is part of the long painful background to the Mabo case. They had no pottery, they had implements of wood and bone and stone but none of metals, they had no paper and no writing, though they were skilled at a variety of other signs. They had no organisation embracing more than say 3000 people and probably no organisation capable of putting more than 200 people into a battlefield at the one time. They had few, if any, permanent villages, and only a token ability to hoard food. They believed in a living, intervening god – here was a close resemblance – but not the God seen as the correct one. It was a society with many distinctive merits, often overlooked, but it was startlingly different to the one that supplanted it.

'In 1788, Aboriginal Australia was a world almost as remote, as different as outer space. We now think of Aboriginal Australia as having a unity, but it had even less unity than Europe possesses today. There were countless economic and social differences, and an amazing variety of languages. Accordingly the idea, widely voiced now, that the incoming British could have – should have – signed a treaty with the Aborigines, and so worked out rights and compensations, rests on a faith in the impossible. Any treaty would have been one-sided, with the Aborigines as losers.

'Even if the First Fleet had brought out not the dross but the wisest and most humane women and men in England, and even if the Aborigines whom they met at Sydney Harbour were the wisest of all their people, how conceivably could a treaty have been signed – given the differences in language and understanding? And if a treaty were signed, how far inland and along the coast would it have extended? The north and south sides of Sydney Harbour, then as now, had different languages and tribal arrangements. (I do not use this argument, incidentally, to comment on the question of whether there should or should not be a treaty today.) There was a huge contrast between the two cultures, the incoming and the resident. Every Australian still inherits the difficult consequence of that contrast.

'How can we fairly summarise this complex and delicate question: was the treatment of Aborigines an ineradicable stain on Australian history? There are many answers, each of them a part answer.

'... Anyone who tries to range over the last 200 years of Australia's history, surveying the success and failures, and trying to understand the obstacles that stood in the way, cannot easily accept the gloomier summaries of that history. Some episodes in the past were regrettable, there were many flaws and failures, and yet on the whole it stands out as one of the world's success stories. It is ironical that many of the political and intellectual leaders of the last decade in our history, are so eager to denounce earlier generations and discount their hard-won successes.

'Many young Australians, irrespective of their background, are quietly proud to be Australian. We deprive them of their inheritance if we claim that they have inherited little to be proud of.'

# Paul Keating
## *At Redfern*

In 1973 the Whitlam government gave two hectares of inner-Sydney housing, in Redfern, to Aboriginal owners. The Block, as it came to be called, was meant to be a testing ground for practical reconciliation, a symbol of how, separate but equal, Aborigines could interact with the broad community. Three decades on The Block symbolises the end of that vision, eroded and then destroyed when drugs infiltrated the area in the '80s. Many indigenous families, whose numbers had trebled from 1976 to 1981, fled the area, and The Block exploded into rioting in 2004 when an Aboriginal teenager, T.J. Hickey, died fleeing from police.

In 1992, at Redfern Oval, just down the street from The Block, Paul Keating gave a keynote address on reconciliation. Written by Don Watson, Mr Keating's speechwriter, 'It was, and continues to be,' said Aboriginal leader Noel Pearson, 'the seminal moment and expression of European Australian acknowledgement of grievous inhumanity to the Indigines of this land… The prime minister explicitly said it was not a question of guilt, but one of open hearts. How could this acknowledgment have been better put?'

This is what Mr Keating said, in part:

'We non-Aboriginal Australians should perhaps remind ourselves that Australia once reached out for us. Didn't Australia provide opportunity and care for the dispossessed Irish? The poor of Britain? The refugees from war and famine and persecution in the countries of Europe and Asia?

Isn't it reasonable to say that if we can build a prosperous and remarkably harmonious multi-cultural society in Australia, surely we can find just solutions to the problems which beset the first Australians – the people to whom the most injustice has been done?

'And, as I say, the starting point might be to recognise that the problem starts with us non-Aboriginal Australians.

'It begins, I think, with that act of recognition. Recognition that it was we who did the dispossessing. We took the traditional lands and smashed the traditional way of life. We brought the diseases. The alcohol. We committed the murders. We took the children from their mothers. We practised discrimination and exclusion. It was our ignorance and our prejudice. And our failure to imagine these things being done to us.

'With some noble exceptions, we failed to make the most basic human response and enter into their hearts and minds. We failed to ask, how would I feel if this were done to me? As a consequence, we failed to see that what we were doing degraded all of us.

'… It might help us if we non-Aboriginal Australians imagined ourselves disposed of land we had lived on for 50,000 years – and then imagined ourselves told that it had never been ours. Imagine if ours was the oldest culture in the world and we were told that it was worthless. Imagine if we had resisted this settlement, suffered and died in the defence of our land, and were told in history books that we had given up without a fight. Imagine if non-Aboriginal Australians had served their country in peace and war and were then ignored in history books. Imagine if our feats on sporting fields had inspired admi-

'We failed to ask, how would I feel if this were done to me?' *Newspix*

'This generation of Australians is better informed about the injustice that has been done than any generation before. We are beginning to more generally appreciate the depth and the diversity of Aboriginal and Torres Strait Islander cultures. From their music and art and dance we are beginning to recognise how much richer our national life and identity will be for the participation of Aboriginals and Torres Strait Islanders. We are beginning to learn what the Indigenous people have known for many thousands of years – how to live with our physical environment. Ever so gradually, we are learning how to see Australia through Aboriginal eyes, beginning to recognise the wisdom contained in their epic story. I think we are beginning to see how much we owe the Indigenous Australians and how much we have lost by living so apart.

'I said we non-Indigenous Australians should try to imagine the Aboriginal view. It can't be too hard. Someone imagined this event today, and it is now a marvellous reality and a great reason for hope.

'There is one thing today we cannot imagine. We cannot imagine that the descendants of people whose genius and resilience maintained a culture here through 50,000 years or more, through cataclysmic changes to the climate and environment, and who then survived two centuries of dispossession and abuse will be denied their place in the modern Australian nation. We cannot imagine that. We cannot imagine that we will fail. And with the spirit that is here today I am confident that we won't.

'I am confident that we will succeed in this decade.'

ration and patriotism and yet did nothing to diminish prejudice. Imagine if our spiritual life was denied and ridiculed. Imagine if we had suffered the injustice and then were blamed for it.

'It seems to me that if we can imagine the injustice we can imagine its opposite. And we can have justice.

# Pearson

Delivering the Ben Chifley Memorial Lecture to the Labor Party faithful at the Bathurst Panthers Leagues Club on 12 August 2000, the Aborigine Noel Pearson, director of the Cape York Institute for Policy and Leadership, put it bluntly: it was time.

'In recent times I have been thinking about the social problems of my people in Cape York Peninsula. The nature and extent of our problems are horrendous... our society is in a terrible state of dysfunction... Our social life has declined even as our material circumstances have improved greatly since we gained citizenship [and] became dependent on passive welfare. [It has] had a cancerous effect on our relationships and values.

'Combined with our outrageous grog addiction and the large and growing drug problem amongst our youth, the effects of passive welfare have not yet steadied. Our social problems have grown worse over the course of the past 30 years. The violence in our society is of phenomenal proportion and of course there is inter-generational transmission of the debilitating effects of the social passivity which our passive economy has induced...

'The irony of our newly won citizenship in 1967 was that after we became citizens with equal rights and the theoretical right to equal pay, we lost the meagre foothold that we had in the real economy and we became almost comprehensively dependent upon passive welfare for our livelihood... life in the safety net for three decades and two generations has produced a social disaster.

'... the real need is for the restoration of social order and the enforcement of law. What happens in communities when the offenders are defended as victims? Why is all of our progressive thinking ignoring these basic social requirements when it comes to black people? Is it any wonder the statistics have never improved? Would the number of people in prison decrease if we restored social order in our communities in Cape York Peninsula?

'Take another example of progressive thinking compounding misery. The predominant analysis of the huge problem of indigenous alcoholism is the symptom theory. The symptom theory holds that substance abuse is only a symptom of underlying social and psychological problems. But addiction is a condition in its own right, not a symptom... the solution to substance abuse lies in restriction and the treatment of addiction as a problem in itself.

'When I talk to people from Cape York Peninsula about what is to be done about our ridiculous levels of grog consumption (and the violence, stress, poor diet, heart disease, diabetes and mental disturbance that results) no one actually believes that the progressive prescriptions about "harm reduction" and "normalising drinking" will ever work.

'This country needs to develop a new consensus around our commitment to welfare. This consensus needs to be built on the principles of personal and family empowerment and investment and the utilisation of resources to achieve lasting change. In other words our motivation to reform welfare must be based on the principle that dependency and passivity are a scourge and must be avoided at all costs. Dependency and passivity kills people and is the surest road to social decline. Australians do not have an inalienable right to dependency, they have an inalienable right to a fair place in the real economy.'

– Abridged

'… no one actually believes that the progressive prescriptions about "harm reduction" and "normalising drinking" will ever work.' *Newspix*

# Author's Acknowledgments

I am indebted to David Horgan of The Five Mile Press, who suggested I write *Why We Are Australian*; to Maggie Pinkney who oversaw its challenging production; to Janet Pheasant, for her tireless work in obtaining the many images in this book; to Michael Bannenberg for his excellent design; to Susan Gorgioski for her invaluable assistance; and to my wife Suzie Howie whose patience was tested but triumphed. I also owe a debt to the works of such historians, authorities and journalists as Patsy Adam-Smith, Robyn Annear, Geoffrey Blainey, Michael Cannon, Les Carlyon, Don Chapman, Manning Clark, Peter Coleman, Frank Clune, Mike Dash, Keith Dunstan, Geoffrey Dutton, Tim Flannery, Harry Gordon, Richard Haese, Geoff Hocking, Robert Hughes, Clive James, A.K. Macdougall, Andrew Mercado, Diana and Michael Preston, Ian Jones, Cyril Pearl, Andrew Rule, Bernard Smith and Terry Smith, Bill Scott, Gerald Stone, John Silvester, Bill Wannan, Don Watson, Charles White and Evan Whitton.

# Pictorial Acknowledgments

The author and Publishers are grateful to Mark
Knight, of the *Melbourne Herald-Sun*
and David Rowe of the *Australian Financial Review*
for permission to reproduce their masterly cartoons.
We also thank the following organisations and
individuals for permission to publish the images in
this book:

Australian War Memorial, Canberra, pages
   80-81; 101
Ballarat Fine Art Gallery, pages 98-9
Robert Blackman, page 39
The *Bulletin* magazine, page 96
Kobal Collection/Wire Image, pages 64-5
Mark Knight and Herald and Weekly Times,
   page 77
National Australian Archives, Canberra, page 97
National Gallery of Victoria, Melbourne, pages
   10-11, 25
National Library of Australia, Canberra, pages 7,
   26, 26-7, 29, 31, 33, 67, 68-9, 102, 104
National Portrait Gallery, Canberra, page 35
Newspix, pages 17, 18-19, 25, 45, 49, 51, 52, 83,
   84-5, 85, 87, 92-3, 107, 109
Percy Grainger Museum, University of Melbourne,
   pages 71, 72
David Rowe, page 89
State Library of NSW, pages 54-5
State Library of Victoria, page 13
Tasmanian Museum and Art Gallery, Hobart,
   pages 11, 38
Victoria Police Museum, page 23.

# Our Australia
# CULTURE

In memory of my parents, Marie and George,
who started me on 'Banjo' Paterson along with
*Jack and the Beanstalk*; for the grandchildren they read to,
Noah and Jack; and for their grandchildren to come.

**Publisher's Note**

This book originally appeared as part of a larger volume:
*Why We Are Australian* (2007).
It has now been divided into three volumes:
*Our Australia: CULTURE, Our Australia: PEOPLE* and
*Our Australia: EVENTS.*

The Five Mile Press Pty Ltd
1 Centre Road, Scoresby
Victoria 3179 Australia
Email: publishing@fivemile.com.au
Website: www.fivemile.com.au

Text copyright © Paul Taylor, 2007
Copy editor: Sonya Nikadie
Supervising editor: Maggie Pinkney
Designer: Michael Bannenberg
Picture editor: Janet Pheasant

Formatting this edition
SBR Productions, Olinda, Victoria 3788

Printed in China

FRONT COVER IMAGE: Sydney beach scene from late 1960s press advertisement, courtesy *General Motors Holden*

# Our
## Australia
# CULTURE

PAUL TAYLOR

The Five Mile Press

# CONTENTS

# Preface

Australian culture. It's a contradiction in terms some people think – the English especially, still smarting over the fact that we seem to have done very well without them for the last few centuries. (Apologies to the English for that gratuitous insult, but we Australians have a reputation to uphold as down-to-earth blokes and blokessses who hold the 'Mother Country,' as we used to call England, in benign and mild contempt.)

Australia's anti-English bent was defined remarkably soon after the convicts in the First Fleet partied hard – to put it politely – on arrival in Sydney Cove in January 1788. Within two decades disdain for Mother England was common throughout the colony. The children of those first settlers – Cornstalks they came to be called – were, an English visitor wrote home in 1824, 'a different race from the old stock… They have generally light hair, blue eyes and shoot up as fast as mushrooms to a very considerable stature… As they grow up they think nothing of England and cannot bear the idea of going there.' The visitor might have been describing the ancestors of Barry 'Bazza' McKenzie.

Ironically, the creator of Bazza McKenzie, Barry Humphries, has made his home in England for most of his life, but the wellspring of his genius is in the middle class sub-urbs of Melbourne where he grew up. Humphries, an adornment to Australian culture, is one of the great international humorists, a man dressed as a woman who has them rolling in the aisles from Broadway to Bahrain.

When you're talking Culture with a capital C, we can give you sublime singers like Melba and Sutherland. Painters such as Nolan, Boyd and Emily Kame Kngwarreye. Authors and poets like Steele Rudd, Peter Carey, Tim Winton, Les Murray and Judith Wright and actors Cate Blanchett, Noah Taylor and Russell Crowe. (All right, Rusty spent his early years in New Zealand, but we consider him, like Phar Lap, Australian. 'Adopting' New Zealanders, when it suits us, is part of our culture.)

So too is Vegemite – the mysterious Magic Mud. Anzac Day. The Cup, the Melbourne horse race that has been giving the nation an excuse to party for almost 150 years. And our beaches. And of course, our sport. Sport is at the heart of our culture and has been since we first beat the Poms at their own game, cricket.

There it is again, that urge to put the English back in their box. Can't help it. It's uncontrollable. It's ingrained. It's part of our culture.

Paul Taylor, *2009*

# 1

# THE BOOKS

*The Female Eunuch* is the best known and most inspirational book ever written by an Australian. It changed the lives of women around the world. An international bestseller, translated into more than 12 languages, *The Female Eunuch* made its author a household name, the first and still the only Super Feminist. Ask someone – anywhere – to name a famous feminist and the odds are they'll answer, 'Germaine Greer.'

Ironically, Germaine Greer's book is less a handbook for feminists, and much more a call for sexual liberation. Sexual liberation, she argued, was the key to women's liberation. The book, quirky and confrontational, had stunning impact. Women didn't realise how men hated them, she said, and how much they were taught to hate themselves. The way out was sexual freedom. For millions of women the shock of recognition was palpable. The media adored this beautiful and outrageous newcomer to the women's movement – 'A dazzling combination of erudition, eccentricity and eroticism,' said *Newsweek*. 'A saucy feminist that even men like,' *Life* magazine said about its cover girl, and *TIME* said she was an eloquent maniac, seemingly 'obsessed by sex...her triumphant answer to everything.' Overnight she became a celebrity intellectual.

That would have pleased Miles Franklin, the author of *My Brilliant Career,* and a passionate feminist herself. Franklin was also a champion of Australian literature, but despaired that it would ever win worldwide recognition. In the main she was right. Marcus Clarke, Henry Handel Richardson, Martin Boyd, Neville Shute, Patrick White, Christina Stead, Shirley Hazzard, Morris West, Peter Carey, Thomas Keneally, Colleen McCullough, all have had some success internationally and a few have enjoyed the highest acclaim. But with the exception of Greer most have had little impact among Australian readers. And yet Australia is reputed to have more writers – and readers – per capita than any other country.

That paradox surely demands examination in a novel.

# On Our Selection

Steele Rudd – or to give him his more prosaic real name, Arthur Hoey Davis – wrote a book about a family of battlers in outback Queensland. His friends told him it was 'rot'. He half believed them. 'I locked it carefully in a drawer at the office, and left it for months. At regular periods my brother [public] servant reminded me of it. He would insert his head through the door, and, with a grin, inquire what had I done with those "lovely coruscations of wit".

'I took it out one day, to give the solicitor's clerk a treat. He read it, shook his head thoughtfully, and said nothing. Confinement, I was convinced, had not improved it. In a reckless moment I dragged it to the light again, packed it and mailed it to the editor of the *Bulletin*.'

*On Our Selection*, a thinly disguised semi-autobiographical novel based on Davis's experiences growing up on a desperately poor farm in Queensland's Darling Downs, sold 250,000 copies by the time of his death in 1935. A play based on the book was seen by an audience of a million in Australia, New Zealand and London's West End. The Rudd family, and Dad and Dave in particular, became part of the Australian argot, the subject of jokes, radio serials and television comedies. The first of seven movies based on the book was made in 1920; the most recent in 1995, with a cast that included Leo McKern as the hard working short-fused Dad, Dame Joan Sutherland as Mother, Geoffrey Rush as the near silent Dave and Noah Taylor as Joe, the stammering youth with a gift for making comedy amid consternation. A century and more after Arthur Davis summoned up the courage to mail his manuscript to the *Bulletin*, the movie

Arthur Hoey Davis – Steele Rudd – was the eighth of 13 children in a family that inspired *On Our Selection*. Seven film adaptations of his work and a radio series made Dad and Dave household names.

*On Our Selection* was still getting guffaws of delight around the world.

But the book, and most of those that Davis wrote after it and based on the same template of the battlers in the bush, was not intended to be knockabout comedy. *On Our Selection* is very funny, and more so for those who had experienced the life the author described. But it was also a chronicle of the hard, sometimes cruel and sad life that Davis knew and grew up in and *On Our Selection* is at times moving and poignant.

The eighth of 13 children of a transported Welsh convict, Arthur Hoey Davis was born in 1868. He was six when he saw his father's struggles to survive as a farmer on Queensland's Darling Downs. At 18 he joined the public service and by 1890 he was contributing short articles to Brisbane newspapers. In 1899 he astonished himself and all who knew him when *On Our Selection* became the bestseller of the day.

Despite the huge success of *On Our Selection*, the last half of Arthur Davis's life was marked by a run of bad luck and worse business management. In 1903 Government cost-cutting caused him to be retrenched from his public service job. He and his wife Christina had three small children, but he refused opportunities to return to the public service and spent the rest of his life trying to live by his writing. He never recaptured the spark that had made his first books bestsellers, and the monthly magazine he founded failed, leaving him with a heavy financial loss.

At his wife's urging Davis returned to the Darling Downs and invested his considerable fortune in an established farm. His writing degenerated. In 1917 the farm failed; one son came back from World War One injured; and finally, in 1920, Christina, suffering extreme anxiety neurosis, had to be permanently institutionalised.

By the early 1920s Davis was living with his younger children in Brisbane boarding houses and he spent the last decade of his life in near poverty in a one-room flat in Sydney's Kings Cross. He died in Brisbane in 1935, widely acknowledged to be an unfashionable 'has-been'.

Cecil Mann in the *Australian Writers' Annual* dissented from that view.

'A noted Australian literary figure has passed – the creator of Dad, Dave and Mum. There was wide agreement on that. With it went a care not to praise too highly. Steele Rudd's "vaudeville gaucheries" were all very well for the generation that roared at them, but we had advanced a little in literary discrimination since then... And so the author who had evoked more outright laughter than any other Australian writer, perhaps more than any imported writer in his prime, was ushered out with a polite requiem of faint praise.'

The first chapter of *On Our Selection*, reproduced here, is a poignant taste of how the settlers cleared the land we see today, and of our love of comedy that emerges from adversity.

### *Starting the Selection*

It's 20 years ago now since we settled on the Creek. Twenty years! I remember well the day we came from Stanthorpe, on Jerome's dray – eight of us, and all the things – beds, tubs, a bucket, the two cedar chairs with the pine bottoms and backs that Dad put in them, some pint-pots and old Crib. It was a scorching hot day, too – talk about thirst! At every creek we came to we drank till it stopped running.

Dad didn't travel up with us: he had gone some months before, to put up the house and dig the waterhole. It was a slabbed house, with shingled roof, and space enough for two rooms; but the partition wasn't up. The floor was earth; but Dad had a mixture of sand and fresh cow-dung with which he used to keep it level. About once every month he would put it on; and everyone had to keep outside that day till it was dry. There were no locks on the doors: pegs were put in to keep them fast at night; and the slabs were not very close together, for we could easily see through them anybody coming on horseback. Joe and I used to play at counting the stars through the cracks in the roof.

The day after we arrived Dad took Mother and us out to see the paddock and the flat on the other side of the gully that he was going to clear for cultivation. There was no fence round the paddock, but he pointed out on a tree the surveyor's marks, showing the boundary of our ground. It must have been fine land, the way Dad talked about it! There was very valuable timber on it, too, so he said; and he showed us a place, among some rocks on a ridge, where he was sure gold would be found, but we weren't to say anything about it. Joe and I went back that evening and turned over every stone on the ridge, but we didn't find any gold.

No mistake, it was a real wilderness – nothing but trees, 'goannas', dead timber, and bears; and the nearest house – Dwyer's – was three miles away. I often wonder how the women stood it the first few years; and I can remember how Mother, when she was alone, used to sit on a log, where the lane is now, and cry for hours. Lonely! It WAS lonely.

Dad soon talked about clearing a couple of acres and putting in corn – all of us did, in fact – till the work commenced. It was a delightful topic before

When the fire took the fencing.

George W. Lambert, one of the most accomplished artists of the first quarter of the 20th century was one of a number of distinguished Australian artists who illustrated *On Our Selection*.

Some of the other distinguished artists included A. H. Fullwood (above), A. J. Fisher (far right) and Alf Vincent (previous page).

we started, but in two weeks the clusters of fires that illumined the whooping bush in the night, and the crash upon crash of the big trees as they fell, had lost all their poetry.

We toiled and toiled clearing those four acres, where the haystacks are now standing, till every tree and sapling that had grown there was down. We thought then the worst was over; but how little we knew of clearing land! Dad was never tired of calculating and telling us how much the crop would fetch if the ground could only be got ready in time to put it in; so we laboured the harder.

With our combined male and female forces and the aid of a sapling lever we rolled the thundering big logs together in the face of Hell's own fires; and when there were no logs to roll it was tramp, tramp the day through, gathering armfuls of sticks, while the clothes clung to our backs with a muddy perspiration. Sometimes Dan and Dave would sit in the shade beside the billy of water and gaze at the small patch that had taken so long to do; then they would turn hopelessly to what was before them and ask Dad (who would never take a spell) what was the use of thinking of ever getting such a place cleared? And when Dave wanted to know why Dad didn't take up a place on the plain, where there were no trees to grub and plenty of water, Dad would cough as if something was sticking in his throat, and then curse terribly about the squatters and political jobbery. He would soon cool down, though, and get hopeful again.

'Look at the Dwyers,' he'd say; 'from 10 acres of wheat they got 70 pounds last year, besides feed for the fowls; they've got corn in now, and there's only the two.'

It wasn't only burning off! Whenever there came a short drought the waterhole was sure to run

'Look at the shoulder on her! And the loin she has!'

Bearded Bert Bailey spent much of his career playing Dad on stage and screen. The most recent film adaptation of *On Our Selection* had a stellar cast: Leo McKern as Dad, Dame Joan Sutherland as Mother, Noah Taylor as Joe and Geoffrey Rush as Dave.

dry; then it was take turns to carry water from the springs – about two miles. We had no draught horse, and if we had there was neither water-cask, trolly, nor dray; so we humped it – and talk about a drag! By the time you returned, if you hadn't drained the bucket, in spite of the big drink you'd take before leaving the springs, more than half would certainly be spilt through the vessel bumping against your leg every time you stumbled in the long grass. Somehow, none of us liked carrying water. We would sooner keep the fires going all day without dinner than do a trip to the springs.

One hot, thirsty day it was Joe's turn with the bucket, and he managed to get back without spilling very much. We were all pleased because there was enough left after the tea had been made to give each a drink. Dinner was nearly over; Dan had finished, and was taking it easy on the sofa, when Joe said:

'I say, Dad, what's a nater-dog like?' Dad told him: 'Yellow, sharp ears and bushy tail.'

'Those muster bin some then thet I seen – I don't know 'bout the bushy tail – all th' hair had comed off.' 'Where'd y' see them, Joe?' we asked. 'Down 'n th' springs floating about – dead.'

Then everyone seemed to think hard and look at the tea. I didn't want any more. Dan jumped off the sofa and went outside; and Dad looked after Mother.

At last the four acres – excepting the biggest of the iron-bark trees and about 50 stumps – were pretty well cleared; and then came a problem that couldn't be worked-out on a draught-board. I have already said that we hadn't any draught horses; indeed, the only thing on the selection like a horse was an old 'tuppy' mare that Dad used to straddle. The date of her foaling went further back than Dad's, I believe; and she was shaped something like an alderman. We found her one day in about 18 inches of mud, with both eyes picked out by the crows, and her hide bearing evidence that a feathery tribe had made a roost of her carcase. Plainly, there was no chance of breaking up the ground with her help. We had no plough, either; how then was the corn to be put in? That was the question.

Dan and Dave sat outside in the corner of the chimney, both scratching the ground with a chip and not saying anything. Dad and Mother sat inside talking it over. Sometimes Dad would get up and walk round the room shaking his head; then he would kick old Crib for lying under the table. At last Mother struck something which brightened him up, and he called Dave.

'Catch Topsy and – ' He paused because he remembered the old mare was dead.

'Run over and ask Mister Dwyer to lend me three hoes.'

Dave went; Dwyer lent the hoes; and the problem was solved. That was how we started.

# Seven Little Australians

'Ido want Fame – plenty of it,' wrote Ethel Turner in her diary. On her 23rd birthday, a few days later, in January 1893, she made another entry: 'Night started a new story that I shall call *Seven Little Australians*.' Ethel was to have Fame.

Now in its third century, Ethel Turner's enchanting 1894 novel has won the affection of children and adults around the world, sold two million copies in 13 languages and been adapted for stage, film and television. Generation after generation, this classic Australian tale is still loved by adults and children, drawn into the lives of the family at Misrule.

*Seven Little Australians* is the story of Meg, 16, who is suspected of keeping a diary, irrepressible Judy, 13, 'without doubt the worst of the seven' and the other Woolcot children, all of them constantly in strife with their father, the strict army officer, Captain Woolcot. The captain's wife, we are led to presume, died having the girl who is always called Baby, and he has married again, a young and kindly girl, Esther. Only 20, and beautiful, Esther has a baby boy, about 18 months old, who is always called the General. At their rambling home on the Parramatta River the children run wild while struggling to win the affections of their remote father. Once called The River House, the Woolcots know it as Misrule. Through it all, however, love and a healthy dose of the Australian sense of fun holds the family together in the face of tragedy: the death of one of the seven.

Ethel Turner came to Australia from England with her mother and sisters when she was 10 years old in 1880. For more than six decades she kept diaries of her full and eventful life. She married Henry Curlewis, a lawyer, in 1896, and had two children: Jean, who became a writer, and Adrian, a judge. In just five months Ethel wrote *The Family at Misrule*, a bestselling sequel to *Seven Little Australians* and before she died in 1958 had written more than 40 books.

Baby was four, and was a little soft fat thing with pretty cuddlesome ways, great smiling eyes, and lips very kissable when they were free from jam. She had a weakness, however, for making the General cry, or she would have been really almost a model child. Innumerable times she had been found pressing its poor little chest to make it 'squeak' and even pinching its tiny arms, or pulling its innocent nose, just for the strange pleasure of hearing the yells of despair it instantly set up. Captain Woolcot ascribed the peculiar tendency to the fact that the child had once had a dropsical-looking woolly lamb, from which the utmost pressure would only elicit the faintest possible squeak: he said it was only natural that now she had something so amenable to squeezing she should want to utilise it.

Bunty was six, and was fat and very lazy. He hated scouting at cricket, he loathed the very name of a paper-chase, and as for running an errand, why, before anyone could finish saying something was wanted he would have utterly disappeared. He was rather small for his age; and I don't think had ever been seen with a clean face. Even at church, though the immediate front turned to the minister might be passable, the people in the next pew had always an uninterrupted view of the black rim where washing operations had left off.

The next on the list – I am going from youngest to oldest, you see – was the 'show' Woolcot, as Pip, the eldest boy, used to say. You have seen those exquisite child-angel faces on Raphael Tuck's Christmas cards? I think the artist must just have dreamed of Nell, and then reproduced the vision imperfectly. She was 10, and had a little fairy-like figure, gold hair clustering in wonderful waves and curls around her face, soft hazel eyes, and a little rosebud of a mouth. She was not conceited either, her family took care of that – Pip would have nipped such a weakness very sternly in its earliest bud; but in some way if there was a pretty ribbon to spare, or a breadth of bright material; just enough for one little frock, it fell as a matter of course to her.

Judy was only three years older, but was the greatest contrast imaginable. Nellie used to move rather slowly about, and would have made a picture in any attitude. Judy I think, was never seen to walk, and seldom looked picturesque. If she did not dash madly to the place she wished to get to, she would progress by a series of jumps, bounds, and odd little skips. She was very thin, as people generally are who have quicksilver instead of blood in their veins; she had a small, eager, freckled face, with very, bright dark eyes, a small, determined mouth, and a mane of untidy, curly dark hair that was the trial of her life.

Without doubt she was the worst of the seven, probably because she was the cleverest. Her brilliant inventive powers plunged them all into ceaseless scrapes, and though she often bore the brunt of the blame with equanimity, they used to turn round, not infrequently, and upbraid her for suggesting the mischief. She had been christened 'Helen', which in no way accounts for 'Judy', but

then nicknames are rather unaccountable things sometimes, are they not? Bunty said it was because she was always popping and jerking herself about like the celebrated wife of Punch, and there really is something in that. Her other name, 'Fizz', is easier to understand; Pip used to say he never yet had seen the ginger ale that effervesced and bubbled and made the noise that Judy did.

I haven't introduced you to Pip yet, have I? He was a little like Judy, only handsomer and taller, and he was 14, and had as good an opinion of himself and as poor a one of girls as boys of that age generally have.

Meg was the eldest of the family, and had a long, fair plait that Bunty used to delight in pulling; a sweet, rather dreamy face, and a powdering of pretty freckles that occasioned her much tribulation of spirit. It was generally believed in the family that she wrote poetry and stories, and even kept a diary, but no one had ever seen a vestige of her papers, she kept them so carefully locked up in her old tin hat-box.

A scene from the three-part BBC series *Seven Little Australians*.

# Power Without Glory

Frank Hardy's *Power Without Glory* purports to be a novel. But on the dedication page is a quotation from Horace: 'Let fiction meant to please be living near to truth.'

The question that Australians have been asking ever since *Power Without Glory's* publication in 1949 is: just how near to truth does this fiction live? Increasingly, the answer seems to be 'not very', and certainly not on the key question that made the novel a social, political, legal and literary landmark.

*Power Without Glory* was written as propaganda. From the 1930s into the war years and beyond, communism had a growing influence in Australian politics and trade unions. By the 1950s the Catholic Church was successfully counteracting communism in the unions through the Industrial Groups. The 'Groupers' were offshoots of the Movement, a Catholic organisation formed to combat communism and to influence the Labor Party, the party most practising Catholics supported. The conflict reached its apogee in The Split – the tumultuous and disastrous schism in the Labor Party that was to keep it from office for almost two decades.

But in 1949, five years before The Split, Frank Hardy, a communist, produced a book designed to sully the reputations of Archbishop Daniel Mannix, who had inspired the founding of the Movement, Bob Santamaria, its intellectual leader, and above all, John Wren, the self-made millionaire who was a friend of Mannix and thought by communists – probably erroneously – to be financing it. All three,

John Wren made a fortune from illegal gambling, but he was also a philanthropist – and puritanical in his personal life.

and scores more well-known identities – Labor Party politicians in federal, state and local politics; journalists; sportsmen in the worlds of horse racing, cycling, wrestling and boxing; gamblers and notorious criminals – are portrayed in the book under pseudonyms that scarcely bother to hide the true identities.

A highly readable, fast-paced narrative, *Power Without Glory* is set in Melbourne during John Wren's days of power. Wren was no saint. He had made his money operating an illegal betting tote, but he was not the gangster, racketeer, and abusive husband that Hardy portrays under the name John West. And Wren's wife, Ellen – Nellie – a devout Catholic, was certainly not the woman, 'Nellie West', in the novel. In *Power Without Glory* Nellie

Frank Hardy's court case made him a national figure, reckoned by many to be a heroic literary giant. In 1952 he went to Russia and wrote praising Joseph Stalin, the 'only dishonest book', he later said, that he ever wrote. Hardy campaigned for land rights for the Gurindji, two of whom came to his funeral, along with Gough Whitlam and other prominent Labor Party figures.

West has an affair with a bricklayer working on the family's mansion, and conceives a child, Xavier. When West discovers this he assaults her, ignores Xavier and is jubilant when Xavier dies. Nellie Wren did bear a child named Xavier who died aged three in 1922.

There could be no doubt about Nellie West's true identity and in 1950 John Wren sued for criminal libel. Hardy used the story of Ellen Wren's alleged adultery to attack her husband, and in turn John Wren used his wife to bring criminal libel charges against Hardy.

In the heated political and sectarian crosscurrents of the '50s, the Supreme Court theatre was a sensation. And at the end of it, the jury found Hardy not guilty. The book, the jury decided, was fiction.

Frank Hardy was free and his fame was assured. *Power Without Glory* sold 100,000 copies in quick time. A sequel about the trial itself was a bestseller. All told, with many sales in communist Eastern Europe,

it may have sold a million copies. In 1976 the ABC serialised it: 26 episodes, each of an hour, and it rated far beyond the corporation's most optimistic hopes. Once again the book topped the bestseller list.

'I knew you would come,' she said, leaning backwards a little over the table, wide-eyed, her body taut, her auburn hair swept back from her face, her breasts heaving above her slim waist.

'What are you standing there for?' she challenged him, in a soft, seductive voice.

He opened his mouth but did not speak; then suddenly he placed the billy-can on the floor and closed on her with two great strides. His arms circled her waist and, as their lips met savagely, her arms went around his neck, knocking his hat on the floor. They kissed with wild intensity, until breathlessness parted their lips. Nellie ran her hands through his fair hair.

'I love you! I can't help it! I love you!'

From *Power Without Glory*

# Monkey Grip and The First Stone

Perhaps Australia's foremost contemporary essayist, Helen Garner has written two books that define two very different decades. *Monkey Grip* was immediately recognised as one of the outstanding novels of its time when it was published in 1977. Eighteen years later, at the height of the political correctness of the 1990s, she wrote her first non-fiction book, *The First Stone*. An investigation into an alleged sexual harassment at Melbourne University, *The First Stone* bitterly divided those who saw it as a betrayal of her previously impeccable feminist credentials and those who acclaimed it for its bravery and integrity and agreed with Garner that the young women who brought the sexual harassment case were puritans, naive but destructive.

Garner argues in *The First Stone* that there is a world of difference between sexual harassment in the workplace (the Master of Ormond College was alleged to have touched a student's breast) and sexual assault. 'Between "being made to feel uncomfortable" and "violence against women" lies a vast range of male and female behaviours,' she wrote. 'If we deny this, we enfeeble language and drain it of meaning. We insult the suffering of women who have met real violence, and we distort the subtleties of human interaction into caricatures that can serve only as propaganda for war. And it infuriates me that any woman who insists on drawing these crucial distinctions should be called a traitor to her sex.'

Helen Garner's work draws on her own life and the world around her. Reviewing her collection of essays,

One of Australia's best modern writers, Helen Garner might have been a teacher had she not been dismissed in 1972 for candidly answering her students' questions about sex. *Newspix*

*The Feel of Steel*, Cath Darcy said: 'Helen Garner's world view is more than just her own: it is the voice of a particular generation of artists and social activists who have now reached middle age. As in all Garner's books, her prior history as a radical in Melbourne's 1970s counter-culture underlies the narrative and places her current observations in a socio-historical trajectory. Her passing references to "long-ago acid trips", her "old hippie instinct", and to bringing up her daughter "with her own bare hands" back in '70s Fitzroy when people "slung their kids on the back of their pushbikes and zoomed away" remind us that Garner exists in Australian public culture as a talisman of that social and historical milieu.'

Garner's classic novel of '70s Fitzroy, *Monkey Grip*, is 'The best account of the last moment of innocence before hippydom turned into yuppiedom,' Imre Saluszinsky wrote in the *Australian*. Nora, the narrator, lives in inner-suburban Melbourne with her child Gracie and her friends, a group of writers, singers and actors. She succumbs to an affair with Javo, a heroin addict – a man with 'a monkey on his back' – and struggles to regain control of her life. But the harder Nora and Javo try to pull away, the tighter the monkey grip.

In the back door, across the worn matting, three steps on the lino of the hall, turn to my bedroom door – and Javo was in my bed with a thick white mask of calamine lotion on his torn skin.

'It's all right, Nor!' he burst out eagerly at the sight of my shocked face. 'It's only some pimples.'

I stood staring at him. I saw that he had been in my bed all night. I felt panicky, and tired of it, wanting to escape now, quick, before the water got any deeper.

I turned back to the kitchen, and found Clive and Georgie sitting at the table drinking coffee. I slid wearily into a chair. They pushed a cup towards me and looked at me in silence, half-grinning about the white-masked apparition in my room. I grinned too, and shrugged, and felt again the moving of that reluctant love for him, in spite of all reason.

'Imagine,' said Clive, catching his breath and leaning forward to me, 'imagine how it must feel to be someone like Javo, thinking, "Is there anything that prevents her from trusting her life to me?" And knowing that YES, there's this – pumping into the crook of his arm – 'imagine the anguish of knowing that!'

Noni Hazlehurst as Nora, the young single mother who claims, 'I don't want to love anyone forever', and Colin Friels as her lover, the junkie, Javo, in the 1982 film adaptation of *Monkey Grip*.

# A Fortunate Life

From the age of eight, his father dead and abandoned by his mother, Albert Facey went to work – backbreaking, dawn to dusk work – as a farm labourer. At his first job a brute beat him with a stockwhip, so cruelly that the boy almost died. His life was saved by a neighbour, a nurse, but witnesses were too frightened to go to the police. He had a narrow escape from death seven years later, droving cattle in Western Australia's Ashburton River country. For seven days he was lost in the wild country. 'A person would have to be lost like I was to really know what it was like – it was dreadful.' He was forced to eat grass, like his horse, Dinnertime: 'Dinnie was in clover; she didn't seem to mind if we were lost forever.' He was saved by Aborigines, people he had been told frightening tales about when he was a child. 'You would have thought I was a special king or something the fuss they made of me.'

Three more years, and this time, at 18, he is told to clean up a well, 42 metres deep. 'Jock and Bentley refused to go down the well, so that left me.' Near the bottom the rough timber shoring up the well gives way and crashes around him. Twenty metres from the top he sees the windlass rope. 'I stepped gently across and got hold of that precious rope and pulling on it I went up and out in a few minutes.

'When I was well away – about 20 yards or so – I couldn't help it, I cried bitterly and couldn't stop. Yet while I was down the well and in great danger and scared stiff, crying was the furtherest thing form my mind.'

A big, tough young man by now, he travelled as a pug in Mickey Flynn's boxing troupe and when

Despite cruel and crushing experiences Albert Facey could say: 'I have lived a very good life… and I am thrilled by it when I look back'. *Photographer: Roger Garwood*

World War One started, enlisted in the AIF and went to Gallipoli. 'I'd have stayed behind if I'd known,' he wrote, but his account of his time at the battlefront is a moving record of mateship – and a remarkable and romantic story founded on a pair of socks.

'… we received some trench comfort parcels from home. Everything was very quiet this day, and a sergeant-major and several men with bags of parcels came along our line and threw each of us a parcel. I got a pair of socks in my parcel. Having big feet – I take a 10 in boots – I called out to my mates saying that I had a pair of socks that I would be glad to swap for a bigger pair as I didn't think they would fit. Strange as it seems, I was the only person in my

19

Albert Facey's humble homestead, relocated to the Wickepin town centre in Western Australia's wheatbelt, somehow conveys the character of the man.

section to get socks; the others got all kinds of things such as scarves, balaclavas, vests, notepaper, pencils, envelopes and handkerchiefs... I found a note rolled up in my socks and it read: "We wish the soldier that gets this parcel the best of luck and health and safe return home to his loved ones when the war is over." It was signed, "Evelyn Gibson. Hon. Secretary, Girl Guides, Bunbury, W.A." A lot of my mates came from Bunbury so I asked if any of them knew an Evelyn Gibson. They all knew her and said she was a good looker and very smart, and that she came from a well-liked and respected family. I told them that she was mine and we all had an argument, in fun, about this girl and we all claimed her.

'The socks, when I tried them on, fitted perfectly and they were hand-knitted with wool. That was the only parcel I received while at Gallipoli.'

Late in 1915, Bert Facey, badly wounded and invalided out of the army, met the girl who had knitted the socks. She was walking with another girl down Barrack Street, Perth, when he and a mate got into conversation with them. 'I then asked the girl who had spoken to me her name. Now, what a shock I got. She said, "My name is Evelyn Gibson."... Although I had never had any real schooling I knew what the word providence meant and here it was now. Evelyn was the most beautiful

girl I had ever seen.' In 1916 they married. Still to come was the loss of his farm in the Depression and the death of their son in World War Two. *A Fortunate Life*, Bert Facey's autobiography, might, then, be presumed to be a deeply depressing story. On the contrary. The title of his book is not intended to be ironic and the happiness of his life after his marriage to Evelyn Gibson can be seen in this simple sentence, written about her death in 1976: 'We had been married for 59 years, 11 months and 12 days.'

That was Bert Facey's fortunate life, a life that was a celebration of his simple honesty, compassion and courage.

Bert Facey, of course, had to teach himself to read and write and he was 87 when the Fremantle Arts Centre Press published his book in 1981. He died the following year, but he lived long enough to know it won the NSW Premier's Literary Award and unanimous and sweeping praise – and deep admiration and affection for its author – from all who read it. *A Fortunate Life* has sold more than a quarter of a million copies.

# 2

# THE RADIO

'On June 15th of this year the *Daily Mail* of London inaugurated the first "world" concert, in conjunction with the famous opera star, Madame Nellie Melba, transmitting her voice over vast distances.' – *Radio News*, September 1920

In 1920, Dame Nellie Melba sang in a radio broadcast heard as far away as Paris. The shock of hearing the diva's disembodied voice emerging from a wooden box – the wireless – so stunned her secretary that she had a fit of the vapours. Nineteen years later, when Prime Minister Menzies advised that it was his melancholy duty to inform us that Australia was at war he was heard on radio sets in millions of Australian homes. And for the next 20 years 'the wireless' – about as tall as a ten-year-old and considerably wider, a stained timber cabinet with fretwork and fabric covering the speaker and a glowing dial - was a beloved part of the family.

From it we heard an endless stream of drama, comedy, music, sport, brand-names, catch-phrases and adored 'personalities'. Jack Davey's 'Hi ho, everybody!' *Blue Hills*. Carter's Little Liver Pills. *Ada and Elsie*. Bob and Dolly Dyer ('Howdy, customers!'). Buckley's Canadiol Mixture. Jim Gussey. *Cop the Lot*. Dick Fair. Terry Dear. Harry Dearth. Rinso. Willie Fennell. *When a Girl Marries* ('For all those who are in love and for those who can... remember'). *The Amateur Hour*. Joy Nichols. *The Goons*. Jim Davidson. *The Lux Radio Theatre*. Bonnington's Irish Moss. *Dr Paul. Mary Livingstone, M.D. Martin's Corner*. The cricket, the footy, the races. Smoky Dawson. *The Hit Parade. McCackie Mansion*, ('Cop this, young Harry!'). *Pick-a-Box. Nightbeat*. Bob Rogers.

Television, of course, brought the golden age of radio to an end. By then 'the wireless' had become 'the radio,' just as 'the pictures,' were to become 'the cinema.' Radio sets shrank and came housed in sleek bakelite and were found on Laminex kitchen benches, out in the shed, in teenagers' bedrooms: and, in time, when it truly *was* wireless, on the beach and in shirt pockets. Its function had taken on a new form, too. Once we listened. Today we talk back.

# The cricket

Before Tony Greig's car key, before Bill Lawry's insistence that it is all happening, before Kerry O'Keefe's mad scientist cackle – even before Richie – there was the synthetic cricket commentary.

In 1932–33, when Richie was a two-year-old toddler, the Australian Broadcasting Commission was formed, just in time to broadcast the bitter and brutal Bodyline Tests. The revelation that you could hear the result of every ball bowled in a Test match caused huge public interest and established the ABC as the national broadcaster in the minds of Australians.

But the following year the Australian side went to England to regain the Ashes, and the ABC was stumped. How could it broadcast the matches when the overseas short-wave transmission wasn't reliable enough to send live commentary back to Australia?

The answer, the ABC hit upon, was the "synthetic" broadcast.

The ABC's cricket commentator Jim Maxwell explained how it worked to Radio National:

'Well they had a crack at it in 1930; it was actually a combination of two commercial stations, Melbourne's 3DB and Sydney's 2UW, that came up with a way of getting the information across, but they didn't do what became known as the "synthetic" broadcast. Because the commercial stations saw some novelty value in having a mix of cricket and live entertainers, comedians, they didn't do what the ABC became famous for.

'And the ABC actually had 13 people between those that were interpreting the information, the technicians and the broadcasters in and around the studio to do this kind of synthetic or ghost

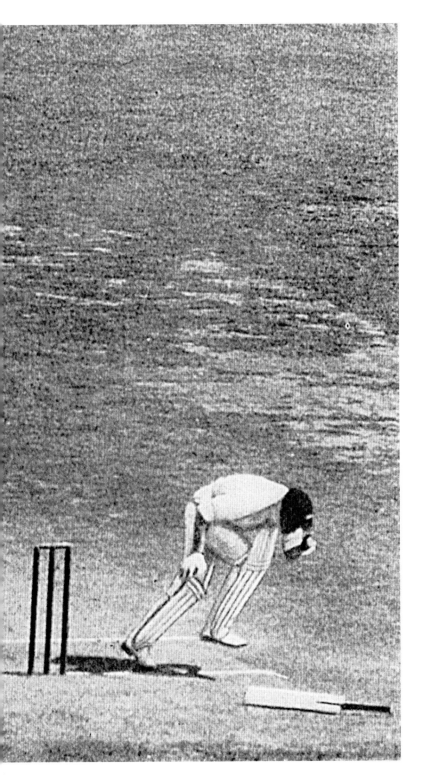

broadcasting of the game. And they'd adopted a code from which the commentators were able to come up with some invention about what occurred on a particular ball.

'Every couple of minutes, someone would dash into the studio with message Number 46, let's say, and on that piece of paper there would be a code for the six balls of the over.

'Now remember the commentator's sitting there with a picture of the ground, and for each bowler he knew which fieldsman, say it was Australia in the field, was in which position. So the code might come through with the word "unchance", and this indicated that the ball had been hit on the full, past the bowler for four runs.

'And so then he would go into a description that led him through that. "Fleetwood-Smith comes into bowl, and Hammond's down the pitch; he's hit it on the full, straight past the bowler, down the ground for four", and up would come the applause from the sound effects created by Dion Wheeler or Des Turner, who was sitting across from the commentator with a couple of disks.

'Imagine the timing that was involved in this to bring up off disk, dropping the needle in the right spot, to get those sound effects, and the commentator who sat there with a pencil, and whacked it on a little wooden device in front of him, to make the sound that was similar to a bat hitting a ball as he described:

"Bowes comes in and bowls to Bradman, and Bradman (WHACK) hits it through the covers for four", and so it did sound very real. And there was a point during this sort of cricket charade that

The defining image of the Bodyline series. At the Adelaide Oval in 1933, the Australian wicketkeeper Bert Oldfield, reels after being struck on the temple by a ball from Larwood. Oldfield was carried unconscious from the field. The broadcast of the incident inflamed listeners around Australia.

Charles Moses, who was one of the instigators of it all, had to go and shoot a Movietone thing for the newsreel to explain to everybody "This is what actually happens; we're all sitting in a studio, we're not at the ground. So although you may think we're giving you a live commentary of the game, we are actually in a studio, we're making it up." But radio being the illusion that it is, they could get away with it, and they did.'

The commentators had to learn to pace themselves though, as Alan McGilvray discovered.

'It was a peculiar experience to sit down for the first time and try and do,' McGilvray said after his retirement in 1985. 'You've got the cable, six balls on it, and I'd dash through it, I'd get through those in about two minutes, and it took me a long while to realise, and in fact it took all of us a long while to realise, that the over would take about four and a half to five minutes.

'So when we finished those six balls, we had no further information, no cables, and so we used to look at the door for this young runner they had, to come in from the decoding room and give me a bit of paper with some particulars on it. And then suddenly, someone woke up and said, 'Look, we're getting through this in two minutes; that means we have a lot of padding to do.'

Today, with Kerry's cackles and Tony's car key we don't have that problem.

# McCackie Mansion

Mo McCackie has a lot to answer for: Gra Gra, Sir Les Patterson and Barry McKenzie, Hoges and hundreds more Australian comic figures; they all owe Mo.

Mo resembled none of them in the slightest way. His chalk white face ringed by a coal black five o'clock shadow, spittle flying over the radio station microphone and into the studio audience, he was a caricature that could not be contemplated today – certainly he was not an 'Aussie' that we could relate to. But he showed the way to what has emerged as a distinct strain of comedy: iconoclastic, vulgar and immensely funny – and above all, Australian.

Mo – Roy Rene – had been Australia's foremost vaudeville comedian when, in 1947, in his mid-50s he tired of touring and left the stage for the radio studio. Rene was always slightly insecure. He could be mystified at times by exactly why he had people helpless with laughter. And radio, new to him, was worrying. Mo could have a theatre audience in fits simply by mugging but mugging couldn't be seen over the wireless. His humour, Rene feared, could fall flat on an audience that couldn't see his face. And there was the matter of his 'blue' humour. Almost everything Mo said, somehow, came out 'blue'. It wasn't his fault, he would insist: 'They're the ones with the dirty minds!'

Fred Parsons, his writer, confirmed this. Mo never said a word a child couldn't repeat at home, Parsons said. Inference, with Mo, was everything.

*McCackie Mansion's* Hal Lashwood ('Lasho') adopts the trademark beam and bowler hat of movie star Stan Laurel as Roy Rene ('Mo') leers.

Rene needn't have worried about his facial expressions. By this time Mo had one of the most recognisable mugs – as he would say – in the nation. *McCackie Mansion*, the final segment of an hour-long show, *Calling the Stars*, was broadcast in front of an adoring studio audience guaranteed to laugh at Mo's slightest facial tic. The segment was so popular that it kept cinema audiences down. And every Tuesday night for listeners of 2GB and its 59 associate stations on the Major network it was part of the fun visualising Mo, fake five o'clock shadow, prominent proboscis shading his real 'mo', in his trademark battered top hat, sagging trousers and long-sleeved singlet and lisping as he opened the door at McCackie Mansion:

'Who's that banging at my doorbell?'

In the studio and around Australia, waiting for the formal response, the audience could barely contain itself as the mincing Harry Avondale – as the agog studio audience discovered, en pointe, like a prima ballerina – replied in his camp, lilting way...

'It's little me. Spencer the garbage man!'

Rolling laughter of delighted recognition. Sustained applause.

Then, Mo (spluttering): 'Come in, Spencer dear, but stand downwind of me... You smell like a bucket of prawns that's been left too long in the sun. Peeeouw!'

Collapse of hysterical listeners.

*McCackie Mansion* (Rene chose the name McCackie because he knew from vaudeville days

that he only had to say the word for an explosion of laughter) was scheduled for six weeks but went on to run for almost three years. Its characters, the ratbag Mo McCackie, his son, Young Harry, the outrageously camp garbage man Spencer, and the next-door neighbours, Horrible Herbie and whining Mr Lasho, gave us a legacy of expressions that can still be heard six decades on: 'Strike me lucky!'; 'Don't come the raw prawn with me!'; 'Cop this, Young Harry!'; 'One of my mob' and 'You little trimmer'. But Roy Rene's great legacy was the revelation he gave Graham Kennedy and Kennedy in turn passed on: Australians love comedy when it's irreverent, doesn't speak down to them, goes way beyond the limits – and is in the Australian vernacular. Kennedy saw Roy Rene on stage only once but must have heard him on *McCackie Mansion* hundreds of times. With his 3UZ radio mentor, Nicky, Kennedy was clearly influenced by Rene's outrageous style. Here's a moment from *McCackie Mansion* that could equally be a moment 10 years later on *In Melbourne Tonight*, with Bert Newton as Spencer and Graham as Mo:

Spencer: *Oh, mercy me, I nearly forgot! The postman came up and thrust an epistle into my hot little hand.*

Mo (slavering, eyes bulging): *The filthy beast!*

If you can hear and see Kennedy saying that you've had a glimpse of the comedy trailblazer, Mo.

For three decades *The Argonauts* was an integral part of the daily lives of hundreds of thousands of Australian children. Today its place has been taken by *Big Brother* and *Home and Away*.

# The Argonauts

The Argonauts, first broadcast in Melbourne in 1933, encouraged children's contributions of writing, music, poetry and art, and became one of the ABC's most popular programs, running six days a week for 28 years. At its peak it had more than 50,000 members – one Australian child in every 20 – with 10,000 newcomers joining each year in the 1950s.

One of those members was 12-year-old Barry Humphries.

*The Argonauts*, Barry Humphries wrote in *My Life As Me*, were his 'preferred family', his cultural mentors. He idolised them. So when they came to Melbourne to broadcast at the Royal Show Barry begged his father to take him. His heart pounding with anticipation, he joined the crowd of fellow Argonauts craning their necks at the window looking into the studio, filled with anticipation of their first glimpse of their heroes, the beautiful Elizabeth, Jason, Mac and Joe.

'We seemed to wait a long time, during which other people entered the studio, through a door lined with perforated acoustic panels. An older man in a rumpled suit, with a ginger moustache, sat down and rather crossly examined some papers. A fat bald fellow wearing an old cardigan lit a cigarette and glanced casually through the glass windows at the crowd. A fair-haired woman in a beige twin-set came in and started talking to one of the technical people.'

And then the theme music started and the chorus sang: 'Adventure ho, Argonauts, row, row, row!' and to Barry's astonishment the old man with the moustache was talking, reading from his lines, greeting the woman in the twin-set: 'Oh and here's Elizabeth coming into the studio. Hello, Elizabeth!'

But she had not just come into the studio! And why were they reading as they spoke?

'Hello, Mac! Hello Joe!' Elizabeth said, following her script.

Barry was devastated. 'Had those funny, friendly exchanges I had listened to with such pleasure at home been written by someone else and typed out?

'There were tears of disappointment in my eyes as I watched these very ordinary, even somewhat shabby people – they had probably travelled all night from Sydney – prosaically reciting their lines... It was a day of disillusionment; far worse than the day I discovered that my parents wore dentures.'

Ten years later, he renewed acquaintance with the Argonauts. In Sydney, and performing with the Phillip Street Revue, he tried to get work in radio but found it difficult. He struggled with the demands of ensemble acting, dialogue going to and fro between the actors grouped in the confines of a studio. But once, he was cast in a minor role in *The Argonauts.*

'Once again I beheld some of my former idols, now much aged, grizzled and irascible, around the microphone. But with what facility they dispatched their silly lines, and with what insouciance they managed to impersonate children and Chinamen, crones and cowboys! Meanwhile they smoked copiously and, as they read their scripts, adroitly let the old pages flutter silently to the studio floor.'

Athol Fleming, who was known to generations of young Australians as 'Mac' and 'Jason', co-hosted *The Argonauts* for its entire 31-year run until one Easter in 1971, Mac, Jason, Jimmy, Gina, Joe, Sue, Barbie – in fact all who sailed with Jason and the Argonauts – row, row, rowed into the unknown. The ABC had decided to put an end to the series and bemused club members who tuned in heard an entirely new children's program based on pop, interviews and topical items of interest.

Barry, like them, would not have been pleased.

# Jack Davey

Jack Davey: I picked young John Howard, he's a nice sort of lad and he's been here two nights now battling away and he just hasn't much luck. How are you John?

John Howard: Not bad thanks, Mr Davey.

Jack Davey: That's alright. What do you do for a living?

John Howard: I still go to school.

Jack Davey: Oh you do. What school?

John Howard: Canterbury Boys High School. [He laughs.]

Jack Davey: Who are they?

John Howard: Oh, that's just my brother; he went to Canterbury too.

Jack Davey: Oh he did hey?

John Howard: And he's got a wife down here with him too. She didn't go to Canterbury.

Jack Davey: I got to say these co-educational schemes are quite alright! Now you know what we've got to do, don't you, John?

John Howard: Yes... Velvet packets, rather.

Jack Davey: That's a boy, Velvet packets, yes. Right, let's get busy. Where do you find a mortar board?

John Howard: Oh, on a school teacher's head.

Jack Davey: That's the best way for it, yes. Right, that's exactly 10 bars of Velvet Soap you've got. In botany, a tree whose leaves fall in autumn is called a what sort of tree?

John Howard: A shedding tree.

Jack Davey: I could not look you straight in the face, John, and say that it was not a shedding tree because there it is, busily shedding. So therefore it

Jack Davey, surrounded by fans and in a rare moment of low energy, pictured during one of the stops on the gruelling round-Australia saloon car race, the Redex Trial.

is. It's called a deciduous tree, but you've got the right idea, you've got 20 packets now.

Venus is another name for the goddess of what?

Don't pull a face like that, you're a bit young yet but you'll come good.

The goddess of what – Venus? No good looking at your brother, he's married.

John Howard: Oh! The Goddess of Love.

Jack Davey: Who composed the oratorio *The Messiah*?

John Howard: Handel.

Jack Davey: You're a nice boy, glad you came John. Afraid you haven't won a washing machine but you're going to keep Mum Howard pretty happy for a long time because you got 90 – give him another 10! – you've got 100 bars of Velvet Soap!

Apart from Jack Davey's unwitting description of John Howard's political future until he finally won office – 'he's been here two nights now battling away and he just hasn't much luck' – this transcript from 1955, radio's last, golden year, shows something of the future prime minister of Australia's stubbornness and innate confidence. On the Macquarie Network's *Give It a Go*, broadcast nationally to millions, he scored laughs off the nation's favourite comedian.

The transcript also shows the wit and warmth of Jack Davey.

Jack Davey's Golden Voice, light, clear and seemingly always young, had a quality that promised listeners friendship – and fun. It appealed equally to men, women and teenagers like the 16-year-old from Canterbury Boys High school (who was so at ease that he got a laugh at Davey's expense). Davey was lightning fast with an ad lib, but other radio stars, too, had quick wits:

Bob Dyer, his only real rival, was a consummate and amusing showman. What set Jack Davey apart, what made him Australia's best-loved radio personality, was the warmth and friendliness of his humour. His natural charm, married to an impish wit, was unmatched. On television only Bert Newton has had the same gifts.

A failed signwriter and used car salesman, Jack Davey arrived in Sydney from New Zealand in 1931 and within two hours had found a flat in McLeay Street, with a harbour view and a landlady who was prepared to lend him £2. His first radio audition flopped. ('You've got a wonderful ego son, but you've got to have more than that.') He wanted to be a crooner, and he landed a job as singer with 2GB. Within three months he had his own breakfast show and then his first jackpot quiz program, *That's What You Think!* For the next quarter of a century Jack Davey was Australia's favourite entertainer, adored by young and old. His 2GB programs were broadcast throughout Australia four nights a week at 8 p.m., prime time, and on *The Ampol Show, Give It a Go* and *The Dulux Show* his famous, 'Hi ho everybody!' was heard by up to five million Australians every week and he was earning five times the prime minister's salary.

Davey was a playboy who lived life at a roaring pace. His philosophy was, 'Bite off more than you can chew, and chew like buggery!'

How he chewed! At his peak Davey did 680 shows a year, his voice was on Movietone newsreels and commercials for everything from Aspirin to radio valves, and all this while he competed in the dangerous and exhausting round-Australia car reliability trials. He spent his colossal wage faster than 2GB could bank it. He had a stable of fast cars and he sailed a cruiser, the Sea Mist: 'Seventy feet of pure extravagance' his personal assistant Lew Wright called it. He would tip a waiter the man's monthly wage for telling him the time. He would win and lose huge sums at the poker table and Sydney's illegal gambling clubs. 'He had absolutely no idea at the time whether he had one pound or one thousand pounds in the bank,' Lew Wright said, 'yet he always spent as though it was £10,000.' Wright also tells of an incident that shows how careless Davey was with his life. Worn out by his all-stops-out work and play regime, with a few drinks inside him fuelling a street argument with friends, Davey threw himself in front of taxi. The driver swerved and Davy staggered off. 'Wasn't that Jack Davey?' the driver said. 'No, he just looks like him,' Lew Wright said, and gave the driver £5.

His reckless lifestyle caught up with him just four years after he interviewed young John Howard. As he lay dying, on 14 October 1959, aged 49 and leaving virtually nothing, Jack Davey told Lew Wright: 'Don't cry for me Lew. I'm the leader of my profession and in five years' time the up and coming boys like Bobby Limb, Graham Kennedy, and Brian Henderson will be pushing me off the top rung of the ladder.'

He made Wright promise that he would tell Australia that he had died peacefully. 'People will be watching the way I die, so as to help others later on, always say I died peacefully. No matter what happens I must die peacefully...

'Have I run a good race?'

Wright swallowed, and said: 'Jack, you ran a beaut!'

Davey's only rival, Bob Dyer, successfully made the transition to television with his quiz show, *Pick-A-Box* and the help of an all-knowing and pedantic young contestant, Barry Jones, later to become a Labor MP.

# The pop boycott

Elton John and Bernie Taupin were writing songs for others for £10 a pop; AC/DC were new to the charts; Janice Joplin was working with a new band and had just months to live; the Beatles were striding across Abbey Road; and in May of that year, 1970, Molly Meldrum spluttered in *Go-Set* magazine: 'From this week on you won't be hearing any more of your favourite Australian or English records on commercial radio. No Beatles, no Zoot, no Johnny Farnham, no Rolling Stones, no Led Zeppelin, no Russell Morris, no Doug Parkinson, no Lulu, no Tom Jones, no Edison Lighthouse, no Alison Durban, no Flying Circus.'

The awful prospect of the airwaves without Lulu was the result of a Mexican stand-off between the 114 Australian commercial radio stations and the six European record company giants. The record companies, 14 years after striking a deal with the Federation of Australian Commercial Broadcasters, suddenly demanded one per cent of the radio stations' revenue in return for the use of their music. The federation refused, and all British and Australian records controlled by the big six – EMI, Festival, PolyGram, RCA, CBS and the Warner group – went off the air.

The 1970 radio ban lasted five months. But it changed the musical map. The stand-off ended when both sides buckled. The big companies needed radio, and radio needed them. In the end it was a win for the recording companies and pay for play became the norm. But in those

Molly Meldrum as few know him. At the office of *Go-Set* magazine, without his hat, around the time he warned of the record giants' impending radio ban. *Photograph courtesy of Jim Colbert*

five months enterprising local record producers, led by Melbourne's Ron Tudor and his Fable label, jumped in to fill the breach, getting weekly shipments of British releases and doing note-perfect cover versions using local talent.

Idris Jones, lead singer of The Mixtures, told ABC TV: 'Ron Tudor came to us and said, "There's this ban on UK records. I think you're a good band. Do you want to record something?" We said, "Sure, we'll give it a go." No one else was beating down our door.' Tudor told them not to be fancy. 'Just copy the bloody thing.'

It was that prosaic. But it was a landmark moment in Australian radio. Overnight, radio found a way to survive the boycott and local 'unknown' artists – Liv Maessen, the Mixtures, Jigsaw, Maple Lace, Autumn, Matt Flinders, the Strangers, Frankie Davidson and others – became famous. Home-grown pop stars.

Liv Maessen, a mother of two, covered Mary Hopkin's Knock, Knock, Who's There? and sold 50,000, the first Australian female pop singer to get a Gold record. The Mixtures' 'In the Summertime' shot to Number One. By October 3 Fable had the top two songs in the charts and nine of the Top 20. It was an astonishing turnaround. A fortnight later the big companies lifted the radio play restrictions. But there was no going back now.

In 1971 The Mixtures came up with an original, a jaunty number Jones's brother Evan had written. 'The Pushbike Song' went to the top in just three weeks and under licence from Fable and was top of the charts in the UK, the first Australian recording to become an international hit. By the close of the decade Fable had become the dominant Australian record label.

It was a short-lived revolution, but it changed the Australian recording scene. Ron Tudor and his indie label, Fable, had shown the big companies – and radio – that the days when overseas talent was automatically assumed to be superior were over. Pay for play is still an irritant for both radio stations and recording companies. But the question of Australian recording talent has long been answered.

# 3

# THE PAINTINGS

Brett Whitley's *Opera House*, on display at Sotheby's, Sydney, was expected to set a new record for an Australian painting when it went to auction in May 2007. It sold for $2.8 million but then John Bracks's painting in the background, *The Old Time*, set a new benchmark – $3.3 million – until, one month later it was passed by another Whiteley. And the prices keep climbing. *Newspix*

It took a little more than a century for Australian paintings to be recognisably Australian. The Heidelberg School, young, enthusiastic mates who spent weekends painting in the small town of Heidelberg, overlooking Melbourne's Yarra Valley – like their contemporaries, the controversial French Impressionists –preferred to paint outdoors. And for the first time the scenes they painted depicted Australia's landscape as it really is.

Tom Roberts, Arthur Streeton, Frederick McCubbin and Charles Conder were passionately nationalistic. And despite mixed reviews, their work, first exhibited in 1889 in the *9 by 5 Impression Exhibition*, sold well. Today their masterpieces, paintings such as Roberts's *Shearing the Rams*, McCubbin's *Down on His Luck* and Conder's *A Holiday at Mentone* are national treasures, beyond price. So too is the Aboriginal rock art, thousands of years old. Like the contemporary work of Aborigines, the rock artists' place is only now beginning to be fully appreciated. Today, the prices for masterpieces from painters such as Clifford Possum Tjapaltjarri and Emily Kane Kngwarreye, who, in 2007 topped the $1 million mark for a painting, match those of all but a few Australian artists.

Sidney Nolan, Russell Drysdale, Fred Williams, Arthur Boyd and John Olsen drew on the inspiration of the Heidelberg School and painted new and popular visions of the Australian landscape. So too did Brett Whiteley, the Peter Pan of Australian art. His lush semi-abstract nudes, all bottoms and busts, and his sweeping and seductive landscapes of Sydney Harbour with its signature deep-blue, have buyers queueing to pay multi-millions for paintings that, almost universally, critics recognise as the work of a genius.

But are they?

The critic John McDonald says not. 'For the whole nation, but especially for Sydney, to separate the talented artists from the egregious myth is a necessary rite of exorcism... critics have been making excuses for him for a very long time.'

# Indigenous Art

Perhaps 50,000 years ago Aboriginal Australians were creating visual art: rock paintings far older than the cave art of Europe, and which can be seen still at hundreds of locations across the continent. Yet only in the last few years have we come to appreciate their priceless legacy.

More than any other people, Australia's Aborigines put art at the core of their life. Art links Aborigines with their Dreaming – the religion and culture that gives them connection to the cosmos – and illustrates the themes of spiritual identity with their ancestors and totems. Indigenous art was purely concerned with these cultural depictions until the arrival of the First Fleet, and it remained largely so until a pivotal moment in the history of art in Australia...

In 1971, a young schoolteacher, Geoffrey Bardon, was sent to Papunya, 250 kilometres north-west of Alice Springs, in the same Central Desert region where, in the 1950s, Albert Namatjira had become Australia's first, and, for a long time, only popularly known Aboriginal artist.

Bardon arrived 12 years after Namatjira's death. The government settlement at Papunya mirrored his depressing story. Established under the assimilation policy, the settlement was where 1400 Aborigines – Arrernte, Luritja, Anmatyerre, Pitjantjatjara and Pintupi – lived a life marked by high death rate, drunkenness, brutal riots, despondency and despair. Once semi-nomads, they struggled to find meaning in their new sedentary existence. They found little support from a government administration that considered the people and their culture to be dying.

Papunya was a community without hope. Bardon, shocked by what he found when he arrived to teach art at Papunya's school, determined to give them hope. He began by encouraging his pupils to stop drawing in the western style, and instead create images of their own culture. Next he suggested to the men working in the school yard – sweeping, chopping wood and performing other menial tasks – that they paint a mural of their ancestral designs and Dreamings.

There was debate among the elders. Should they allow their images, traditionally painted only on rock walls, on the ground, or on bodies for ceremonies, to be seen on the walls of the school?

Papunya was a site of the Honey Ant Ancestor. Old Tom Onion Tjapangati, the owner of the Honey Ant Dreaming, gave his permission and Charlie Tjararu Tjungurrayi summed up the feeling: 'If I don't paint this story some white fella might come and steal my country.' Charlie, Long Jack Phillipus Tjakamarra, Billy Stockman Tjapaltjarri, Old Mick Tjakamarra and others set to work.

The Honey Ant Dreaming mural survived only a year before it and others the men painted were destroyed. The school walls, the authorities said, needed to be returned to their former state. But Honey Ant Dreaming was the first major public display of the ancestral designs. The children and their parents understood that it was an affirmation of their cultural identity. And by now others – around 20 – were creating often astonishing art, using synthetic paints on Masonite boards and building scraps given to them by Bardon. Soon they were showing their paintings in Alice Springs

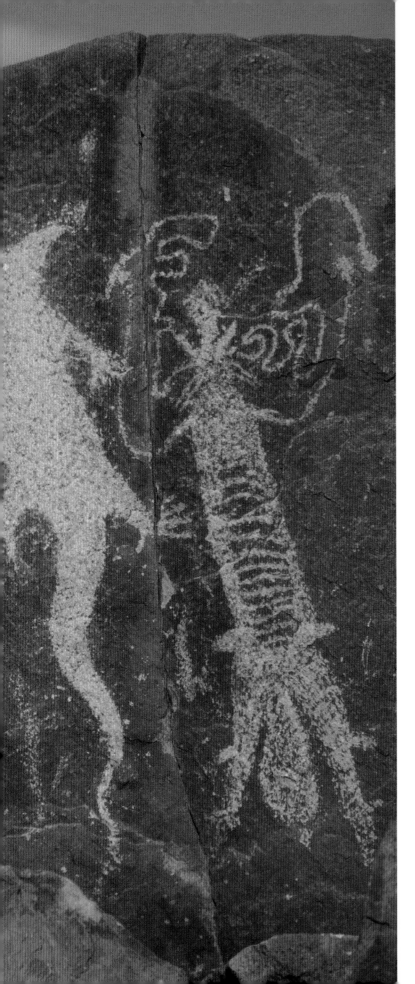

and then forming a company – separate from the white administration – called Papunya Tula (the Honey Ant Meeting Place).

'The rising of the painters' spirits in 1972 was to make the painters new men like warriors of old,' Bardon said. And the success of Papunya Tula inspired other Aboriginal communities. Soon hundreds of Aboriginal artists around Australia, from the Tiwi Islands, Cape York and Arnhem Land in the north to Carrolup and Coranderrk in the south were showing their work. By the 1990s collectors were paying large sums – the record price for an Aboriginal painting, $780,000, is held by Rover Thomas – for paintings on canvas by such artists as Emily Kame Kngwarreye, Kitty Kantilla, Ginger Riley Munduwalawala, Susie Bootja Napangarti, Anatjari Tjampitjinpa and Clifford Possum; bark painters by such as John Mawurndjul, Paddy Fordham Wainburranga and Ivan Namirkki; town and city painters such as Judy Watson and Gordon Bennett; and those like Lin Onus and Robert Campbell who depict the interplay between indigenous and non-indigenous cultures.

The Western Desert painting movement is a landmark in visual art, irrevocably changing the way the world sees Aboriginal art and culture. But it took a courageous and idealistic young white school teacher, a group of black men doing menial work in his school yard, and a painting heritage that may pre-date any other to begin what has been described as the last major art movement of the 20th century.

Australian rock paintings, pre-dating any in Europe, are belatedly coming to be treasured and, even more slowly, protected.

# Albert Namatjira

He was Australia's most popular living painter, a watercolourist whose landscapes hung in reproductions on the living room walls of scores of thousands of suburban homes around the nation.

He was also Australia's best-known Aborigine: the only Aborigine, in fact, that all Australians knew by name: Albert Namatjira, the embodiment of assimilation, a living symbol of what Aborigines might accomplish with encouragement and tuition. Yet within a few years from the day he was proudly presented to the queen, an admirer of his work, Namatjira was sentenced to jail, and soon after, at the age of 57, he died of hypertensive heart failure, a legacy of the difficulty of straddling the gulf between two cultures and the disillusionment and bitter disappointment that came with success and the colour of his skin.

Albert Namatjira's work was derided in art circles and, eventually, almost forgotten by the public who had once avidly collected it. By 1991 the definitive *Australian Painting 1788–1990* could give 20 pages to a chapter on Aboriginal painting but fewer than 20 lines to Albert Namatjira. (Today his significance as a painter has been reappraised and the experts say that, far from being copies of the western landscape style, his watercolours – which sell at around $30,000 – hold a strong indigenous message, his personal visage of his ancestral landscapes. Albert Namatjira would have liked to have heard that half a century earlier.)

Born into the Arrente tribe, he was christened Albert by his Christian parents and was raised on the Hermannsburg Lutheran Mission near Alice Springs. Young Albert was given an elementary education but at 13 he disappeared with some of the tribal elders, underwent initiation rites and was taught the traditional culture of his tribe. Five years later, he again disappeared, this time eloping with Ilkalita, a girl from another tribe – something taboo. The Arrente ostracised him.

For the next three years, until the taboo was withdrawn, the couple worked on cattle stations – Namatjira was a skilled builder and saddler – and when they returned to the mission Ilkalita became a Christian, baptised Rubina.

In 1934, working as a camel driver, Namatjira took a landscape artist, Rex Batterbee, on camping trips where Batterbee taught him to paint in the European way. Namatjira proved to have an astonishing facility for painting. His first one-man show, in Melbourne, was a sell-out and within 10 years he was nationally known. His watercolours of the MacDonnell Ranges and the desert he had roamed in his years camel driving and working on stations were highly prized by private collectors but held in contempt by many in the mainstream art world. They saw his distinctive, colourful landscapes as second-rate examples of the 'Gum Tree School' of Australian art: depictions of the landscape that usually showed two or more noble eucalypts and a scattering of cattle.

By 1950, however, he was a wealthy man, supporting at Hermannsburg, Pastor Albrecht of the Lutheran mission reckoned, up to 580 of his people a week. There were tax problems, and he was refused permission to buy a house in Alice Springs: legally, as an Aborigine, he was not allowed in the town after dark. There were forgeries, too, and unscrupulous businessmen. Dejected, he said, 'I was happier before I was a rich man.'

In 1956 he sat for William Dargie's Archibald

Prize-winning portrait. The painting shows a tired, dispirited man, yet imbued with great dignity. The following year he and Rubina were granted citizenship, the first full-blood Aborigines to be given the right. It was an ambiguous 'gift'. He could buy and consume alcohol, but he could not share it or give it to members of his tribe. He could buy his house in Alice Springs, but his children could not live there with him.

He began drinking, and on a taxi ride between Alice Springs and Hermannsburg, shared a bottle of rum with a fellow Aboriginal artist. He was charged and went before an Alice Springs magistrate who said that, 'The whole principle of the law is to protect Aborigines against themselves,' before ordering Namatjira to six months' imprisonment.

The sentence caused national outrage. There were few who agreed with the *Northern Territory News*: 'It must be clear that it was a mistake to give Namatjira his citizenship passport, despite the fact that he had proved he could "walk with kings", earn more than most whites, and had dignity and ability. Surely an essential measure of whether a native should get "full rights" must be his proven ability to bring up his family to the acceptable "white standards". This was not the case with Namatjira.'

On appeal Namatjira's sentence was halved and on the order of the Minister for Territories, Paul Hasluck (later the governor-general), served his time in open detention and in his own Papunya country. He was freed in May 1959, but he never again painted and died three months later.

The first Aboriginal artist to win widespread popularity, Albert Namatjira. His face foretells the tragedy fame and fortune would bring him.

# William Dobell

In 1944 the Australian art world went to war. The conflict was sparked by a painting of the artist's friend that the friend – and other artists – took exception to. It erupted into a controversy that made front page news day after day. At a time when the Soviet armies broke through to Leningrad, lifting the 900-day siege, and Douglas MacArthur started to push back the Japanese in the Pacific, people were arguing about the aesthetic merits of William Dobell's Archibald Prize-winning portrait of Joshua Smith. Had Australia's most prestigious prize for a painting of a portrait been given for a painting of a portrait? Or was it a caricature?

Dobell had entered three paintings in the 1943 Archibald: *The Billy Boy, Brian Penton* and *Portrait of an Artist Joshua Smith*, any one of which could have won the prize. Tragically, the prize went to the painting that would become the most notorious in our history. It ruined the lives of some of the main players and it robbed Australian art of a decade and more of potentially great art from Dobell.

William Dobell knew and counted Joshua Smith as a casual friend, a man he had known for four or five years. They were both artists and had shared a tent while working their way around Australia as camouflage painters of military bases and buildings for the Department of the Interior.

Years later, Dobell revealed, 'I was apprehensive even when I won it [the Archibald]. Everything started to happen so quickly. First Joshua's reaction – he congratulated me when I painted it – he loved it at first, but then it won the prize and offended his parents so much that he hasn't spoken to me since. They arrived one morning at 7.30 – no, earlier than that because I wasn't out of bed. They wept all over the flat. Being a poor housekeeper I had no handkerchiefs to offer them, so I got a towel. They were handling this wet towel and washing their eyes, begging me to never exhibit it again.'

Dobell promised he wouldn't exhibit the portrait again if they didn't reveal the pact to the press. When they did, Dobell considered the agreement broken.

'Smith was a thin, bony man with prominent features,' the art historian and critic Bernard Smith wrote in *Australian Painting*. 'Dobell produced a portrait which, though not unsympathetic, adopted a manneristic attenuation of form and an expressionistic intensity of colour more rigorous and thoroughgoing than anything he had painted previously. There was an expression partly of wonder and partly of self-pity upon the face but the figure sat erect with a natural, if uneasy dignity.'

Two unsuccessful entrants, neither very distinguished painters, would have disagreed with this appraisal. They claimed the portrait was a caricature, 'a representation of a person whose body, limbs and features are grotesquely at variance with normal human aspect and proportions', and they took their claim to the Supreme Court in a bid to overturn Dobell's award.

Archibald winners have been taken to court on three occasions. In 1976 John Bloomfield's portrait of film-maker Tim Burstall won the prize but shortly after was declared ineligible when the Archibald trustees discovered the portrait had been painted from a photograph. Bloomfield sued and lost. In 2006, the self-described starving artist Tony Johansen took legal action against the trustees of the Art Gallery of New South Wales on the grounds

William Dobell's portrait of his painter friend Joshua Smith pleased Smith at first, but later ruined the friendship and blighted the lives of both. *Newspix. Private collection*

that the 2004 winning portrait of David Gulpilil was a drawing, not a painting. Legal costs for the case were estimated to top $500,000. Johansen lost.

'The Archibald Prize thrives on controversy, argument and debate,' Edmund Capon, the director of the Art Gallery of New South Wales, has said, but the Dobell case is a tragedy, a case of a great, landmark painting held up to ridicule and ultimately almost physically destroyed.

The Sydney poet Kenneth Slessor called the case Dumbell v. Dobell and wrote, 'Sober comment would scarcely seem to be required on the naive assumption that good or bad in terms of art can be determined by a number of gentlemen in wigs asking questions and expounding precedents in a court of law.' And the case, indeed, took on a Monty Python character.

J.S. MacDonald, the first witness for the plaintiffs, was a former director of the Art Gallery of New South Wales. He gave his opinion that the last good English portrait painter had died in 1830, and the Dobell was 'a pictorial defamation' of the Joshua Smith he knew. The Joshua Smith depicted 'did not look like a man who could paint a portrait fit for entry into the Archibald Prize'. (A few months later Smith was to enter that year's Archibald Prize – and, surprise – win it, with a bland portrait of the Speaker of the House of Representatives.)

The former acting director of the Art Gallery of New South Wales was just as caustic. 'Well, of course, someone said that a portrait is a picture in which the mouth is always bad,' said John Young, his own mouth, no doubt, pursed, 'but I think in this case that it is obviously not like Joshua Smith's mouth at all. I feel that it seems to be, by some fantastic direction, that the mouth has become as

though he has a hare lip. The nose has become – as I know Joshua's nose – it has become flattened... Joshua sometimes smiles at his own faults. Now, I could only think that there would be a ghastly and hideous grimace if the mouth was asked to smile.'

Another witness said the picture was a 'biological absurdity' and a doctor gave his opinion that it represented the 'body of a man who had died in that position and had remained in it for some months and dried up'.

When it came Dobell's turn to take the witness box he talked about Joshua Smith, the subject of his painting:

'I respected him and I still respect him, but I always regarded him as a rather diffident type of person and one who naturally seems to call for people's sympathy, but when I worked with him as a camouflage labourer, I had to share the same camp with him for almost 12 months, and I got to know his real character and I found that there was a determination that amounted to stubbornness.'

It was this duality that Dobell tried to depict in his portrait.

It was war in the court room, too. Under intense cross-examination by counsel for the plaintiffs, Dobell, riled, replied to one line of questioning: 'You are taking it bit by bit, and I am taking it as a picture. I might just as well criticise the conduct of your case by the angle of your wig!'

The defining exchange came when the counsel asked Dobell: 'As he sat before you, did he physically appear to your eyes as he appears now in that canvas?'

Dobell: 'Yes, within those limits I have already mentioned. You cannot answer a question like that "Yes" or "No", not on an artistic point of art.'

Counsel: 'Leave art out at the moment.'

Dobell at work (above) and Smith (below) who won the Archibald the year after Dobell's portrait of him.

Dobell: 'You cannot leave art out!'

Mr Justice Roper took that point very clearly. In his plain-speaking judgement against the plaintiffs he said: 'The picture in question is characterised by some startling exaggerations and distortion clearly intended by the artist, his technique being too brilliant to admit of any other conclusion. It bears, nevertheless, a strong degree of likeness to the subject and is, I think, undoubtedly a pictorial representation of him. I find as a fact that it is a portrait.'

'Portrait or caricature: the fields were not mutually exclusive,' Bernard Smith wrote.

'...if the word caricature has any meaning at all in the normal English usage Dobell's painting of Joshua Smith was most certainly a caricature, but a caricature which was also a portrait of the highest artistic quality.'

The effect of the controversy was devastating for both men. It ruined their friendship. Smith, upset by the constant attention from those wondering if he actually did look like the portrait, became a recluse and, though Dobell again won the Archibald in 1948 with a portrait of his friend, the painter Margaret Olley, it took another decade before he once again began producing outstanding art: the dazzling portrait of Helena Rubinstein; the Menzies portrait for the cover of *TIME* magazine; The Strapper and the like, which cemented his place as one of Australia's finest artists.

The Archibald portrait itself suffered because of the court case. Dobell hid the painting and, partly eaten by silverfish and then largely destroyed by fire, *Portrait of the Artist Joshua Smith* went into private hands.

Dobell, too, never really recovered; like Joshua Smith he became a near-recluse, and died at his Newcastle home in 1970.

# *Ned Kelly by Sidney Nolan*

One of the signature paintings of Australian art, Ned Kelly rides into the seemingly limitless plain, an alien figure yet strangely in harmony with the landscape. Through the visor of his helmet he sees – and we see – the big sky of his big country.

Sir Kenneth Clark, the recently retired director of the National Gallery in London, was in Sydney and viewing the Wynne Prize Exhibition of 1949. 'I was taken to visit an exhibition of contemporary landscape painting,' he wrote in his memoirs, 'and it was sad to see how the excellent Australian landscape painters of the late 19th century had exhausted the genre. As I was leaving the exhibition I noticed, hung high up above the entrance stairs, a work of remarkable originality and painter-like qualities.

'I asked who it was by. "Oh, nobody." "But you must have his name in your catalogue." "Let's see; here it is, Nolan, Sidney Nolan. Never heard of him." I said I would like to see some more of this work. "Well he's not on the telephone." "But you must have his address." More angry scuffling finally produced an address in a suburb of Sydney. I took a taxi there that afternoon, and found the painter, dressed in khaki shorts, at work on a series of large paintings of imaginary birds. He seemed to me to be an entirely original artist and incidentally a fascinating human being. I bought the landscape in that exhibition, not that it was necessarily the best, but in order to annoy the exhibition secretary, and was confident that I had stumbled on a genius.'

Sir Kenneth Clark went on to make a television series that established him as the world's foremost art critic. And Sidney Nolan went on to be generally accepted as the greatest of all Australian painters in the European tradition.

Nolan, too, established his reputation with a series: 27 paintings of the Ned Kelly saga, done between 1 March 1946 and 2 July 1947, all but one painted on the kitchen table at Sunday and John Reed's Melbourne home, Heide.

The Reeds were the patrons of a number of Melbourne artists later to become famous, and Nolan, who lived for a considerable and formative time at Heide, had a tumultuous affair with Sunday. John Reed, who was aware that his wife and Nolan were lovers, never wavered in his admiration for the painter.

At Nolan's first exhibition of the Kelly series, Reed wrote an unequivocal and astonishingly confident assessment of the unknown painter. In the exhibition's unassuming eight-page stapled pamphlet, illustrated with a single black and white photograph, Reed said, 'For those of us who rate Sidney Nolan as one of the two or three painters in Australia of real significance, this exhibition – his first one-man show in a public

The Kelly series of 27 paintings, done on a kitchen table over 16 weeks, established Nolan's reputation internationally.

Sidney NOLAN
born Australia 1917 died England 1992
*Ned Kelly* 1946
Painting enamel on composition board
90.8 x 121.5 cm
Gift of Sunday Reed 1977
National Gallery of Australia, Canberra

gallery – is of quite outstanding importance.
We believe its value in the history of Australian
painting is already assured.

'Australia has not been an easy country to
paint. A number of artists have sensed something
of what it holds and one or two – the early
Roberts and Streeton – have succeeded in giving
us glimpses of it which were movingly true;
but we have waited many years for a mature
statement to cover both the landscape and man
in relation to the landscape.

'In my opinion this has now been achieved
by Sidney Nolan in the group of 27 paintings
exhibited, and it is a remarkable achievement
indeed, necessitating as it has the most sensitive
and profound harmony between symbol,
legend and visual impact. That this has been
accomplished in language of the utmost
simplicity is in itself an indication of the strength
of the artist's vision and discipline, while at
the same time it should allow those who are
responsive to the elemental things which move us
all to find ready responses in themselves to what
the paintings have to give.'

# *Blue Poles by Jackson Pollock*

*TIME* magazine called Jackson Pollock the Shock Trooper of modern painting. A big, hard drinking tough guy born on a sheep ranch in Cody, Wyoming, Pollock invented 'action painting'. Cigarette dangling from his mouth, he would attack canvases on the floor, dripping paint, sprinkling sand and scattering broken glass over them, smearing and scratching, so that he came to be dubbed by the press Jack the Dripper.

But he caught the eye of the hottest dealer of her day, Peggy Guggenheim, and when *TIME* showed photographs of him at work, spattering paint seemingly at random, his reputation soared. Pollock blazed a trail for abstract artists in America: after Pollock it was impossible, it's been said, for an artist to confront a canvas in the old way. In 1956, drunk, he ran his car off the road and was killed.

Pollock's fame was now assured.

In 1972 Gough Whitlam told James Mollison, the director of the yet-to-be opened National Gallery of Australia, to buy 'exemplary objects' for the collection. Mollison, delighted, went shopping. Among his purchases was one of Pollock's masterpieces, *Blue Poles*. The sale ignited a clamour. It was a defining moment in Australian cultural history. The cost, $1.35 million (then a world record for a contemporary painting), was seen as evidence of the Labor Government's economic ineptitude and the painting itself was mocked by editorial writers and cartoonists across the nation.

Gough Whitlam with Blue Poles, the painting he wittily defended and that may be seen as symbolic of his own controversial, colourful and confrontational style. *Newspix*

47

In Parliament the leader of the Country Party confessed that he couldn't comprehend the merit of the painting. Mr Whitlam replied, 'If Australian galleries were limited by the comprehension of the Right Honourable gentleman they would be very bare and archaic indeed.'

Mr Whitlam later recounted: 'W.C. Wentworth IV pored over the myths of the painting's creation to produce the last question, which was directed to the Speaker on 4 December: "Do you agree that the aesthetic impact of a work of art is increased by the contemplation of it in the circumstances in which it was created? When the bargain-priced masterpiece *Blue Poles* reaches its fortunate purchasers in Australia, will you discuss with the president of the Senate the possibility of having the painting laid out on the floor of Kings Hall so that honourable members and senators can view it from the viewpoint of its inspired creator?

'"Will you further arrange for free drinks to be served in King's Hall so that honourable members and senators can share to the full in the inspiration of the artist or artists?

'"If the painting is so exhibited, will you ensure that it is securely fenced off in order to shield us from the temptation to take off our shoes and affix addendums to it in the same manner in which the basic painting was allegedly done?"'

Mr Whitlam said the Speaker, Jim Cope, 'answered in his best style: "I will do so, providing the honourable member agrees to sit on the biggest pole for some time." Silly Billy was knocked off his perch and Margaret and I had Blue Poles featured on our 1973 Christmas Cards.'

Was *Blue Poles* over-priced?

Robert Hughes, *TIME* magazine's art critic, said in Chicago in 1984: 'My fellow countrymen were rather proud of beating [the] creative asking price down [from US$3 million to US$2 million]. Nobody had even thought of asking so much for a Pollock; but of course the market gratefully rallied behind this heroic example and every Pollock in the world quintupled overnight, thus enabling the National Gallery of Australia to announce that *Blue Poles* was really cheap.'

Is *Blue Poles* a great work of art?

Pollock's supporter Clement Greenberg claimed that the painting was 'an absolute failure and a ridiculous thing to buy'. And author John Updike was even more scathing. 'This intensely awkward canvas, with its unhappy discovery of orange paint, found its way to Canberra, Australia, whence its harsh expanse will come but rarely to trouble American museum-goers.'

On the other hand the New York-based Australian art dealer Max Hutchinson, who brokered the sale, declared that '*Blue Poles*, along with Picasso's *Guernica* and Monet's *Water Lilies*, is one of the five or six great works of art painted since the Renaissance.' In which case Australia got the art bargain of all time.

# 4

# THE STAGE

World Heritage-listed, the Opera House is one of the architectural marvels of the world. Yet inside, like the Australian theatre, it fails to deliver on its promise.

'If you don't do it, I resign,' Jørn Utzon told the Minister for Public Works and the Minister replied: "I accept your resignation. Thank you very much. Goodbye.' A regrettable difference of opinion between the architect of the Sydney Opera House and the NSW government, the fallout has had lasting consequences that will cost around $500 million to resolve.

The Opera House, the symbol and soul of Sydney, is one of the 20th century's most sublime buildings And yet... and yet... the Sydney Opera House is disappointing and inadequate inside.

The Opera House can also be seen as a symbol of the Australian theatre. On the surface our theatre is thriving. Melbourne has one of the three or four biggest theatre districts in the world. Adelaide, Brisbane and Perth all have large, modern theatres. A blockbuster musical will be seen by millions around the country.

Yet the theatre in Australia itself has produced only three performers who can be said to be 'superstars' and two of them – Melba and Sutherland – were singers. The third, Barry Humphries, is the only one whose art is recognisably 'Australian.' Half a century ago Ray Lawler's *Summer of the Seventeenth Doll* was described by the London *Times* as 'the best play ever written about Australia – purely Australian but in quality to be compared with the work of Tennessee Williams, Arthur Miller and Sean O'Casey.' After *The Doll*, playwrights like Jack Hibberd with his bawdy *Dimboola*, Bob Ellis and Michael Boddy with *The Legend of King O'Malley* and David Williamson with his early works, wrote plays that were performed in back-street venues such as La Mama, The Pram, Nimrod and Jane Street. They ignited an exciting, potentially great era for Australian drama.

It failed to materialise. In the following decades a handful of Australian plays, like *The Doll*, were staged in London's West End and even fewer on Broadway. Like the Australian cinema, our theatre can produce fine actors, directors, set designers and the like, but the scripts too often, play safe: the great themes elude.

The first theatre in Australia opened 177 years before we got the Sydney Opera House. We are still waiting for the Great Australian Playwright.

# The Recruiting Officer

*The Naked Island*, Russell Braddon's account of his time as a prisoner of war of the Japanese, is a dark record of torture, disease and deprivation, at times almost too horrifying to contemplate.

Yet in the midst of this horror there is one glimpse of sanity and hope and even happiness: the Concert Party. 'There are few men who were captured in Singapore in 1942 and who survived till 1945,' he wrote, 'who do not now remember and will not always remember the skill of John Wood, the songs (topical and tuneful) of Slim de Gray and Ray Tullipan, the harmony of Geoghegan and Woods and that plaintive cry of our most melancholy comic: "You'll never get off the island". No matter how black the news nor how depressing the atmosphere, Harry Smith, universally known as Happy Harry, had only to turn his long face full at the audience and wail the apparent truism, "You'll never get off the island," for complete hilarity to be restored.'

The British fondness for theatrical high jinks is a thread that runs through many a prisoner of war movie, but it is real for all that. And it is a thread that goes back to its first recorded appearance in Australia, on 4 June 1789, at Sydney Cove. On that day, 11 convicts, with the permission of Captain Arthur Phillip, performed *The Recruiting Officer.*

*The Recruiting Officer*, written in 1705, was an 18th century favourite, and as with prisoner-of-war theatre, it was comic, enlivened by wry and topical references to the miserable and oppressive circumstances in which it was staged.

'That every opportunity of escape from the dreariness and dejection of our situation should be eagerly embraced will not be wondered at,' Captain Watkin Tench, the chronicler of the First Fleet's settlement, wrote, a sentiment expressed by Russell Braddon a century and a half later.

'The exhilarating effect of a splendid theatre is well known: and I am not ashamed to confess, that the proper distribution of three or four yards of stained paper, and a dozen farthing candles stuck around the mud walls of a convict hut failed not to diffuse general complacency on the countenance of 60 persons of various descriptions who were assembled to applaud the representation.'

How was the show?

'Some of the actors acquitted themselves with great spirit,' Tench wrote – in his capacity as the performance's inadvertent reviewer – 'and received the praise of the audience: a prologue and an epilogue, written by one of the performers, were also spoken on the occasion: which although not worth inserting here, contained some tolerable allusions to the situation of the parties, and the novelty of a stage representation in New South Wales.'

By Permission of His Excellency.
At the THEATRE, SYDNEY,
On Saturday March 8. 1800. will be Presented,
The COMEDY of
The Recruiting Officer.

Plume . . . . . . . . . W. Smith.
Worthy . . . . . . . . W. Richards.
Ballance . . . . . . . G. Hughes.
Bullock . . . . . . . . I. Cox
C ſtar Pearmain . . . H. Parſons.
Thomas Appletree . . B. Smith.
Kite . . . . . . . . . . J. White.
Melinda . . . . . . . Mrs Barnes.
Roſe . . . . . . . . . . Mrs. Radley
Lucy . . . . . . . . . . Maſter Haddocks
Sylvia . . . . . . . . . Mrs. Parry.

To which will be added
A Muſical Entertainment called
The Virgin Unmaſked.

Bliſter . . . . . . . . . W. Smith.
Godwill . . . . . . . . H. Parſons.
Quaver . . . . . . . . G. Hughes.
Coupee . . . . . . . . J. White.
Thomas . . . . . . . . Mrs. Parry.

'The Doll', now more than half a century old, reaffirms its classic status whenever it is revived. It remains Australia's finest play. This scene is from the Melbourne Theatre Company's 1995 production of the play.

# Summer of the Seventeenth Doll

It was the year Laminex began its slick, quick conquest of Australian kitchens; the year of the ALP Split; the year Sydney said goodbye and Cheers! to the six o'clock swill; and the year of *Summer of the Seventeen Doll*. 'The Doll's' premiere, in November 1955, was – and was quickly recognised as – a landmark in Australian theatre. Leonard Radic, one of Australia's most respected theatre reviewers, calls it 'Australia's finest play. In a very real sense, the history of the modern Australian theatre begins with it.'

Staged at Melbourne University's Union Theatre, Ray Lawler's *Summer of the Seventeenth Doll* is a play on themes that until then had been completely unexplored by Australian playwrights: the inability to distinguish between reality and illusion and the disintegration with age of youthful dreams.

Barney and Roo (Lawler played Barney in the original production) are two Queensland cane-cutters, good mates who each year come south to Melbourne for five months, their lay-off period. Wallets bulging, they stay in the two-storey terrace house owned by the barmaid, Olive's mother – and 'make whoopee' with Olive and her fellow good-time girl, Nancy. For 16 summers the self-indulgent annual reunion has worked beautifully. Then Nancy calls it a day and gets married, and the prudish Pearl takes her place. By now the boys, Barney and Roo, are in their 40s and the 'five months of heaven' that Olive gushes to Pearl about is beginning to fray. Roo talks of getting work while they're in Melbourne and Barney is flabbergasted. They 'blue'. Pearl, disillusioned, packs and goes and Olive's mother reminds them: 'There's a time for sowing and a time for reaping – reapin' is what you're doin' now.' Only Olive can't understand that. 'I want what I had before,' she cries, refusing to face the truth that her dream – all their dreams – must unravel with age.

In the US, Arthur Miller was exploring similar themes in *Death of a Salesman*, and Lawler's play stands comparison with that masterpiece. *The Doll* toured Australia and went to London's West End where it was well reviewed. But Ray Lawler's place in Australian theatre history will always be assured because for the first time, his play showed audiences a slice of Australian life; recognisably and richly idiomatic but universal for all that.

# *Barry Humphries*

**B**arry Humphries is that rarity, a peerless performer who has no discernible influences. There has never been another like him. And it can be argued there never has been a theatrical comic to match him. The influences of almost all great artists can be traced, usually without difficulty. In theatre, we can follow the straight and clear line back through two centuries from Olivier to Garrick to Kean. In literature, Hemingway could be said to be unique, until you factor in Gertrude Stein, repeating phrases over and over with slightly different wordings, and the he-man writer Jack London, whose fingerprints are all over 'Hem's' work. In art, Picasso's influences can be found in Cezanne, Matisse and African tribal masks going back a thousand years. Ballet dancers do it as they've done it for a century or two, clowns go back to the Colosseum and beyond.

But Barry Humphries' theatrical roots... well, Sir Les Patterson would no doubt have a view on the matter, but for the rest of us, they're not at all evident.

Dr Sir Leslie Colin Patterson KBE, Dame Edna Everage and Sandy Stone, the three unique characters Humphries invented, stand alone in comedy. Too hard an act to follow, they have no rivals and no pretenders to their shared throne. They have ensured Barry Humphries' place among the geniuses of entertainment. Dame Edna has now conquered almost the entire English-speaking world, been seen on stage by millions and on television and in films by many millions more.

Barry Humphries may be the most successful theatrical comic in history. Certainly he is unmatched for his daring – he works without a 'net', using the audience to inspire and feed his performance. His timing is wondrous and his physical comedy – spanning Sandy Stone's somnambulant immobility to Sir Les Patterson's eye-catching and wickedly independent member – is

Once a simple mauve-haired lass from Moonee Ponds, the gigastar Dame Edna turns her saurian eyes toward us. Best to look away quickly.
*Photograph: John Timbers*

consummate. And he's done it for decades. From his teenage years he's had the ability to have an audience in convulsions of laughter.

The role models for Edna, Les and Sandy and all the many characters created by Humphries are clear enough: real-life megastars; gross politicians; the prematurely old outer suburban man; the hypocritical inner suburban Leftie; used car salesmen turned art collectors; intellectual poseurs; crass and corrupt captains of commerce and venal union officials, and, of course, the wellspring, Humphries' mother and her circle. They are his muse and his targets, but the secret of Humphries' extraordinary half century of success lies in his private delight in taking an already outrageous joke far too far and doing it all with the skill of a poet.

Barry Humphries was confounding people as a schoolboy. At Melbourne Grammar, the private school he once derided in his *Who's Who* entry – 'self educated, attended Melbourne Grammar School' – he is remembered for such incidents as the Parade Ground Request. Grammar's cadet corps was standing stiffly to attention being inspected by a notable old boy, an army general. Khaki uniforms pressed and spotless, belt buckles Brassoed to a high gleam, boots laboriously blacked and buffed, webbing immaculately white, .303 rifle barrels pulled through a dozen times, the cadets stood quivering at attention as the eminent old soldier strode along the ranks.

Lanky young Private Barry Humphries didn't bother to disguise his loathing of being a cadet. His slouch hat was on the wrong angle, his jacket drooped over his grubby belt, his canvas ankle gaiters were only partly fastened.

Private Humphries stepped from the ranks.

'Excuse me, General,' he said as the great man was a pace away, 'could you please help me with my gaiters?'

Humphries' retinue of original practical jokes is now known throughout the civilised world. There's the early classic: a university student, he boards a suburban train and has accomplices stationed all along the route. At each station as the train draws to a stop a waiting accomplice is positioned to pass his breakfast through the window. No words are spoken. Barry simply accepts his orange juice and his plate of grapefruit slices at the first stop and has them while fellow passengers in his carriage goggle. Next stop, cornflakes. At the next, toast and marmalade. Then bacon and scrambled eggs and finally coffee.

He liked trams. On a tram you could do your trick, get off and watch it lurch away before stunned passengers could react. He once boarded a rush-hour tram behind an accomplice on crutches, his leg in plaster. People squeezed up to make room for the young man with the broken leg. Humphries lunged, just too late, for the seat. Then, standing above the handicapped young man, a copy of *Mein Kampf* in his free hand, he gripped the overhead rack and in a coarse and cruel German accent, freely showering spittle, he demanded that the cripple move over. The handicapped young man looked terrified but stayed where he was. As the tram came to the next stop the German's exasperation boiled over. He kicked the cripple's bandaged leg and stormed off the tram swearing frightful German oaths while the passengers, impotent with rage, watched him escape.

He arranged for an actress, young and sweet, to dress in a school uniform and sit in a seat by the tram door. Humphries pulled up alongside the tram in a red MG sports car and began ogling the

schoolgirl. At each stop he continued what was now, clearly, the silent and apparently increasingly successful seduction of a minor. Finally the schoolgirl hopped from the tram and sped off with him. In staid Melbourne, in the late '50s, the shock wave that shuddered through the tram was palpable.

He would go into a shop and say, 'I'd like to buy a cake of soap.' When it was given to him he'd return it, saying, 'Oh no, I don't want the soap, you keep it. I only wanted to buy it.' His in-flight vomit routine – eating coleslaw from his sick bag – is legendary. But he also likes spontaneous practical jokes that only he understands or ever knows about. In New York, an unknown, he was appearing in the musical *Oliver!* A correspondent for the Melbourne *Sun News-Pictorial* left the newspaper's Times Square office and was taking a lunchtime stroll down 44th street when he came upon a crowd gathered around what transpired to be a pedestrian, mildly injured in a brush with a car.

On the fringe of the crowd an agitated young man with black, shoulder-length hair was grabbing passers-by and babbling, 'They've caught a Communist! They've caught a Communist!' Humphries had no way of knowing that a reporter who knew who he was would chance by just at that moment. He was simply filling in the time, amusing himself, between the matinee performance and the evening show.

Humphries is an improviser, and there is a poetry there, underlying it all.

Barry Humpries is an accomplished painter. His self-portrait in the National Portrait Gallery, Canberra, shows us how he would like to be seen.

Self-portrait 2002
by Barry Humphries
oil on canvas
Collection: National Portrait Gallery, Canberra
Gift of the Margaret Hannah Olley Art Trust 2003

He is at his most poetic, and most moving when he is Alexander Horace 'Sandy' Stone, the old digger who was 'gathered' in his sleep and has returned as a ghost to haunt us with his memories of...well, nothing to speak of, really. Almost the last thoughts Sandy had were, 'The Harpic is cleansing while I sleep,' before he passed away: 'deceased, with the resultant consequence that there has been a considerable change in my lifestyle. I've never had a day's illness in my life, so this little setback came as much as a surprise to me as it did to Beryl, my good wife...'

Poet Laureate John Betjeman loved 'dear old Sandy' and knew his lines by heart. Sandy, Betjeman wrote, was 'a very kind man with no taste and much sensibility.' Clive James described him as 'Ezra Pound with the power off'.

In the voice common to many Australian men of his generation – 'like the scratch of a match,' Humphries has said – Sandy tells us, 'Beryl had cut some delicious sandwiches. Egg and lettuce. Peanut butter, Marmite and walnut, cheese and apricot jam. And lots of bread and butter and hundreds and thousands – and one of her specialties – a chocolate and banana log. She'd only baked that morning and the kiddies were most intrigued. Beryl said that if they promised to behave themselves at Wattle Park they could lick the beaters...'

As if we care. But, strangely, we do care.

In The Holy Trinity Op Shop he finds an old family album with snaps of World War One servicemen. They had 'the sort of faraway look on their faces like they knew they was never coming back.' Then he picks up an album of more recent family photographs, people in their Sunday best, faces screwed up against the sun. 'They wouldn't have bothered, would they, if they'd known they

was all going to end up around an opportunity shop with "15 cents" in chalk scribbled across the happiest days in their lives.'

Sandy's own photographic records of happy times ended in an incinerator when his neighbour Clarrie Lockwood married the widowed Mrs Stone – 'He'd had his eyes on Beryl's cumquats for years.' The Lockwoods sold Kiaora, 36 Gallipoli Crescent, Glen Iris, and moved to a Gold Coast condo. Tidying up they came across an old Stone family album, damp and crawling with insects, with 'faded snaps the color of tea that you made with condensed milk'. Clarrie took it to the incinerator on a shovel and 'It was a beggar to burn. He had to delve into the incinerator with a garden fork, turning the pages and sticking them through...1936 ...1937...1938...'

Sandy Stone, the Melbourne writer Keith Dunstan said in 2006, will become one of the great characters of Australian folklore. You could compare him with Ginger Mick, the Sentimental Bloke, Dad and Dave or Clancy of the Overflow.

Edna and Les have people weeping with laughter but Sandy's melancholy monologues, delivered in a quavering monotone as he sits slumped in an old, deep, Genoa velvet armchair in dressing gown, pyjamas and slippers, hottie on his lap, have another, extraordinary effect on audiences. Between the laughter in the hushed theatre – and Sandy is very funny – you can catch people sobbing.

That is why Barry Humphries is unique.

I'm redecorating now and I need input. I need new ideas. What colour is your bedroom, Fay darling? Beige, oh, lovely. Presumably a nice shade of beige, is it? Beige walls, are they Fay? Are they papered or painted? Painted, lovely. Matte

Of all the characters Humphries has created, Sandy Stone, with his monotone monologues is the most likely to last in our affection. Sandy, an extremely boring man, somehow has the power to move us to tears.
*Photograph: John Timbers*

or a gloss finish? What darling? A matte beige. Oh lovely. And do you have a double bed, Fay? Do you? Oh, you're an optimist anyway, Fay. And curtains, what colour? Cream. No windows, but curtains, that's unusual...But the curtains are very different, aren't they? They need to be, because you might just try to put your head out the window and you'd bash your head against the wall. You look as though you might have done that a few times too. However, what type of carpet do you have, Fay? Fay? A green carpet. Is it a deep green or a pale green, Fay? A pale green. Is it a Wilton, a berber or shag, Fay? It's a Wilton. I'm glad because frankly I don't like a shag in a

bedroom, I don't. What is the matter with you people? You're over-tired, you're over-excited.

Now, Fay, do you have an en suite bathroom, Fay? No, well a walk never hurt anyone, Fay. Oh Fay, I'm fond of you. You're lovely. That fabric, it's absolutely adorable, isn't it? You were lucky to get so much of it, Fay.

You're going to love Fay when she's on stage in a minute. You are. Fay has gone pale green now... not yet, Fay, but soon. So soon, that if I was you I would start tensing up now. You wouldn't be here alone, anyway, Fay. Matthew and Linda will be up here. They will. Matthew and Linda. Our late-comers. They'll be up here writing their essays: Why we were late.

Did you see my bridesmaid here a little while ago, did you, Fay? Madge... she's a worry. She was my bridesmaid. She caught my bouquet. On the back of the neck as it happened. It wiped out an entire nerve centre and she has been dependent on me ever since. Well, she's a New Zealander. Have you ever been in a disabled toilet, Fay? Have you? Ever had a peep in one? It's another world in there, it is. It's like a gymnasium in there, it is. Expect to see people doing aerobics, you do. And there's a chrome ladder going up the wall. What do they do in there? They spin in, they snip the door, and shin up the wall. That's what they do. And they peep over at us, I'm sure that they do. And I mean this lovingly. I do. I mean this compassionately.

And if there's anyone here that came on wheels tonight, anyone with a hint of chrome, a touch of Richard III about them, please, I'm not a healer. I have to say this, I cannot heal. Oh, how I wish I could heal, but I can't, I'm sorry, but I can't. So don't bring your sore bits around to me later.

# Hair

Hair, more than any other musical, captured an audience waiting for it to happen: the people of the '60s. Young and old, rich and poor, left and right, almost everyone was swept up in the '60s revolution and its attitudes to the Vietnam War, protests, drugs, rock 'n' roll, sex.

Hair was a harmless enough musical – in retrospect – but it was part of the revolution that saw Australia finally say goodbye to the somnambulism of the Menzies era.

The revolution happened almost overnight late in the decade. It began when women old enough to qualify for a senior citizen's pass to the cinema took to squeezing themselves into 'mini skirts'. And it ended in the mid-'70s when your Commonwealth Bank Manager, Merv Staircase, sloped out of his office one day for you to discover that since you'd last seen him he'd let his comb-over go right over, so that he now had locks – oily, greasy hair – down to the dandruff on his shoulders. And he was giving you the 'peace' fingers! Then and there you decided you were going to get rid of the Lennon spectacles, renew acquaintance with your barber, if he was still in business, and stop calling everyone 'man'.

But until then, and even then, you could still be a vicarious part of it all by going to the happening musical, Hair.

The Sydney opening night of Hair at the Metro Theatre in Kings Cross on a cold June night in 1969 generated unsurpassed anticipation and excitement. Leslie Walford, the Sun-Herald's social columnist, could barely contain himself: 'Every piece of tat or glamour was glittering... The men were peacocks – garbed in velvet, in gold, in cast-

offs, in leather, in kaftans – letting their egos run wild. Harry Miller wore a painted white suit, a sort of Joseph's coat of many colours... After the audience had danced with the cast on stage in a final personal involvement, nearly everyone went to the party.'

At the core of the excitement was the promise that the entire cast – the members of The Tribe: Sheila, who fancies Berger, who in turn is fancied by Claude, whose girlfriend Jeanie is pregnant by ...well, the plot really wasn't the point – all of The Tribe crawl and duck under cover of a huge white sheet, shuck their clothes in an ungainly and awkward strip that has the sheet bobbing suggestively and, finally naked, throw it back to stand, for perhaps 10 seconds...revealed!

*Hair* 'became the immediate sensation the Harry M. Miller production house anticipated,' Reg Livermore, who took over the role of Berger in 1970, wrote in *Chapters and Chances*. 'They advertised that it would not be staged anywhere but Sydney at the Metro... They came in droves from all over Australia... you wouldn't have been able to wipe the grins off the faces of those who had been invited in as investors – Graham Kennedy famously among them. The show was breakfast, lunch and dinner conversation, crossing all boundaries. Who could afford not to be there or be square?'

Director Jim Sharman cast his *Hair* 'Tribe' mainly from theatrical newcomers, because, he said, 'they had something of the street savvy and something of the edge that the piece itself had.' Most were never again heard of. But The Tribe included John Waters and Marcia Hines, Lindsay Field, and, not long after, Reg Livermore. Livermore saw it in preview: 'when the lights came up afterwards, I could not for the life of me stop blubbering and howling', and he vowed then and there that he would join The Tribe.

Eric Willis, the Chief Secretary of New South Wales, who also went to see a preview, had the power to censor the nude scene. He did not blubber. But he also did not howl. 'I told them it was not my kind of show. That it denigrated all of the basic standards of life that we had been reared to believe were correct... the nude scene in my opinion was completely unnecessary... but it was so brief that, you know, I just thought it was harmless.'

# Cameron Mackintosh

The musical theatre in Australia, Michael Edgley pronounced, was dead. And, as Australia's most successful entrepreneur, he would know.

Michael Edgley had a meteoric beginning to his brilliant career. In 1976 his father Eric was in the process of completing arrangements to bring a Russian circus to Australia when he died suddenly. Michael, 23, took over and when the circus arrived in Australia set off on the national tour at the wheel of his Morris Oxford. When it returned to Melbourne at the end of a very profitable tour Michael Edgely was driving a Rolls-Royce.

For the next 15 years Edgley had gone on to bring Australian audiences a succession of Russian shows – Moscow circuses, Georgian dancers, the Red Army choir, Nureyev and Fonteyn and other principals of the great ballet companies. He toured scores of rock stars, often in collaboration with Kevin Jacobsen: Billy Joel, Alice Cooper, Meat Loaf, Kiss, Simon and Garfunkel and such disparate personalities as Peter Allen, Sammy Davis Jnr, Evel Kneivel, Shirley Bassey and Marcel Marceau.

At the end of the '70s Edgley successfully presented two major musicals, *A Chorus Line* and *Annie*, but each of them was expensive to mount and needed near-capacity houses to return a reasonable profit. By 1980 he turned his back on musicals and focused on interests in *The Man From Snowy River, Phar Lap* and other Australian feature films. Among those Edgley had collaborated with during his music theatre interlude was a

*Masquerade!* One of the spectacular highpoints of a musical built on spectacle.

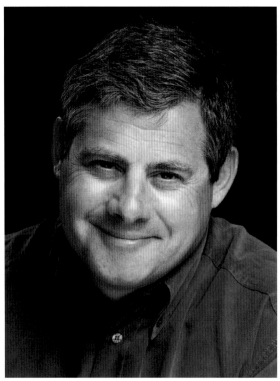

Cameron Mackintosh, knighted for his services to the arts, has been a generous benefactor to musical theatre in Australia and the UK.
*Photograph © Michael Le Poer Trench*

young English producer, Cameron Mackintosh. Together they had bought Mackintosh's West End hit *Oklahoma!* to Australia and in 1984 Mackintosh invited Edgley and other investors to help him stage his new production, *Cats*, here. Edgley, like almost all the Australian investors Mackintosh approached, declined. Mackintosh found the money in New Zealand. For years after, grateful New Zealand investors, many of them former dentists, would arrive (usually by way of their ocean-going yachts) at the nearest port of call to Mackintosh's celebrated opening nights of *Cats*.

Cameron Mackintosh (he was knighted in the '90s but prefers to be called Cameron) had been stage-struck from the age of eight when he was taken to see *Salad Days*. He has done it all in the theatre. He started backstage on props at London's vast and famous Drury Lane, the crucible of the musical theatre. 'You only got £7 a week but I managed to make another £7 by volunteering to work in the mornings cleaning the foyer carpets and polishing all the brass around the dress circle. The trouble was that I have always hated getting up early, so I used to bribe a friend to go along early and just plug in the Hoover, so that the theatre manager would hear the noise and assume I was already at work.' He was a born impresario.

By the time he was 21 he had an almost complete education in musical theatre – he had learned, along the way, that he couldn't act – and by the time he met Michael Edgley his knowledge had been underpinned by more than 500 productions: dismal failures, smash hits, he'd produced them all. Today, of course, Mackintosh is the most successful producer the theatre has known.

Cameron Mackintosh set the template for the modern musical and in the process revived and revolutionised theatre in Australia. A master of marketing, Mackintosh attracted millions – around one in every five Australians and up to 100,000 New Zealanders – to just three 'blockbuster' productions. For 13 years, in an almost unbroken line, from 1985 until 1998, *Cats, Les Miserables* and *The Phantom of the Opera*, dominated Australian theatre. They remain, by far, the three most successful theatre productions staged in this country.

The revolution began when *Cats* made its spectacular debut at Sydney's Theatre Royal in November 1985. It was an opening night to remember. 'The audience was loving it,' Debra Byrne recalled in her autobiography, *Not Quite Ripe*. 'The cats were performing the introduction to "The Jellicle Ball", more than 12 minutes of singing,

*The Phantom of the Opera may be the longest running show on the Australian stage, but on and off, Federici, the Phantom of the Princess, has been playing at the theatre for almost 120 years.*

*The Princess has its own phantom – Federici, a basso baritone who in 1888 made a spectacular exit on the opening night of Gounod's* Faust. *As the opera reached its climax Federici, as Mephistopheles, swirled his scarlet cape around him and in a cloud of sulphurous smoke vanished to the nether regions – through a hidden trapdoor on stage. As he went down the trapdoor, Federici may have hit his head. Or he may succumbed to a heart attack. Whatever the cause by the time the trap reached the cellar floor he was dead.*

*Federici's ghost made its first appearance that night: some cast members swore that he took his curtain call with them and continued to do so on other nights. He was next seen at the Princess during a season of* Macbeth *by a fireman patrolling the empty theatre – one of many sightings by firemen. In 1911, when one of them failed to send his 'all's well' signal to the fire station the brigade rushed to the theatre. They found their man, who had seen Federici standing on stage in a shaft of light, cowering in a corner of the dress circle petrified with fright.*

reciting, dancing, tumbling and somersaulting... I waited at the back of the stage to make my entrance. I saw Cameron Mackintosh in the wings. I knew something was wrong. The dance was coming to its climax and I saw Cameron edging his way towards the stage. He saw me, and just as he was about to motion to me, one of the stage managers approached and told me we had to stop the show.

'Seconds later, the dance was over. When I should have entered Cameron did instead. The cats behaved brilliantly in character: they snarled, crept and huddled together, they hissed and scratched at the intruder. Cameron turned to the audience and calmly explained that there had been a bomb threat and everyone had to leave the theatre until we were given the all clear.'

Stunned, the audience filed out. Debra Byrne, who starred as Grizabella, the cat who ascends to the Heaviside Layer, and who got to sing 'Memory', ironically the musical's one memorable song, found herself in an office nearby with the composer, a pale Andrew Lloyd Webber and, puffing on a cigar, the prime minister, Bob Hawke.

*Cats* transformed the Australian theatre. Lloyd Webber's musical was based on some whimsical and obscure verse by the po-faced poet T.S. Eliot and had an almost non-existent plot line. That was why investors ran from it. But Mackintosh turned it into an experience, a musical that went on to run for a record 7486 performances on Broadway. (*Cats'* record was broken in 2006 by *The Phantom of the Opera*.)

Cameron Mackintosh's 'blockbusters' famously have one big talking-point: the all-enveloping garbage dump set of *Cats*; the barricades of *Les Miserables*, the crashing chandelier of *The Phantom of the Opera*, and the helicopter of his *Miss Saigon*. But within the Australian theatre industry the real talking-point was how the English impresario set about selling his blockbusters. He released tickets in 'blocks' so that seats were always in demand. He marketed his musicals interstate and in New Zealand, and, with Qantas, established attractive travel packages worth millions to the cities that hosted his musicals. A hands-on producer, Mackintosh involved himself in every aspect of the production, from the logo to the lighting. No detail was too small to avoid his attention.

Mackintosh, who loves theatres, and old theatres in particular, caused the resurrection of some that were once Melbourne's and Sydney's grandest. He gave Sydney a wonderful new Capitol theatre, reborn from the old Haymarket cinema.

In Melbourne he inspired property developer David Marriner to restore the most glorious of all Australian cinemas, the Regent, slowly rotting after a union ban stopped its demolition. And he persuaded Marriner to re-open the century-old Princess, a theatre that had been 'dark' for years. Mackintosh promised that he would put *Les Miserables* into the Princess in 1988, after its season in Sydney, and would follow it in 1990 with the Australian premiere of the hottest musical of all.

*The Phantom of the Opera* had its Australian premiere on 9 December 1990 with Anthony Warlow in the lead role of the Phantom. Hiding his hideously disfigured features behind a mask, the bitter and very twisted Phantom causes murder and mayhem at the Paris Opera of the late 18th century. Marina Prior played Christine, the young girl from the opera ballet who hears the Phantom's seductive 'Music of the Night' and, transformed into the opera company's diva, becomes the toast of Paris.

Romantic, thrilling and gorgeous – the budget was $10 million – the musical was a sensational

Mackintosh had a hard time finding backers for his first blockbuster, *Cats*. Foolish Australian investors turned him down.

success. For the first two-and-a-half years of its season the blockbuster to beat them all was sold out every night.

It took $82 million at the box office – each announcement of a new block of tickets had queues snaking a block long – and drew 400 tourists a week to the city, making it worth half a billion dollars to the Victorian economy. More than one-and-a-half million saw 1048 performances at the Princess until the curtain finally came down in June 1993. And another 300,000 saw the show when it returned to Melbourne in 1997-98.

In July 2007 it came back for a third time, opening at The Princess Theatre where, 17 years before, it had such a triumphant premiere. This time it was produced by Andrew Lloyd Webber's Really Useful Company, and once more it starred Anthony Warlow as the Phantom.

*The Phantom of the Opera* is the biggest box office grossing entertainment ever – bigger than any film. It grossed $247 million in Australia alone before it closed in Perth in September 1998, and overall it has played in 110 cities around the world to more than 80 million theatre-goers. Nothing comes remotely close to *The Phantom of the Opera*.

# 5

# THE ICONS

'The Little Digger' statue in Anzac Park, Port Douglas. Its like can be seen in towns around Australia. Below the usually half life-size statue of an infantryman of World War One, head bowed and hands cupped over his rifle in the reverse arms position, the roll of honour on the plinth never fails to move: listed are the men from that district who never came back.

An icon, in today's terminology, is someone or something that is universally and uncritically admired by a nation. The courageous PoW surgeon 'Weary' Dunlop was such a one. Vegemite is such a thing. (If there is any criticism of Vegemite it is that more is less.) The Holden car was another. Prime Minister Ben Chifley unveiled 'our' car in November 1948 and it soon had almost half the market share. In *Melbourne on My Mind* Keith Dunstan recalls, 'My father received his No. 1 Holden that Christmas. The waiting list had already grown to two years and the prestige of having the first Holden was even better than owning a Rolls-Royce. And how advanced it was; no chassis. It had what they called a monocoque construction, a "development of the streamlined aircraft construction." There were some interesting variations from aeroplanes. We noticed that when we slammed the door hard all the door handles popped off on the inside.'

Holden still sells around one in five passenger cars in Australia, but its status is not what it was. Like other iconic products, Victa lawnmowers, Violet Crumble bars, Bushells tea and Hills Hoists, the bloom has faded.

Perhaps no other Australian icon is as indestructible as our national song, 'Waltzing Matilda'. Paul Keating has said: 'I suspect there is no one who has not at some time, somewhere in the world, heard or remembered the tune and felt deeply affected by it. I'm sure it has brought Australians home before they intended to, and given others the strength to stay away a bit longer.

'For a century it has caused more smiles and tears, and more hairs to stand up on the back of Australian necks than any other thing of three minutes duration in Australian history... "Waltzing Matilda" is Australia's song and it always will be.'

# The Melbourne Cup

A long-stemmed white rose within the veggie patch, Jean Shrimpton outraged the Melbourne Establishment at the 1965 Cup carnival. Photographed on Derby Day, 1965, the Saturday before the Cup, 'The Shrimp's' short skirt – 10 centimetres above the knee – sent the nation's young women straight to their sewing machines. But it was not her fledgling mini that caused the furore, more the fact that the world's most famous model had not seen the need to come to Derby Day in hat, gloves or stockings.

After 1965 the Cup Carnival began to party once more, as it had a century before when Sydney – indeed all Australia – took the Melbourne Cup to its heart. In 1885 (Sheet Anchor's year) the *Sydney Morning Herald* railed that this 'worst occasion and cause for a national gathering, is naturally allied to more that makes directly for human degradation than any other public sport or pastime that could be named'. Alas, the horse had bolted long before. By then, two decades after Archer won the first race, the Melbourne Cup was a blazing success, an extraordinary sporting event that involved most of the Australian community in a social celebration without peer.

'It is the Melbourne Cup that brings this multitude together,' Mark Twain wrote after his tour of Australia in 1895 (Auraria's year). 'Their clothes have been ordered long ago, at unlimited cost and without bounds as to beauty and

The *Australasian Sketcher*'s man at the 1873 Cup captures the Fashions on the Field.

magnificence, and have been kept in concealment until now, for unto this day are they consecrated. I am speaking of the ladies' clothes, but one might know that.

'And so the grandstands make a brilliant and wonderful spectacle, a delirium of colour, a vision of beauty. The champagne flows, everybody is vivacious, excited, happy; everybody bets and gloves and fortunes change hands right along, all the time. Day after day the races go on, and the fun and the excitement are kept at white heat; and when each day is done the people dance all night so as to be fresh for the race in the morning.

'And at the end of the great week the swarms secure lodgings and transportation for next year, then flock away to their remote homes and count their gains and losses, and order next year's Cup-clothes, and then lie down and sleep two weeks, and get up sorry to reflect that a whole year must be put in somehow or other before they can be wholly happy again.'

Nothing has changed. Today almost 400,000 go to the four days of the Melbourne Cup Carnival, and around the nation that many again dress up and celebrate as if they were at the Cup. More than 2.5 million viewers – 92 per cent of the available audience – and 700 million people worldwide, watch the big race on television.

'There she was, the world's highest paid fashion model, snubbing the iron-clad conventions of fashionable Flemington with a dress five inches above the knee, NO hat, NO gloves and NO stockings!' Barry Watts wrote on 1 November 1965 on the Melbourne *Sun News Pictorial*'s front page.

'The shockwaves were still rumbling around fashionable Melbourne last night when Jean Shrimpton – The Shrimp – swore she hadn't realised she was setting off such an outraged upheaval at Flemington on Saturday.

'"I don't see what was wrong with the way I looked," she said. "I wouldn't have dressed differently for a race meeting anywhere in the world."

'For my money, she looked tremendous – but Flemington was not amused. Fashion-conscious Derby Day racegoers were horrified. "Insulting"... "a disgrace"... "how dare she?" ... If the skies had rained acid not a well-dressed woman there would have given The Shrimp an umbrella.'

# Anzac Day

'It's just about one long grog-up,' the son of the World War Two Digger shouts in *The One Day of the Year*. 'We're sick of all the muck that's talked about this day... It [Gallipoli] was doomed from the start, it was a waste. Every year you still march down that street with that stupid, proud expression on your face, you glorify the wastefulness of that day.'

His father hits back: 'You'd take away everything. You'd take away the ordinary bloke's right to feel a bit proud of himself for once.

'Every city, every little town in this country puts on its service and its march on that day. Every day for 40 years they've done it and they always will do it. You don't get there to show what a great soldier you was; you're there as mates; you're there to say it was a job you had to do and you done it – together.'

Alan Seymour's landmark play, about a father and son at war over the commemoration of the landing at Gallipoli (and all the wars Australians had fought in) articulated the changing attitudes of the young towards Anzac Day. In the coming decade and in the wake of Vietnam those attitudes were exacerbated, so that by the 1980s there were some who felt that Anzac Day was a relic destined to disappear by the turn of the century.

How wrong they were.

'The dawn service draws about 15,000 pilgrims,' Les Carlyon writes in *Gallipoli* of the April 25 commemoration of the 1915 landing on the beach. He was on the beach almost 90 years on, among '...old men with their uncles' medals jangling on

sports coats, Vietnam vets with medals pinned
on yellow rugby guernseys, backpackers lumping
bedrolls, 20-year-olds with Australian flags draped
over their shoulders, school kids on trips, matrons
from Sydney's North Shore...'

Back home, at hundreds of Anzac Day
commemorations, the same kind of people – the
old men with their medals, the young with their
flags – are sharing the same visceral thoughts and
emotions. In small towns in far north Queensland,
palm trees framing the Coral Sea behind them,
they have gathered in the hot sun before the small
sandstone statue of a World War One soldier.
Thousands of kilometres south, the weather is bitter
cold, much like the winters on the Western Front
of 1916, but it's much the same small town park;
much the same 'little Digger' statue; much the same
crowd. At Avenues of Honour in the midlands of
Victoria, in Perth, before marble rolls of honour,
at the Cenotaph in Sydney's Hyde Park – across
the continent we stand for one minute in silence.
A bugle call sounds the Last Post. Some honoured
dignitary recites:

*They shall grow not old, as we that are left grow old:*
*Age shall not weary them, nor the years condemn.*
*At the going down of the sun and in the morning*
*We will remember them.*

Anzac Day. Lest we forget.

Wreaths of red poppies, laid on Anzac Day, 25 April and Remembrance Day,
11 November, are poignant reminders of the same flower seen by soldiers at
Gallipoli, the Somme and Palestine, where this Light Horseman stoops to
pick them in 1917. *AWM P03631*

# Beaches and Bondi

O n a hot summer's day in 1906, with marvellous symmetry, two newly emerging Australian icons took their bow – thanks to an ancient, third icon.

It was 3 January, and an Australian invention was about to give the first dramatic presentation of its potential. Bondi surf lifesaving club was on the eve of being formed and one of its founding members, Lyster Ormsby, had come up with a device he believed could save lives. It did so on that day. Attached by a belt to the reel of rope, a man plunged into the surf at Bondi and swam out to rescue three kids in trouble. One of them was a boy, Charlie Smith – later to be known as Sir Charles Kingsford Smith, and later still, ironically, to be claimed by the sea in the Bay of Bengal.

Like millions of Australians then and now, Charlie Smith was spending his summer holidays on the beach. It's what we did when we were kids, and what we do, if we're lucky, when we're adults. Surf, sun, sand – the bliss of the beach is deep in the Australian psyche.

We all of us have our 'special' beach: Coolangatta, Portsea, Burleigh Heads, St Kilda, Scarborough, Coogee, Brighton, Surfers Paradise, Bells, Maroubra, Noosa, Lorne, Lady Jane, Sorrento, Four Mile, Sandy Bay, Bronte, Cottesloe, Manly, Glenelg, Southport, Newcastle, Point Lonsdale, Freshwater, Albert Park, Balmoral, Torquay, Tweed Heads... The list is almost endless, but in that

An iconic cornucopia pictured in this late 1960s press advertisement: beach, blondes, bikinis, surfboards and the latest Holden station wagon.

special roll call one beach stands alone.

Bondi.

Why is that? Bondi's surf is nothing to write home about, unless you're from Japan or Great Britain. The setting is less than spectacular and the architecture along Campbell Parade teeters on the edge of tackiness. Yes, it's conveniently close to the centre of a great metropolis, but that too can be a drawback when the temperature soars and Bondi's wide span of sand becomes a blanket of bronze, salmon pink and off-white flesh (that last would be the good people from Great Britain.)

For most of us, the beach we grew up on will always be our private Aussie icon. Yet Bondi, we unanimously agree, is the international icon, the one we're proud of. Why? Because Bondi represents the Australian character. It's big, brash and beautiful; sunny and sensuous; welcoming and tolerant. More than any other beach, Bondi is egalitarian. At Bondi you can find yourself bodysurfing into the beach alongside Miss Australia, a backpacker from Dublin, a Stock Exchange secretary taking a sickie, an alarmingly tattooed Maori front-row forward, James Packer and his partner and ten Redfern kids from The Block. And you can get to your feet, turn and head back into the breakers with them to do it all over again.

Bondi Beach... international icon. *Newspix*

# Vegemite

Non-Australians are nonplussed by our universal addiction to the mysterious black substance in the squat jar. It is said that there are some of us who find the taste of Vegemite too salty, but this – surely – is a folk myth, or possibly, a despicable canard put around by New Zealanders who prefer the English rival, Marmite. We acquire the Vegemite taste from an early age and we remain happily hooked for as long as we live. Like that other wonder drug, penicillin, Vegemite is the result of an accidental discovery of an unexplored use for yeast; spent brewers' yeast, used in the manufacture of beer. Spent yeast was often discarded, but it contained nutrients and vitamins. Could there be a use for it? At the Melbourne factory of the Fred Walker Cheese Company, food technologist Dr Cyril P. Callister took some leftover brewers' yeast, added various vegetable and spice additives and, in 1923, discovered... well, what is it?

Fred Walker ran a competition to name the mysterious new... stuff. An unlikely legend has it that as Fred and his seven-year-old daughter Sheilah were sorting through the entries she came up with the name on the spot. Whatever was she thinking?

The following year the company became the Kraft Walker Cheese Company, now simply Kraft Foods. Although it is now American owned, the magic mixture is still made only in Melbourne and by only 26 people. Between them they make enough to export to 16 countries, and supply the home market's insatiable appetite. Australians buy the black gold at the rate of 44 jars every minute.

Vegemite is lodged in our vernacular. In the 1940s, beaming little Aussie kids chorused, 'We're happy little Vegemites' in an enduring radio advertising campaign that graduated to television and went on to enjoy various reincarnations. And these days we describe another's feelings by way of saying: 'He's a happy little Vegemite.'

Unhappy little Vegemites by the thousands wailed when they heard the news that kosher Vegemite, on the market for 20 years, was to be scrapped. Tim Blair's blogsite carried the grim news:

Hundreds of families have been scouring supermarkets for the last kosher jars of the famous spread. One mum bought 75 jars in one shop.

Dad Mark Chaskiel said the family have run out of kosher Vegemite after panic-buying 35 jars. 'I was brought up on Vegemite,' Mr Chaskiel said. 'I can sacrifice lobster and prawns for kosher but I can't give up Vegemite. It's an Australian birthright.'

Blair sympathised and went further: 'If I were denied Vegemite for religious reasons, I would give up religion.'

# Sydney Harbour Bridge

It was going to cost the astronomical sum of four million, two hundred and seventeen thousand, seven hundred and twenty-one pounds, eleven shillings and ten pence, but for what it gave Australia it was cheap at half the price (and the price, of course, for the Sydney Harbour Bridge, more than doubled before it was finished). But what a bargain. Envied by other capitals though it has been and always will be, the bridge has been part of our common story ever since. It gave Australia its first national monument.

The bridge had been a long time coming. The great convict architect Francis Greenway had designed a bridge to span the harbour in 1815. But it took almost a century before a government engineer, John Job Crew Bradfield, was commissioned to build a bridge between Dawes Point in the city and Milson's Point on the northern shore. Bradfield's design called for the marriage of two halves to make the largest and heaviest steel arch bridge ever built. Two cantilevered half arches, anchored by 128 immense wire cables, would be built from either shore. The arches would reach over the water until they came almost close enough to touch; less than a metre apart. Then a long pilot pin would be inserted between them, the cables would be gradually slackened and the two halves would meet as one. The riveters would then seal the marriage of 650,000 tonnes of steel. Beneath the

The Sydney Opera House is unquestionably a glorious structure: one of the modern wonders of the world. But it belongs to Sydney. The beauty of the Sydney Harbour Bridge lies in what it symbolises. Practically speaking, it is a road between the city and the north shore, but the Sydney Harbour Bridge is much more: it is a link that joins us all. It belongs to all Australians. *Newspix*

HAPPY NEW YEAR!

arch, 440 feet high, gigantic girders would hang to support the eight-lane roadway and two-lane rail track below.

Simple as that.

Of course it didn't quite turn out that way. Sixteen workers died building the bridge, some of them unqualified men who took the job in desperation during the Depression. And the grand opening of the bridge on 19 March 1932 was going very well, with Mr Jack Lang, the state's firebrand socialist premier announcing, '...in a few moments I shall complete the opening ceremony by severing the ribbon stretched across the highway,' when someone did it for him.

A curious Irishman, Captain Francis De Groot, an antique dealer and former army officer, had somehow got among the premier's mounted guard of honour. Wearing his antique army uniform and wielding a sabre, De Groot spurred his forlorn steed, found for the purpose at the last moment, galloped up and slashed through the ribbon. 'I declare this bridge open in the name of the decent and respectable citizens of New South Wales!' he shouted as he was dragged from the horse by the Police Commissioner. A member of the extreme right-wing New Guard, De Groot said his intention was 'to bring ridicule upon Mr Lang, cause no injury to anyone and make the whole world laugh'. A pioneer in the increasingly long and crowded line of pestilent protesters, De Groot was fined £5 and had his sabre returned.

Thanks to a television commercial, most Australians now know that the inspiration for Bradfield's bridge was sparked by half a slice of lemon dropped into a gin and tonic; and gullible viewers may even believe that. But the truth is that the design had been a matter of controversy since 1926, a debate reignited in the *Australian* in March 2007, just a week before the 75th anniversary of the bridge's opening. The newspaper reported that an Australian engineering firm claimed that the final design was the work of an Englishman, Ralph Freeman (a claim supported by the *Encyclopedia Britannica*.)

'No other bridge in the world can match it as the centrepiece of a city,' said the London *Guardian* in an editorial marking the bridge's 75th anniversary. 'Other bridges are longer, higher or carry more traffic, but none dominates a city likes Sydney's giant steel arch.' But the bridge has had the odd critic. 'Sydney Bridge [sic] is big, utilitarian and the symbol of Australia,' the American novelist James Michener wrote on a visit to Australia in 1951. 'But it is very ugly. No Australian will admit this.' Certainly not! Painters – from Grace Cossington Smith, with her masterpiece, *The Bridge in Curve*, to Brett Whitely and, yes, Ken Done – portray the bridge as a beauty. Millions of photographers have tried to capture its monumental majesty, and some, like Henri Mallard, who filmed the progress of the colossus, and photographer Harold Cazneaux who celebrated the light and shade of its steely heart, have succeeded brilliantly.

But above all what James Michener failed to see is plain to the eyes of all Australians. The bridge stands where the First Fleet settlers established the infant colony – a spectacular reminder that in less than a century and a half the 'colony of thieves' as it was once called, had transformed itself into a great nation.

# 6

# THE TELEVISION

'Look at moiye!' And from Finland to Frankston we're looking. Created by Gina Riley (left) and Jane Turner, (right) the dysfunctional daughter and mother stars of *Kath & Kim* took Australian comedy to the world, where Fountain Lakes, Melbourne's fictional suburb, clearly has many clones.

'Good evening and welcome to television,' the handsome, urbane man in the well-cut dinner suit, a white carnation in his buttonhole, purred at us one Sunday night in September 1956. We said nothing in reply. We just gawped, lost for words at the wonder of it all. The man was talking to us – looking us straight in the eye – from a glowing tube in a luxurious wooden cabinet. Life, we knew, would never be the same. What we didn't know, and desperately wanted to know, was how soon we could get a telly!

Within a year each city had one national and two commercial stations and by 1960, when quizmaster Bob Dyer – 'Howdy customers!' – won the Gold Logie, 'the Box' was on day and night in hundreds of thousands of homes around the nation. Despite the fact that a 21-inch set cost around $15,000 in today's terms, almost eight out of ten homes were under its spell.

Today the spell is broken. The networks can no longer compel us to watch programs at the time they want us to. People can now decide what they will watch and when, downloading the hot TV series only hours after it has screened in New York and before it is seen in San Francisco, let alone Sydney.

TV is no longer the focus for the entire family. Now there are numerous options. By 2010 one in three Australian homes will have a broadband-based wireless IT network targeting demographic niches that demand limitless sport, 24-hour news, Shakespeare, Shelley and Shostakovich and round-the-clock porn. But overriding all is the internet video revolution led by YouTube, MySpace, Yahoo, MSN and the like, where, every day more than 150 million international viewers watch short and sharp clips – home movies and amateur comedy and dramas, music videos, clips from past and current movies and famous television moments – at video-sharing websites. In 2005 online video services generated $US230 million. By 2010 that figure will be $US1.7 billion. DIY programming.

Good evening and goodbye to television as we knew and loved it.

# Graham Kennedy

T he King died at 4.30 a.m., on 25 May 2005. At his funeral service his mourners sang this song:

*Being a chum is fun*
*That is why I'm one,*
*Always smiling, always gay,*
*Chummy at work and chummy at play,*
*Laugh away your worries,*
*Don't be sad or glum,*
*And everyone will know that you're a*
*Chum, chum, chum.*

A thread in Graham Kennedy's life for 55 years, the song contains a number of ironic references that none of the mourners, many of them famous in their own right, would have missed. Graham Kennedy was the King of Television but the crown came at a bitter price. His life in television was not fun, he said. 'I was terrified for 40 years.' He was gay, but he lived alone, without a chum. He was not always smiling, he was often sad and glum. Intensely private he was not always chummy at work and play; he couldn't laugh away his worries.

But probably more than any other Australian entertainer, he had the love of millions of Australians who saw him as one of the family. The naughty one.

Gra Gra, as he came to be known, to his irritation, first sang the Chum song in 1950 when he joined radio station 3UZ in Melbourne. He'd left school in 1949. He was 15 and got a job as a copy boy with the ABC. That led to a job as a turntable operator with 3AW and, within a year, to the record library at 3UZ where Cliff Nicholls was

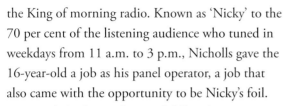

the King of morning radio. Known as 'Nicky' to the 70 per cent of the listening audience who tuned in weekdays from 11 a.m. to 3 p.m., Nicholls gave the 16-year-old a job as his panel operator, a job that also came with the opportunity to be Nicky's foil.

Kennedy had an unhappy childhood. His parents had fought bitterly. When they divorced, in 1939, the five-year-old boy was mainly brought up by his grandmother, whom he greatly loved. Nicky, Graham acknowledged, became like a surrogate father, and from Nicky he learned much of the magic that made him the biggest television star Australia has known.

Nicky talked directly to his listeners, the housewives of Melbourne. Leaning close to the microphone on *Chums Club* he'd call them 'mum', 'darl', and 'luv', as if he knew them all, was cosy with them, treated them, as the Club theme song had it, as if they were his chums.

And he'd mock the commercials. No one on radio had ever mocked the commercials, they were sacrosanct. Nicky would get Graham to blend jingles, so that a cure for corns would be wed to the answer to constipation, Laxettes, one of the great advertisers of the '50s. He'd speed up the commercials, slow them down, deride them, even – to the shocked delight of his fans – physically destroy the sponsor's products.

Soon Graham was in on the act. On air with Nicky he showed he had a quick wit and a mischievous sense of humour every bit as anarchic as Nicky's. The combination, Nicky and Graham, became perhaps the greatest double act in radio history.

Then, in 1956, the year that television began in

Gra Gra began in radio, where he quickly became a star, but his spiritual heritage was vaudeville with its risqué humour and direct connection to the audience. Later he proved to be a fine character actor in feature films. *Newspix*

Australia, Cliff Nicholls died, aged 51. Graham successfully carried on – *The Graham Show*, 3UZ after very little thought called his slot – and the vaudeville comedian Happy Hammond joined him as his partner. Graham's ribald, often smutty, sense of humour had its seeds in the vaudeville theatres that were a part of the suburban landscape of Melbourne and Sydney, and the vaudeville great, Roy Rene, 'Mo', who became a star of radio comedy, was another undoubted influence on the teenager. Mo and the others taught Kennedy, as he told a viewer complaining about his innuendoes, 'There are no limits, luv. There are no limits.'

A year after Nicky's death, Channel Nine invited Graham to present an evening television variety show, *In Melbourne Tonight*. He was 23 and knew nothing of television, but then who did? He brought home his first payslip and proudly showed it to his grandmother. She was appalled. It was too much, she said; he should return it. His boss in later years, Sir Frank Packer, would have liked him to return his pay. He had a suspicion that Kennedy was homosexual and wanted him sacked, but the success of *In Melbourne Tonight* and Graham's extraordinary power to have the town talking the following morning – 'Did you see Graham last night?' – made that impossible and for the best part of 30 years Graham Kennedy earned millions for himself and many more for the Packer family.

His formula was a blend of audacity, irreverence, innuendo, iconoclasm and physical comedy, all wrapped in the persona of a naughty boy having fun and sharing it with the viewers.

He drew around him a band of seasoned performers – Joff Ellen, Buster Fiddess, Rosie Sturgess, Noel Ferrier, Mary Hardy, many of them from vaudeville. And for his sidekick he had the ideal foil: Bert Newton. Newton, his radio rival, was every bit as quick-witted as Kennedy, and where bug-eyed Graham, cheeky tongue in a gaping mouth, was forever – seemingly – teetering on the verge of losing all control, handsome Bert was calm and suave, the perfect butt for Graham's uniquely anarchic comedy.

The pair made a comedic art form from reading live commercials. *Bert! Bert Newton's Own Story*, recounts how 'The blood would drain from the face of Pelaco shirt-wearing executives in television, advertising and business until they realised that instead of televisual suicide, this skinny little wiseguy was commercial gold. And then they liked his brand of humour a lot.' The two of them made products famous overnight and, an advertiser's ultimate fantasy, they once turned a 30-second commercial into an unscripted 22 minutes of uproarious comedy.

Graham had a Labrador, Rover, who was sometimes enlisted to perform in the live reads for a dog food. Rover would usually distinguish himself. Once he refused to eat the sponsor's dog food and Kennedy hopped into it with relish. Another time Rover relieved himself on set: a long, long, time. Both routines were undoubtedly contrived, but the audience shrieked with delight as they did every night on *In Melbourne Tonight*. People asked Kennedy for the next 20 years, 'Whatever happened to Rover?' 'He was a dog,' he snapped when a viewer asked the question on *Graham Kennedy's News Hour* in 1989. 'What do you think happened to him?'

(He loved animals. When he retired to a property near Bowral he kept Clydesdale horses and a golden retriever, Henry. One of the horses died. Kennedy buried him on the property and when his

'There are no limits, luv. There are no limits.' Deadpan, Kennedy begins one of his classic commercials. When inspired he could devote up to 20 minutes mocking a sponsor's product. Overnight, sales of the product would soar. *Newspix*

housekeeper told him that Henry was digging up the horse, Kennedy said, 'Oh, good. I'd like to see him again.')

Graham Kennedy was a perfectionist and his comedy routines were meticulously rehearsed. Then, when they went to air, his fellow performers, Joff Ellen, Pete Smith, Rosie Sturgess, Buster Fiddess, Bert, would find that Kennedy was acting to a script of his own: a script that was a work in progress in front of a studio audience and millions more watching at home, and that had everyone, themselves included, in stitches.

His biographer Graeme Blundell says Kennedy

'created a particular kind of urban comedy... There was no reality that he appeared to believe in when he performed; he'd ridicule everything. We take it for granted now because everyone does what he did. "They've all stolen my act," he used to say in the '90s.

'He understood that it was the telling that was funny. There was no punch line as such, he would digress, he didn't know where he was going but it was just hysterical.' Kennedy refused to be interviewed for the book, *The King*, and, according to Blundell, read the early chapters of the book and liked it. He declined to read more, however, 'because I know how it ends'.

Seat of the pants comedy like Kennedy's wears the nerves. After 13 years at the top of television he quit *IMT* in 1969 and retired for what he later described as 'two years of misery' (Stuart Wagstaff once said that 'Graham's life off camera is one long stage-wait) and in 1972 he was back in *The Graham Kennedy Show*. (Like 3UZ, the creative department at Nine saw no point in agonising over the name.) By now what had been shocking a decade earlier was no longer the subject of water cooler conversations the following morning and Graham was forced to push things a little harder.

In March 1975 he imitated a crow call during a live read of a commercial by the squeaky clean Rosemary Margan. The crow call was a favourite of his at the time. It went like this: 'Faaaaaaaaaaaark.' It was not particularly funny and it had gone unremarked when he had done it on other occasions, but on 5 March 1975 it led to Nine getting, the network said, hundreds of calls of complaint. Nine insisted that from then on Kennedy's shows would have to be pre-recorded. A few weeks later he left Nine.

Kennedy was sacked or quit, Graham Blundell believes, not over the crow call, but after he had launched a vitriolic attack on the Labor government's Media Minister, Doug McClelland, for his failure to support local content on TV. The attack was edited from the tape that went to air. It shows a beleaguered side to Kennedy that was increasingly getting darker. In part, Kennedy said:

Good evening. Little serious bit to start with: Senator Douglas McClelland, ah, is really copping it in the press at the moment. All this week, every paper you pick up, there's a, there's a roast for the senator.

And like most Australians I hate to kick a man when he's down. But in Doug McClelland's case

I happily make an exception.

He has failed, and he knows it, too. Now the public know it.

This misguided minister took credit for a mythical boom in television production. Now there is no boom. Employment in television production is down this year by over 30 per cent. And that's a fact.

... We are all suffering from the lack of local content at the moment. I'm being trashed in the surveys because constantly being thrown up against me are shows like the Academy Awards, and cheap television series, all purchased for a few hundred dollars from the Yanks.

... I know I can speak for a lot of my colleagues in the industry, and several other industries in the entertainment field, when I demand, here, tonight, nationally, that Senator McClelland be dismissed from office; and I would suggest most strongly that the portfolio itself be dropped.

That's all I want to say.

In 1977 Kennedy returned on Channel 10, hosting a comedy show, *Blankety Blanks*, that ran for two years with guest panellists such as Noeline Brown, Barry Creyton, Ugly Dave Grey, Carol Raye and Stuart Wagstaff. It won Kennedy the 1978 Gold Logie – his seventh – for the most popular personality on Australian television. The program's smut quota was high.

Ten years on, back at Nine, he was reading the news, first with a bewildered Ken Sutcliffe and then John Mangan. On the show, nostalgically, he reprised the Chum song. The show, of course, had very little to do with news. It was Graham's slant on the news. Queen Elizabeth, he broke off from reading a news item, 'didn't have bad breasts... for a woman of her age,' and when the whim took him he'd stand from behind his desk to reveal that from the waist down he was trouserless.

He did Graham Kennedy's *Funniest Home Videos*, but by now there was a note of desperation in it all. 'The most devoted youngster I have ever met, he eats and sleeps TV,' Bob Dyer, the quiz show master, had said four decades before when he took the scrawny young star on a fishing trip. 'He is probably the loneliest young man in Australia.' In 1991 he retired, this time for good. His legacy was four shows voted by 100 people in the industry as among the 50 best Australian productions. *In Melbourne Tonight* topped the poll.

Three years later Graham Kennedy made his final television appearance, an interview with Ray Martin. He was embittered by it. He felt Martin had 'ambushed' him with probing questions about his private life. Television had finally consumed him.

His private life was shared by a small circle of friends. A recluse, he would communicate with friends by fax. He sacked his long-time manager Harry M. Miller by fax. Miller sued him, lost the case and had to pay Kennedy $75,699. It was a bitter end to a friendship of three decades.

A diabetic, Kennedy drank and smoked heavily and his health declined alarmingly. He injured himself in a fall down stairs, had to sell his property, and went, finally, into the Kenilworth nursing home at Bowral. His oldest friend, Bert Newton – they had known and liked each other for almost 50 years – visited him when it was clear the end was getting near.

The King had his 70th birthday in a wheelchair. Three months later he died.

# Number 96

In big bold type the headline for the press ad trumpeted: Tonight at 8.30 television loses its virginity!

For once, that was no exaggeration. Australian television lost its innocence on 13 March 1972 when *Number 96* went to air. Until then we'd only really known the sedate soap, *Bellbird* – 'not so much a drama, more a reassuring habit like thumb sucking' as Phillip Adams said – but *Number 96* changed all that.

The show revolutionised television in Australia. From its nudge-nudge, wink-wink title to its full frontal nudity and the subjects like homosexuality, adultery, drugs, domestic violence and rape that were its staple, *Number 96* was camp, candid, and for all its melodrama, its black masses and bombs, a real reflection of Australia in the early '70s.

*Number 96* ranked Number 9 in the poll of the Top 50 Australian television shows but at Ten it deservedly ranks much higher. It saved the network.

Ten, lagging badly behind Nine and Seven, unable to match their buying budgets for overseas programs and its advertising revenue plummeting along with its ratings, was desperate when program manager Ian Holmes commissioned a locally made soap. He saw the show as *Coronation Street* – with sex. 'Sexuality and other previously taboo subjects had been part of the brief,' he has acknowledged, and the independent producers Don Cash and Bill Harmon, and writer David Sale, answered the brief brilliantly.

Abigail's nude scenes as Bev Houghton made her Australian television's first and most enduring sex symbol. Most sensational of all, however, was Abigail's abrupt departure from the series. *Number 96* carried on next week with a new Bev but somehow the show was never the same. *Newspix*

In an existing block of eight flats in 83 Moncur Street, Woollahra, David Sale set his characters and his concept. There was South African former call-girl, Vera (Elaine Lee), the tarot card reader forever unlucky in an endless series of affairs. She was raped by her ex-husband Harry Collins (Norman Yem) in the first episode, and she was to be raped again and yet again. There were her next-door neighbours, Lucy and Alf (Elisabeth Kirby and James Elliott), the middle aged immigrants from Lancashire. In Flat 4 were teacher Mark Eastwood (Martin Harris) and his pregnant wife (Briony Behets). There were superbitch Maggie Cameron (Bettina Welch) and the homosexual lawyer Don Finlayson (Joe Hasham), the one character who could be relied upon to do the right thing always. There was the comic couple Herb Evans (Ron Shand) and his wife, the concierge Dorrie (Pat McDonald), the bumbling Hungarian Jew, Aldo Godolfus (Johnny Lockwood) in the deli downstairs, the mysterious brother and sister, the Vansards (Joe James and Lynn Rainbow), who ran the chemist shop opposite, soon to become a wine bar, a popular meeting point for the residents of 96, and the flatmates Janie Somers (Robyn Gurney) the actress, and the virgin and virtuous Bev Houghton, a harbour cruise hostess.

Bev was played by Abigail (her surname, Rogan, was never revealed). Abigail, overnight, became something that Australia had never had: a sex symbol. Over the next five years dozens of characters – Bev among them – were to come and go, and Pat McDonald as Dorrie won more Logies than any other *96* performer, but it was Abigail who made *Number 96* Australia's top rating show.

When she abruptly left the series in June 1973 it was front page news. Did she go, as Abigail insisted, because of differences with the producers? Or was it, as Andrew Mercado says in *Super Aussie Soaps* that she was fired because of a roll of film? 'The real story, according to David Sale who was in the office when Bill Harmon fired his biggest star, can finally be told,' Mercado says.

'Abigail had left behind in a taxi a handbag that contained a roll of undeveloped film that featured her in some very compromising situations. How the photographs got into circulation remains a mystery but the fact that they were doing the rounds was enough for Bill Harmon to decide that was enough.'

Harmon, a tough, down-to-earth producer, had no compunction about replacing Abigail in the role of Bev. So viewers saw Abigail's Bev walk into a bedroom and, the next night, Vicki Raymond's Bev emerge. Abigail was obliged to take her talents to the theatre where, twice nightly in *The Saga of San Peel* at the Barrel Theatre in Kings Cross, playing an evangelist at work in a brothel, she took a bath on stage.

Sounds like a script from *Number 96.*

The show ran for 1218 episodes, and in the end became an outrageous and often very funny spoof of itself and the rival soaps the other networks rushed into production. But it set new benchmarks in many areas of television. It invented the cliffhanger to keep viewers on edge over the summer break. And it undoubtedly shaped – for the better – Australians' attitudes to homosexuality, race and our sense of fun.

# Paul Hogan

**P**aul Hogan, 32, was up on the Harbour Bridge working as a rigger when his mates dared him to go down and send up those pompous whackers on the TV talent quest, *New Faces*. He came down as Hoges, an ocker: a laconic but sharp observer of life, a pub philosopher in football shorts, sleeveless shirt, long white socks and brickie's boots.

It was 1972, it was time for the Whitlam government, and there was a palpable feeling that the Australian identity, after a decade of cultural cringe under the anglophile prime minister, Sir Robert Menzies, was coming back into focus, confident and can-do. Hogan's *New Faces* act was simple: he played himself, a shrewd representative of the new breed of Australians who were proud to call themselves Aussies.

'Hoges is not too far from me,' he told the *Australian* some time later. 'He lives a few streets away from me, but he does not live with me.'

For a brief period he was working on the bridge and appearing on TV. 'I was poor and famous,' he told the *Age*. 'That was really awful. I thought, "I'm not going to go on the television again." I was on television, and people would see me and recognise me everywhere, but I was still going to work on the bus and the train.'

'It's one thing to wave to the crowd and get into your Rolls-Royce, it's another to sit on the bus, and some bloke beside you goes, "Saw you last night. Yeah, it wasn't too bad." Yeah, thank you. I thought, "This sucks, I don't want to do this any more." But

An early photograph of Paul Hogan before he gave up his day job to become Hoges. The two, Hogan and Hoges are quite close – Hoges, he says, 'lives near me', and, though this is debatable, 'Neither of us gives a bugger what people think'. *Newspix*

he never went back up the bridge. In short time Paul Hogan emerged as the national spokesman for the new Australian pride, a bloke speaking in a broad, slow accent that Australians identified with because most of them spoke like that.

Soon he had a comedy sidekick, Strop, an unadulterated dill in a surf lifesaving cap. John Cornell, who played Strop, became Hogan's real-life friend and business partner, a calculating, ambitious man a million miles removed from the prognathous-jawed Strop. Cornell was a TV producer for *A Current Affair* when he saw Hogan's potential and gave him a slot on the show. Hoges's bloke in the pub's slant on the news became compulsive viewing. And, carefully guided by Cornell, the marketing of Paul Hogan began.

Winfield cigarettes built one of the most famous and successful of all Australian advertising campaigns around his image and one word, 'Anyhow...' Kerry Packer invited him to create his own comedy sketch series for the Nine Network. And within five years Paul Hogan was the most admired man in the nation.

In 1981, he and Cornell sold 26 episodes of edited highlights from the Australian shows, first to the Americans and then to Britain's Channel 4, in the prime-time slot at 8.30 p.m. But Hogan's greatest exposure to the international markets that he was shortly to enthral came when he did TV commercials for Australian tourism in the US, and Foster's Lager in the UK. The laid-back larrikin Hoges character came across just as it had in Australia – warm, funny and likeable. The proof was plain to see. He had already made Winfields the number one brand in Australia; in Britain Foster's Lager became the second-biggest-selling beer, and in America tourist bookings for visits to Australia doubled in four years in the wake of his 'throw another shrimp on the barbie' commercials.

Now he and Cornell were ready to go for the jackpot. He gave straight acting a try in the Australian mini-series, *Anzacs*, and then, in 1985, he began filming *Crocodile Dundee*. His character – the usual Hogan persona now called Michael J. 'Crocodile' Dundee – was a bushman who conquered New York with a ready grin and a big knife. In turn Hogan conquered millions of moviegoers. The film's $328 million gross was the 10th biggest in history and introduced what could be said to be the essential Australian character to the world.

'Australia has a new roving ambassador,' Sydney's *Daily Mirror* said, 'the phenomenally successful Crocodile Dundee, otherwise known as Paul Hogan. And every one of his interviews is a plug for Australia – a positive, bright, breezy Australia bristling with energy and talent.'

He made two more 'Croc' movies – an apt description most critics thought – and a handful of others. None matched, or could hope to match, the extraordinary success of the original.

His marriage broke up and it seemed to sour Australia's love affair with him. Hogan once claimed that one of the things he shares with Hoges is that 'neither of us gives a bugger what people think'. The disappearance of the laughter wrinkles that gave Hogan's face its craggy appeal suggest that Paul Hogan has parted with Hoges on this matter.

No matter. What hasn't changed is the confidence and the pride in their country that he helped engender among Australians. We still owe you for that, Hoges.

On yer, mate!

# Neighbours

A soap series based on everyday people living in an uber-suburban cul de sac? 'It will never, ever work!' said Ian Smith, and he would know. A scriptwriter himself, an actor from *Bellbird*, an associate producer on *Prisoner*, Smith's opinion was shared by other shrewd judges.

More than two decades on Ian Smith is, apparently, a permanent fixture on the television landscape. As the widower Harold Bishop, who came to Ramsay Street, opened a health food shop and boarded with Mrs Mangel, he became a pivotal figure in the unending story that is *Neighbours*. Harold wooed and won Madge Ramsay (Anne Charleston) and they wed in 1989. The two settled down to a life of soap domesticity until, as is the way of things, he was washed out to sea, lost his memory, joined the Salvation Army and was finally reunited with Madge.

He had been her first boyfriend when they were teenagers in Brisbane, and he was by her side when she tragically died. It was an episode that had millions sobbing along with him, and grief-stricken though they were, wondering why Madge's tomboy daughter Charlene (Kylie Minogue) and her ex-jailbird son Henry (Craig McLachlan) weren't there, wringing their sodden hankies along with them.

Well, why weren't they there?

It's a long story. Thousands of episodes on it's hard to keep track of things. Here, for example, is how, in *Super Aussie Soaps*, Andrew Mercado summed up just

The new kid on the block, tomboy Charlene Mitchell (Kylie Minogue) set *Neighbours* on its triumphant march through the television decades. Charlene's romance with Scott Robinson (Jason Donovan) cemented the series and their wedding in July 1987 remains one of the highest-rating soap opera episodes in Australia. In the same year Kylie recorded 'Locomotion'. *Newspix*

one episode of *Neighbours*, the first, screened at 5.30 on Seven on Monday, 18 March 1985:

... it all began with a noisy bachelor party thrown by Des (Paul Keane) which was keeping everyone awake in Ramsay Street, Erinsborough. Maria Ramsay (Dasha Blahova) tried to stop her hot-headed husband Max (Francis Bell) from calling the police, while their eldest son Shane (Peter O'Brien) was across the road ushering in the 'special' entertainment for Des.

Max stormed over to confront the revellers just as stripper Daphne (Elaine Smith) began her routine. He shut the party down, Daphne told him to 'drop dead' and a drunken Paul Robinson (Stefan Dennis) was helped home to father Jim Robinson (Alan Dale) and grandmother Helen Daniels (Anne Haddy). Jim was a widower with four kids, while stylish Helen was the mother-in-law who had moved in with the family after her daughter died.

Des's future bride Lorraine (Antoinette Byron) was having a sleepover with Jim's eldest daughter Julie (Vikki Blanche), who had previously been engaged to Des. After Julie spent all night discussing Des's shortcomings, Lorraine decided to call off the wedding the next day. As Des sank into despair, Daphne showed up to search for a lost watch and ended up moving in to help out with his mortgage. Max was horrified that a stripper was living in Ramsay Street (he felt it was his street because it was named after his grandfather).

Over at the Robinsons', youngest daughter Lucy (Kylie Flinker) provided cute relief while other son Scott (Darius Perkins) was best mates with next-door neighbour Danny Ramsay (David Clencie). Their friendship was about to be tested over Scott's burgeoning relationship with shy schoolgirl Kim Taylor (Jenny Young) who was rebelling against the over-protective ways of her strict parents.

Have you got that? That's the first half hour. Thousands more to come, and the story, more than 20 years later, is still unravelling.

And yet the most successful show in Australian television history was twice almost buried where soaps go to die. *Until Tomorrow; The Unisexers; Arcade; Holiday Island; Taurus Rising; The Power, The Passion; Richmond Hill; Echo Point*... remember them? They failed the ratings test. So too, for a crucial time, did *Neighbours*.

On 12 July 1985 Seven called it quits. The show was popular enough around the country, but not in Sydney. The network announced it was closing *Neighbours*. No sooner had the execution taken place than the Ten Network announced that *Neighbours* would continue on its channel. Grundys, the producers, had been talking to them and Ten's Tom Warne said, 'I think a lot of programs have been cancelled prematurely. *Neighbours* will continue basically as it appears on television at the moment.'

Alas, that couldn't be. Seven told a sceptical Ten that the sets had been accidentally destroyed in a fire, leaving their rivals embittered, but with the opportunity to re-think things. The break caused Ten to decide to increase the comedy component, making the comedy/drama balance of the series 50-50. And it made a crucial casting decision, replacing Darius Perkins in the role of Scott Robinson with Jason Donovan. Oh, and the network also signed an unknown 17-year-old for 12 weeks with

an option. Kylie Minogue was cast as Charlene, Madge's daughter, a tomboy who came with overalls and attitude.

On 20 January 1986 the new, improved *Neighbours*, with added Donovan, premiered on Ten. Then Charlene came down from Coffs Harbour to join her mum on 18 April 1986, punched Scott Robinson on the nose and sent Ramsay Street property values soaring.

Within months the press couldn't get enough of Kylie and Jason, whose on-screen teenage romance was carried on off screen. Teenagers were obsessed with them and the show. The cast made an appearance at the Royal Easter Show and five children were injured in a stampede to get to them. Six months later, in October, *Neighbours* went to the UK, where BBC1 in its wisdom screened it at 1.30 p.m., and 9.05 a.m., slots guaranteed to be teenage-free. But 15 months later, bombarded with

demands, the BBC relented and gave *Neighbours* the ideal 5.35 p.m. slot. Sixteen million viewers tuned in. (Among them, it was said, were the Queen, Princess Di and Prince William.)

The Seven network eventually made amends for its blunder when it came up with an answer to *Neighbours*. Head of Drama, Alan Bateman, driving through a small country town in New South Wales, stopped for ice creams for the kids. The locals, he found, were furious at plans for a home for city foster children in the town. Bateman wondered how those city kids would fit in and the idea of *Home and Away* was born. Today *Home and Away* out-rates *Neighbours* in Australia and it too is a hit in the UK.

But there's no going past the fact that everybody still needs good *Neighbours*.

*Neighbours* brings English pilgrims by the busload to Melbourne's fictional Ramsay Street (real street name Pinoak Court in the outer Melbourne suburb of Vermont South). In 2007 Britain's Channel Five paid $720 million to grab the series from the BBC.

# Bert Newton

George Negus: 'Yeah, just going through the research notes – it's pretty embarrassing your... your success. Fifteen Logies, co-hosted the thing 18 times, 2500 shows, talked to over 20,000 guests.'

Bert Newton: 'Can I have a look at that? You've got Don Lane's. His wish list.'

No television personality has ever matched Bert Newton's quick wit. On US television, neither Johnny Carson nor his successors and rivals. Letterman? Not in the same ballpark. Leno? Please! On English television not David Frost, not Parkinson, not... look, the truth is, television hosts, from Groucho Marx back in the early '50s to whoever's hosting this year's late night show, almost always have their ad libs, their every comic move, carefully scripted and often rehearsed. Not Bert.

'He can turn a sneeze into a gag or dress up a camera glitch,' said Patrick Carlyon in the *Bulletin*. 'He can swap silly for earnest – Benny Hill for Kerry O'Brien – in an instant.' Rob Sitch, one of the team behind *Frontline, The Castle* and *The Dish*, says, 'Given a pregnant moment in live television, Bert is the best user of the following five seconds of anyone in the world.'

So he's quick on his feet. So, probably, is Woody Allen. But then, there's Bert's warmth. Very few have his warmth.

And none – not one major television star – has endured so long. He has been on television in Australian homes almost since it began, half a century ago. Most extraordinarily, no one – not even his fellow performers – dislikes or is jealous of him. Almost as amazing, as he gets older, his fans seem to get younger. They have no idea of what

*In Melbourne Tonight* was, or who or what the hell Don Lane is: a kind of salami?

But Bert? Bert, they like. Bert, they instinctively know, deserves respect. Graham Kennedy may have been The King, but Bert rules, OK?

Bert and Graham's careers will always and inevitably be compared and contrasted. Friendly radio rivals before they worked together, they grew up with television and shaped it and us. Graham lived for television and left it a burnt-out case. Bert goes on. On 16 December 2005, he wound up on the show he created, *Good Morning Australia*, and after 14 years returned to Nine, the network that fired him in 1985 and where Bert learned that he'd been dumped after a reporter phoned him for a comment. He'd been with Nine for 26 years.

Albert Watson Newton was 11 when his father died. His dad, Joe, had come back from the war after serving in Greece, Crete, the Middle East and New Guinea. Little Bertie had opened the door to their house at 29 Holden Street, North Fitzroy, and saw a stranger. 'I didn't recognise my own father,' he remembered. 'I wouldn't let him in.'

Four years later, worn out and suffering recurring attacks of malaria, Joe died. Bert, encouraged by his mother and his elder sister, discovered an engrossing distraction from his grief. He became part of the regular studio audience of *Peter's Pals*, a children's show on Melbourne's 3XY. Soon he was part of the show, writing radio plays and reading commercials. At 14 he was performing as a clown on 3XY's Saturday morning show for children, and when he left school at 16 he went straight to work at the station as a turntable operator and junior announcer.

The only television star in the world with a career spanning half a century, Bert, as everyone calls him, was named Number One when Nine screened a commemorative program, *50 Years 50 Stars*. He has won 18 Logies including four Gold and one Special Gold. *Newspix*

(The idea of continuing his education probably never crossed Bert's mind. The Marist Brothers, who taught and fondly remember him, treasure Bert, explaining, on yet another occasion, why he hadn't done his homework. 'Sorry, Brother. But my grandmother died yesterday.'

Brother Cleophas considered this. 'Another one! Already this year you've lost two grandmothers.'

Young Bert hesitated for just a beat: 'Yes, Brother, that's right. My grandfather remarried.')

In 1957, Channel 7 offered him an on-camera job and Alice, his oldest sister (he was the youngest child of six) urged him to take the offer. He and Graham Kennedy were late night DJs on rival radio stations – Bert was 18 and Graham 23 – and they'd first met over a few beers after work. Now, within two months, they were each offered jobs on the new, unexplored medium, Graham, with Nine as host of *In Melbourne Tonight*, and Bert with Seven as host of *The Late Show*. By 1960 they were working together, creating entertainment history on *In Melbourne Tonight*.

The two stayed mates but while Graham increasingly retreated into himself, Bert was happy to share his public life with his fans. He is amused by the pretensions of some celebrities. 'If you don't want to get mobbed or be given a hard time, don't wander through the airport wearing dark glasses and humming your theme song.'

Unlike Graham, Bert was close to his family – he'd lived at home with his mother, Gladys, a sister and a brother until he was 36. In 1974 he married Patti McGrath, whom he'd met when she was a child, singing and tap dancing on his 3XY show. Graham was best man, there were 100 invited guests and there were 10,000 outside the church. He's still married to Patti and he still goes to Mass. His family and his faith have sustained him throughout his life.

There were other disparities between Bert and Graham, but each shared a talent for acting. Graham, in hindsight, might have been better advised to look to cinema. Critics praised his performances in such films as *Travelling North, The Club* and *Don's Party*. Bert made two or three films but his first love is theatre. His big sister Alice took him to see *Annie Get Your Gun* when he was nine. 'It was magical,' he says. In the '90s he emerged as a music theatre star in *The Wizard of Oz, Beauty and the Beast, The Sound of Music* and *The Producers*, where, Mel Brooks said, he gave the definitive performance as the nutty Nazi playwright, Franz Liebkind.

Bert never strayed from playing the straight man to Graham's wild and unpredictable on-screen character. Was he tempted to have his own show? In 1963 John F. Kennedy was shot. A Melbourne advertising executive remembers travelling in a taxi and saying to the driver, 'Kennedy's been shot and killed. Isn't that awful!'

'Ah, well,' said the driver, 'at least Bert Newton will get his chance now.'

Bert was 'second banana' to Graham, and when Graham went, to Don Lane. But by then we were all aware that it was Bert who was the star, Bert who made it all happen. In his interview with George Negus, Bert said, 'I don't think that there's as much pressure when you're number two [but] the second banana has to know more than the first banana, because he's got to know what he's going to do, and he's also got to know what possibly we have to search for, too, and make sure that they're coming out okay.'

They've been coming out okay for Bert for 50 years now and there's no reason to think they'll stop. Bob Hope once described Bert as Australia's Bob Hope – without the team of comedy writers. And Hope lived to 100.

# 7

# THE FILMS

A still from the world's first feature film, *The Story of the Kelly Gang*, showing – wildly inaccurately – Ned's capture.

Australia's oldest surviving film – and this may not come as a surprise - is of Newhaven's Melbourne Cup win. It was filmed on 3 November 1896 by Maurice Sestie, sent to Australia to introduce the Lumiere Cinematographe, a device that could take and project film. Within four years Joe Perry and General Herbert Booth, son of the founder of the Salvation Army, had produced *Soldiers of the Cross*, our first, and some claim, the world's first feature film. In fact it was more a multimedia presentation combining film, music, lantern slides and commentary about early Christian martyrs. The honour of being the first feature film belongs, however, to another Australian production, *The Story of the Kelly Gang*, the first true narrative feature film and the 1906 precursor to a million 'cowboy' movies.

Either way, the Australian film industry was off to a wonderful start.

So what went wrong?

More than a century after *The Story of the Kelly Gang* our movie industry is one area in which Australia merely muddles along. Of course we have produced a score or more wonderful films, from the silent classic *The Sentimental Bloke* to the quirky and very funny Kenny, the film that lifts the lid on the port-a-loo industry. (Quirky is a word often applied to Australian films that try, but fail, to be funny.) The fault, many in the industry say, lies with insufficient government funding. Others point to the international success of films such as *Crocodile Dundee*, our highest box-office grosser, made, like *Kenny*, with private funding.

The question was bluntly posed by Senator Fierravanti-Wells to the then head of the Film Finance Corporation: '... the Film Finance Corporation... has invested in over, say, 900 titles, 12 of which have made a profit... the Film Finance Corporation has received $70.5 million in Commonwealth funding and saw a return of a little over $1 million for its film investments... Just to look at one commentator's opinion... the films we subsidise now are so darkly unwatched that all we promote is the notion that Australian films really stink.'

Are subsidised Australian films on the nose? Perhaps Kenny holds the answer to that question.

# Kokoda Frontline

'...the war, we thought, was still far away, an exciting picture show put on for the impressionable schoolboy I then was, and a lot more interesting than Maths, Latin or French irregular verbs.'

That's the expatriate Australian journalist Murray Sayle, recalling in *Quadrant* the time when 'Urban Australians first saw Damien Parer in that never-to-be-forgotten year of fear, 1942, the year that changed our view of the world forever, and should have changed it more...'

In September 1942 young Murray and his Sydneysider mates were at the Saturday arvo flicks, the movies at Hoyts. First came the cartoon, then the Cinesound Review, 'with its endearing ear-twitching kangaroo', a cousin of MGM's roaring lion, leaping out of frame.

'This newsreel was like nothing we had ever seen before. No gun flashes, no crashing bombs. Intrigued, our chiacking fell silent. The title *Kokoda Front Line* came up, with a short explanation: "Damien Parer [a name new to us] ace war correspondent, in four weeks took his cameras to the far corners of New Guinea, securing many amazing pictures... He is an experienced and reliable observer."

'Still no bang-bang. Instead, we see what looks like a suburban lounge room with books and a vase of flowers. A serious young man seated on a stool gazes squarely at the camera. He is in uniform, and at first we think he might be some sort of official spokesman. He uses a quiet, measured tone, remote from the spurious excitement of most war commentaries, then and now. He speaks unobtrusive but unmistakable Australian. To our

ears he is one of us, delivering the most eloquent to-camera speech in our history:

'"Eight days ago I was with our advance troops in the jungle facing the Japs at Kokoda. It's an uncanny sort of warfare. You never see a Jap even though he's only 20 yards away. They're complete masters of camouflage and deception. I should say about 40 per cent of our boys wounded in those engagements haven't seen a Japanese soldier, a live one anyway. Don't underestimate the Jap, he's a highly trained soldier, well disciplined and brave, and although he's had some success up to the present, he's now got against him some of the finest and toughest troops in the world – troops with a spirit amongst them that makes you intensely proud to be an Australian. I saw militiamen fighting over there, fighting under extremely difficult conditions alongside the AIF, and they acquitted themselves magnificently. When I returned to Moresby I was full of beans. It was the spirit of the troops and the knowledge that General Rowell was on the job and that now we had a really fine command. [A half-smile lights Parer's face as he names Rowell – praise that was indirectly to cost Parer his life two years later.]

'"But when I came back to the mainland, what a difference. I heard girls talking about dances, men complaining about the tobacco they didn't get. Up at the front they were smoking tea some of the time. There seems to be an air of unreality, as though the war were a million miles away. It's not. It's just outside our door now. I've seen the war and I know what your husbands, your sweethearts and brothers are going through. If only everybody in Australia could realise that this

country is in peril, that the Japanese are a well-equipped and dangerous enemy, we might forget about the trivial things and go ahead with the job of licking them."'

Damien Parer was Australia's first Oscar winner: A Best Documentary Academy Award for *Kokoda Frontline*. The film showed Australians for the first time what their soldiers faced in fighting the Japanese in New Guinea – ghastly fighting taking place just a few hundred kilometres from their shores. *Kokoda Frontline* had huge impact on young Murray Sayle and every Australian who saw it.

Three months before, Japanese mini submarines had attacked Sydney harbour, and in February Darwin had been bombed. After *Kokoda Frontline*, men began digging trenches and air raid shelters in their family backyards. Children were taught air raid drills and shown how to wear gas masks.

'It was startlingly clear to everyone in Australia that the British Empire, in which we had considered ourselves among the colonisers, not the colonised, was a military house of cards, and we must now fend for ourselves,' Sayle said.

Murray Sayle's reference to the half-smile that lit Parer's face as he named General Rowell – 'praise that was indirectly to cost Parer his life two years later' – is an aside on the mounting feud between two Australian generals, Rowell and Blamey, the man America's General Douglas MacArthur had insisted should replace Rowell in New Guinea. Rowell felt Blamey was incompetent. Damien Parer's dislike went further. 'He distrusted Blamey,' Parer's biographer, Neil McDonald, says.

'Parer indicated he believed he'd [Blamey] been

Damien Parer's admiration for one general and his detestation of another – Blamey – ultimately led to his death, machine-gunned amid US troops on a Pacific island.

drunk in Greece; there is an odour of alcohol about the Greece campaign and about Blamey's conduct there. General Rowell made it possible for Damien to go up the Kokoda track and he was a loyal friend and he was a mate. This is Australian mateship at work here. So Parer goes down and puts a tribute to Rowell at the head of *Kokoda Frontline*.'

Three days after *Kokoda Frontline* opened to packed houses in Sydney on 22 September, Blamey sacked Rowell and banished him to Cairo. Blamey's rage was such that he would have demoted him to colonel had Prime Minister Curtin not stopped him. His anger didn't stop there. When Blamey learned that the army had ordered prints of *Kokoda Frontline* to use for training, and that the troops cheered when Rowell's name came up, he had the prints removed and Parer's reference to Rowell deleted.

This, and a falling out with bureaucrats back home, led to Parer's decision to join the Americans on the battlefield, working for Paramount Pictures and *Life* magazine. His friend and war correspondent colleague Maslyn Williams said, 'It broke his heart to work with the Americans. He did it because the peanuts who were running our organisation would not let him do what he had to do.' (At the same time Chester Wilmot, another famous Australian war correspondent, was forced out of Papua by Blamey because Wilmot urged Curtin to reinstate Rowell. Wilmot went to work with the BBC and went behind the lines on D-Day. His *Struggle for Europe* was an international bestseller.)

Damien Parer, inevitably, was killed in the fighting, cut down by a machinegun firing from a concealed pillbox. He had not long been married and had a son he'd never met.

He had always operated on the principle that the best way to record the war was to get between the

*Kokoda Frontline.* '…the images of mateship that was there; Lofty and Stumpy sharing a cig under a cape… he gave them that… That was the most important thing about him.' *AWM 013287*

combatants. A deeply religious man, Parer once told his brother, 'I think that before the war ends I will die if I continue taking photographs the way I am doing. I feel that it is my duty to try to portray the truth and the honesty, the justice and the beauty in the soul of every soldier that dedicates his life to fight, and if necessary, die for his country. I will go on taking photographs the way I know I should, even though I die taking them.'

Damien Parer expanded the Anzac legend. 'He created his own icons of mateship. The man with a cape, the soldier on the stretcher looking to his friend… the images of mateship that was there; Lofty and Stumpy sharing a cig under a cape… he gave them that… That was the most important thing about him.'

Chester Wilmot said, 'He made the cameras speak as no other man I've known and his films gave an immortal portrait of the Australian soldier of this war.'

# The Overlanders

In 1942 bureaucrats from the Federal Food Office ordered stockmen of the Northern Territory to slaughter 100,000 of their cattle to prevent them from falling into Japanese hands in the event of an invasion. The stockmen were outraged. They decided, instead, to drive their cattle to safety 300 kilometres inland.

An English film director, Harry Watt, was in the Northern Territory at the time, looking for inspiration. Watt had made a number of wartime propaganda films for the British Government – *London Can Take It* and the like – and their success confirmed his belief in films set against contemporary, authentic backgrounds. The idea for *The Overlanders* was born. Ealing Studios gave the movie their backing and with it an expert producer, chief cameraman and film editor.

It was a big commitment for Ealing. Set against the epic cattle trek, *The Overlanders* took more than two years to make and cost £80,000. But it returned its budget 10 times over in Australia alone and much more in the UK and the US. Like *The Man From Snowy River*, the movie showed international audiences a landscape – and a people – new to their eyes. 'It puts Australia on the film map as never before,' said London's *Daily Herald*, and the *Times* pronounced, 'This is a film that must be seen. It is a fresh and lovely film and a study in artistic self-restraint.' Watt's own praise was for 'The sunshine, the marvellous locations and fascinating outback Australians who live in the bush', and, in a masterstroke, the man he had cast in the lead role, Chips Rafferty.

Rafferty, Watt thought, was 'the typical Australian. His height, his slow smile, his laconic talk, the way he moves and the way he stands are characteristic of Australians.' Chips Rafferty was the Paul Hogan of the 1940s, and *The Overlanders*, whether or not the producers of *The Man From Snowy River* and *Crocodile Dundee* knew it, was the father of both those international smash hits.

# The Man From Snowy River

*T*he *Man From Snowy River* is that movie curiosity, a 'horse opera' remembered more for the soundtrack and the horses than its story. Bruce Rowland's stirring theme seems to be the 'music under' whenever the national spirit needs to be summoned, most famously at the opening ceremony of the Sydney Olympics. That spectacular began when a lone High Country horseman cantered into the stadium, reared his horse and cracked his stockwhip. The music that followed was almost compulsory: the theme from *The Man From Snowy River.*

The 1982 big budget movie starred a Hollywood 'name' – Kirk Douglas – without which, it was thought, worldwide sales would be impossible. It was up to the scriptwriters, after that, to weave an American into the story based on Banjo Paterson's epic. Douglas played two key roles: as twin brothers who haven't spoken for years. Tom Burlinson, a little known soapie actor, played the role of Jim Craig, the 'stripling on a small and weedy beast',

'And he raced him down the mountain like a torrent down its bed.' Tom Burlinson as Jim Craig – the 'Man' – in the film's finest moment.

whose triumphal return of the prize horse that got away wins him everlasting renown as the Man from Snowy River, and Sigrid Thornton played the girl torn between... but the story was never important. What mattered were the horses, the music and the magnificent High Country where the movie was shot.

There were mutterings about the casting of Kirk Douglas but the star quickly put paid to that. On arrival in Australia he challenged the media throng, who were demanding he explain his intrusion in a sacred Australian poem. 'OK,' said Douglas, 'Can anyone here recite some verses – any verse – from your famous poem?' Embarrassed silence. Douglas

launched into the opening, 'There was movement at the station,' and the producers knew they had a hit.

At the two-day premiere celebrations, in the bush town of Mansfield, Prime Minister Malcolm Fraser came down to lend a hand with publicity – he obligingly mounted a horse and galloped into the horizon for the cameras – and *The Man From Snowy River* was away. It went on to be much bigger than anyone dreamed of, a huge international hit, the first Australian movie to reach the box office Top 10 in the US and the UK.

Excerpt from 'The Man from Snowy River' by A.B. 'Banjo' Paterson. This poem inspired the creation of the classic movie.

## *The Man from Snowy River*

There was movement at the station, for the word had passed around
That the colt from old Regret had got away,
And had joined the wild bush horses – he was worth a thousand pound,
So all the cracks had gathered to the fray.
All the tried and noted riders from the stations near and far
Had mustered at the homestead overnight,
For the bushmen love hard riding where the wild bush horses are,
And the stock-horse snuffs the battle with delight.

There was Harrison, who made his pile when Pardon won the cup,
The old man with his hair as white as snow;
But few could ride beside him when his blood was fairly up –

He would go wherever horse and man could go.
And Clancy of the Overflow came down to lend a hand,
No better horseman ever held the reins;
For never horse could throw him while the saddle-girths would stand –
He learnt to ride while droving on the plains.

And one was there, a stripling on a small and weedy beast;
He was something like a racehorse undersized,
With a touch of Timor pony – three parts thorough bred at least –
And such as are by mountain horsemen prized.
He was hard and tough and wiry – just the sort that won't say die—
There was courage in his quick impatient tread;
And he bore the badge of gameness in his bright and fiery eye,
And the proud and lofty carriage of his head.

# Crocodile Dundee

Crocodile Dundee is and almost certainly always will be the most financially successful Australian movie. *Shine* won far more awards. But *Crocodile Dundee* won the money. Released in 1986, it cost close to $9 million to make, a record at the time for an Australian movie. But it took almost $400 million worldwide, then the 10th highest gross in cinema history. In the US it was the most successful foreign film ever, out-grossing the James Bond films and leaving others such as *Chariots of Fire* panting in slow mo, far behind. It was the second-highest grossing movie in the States and it topped the box office grosses in unexpected places such as Stockholm, Paris and Rome. London loved *Crocodile Dundee* and Australia, of course, adored it.

What made the movie such a success? Three elements. It had a story as old as the pyramids: the country bumpkin who comes to town, encounters strange people and curious things, and comes out on top. It was brilliantly marketed in a way no one had done before or since. And it had a star with a charisma that crossed all demographics.

Paul Hogan was not the first to explore the comic possibilities of an innocent abroad. Barry Humphries had done it before in a *Private Eye* comic strip that became *The Adventures of Barry McKenzie*, Bruce Beresford's very funny and very successful movie, at least in Australia. Bazza McKenzie was a good-hearted Aussie oaf let loose in London of the Swinging Sixties and totally confused by the Poms he encountered. Mick Dundee was much shrewder, a bloke from the Outback who unexpectedly finds himself mixing

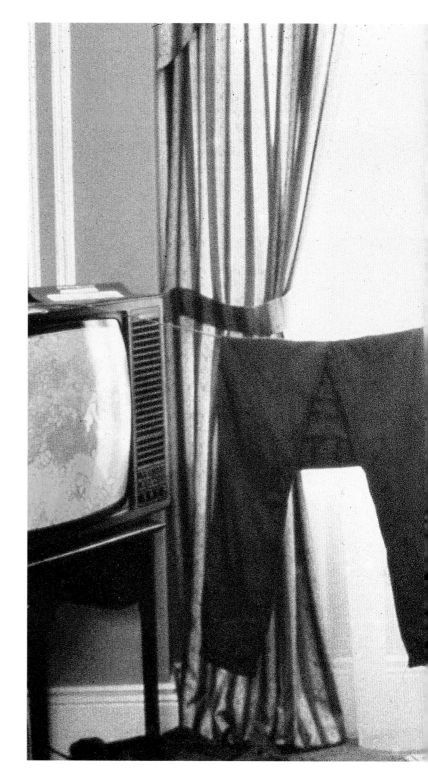

with the sophisticates of New York in the mid-'80s. Bazza might have been the uncle of Mick, but Mick would have shinned up the nearest Fifth Avenue telegraph pole to avoid him.

Paul Hogan, who co-wrote the movie (and got an Oscar nomination for it), consciously or subconsciously may have been inspired by Barry Humphries' success with Bazza. But Humphries, in turn, was following a rich literary vein that Bernard Levin, the *London Times* columnist alluded to when he compared Mick Dundee with 'Beowulf and King Arthur, Roland and Oliver, Candide and Bertie Wooster, Prince Charming and Bilbo Baggins and Robin Hood'. And you certainly couldn't say that about Bazza McKenzie.

Hogan himself said he wanted Dundee to be much more than an ingenuous Aussie abroad. 'The character is an attempt to give Australia a hero,' he was quoted as saying in London's *Time Out*. 'It's a country desperately short of heroes. We haven't got a Daniel Boone or a Robin Hood. All we ever had was Ned Kelly, an Irishman with a bucket over his head who pulled few unsuccessful robberies a long time ago.'

That sounds more like Hoges than Paul Hogan, and the truth is that Mick Dundee is less a hero to us, more like the Australians that many of us know and all of us respect: strong, independent men and women who live by their own values, are quietly self assured, good in a crisis, and can laugh at themselves.

*Crocodile Dundee* was a 'sleeper', a success that caught the movie industry unprepared. But though the scale of its success undoubtedly surprised Hogan and his partner John Cornell – who would have imagined they would make the 10th-highest grossing movie of all time? – the pair had quietly

constructed a brilliant international marketing campaign built around Hoges and Paul Hogan.

Hogan had already demonstrated he could shift markets when he was the face of Winfield, the cigarette of his choice until he gave away the smokes and, in the process, he says, lost the crow's feet and the furrows on his face that gave it such charm and character. Then the Australian Tourism Commission asked Hogan, more or less as a favour, to do a commercial for the US market: inviting Americans to join him in Australia over a barbecue of 'shrimps', a crustacean we are unfamiliar with. The commercial made Hogan's face and easy charm recognisable to millions of Americans (and brought thousands to Australia to enjoy the shrimps).

Then Carlton & United Breweries, looking to make Foster's a force in the UK and the US, asked Hogan to star in a series of commercials. In the UK he played Hoges, a bumbling Aussie at large who somehow gets the better of the Poms at the end. In the US, he was Paul Hogan, laid back, somewhat bemused by the culture he found, but always amused by it and always amusing. The British loved Hoges. The Americans were charmed by Hogan.

Then Hogan doffed the comic beanie he had often worn as Hoges and tried on the diggers' slouch hat he wore as Paul Hogan, the dramatic actor in the epic TV series, *Anzacs*. It was a good fit. Paul Hogan could act, no worries. They were ready to make their movie.

They put the word out to friends like Kerry Packer, Dennis Lillee and Rod Marsh: invest in this, it's a surefire hit.

Publicist Suzie Howie, on location with the movie, knew that *Crocodile Dundee* was going to be a smash from the reactions of New Yorkers. 'In Alphabet City, where we did a scene in a bar, we had drug pushers looking through the windows, calling out delightedly: "Hey dude! Put another shrimp on the barbie!" On Fifth Avenue they'd lean from their limos to get a good look at "that guy in that commercial". Just about everyone seemed to recognise him and everyone who did clearly liked him immensely.'

Paul Hogan has always had that charm. In his typical self-deprecating way, he said in the '90s, 'I've only got a couple of years left, then my hair will fall out, my chest will have gone grey, my belly will stick out and I'll have varicose veins. I'll revel in that [fame] for a couple of years – let ladies paw me in the street – then I'll go back to [TV] comedy again.'

In any event he doesn't look anything like that. Paul Hogan these days looks more like an investment advisor. And, regrettably, he'll never go back to making television comedy. But we'll always have *Crocodile Dundee*.

# *Shine*

*S*hine is, and surely will always be, the only Australian movie that sparked a restaurant brouhaha – a near-brawl, between Hollywood heavyweights. Across a crowded room Harvey Weinstein, the formidable head of Miramax, accused New Line's Bob Shaye of 'stealing' the movie. It was that hot.

The hit movie of 1996, loved by audiences internationally and universally admired by the critics, *Shine* had its flaws: the dramatic intensity dips in the second half. But it went into the Academy Awards with seven nominations – best film, actor, supporting actor, director, script, editing and score – the record for an Australian film at the Academy Awards. In any event *Shine* won only one award. It missed Best Picture – that went to the interminable *The English Patient* – but it won Geoffrey Rush the Oscar for Best Actor. That win presented not only a new film star face to the world but also a new image for the Australian film industry.

*Shine* showed we could make movies that didn't star horses or laconic blokes given to wearing over-the-shoulder crocodiles and keeping the dramatic dialogue to 'Crikey'; movies that didn't need a large wardrobe of period costumes; movies that weren't stamped Quirky; and movies that didn't carry the warning: lightweight, handle with care. *Shine*'s complex and emotionally disturbing depiction of a subject seldom examined in our cinema – love – made it a landmark. It changed the way the world saw Australian movies.

Harvey Weinstein and Bob Shaye knew *Shine* was going to be a huge hit long before the 1995

Noah Taylor as David Helfgott in the climax of *Shine* – his breakdown while performing 'the Rach 3'.

Sundance Film Festival audience was on its feet, tumultuously applauding the unknown Australian entry. But Scott Hicks, the movie's director, had known it for 10 years.

In 1985 Hicks read Adelaide journalist Samela Harris's feature story about David Helfgott, a brilliant pianist performing a classical repertoire in a Perth restaurant. Intrigued, he went to see Helfgott perform, and then met him and his wife Gillian. He learned their story. Jan Sardi's and Hicks's deeply moving screenplay built on that story, although Hicks insists the movie is not entirely biographical.

David Helfgott's father, Peter (Armin Mueller-Stahl) settled in Australia after the war. But his parents and sisters-in-law perished in the Holocaust. Loving, overbearing and obsessive, he is determined to keep his family together, at all costs. Peter's son, David (Noah Taylor), a piano prodigy, is driven hard by his father, his music tutor, who nonetheless forbids him to accept a US scholarship offered by the great violinist Isaac Stern. When David wins another scholarship, to London's Royal College of Music, Peter Helfgott again refuses to let him go. David's only soulmate, the elderly and eminent author Katharine Susannah Prichard (Googie Withers), encourages him, and aware that his relationship with his father may be irrevocably broken, David defies him and goes to London.

There he discovers himself, and life beyond the piano. He lets his eccentric habits hang out and his hair down; he corresponds with Katharine; his talent, under the gentle guidance of Cecil Parkes (John Gielgud), flowers. Then, at the crowning moment of his life, the conclusion of a public performance of Rachmaninoff's devilishly

'No one's ever been mad enough to attempt the Rach' 3.'
'Am I mad enough, Professor? Am I?' Noah Taylor as David Helfgott, the music student in London and in love with life. *Newspix*

demanding *Third Piano Concerto*, the young student has a nervous breakdown.

We next see David (now played by Geoffrey Rush), a decade and more on, a babbling, incoherent bundle of nervous mannerisms. '...So maybe I was a sad cat – was I a sad cat? I was I was, always kissed them kissed them, yes I did, I did, I did kiss them all kissed them all, nice little cat always oh ho, oh ho...' The intellectually curious and wryly amusing young student has gone. In his place is a childlike, manic man, bouncing trouserless on a trampoline, a sometimes alarming figure with a disconcerting habit of unexpectedly fondling women and a candour that borders on Tourette's syndrome. 'I never grew up, I grew down. Har har! I'm a bit of a handful, bit of a handful!'

Before his breakdown David has known only the love of his father – an erratic love by turns tender and cruel. When he meets Gillian (Lynn Redgrave), an offbeat middle-aged astrologer, David discovers love that demands nothing. The film ends with him returning triumphantly to the concert hall.

When news of the planned movie seeped out those few who knew David Helfgott were puzzled. He seemed such an odd subject in every way. Scott Hicks knew better. He had a story with universal appeal and he and Jan Sardi had written a compelling script. An Emmy award-winning director, Hicks was confident of his own ability. But casting would be everything. Hicks wanted Geoffrey Rush. Theatregoers knew Rush as an outstanding actor, but outside theatre he was little known. He wasn't a 'billboard' name. The film's backers were deeply unhappy with Rush.

On the other hand, Noah Taylor, Rush's proposed co-star, was internationally admired. He began in theatre as a teenager and in 1986 made his cinema debut, nominated for best actor as Danny Embling in John Duigan's *The Year My Voice Broke*. Taylor's performance in that movie and in *Flirting*, Duigan's second movie following Danny Embling's life, had earned him high regard, in America particularly.

Hicks got his way. In 1995 he finally found himself working with a superb cast of international and Australian actors, all of whom gave flawless performances. Hicks's stubborn insistence on Rush was rewarded at the Oscars. Seven nominations and there could have been more. Before the nominations were announced, *Entertainment Weekly* commented that if Geoffrey Rush won, 'he'd do well to thank his 27-year-old co-star, Noah Taylor, whose performance as the young Helfgott may be the year's most not talked about. Without him, Rush might never have had the chance to shine.' After the announcements, *Newsweek* put Taylor's situation bluntly: '...did he get screwed in the Oscar nominations...'

In his acceptance speech Rush thanked all the Australian actors he had ever worked with, and the overwhelming winner after those 1996 Academy Awards were Australian actors. In the 60 years before *Shine*, Australian films had been nominated for 49 Academy Awards, only one of them for an acting performance by an Australian – Peter Finch. It was universally agreed, in Australia and beyond, that our actors couldn't cut it against the best. In the 10 years after *Shine*, Australian films won 61 Oscar nominations and actors picked up 10 of them, including four Best Actor/Actress awards. It's got to the point where the media asks peevishly why 'we've' been overlooked if Geoffrey, Cate, Russell, Heath, Naomi, Toni, Hugh or Nicole aren't figuring in the nominations.

These days, internationally, Australian actors shine.

# Author's Acknowledgments

I am indebted to David Horgan of The Five Mile Press, who suggested I write *Why We Are Australian*; to Maggie Pinkney who oversaw its challenging production; to Janet Pheasant, for her tireless work in obtaining the many images in this book; to Michael Bannenberg for his excellent design; to Susan Gorgioski for her invaluable assistance; and to my wife Suzie Howie whose patience was tested but triumphed. I also owe a debt to the works of such historians, authorities and journalists as Patsy Adam-Smith, Robyn Annear, Geoffrey Blainey, Michael Cannon, Les Carlyon, Don Chapman, Manning Clark, Peter Coleman, Frank Clune, Mike Dash, Keith Dunstan, Geoffrey Dutton, Tim Flannery, Harry Gordon, Richard Haese, Geoff Hocking, Robert Hughes, Clive James, A.K. Macdougall, Andrew Mercado, Diana and Michael Preston, Ian Jones, Cyril Pearl, Andrew Rule, Bernard Smith and Terry Smith, Bill Scott, Gerald Stone, John Silvester, Bill Wannan, Don Watson, Charles White and Evan Whitton.

# *Pictorial Acknowledgments*

The author and Publishers thank the following organisations for permission to publish the images in this book:

Australian Broadcasting Corporation, page 27

Arts Centre, Performing Arts Collection,
    Melbourne, pages 51, 52-3

Australian War Memorial, Canberra,
    pages 70-71, 98

Fairfax Photos, pages 22-23, 68, 91

Fremantle Arts Centre Press, page 19

General Motors Holden, cover image and
    pages 72-3

Kraft Foods Limited, page 75

National Gallery of Australia, Canberra, page 45

National Portrait Gallery, Canberra, page 55

National Library of Australia, Canberra, pages 8,
    14, 16, 25, 29, 31, 39, 43 (upper and lower),
    58-9, 66-7, 97

Newspix, pages 17, 21, 41, 46-7, 76-7, 80, 82-3,
    85, 87, 89, 93, 107

Picture Australia, page 20

# Waltzing Matilda

Once a jolly swagman camped by a billabong
Under the shade of a coolibah-tree,
And he sang as he watched and waited till his billy boiled,
'Who'll come a-waltzing Matilda with me?
Waltzing Matilda, waltzing Matilda,
Who'll come a-waltzing Matilda with me?'
And he sang as he watched and waited till his billy boiled,
'Who'll come a-waltzing Matilda with me?'

Down came a jumbuck to drink at the billabong:
Up jumped the swagman and grabbed him with glee,
And he sang as he shoved that jumbuck in his tucker-bag,
'You'll come a-waltzing Matilda with me.
Waltzing Matilda, waltzing Matilda,
You'll come a-waltzing Matilda with me.'

Up rode a squatter mounted on his thoroughbred;
Down came the troopers, one, two, three:
'Who's that jolly jumbuck you've got in your tucker-bag?
You'll come a-waltzing Matilda with me!
Waltzing Matilda, waltzing Matilda,
You'll come a-waltzing Matilda with me!
Who's that jolly jumbuck you've got in your tucker-bag?
You'll come a-waltzing Matilda with me!'

Up jumped the swagman and sprang into the billabong;
'You'll never catch me alive!' said he;
And his ghost may be heard as you pass by that billabong,
'You'll come a-waltzing Matilda with me!
Waltzing Matilda, waltzing Matilda,
You'll come a-waltzing Matilda with me!'
And his ghost may be heard as you pass by that billabong,
'You'll come a-waltzing Matilda with me!'

– A. B. ('BANJO') PATERSON